PHILOSOPHICAL QUESTIONS

An Introductory Anthology

Richard L. Purtill
Western Washington University

Michael H. Macdonald
Seattle Pacific University

Peter J. Kreeft
Boston College

PRENTICE-HALL, INC.
Englewood Cliffs, New Jersey 07632

Library of Congress Cataloging in Publication Data
Main entry under title:

Philosophical questions.

    1. Philosophy—Addresses, essays, lectures.   I. Purtill,
Richard L., 1931-   . II. MacDonald, Michael H.
III. Kreeft, Peter.
BD41.P465 1985   100   84-6968
ISBN-0-13-662305-0

Manufacturing buyer: Harry P. Baisley
Cover design by Lundgren Graphics, Ltd.

Printed in the United States of America

10 9 8 7 6 5 4 3 2 1

ISBN 0-13-662305-0

Prentice-Hall International, Inc., *London*
Prentice-Hall of Australia Pty. Limited, *Sydney*
Editora Prentice-Hall do Brasil, Ltda., *Rio de Janeiro*
Prentice-Hall Canada Inc., *Toronto*
Prentice-Hall of India Private Limited, *New Delhi*
Prentice-Hall of Japan, Inc., *Tokyo*
Prentice-Hall of Southeast Asia Pte. Ltd., *Singapore*
Whitehall Books Limited, *Wellington, New Zealand*

CONTENTS

PART ONE
WHAT CAN WE KNOW?

ONE: CAN WE KNOW ANYTHING? THE PROBLEM OF SCEPTICISM, 29

TWO: WHAT IS REAL? THE PROBLEM OF METAPHYSICS, 58

Comment

THREE: HOW CAN WE KNOW? THE PROBLEM OF EPISTEMOLOGY, *102*

A. Ancient Rationalism

B. Realism

C. Modern Rationalism

D. An Empiricist View

E. Another Empiricist View

F. Idealism

Comment

PART TWO
WHAT SHOULD WE DO?

FOUR: ARE WE FREE TO CHOOSE? THE PROBLEM OF FREE WILL, *147*

A. Strict Determinism

B. Compatibilism

C. The Free Will View

D. An Argument for Free Will

Comment

PART THREE
WHAT MAY WE HOPE?

E. Another Argument for Immortality

F. A Third Argument for Immortality

Comment

PREFACE FOR TEACHERS

Philosophy is one of the most fascinating and important subjects that anyone can study. I am sure that you as a teacher of philosophy will agree with this statement: our problem as teachers is to get our students to see that it is true. Our own enthusiasm for our subject will do part of the job, but we must share that enthusiasm in a way that will let students see the relevance of philosophy to their own concerns and problems. The traditional methods of teaching philosophy put some obstacles in the way of this. Philosophy has a long and complicated history, and the further we follow that history, the more complex and interrelated the problems become. That is why we so often start an introductory philosophy class with the Greek philosophers, who began philosophy as we know it. But we cannot simply stay with the ancient Greeks: too much has happened in philosophy since then. And though classical Greece may be surprisingly like our own times, there are cultural assumptions which make it hard to see why some problems took the form they did.

If we go to the other extreme and stick with contemporary philosophers, we face a different sort of problem. For better or for worse, philosophy in the English-speaking countries has become a rather technical enterprise and the average article in *The Journal of Philosophy* or *The Philosophical Review* or *Nous* will not be interesting to students, or even intelligible to them. Even philosophical articles that seem relatively straightforward and nontechnical will often assume a background that the student cannot be expected to have.

There is no way around it: we must deal with the whole course of philosophical argument on a subject if we are to give students a real idea of the problem involved and the possible answers to it. The problem is how to do this without on the one hand watering down the material or on the other hand giving students material that will bore or unduly puzzle them.

In this book we, the editors, have tried to give the essential readings on major philosophical problems: two thirds of our selections are, and must be, the familiar ones that form the core of any good book of readings in philosophy. To help the student understand these selections, we have done two things. First we have edited the selections so that only the essential parts are given: those passages which you would almost certainly spend most of your time in class talking about. Some of the connecting material has been shortened, or, where possible, omitted. Second, in the introductions to the sections, we have done some of the explanatory work necessary to help students understand the background of the selections and their bearing on the problems. Our aim has been to leave you, the classroom teacher, free to discuss the philosophical issues rather than historical or sociological sidelines.

A number of the selections in this book are not among the standard ones found in most books of readings. These selections are of two kinds. The first are short philosophical treatments of a problem which are not well-known but which have some special virtue of clarity or originality that make them valuable contributions to the problem under discussion. Sometimes, but not always, these selections are by contemporary philosophers. The second kind we have called "Comments." They are drawn from stories, essays, and other sources, which would usually be classed as literary rather than philosophical treatments of a subject, but which illuminate in some way the philosophical issue under discussion. Literary expressions of philosophical positions influence all of us, even those of us who are professional philosophers, and we hope that our literary selections will be useful and interesting in involving your students in the issues involved. Even though they follow the strictly philosophical selections, you may want to have your students read them before you begin discussion of the philosophical selections.

Since most students come into philosophy class with only the vaguest idea of what philosophy is all about, we open with the section, "Why study philosophy?" We start where Western philosophy began, with the Greeks, and go on to a kaleidescope of views on philosophy with which we attempt to show both the diversity and the unity of views about the nature of philosophy through the ages. We end this section with some contemporary views of philosophy.

The main part of the book is organized around three questions which, as Kant said, are basic not only to philosophy but to human life: "What can we know?"; "What should we do?"; "What can we hope?" Under the first heading we have grouped not only problems about knowledge but also the issue of scepticism and questions about truth and reality. The second heading includes not only the problem of how we should behave and how we should live, but also the prior problem as to whether we have freedom to act. Under the third heading we discuss God, immortality, and meaning of life. We have made the three sections independent enough so that they can be taken in any order you prefer, and this is true to some extent of the subquestions under each major question. However, the selections within each subsection should be dealt with in the order in which they are given, since they follow the historical and logical development of a problem.

Our final section shows how philosophy can be applied to some important human problems: you may wish to supplement this section with applications of philosophy to social or intellectual problems especially important to you and to your students.

The editors of this book believe that philosophy is an important and fascinating human enterprise, well worth living for or even dying for, as Socrates did. We hope that this book of readings helps you and your students to carry on this enterprise. Everything in the book—the selections, the introductions, the discussion questions, and suggested readings—are planned with that purpose in mind. We would welcome your comments and suggestions as to how this job could be done better. One of the rewards of being a teacher of philosophy is the opportunity to continue learning about our subject, from our students and our colleagues, as well as from the great philosophers past and present. The model of every teacher should be the "clerk of Oxenford" of whom Chaucer said "and he would gladly learn and gladly teach." We hope that this book will help you to teach a little more gladly and more effectively.

PERMISSIONS ACKNOWLEDGMENTS

Excerpts from the following sources appear throughout the book and are reprinted with permission from the publishers listed.

"The Suicide of Thought" from *Orthodoxy* by G.K. Chesterton. Reprinted with permission of Dodd, Mead & Company, Inc.

On the Nature of the Universe by Lucretius, translated by Ronald Latham. Copyright © 1951 by R.E. Latham. Reprinted by permission of Penguin Books Ltd.

Summa Theologiae by St. Thomas Aquinas used by permission of Benziger Brothers, Inc., a division of Glencoe Publishing Company, Inc.

Discourse on Method by René Descartes used by permission of The Bobbs-Merrill Co., Inc.

Critique of Pure Reason by Immanuel Kant, translated by Norman Kemp Smith. Reprinted by permission of Macmillan, London and Basingstoke.

The Freedom of the Will by J.R. Lucas. Copyright © 1970 by Oxford University Press. Reprinted by permission of Oxford University Press.

INTRODUCTION:
WHY STUDY PHILOSOPHY?

A. THE BEGINNING

Plato: *The Apology of Socrates*

Socrates (c. 470–399 B.C.), the Greek philosopher, was probably the first person to carry on the activity of clarifying, criticizing, and arguing about the fundamental problems that we, in the West, call philosophy. Socrates was Plato's teacher, but probably had no philosophical system of his own and very likely no personal philosophical theories. Our impression of him is largely based on Plato and Xenophon, both of whom fictionalized him to serve as the mouthpiece of their own theories. What emerges is a strong and recognizable personality, fascinated by philosophical problems and ready to question and challenge any assumption or theory. It is this spirit, rather than any discovery or theory, which makes Socrates the spiritual father of all Western philosophy. The selection that follows is Plato's account of Socrates' speech in defense of his way of life, made when he was brought to trial on charges of being antireligious and of corrupting the young men of Athens.

APOLOGY

How you, O Athenians, have been affected by my accusers, I cannot tell; but I know that they almost made me forget who I was—so persuasively did they speak; and yet they have hardly uttered a word of truth. But of the many falsehoods told by them, there was one which quite amazed me;—I mean when they said that you should be upon your guard and not allow yourselves to be deceived by the force of my eloquence. To say this, when they were certain to be detected as soon as I opened my lips and proved myself to be anything but a great speaker, did indeed appear to me most shameless—unless by the force of eloquence they mean the force of truth; for if such is their meaning, I admit that I am eloquent. But in how different a way from theirs! Well, as I was saying, they have scarcely spoken the truth at all; but from me you shall hear the whole truth: not, however, delivered after their manner in a set oration duly ornamented with words and phrases. No, by heaven! but I shall use the words and arguments which occur to me at the moment; for I am confident in the justice of my cause: at my time of life I ought not to be appearing before you, O men of Athens, in the character of a juvenile orator—let no one expect it of me. And I must beg of you to grant me a favour:—If I defend myself in my accustomed manner, and you hear me using the words which I have been in the habit of using in the agora, at the tables of the money-changers, or anywhere else, I would ask you not to be surprised, and not to interrupt me on this account. For I am more than seventy years of age, and appearing now for the first time in a court of law, I am quite a stranger to the language of the place; and therefore I would have you regard me as if I were really a stranger, whom you would excuse if he spoke in his native tongue, and after the fashion of his country:—Am I making an unfair request of you? Never mind the manner, which may or may not be good; but think only of the truth of my words, and give heed to that: let the speaker speak truly and the judge decide justly.

And first, I have to reply to the older charges and to my first accusers, and then I will go on to the later ones. For of old I have had many accusers who have accused me falsely to you during many years; and I am more afraid of them than of Anytus and his associates, who are dangerous, too, in their own way. But far more dangerous are the others, who began when you were children, and took possession of your minds with their falsehoods, telling of one Socrates, a wise man, who speculated about the heaven above, and searched into the earth beneath, and made the worse appear the better cause. The disseminators of this tale are the accusers whom I dread; for their hearers are apt to fancy that such enquirers do not believe in the existence of the gods. And they are many, and their charges against me are of ancient date, and they were made by them in the days when you were more impressible than you are now—in childhood, or it may have been in youth—and the cause when heard went by default, for there was none to answer. And hardest of all, I do not know and cannot tell the names of my accusers; unless in the chance case of a comic poet. All who from envy and malice have persuaded you—some of them having first convinced themselves—all this class of men are most difficult to deal with; for I cannot have them up here, and cross-examine them, and therefore I must simply fight with shadows in my own defence, and argue when there is no one who answers.

I dare say, Athenians, that some one among you will reply, 'Yes, Socrates, but what is the origin of these accusations which are brought against you; there must have been something strange which you have been doing? All these rumours and this talk about you would never have arisen if you had been like other men: tell us, then, what is the cause of them, for we should be sorry to judge hastily of you.' Now I regard this as a fair challenge, and I will endeavour to explain to you the reason why I am called wise and have such an evil frame. Please to attend then. And although some of you may think that I am joking, I declare that I will tell you the entire truth. Men of Athens, this reputation of mine has come of a certain sort of wisdom which I possess. If you ask me what kind of wisdom, I reply, wisdom such as may perhaps be attained by man, for to that extent I am inclined to believe that I am wise; whereas the persons of whom I was speaking have a superhuman wisdom, which I may fail to describe, because I have it not myself; and he who says that I have, speaks falsely, and is taking away my character. And here, O men of Athens, I must beg you not to interrupt me, even if I seem to say something extravagant. For the word which I will speak is not mine. I will refer you to a witness who is worthy of credit; that witness shall be the God of Delphi—he will tell you about my wisdom, if I have any, and of what sort it is. You must have known Chaerephon; he was early a friend of mine, and also a friend of yours, for he shared in the recent exile of the people, and returned with you. Well, Chaerephon, as you know, was very impetuous in all his doings, and he went to Delphi and boldly asked the oracle to tell him whether—as I was saying, I must beg you not to interrupt—he asked the oracle to tell him whether any one was wiser than I was, and the Pythian prophetess answered, that there was no man wiser. Chaerephon is dead himself; but his brother, who is in court, will confirm the truth of what I am saying.

Why do I mention this? Because I am going to explain to you why I have such an evil name. When I heard the answer, I said to myself, What can the god mean? and what is the interpretation of his riddle? for I know that I have no wisdom, small or great. What then can he mean when he says that I am the wisest of men? And yet he is a god, and cannot lie; that would be against his nature. After long consideration, I thought of a method of trying the question. I reflected that if I could only find a man wiser than myself, then I might go to the god with a refutation in my hand. I should say to him, 'Here is a man who is wiser than I am; but you said that I was the wisest.' Accordingly I went to one who had the reputation of wisdom, and observed him—his name I need not mention; he was a politician whom I selected for examination—and the result was as follows: When I began to talk with him, I could not help thinking that he was not really wise, although he was thought wise by many, and still wiser by himself; and thereupon I tried to explain to him that he thought himself wise, but was not really wise; and the consequence was that he hated me, and his enmity was shared by several who were present and heard me. So I left him, saying to myself, as I went away: Well, although I do not suppose that either of us knows anything really beautiful and good, I am better off than he is,—for he knows nothing, and thinks that he knows; I neither know nor think that I know. In this latter particular, then, I seem to have slightly the advantage of him. Then I went to another who had still higher pretensions to wisdom, and my conclusion was exactly the same. Whereupon I made another enemy of him, and of many others besides him.

Then I went to one man after another, being not unconscious of the enmity which I provoked, and I lamented and feared this: But necessity was laid upon me,—the word of God, I thought, ought to be considered first. And I said to myself, Go I must to all who appear to know, and find out the meaning of the oracle. And I swear to you, Athenians, by the dog I swear!—for I must tell you the truth—the result of my mission was just this: I found that the men most in repute were all but the most foolish; and that others less esteemed were really wiser and better. I will tell you the tale of my wanderings and of the 'Herculean' labours, as I may call them, which I endured only to find at last the oracle irrefutable. After the politicians, I went to the poets; tragic, dithyrambic, and all sorts. And there, I said to myself, you will be instantly detected; now you will find out that you are more ignorant than they are. Accordingly, I took them some of the most elaborate passages in their own writings, and asked what was the meaning of them—thinking that they would teach me something. Will you believe me? I am almost ashamed to confess the truth, but I must say that there is hardly a person present who would not have talked better about their poetry than they did themselves. Then I knew that not by wisdom do poets write poetry, but by a sort of genius and inspiration; they are like diviners or soothsayers who also say many fine things, but do not understand the meaning of them. The poets appeared to me to be much in the same case; and I further observed that upon the strength of their poetry they believed themselves to be the wisest of men in other things in which they were not wise. So I departed, conceiving myself to be superior to them for the reason that I was superior to the politicians.

At last I went to the artisans, for I was conscious that I knew nothing at all, as I may say, and I was sure that they knew many fine things; and here I was not mistaken, for they did know many things of which I was ignorant, and in this they certainly were wiser than I was. But I observed that even the good artisans fell into the same error as the poets;—because they were good workmen they thought that they also knew all sorts of high matters, and this defect in them overshadowed their wisdom; and therefore I asked myself on behalf of the oracle, whether I would like to be as I was, neither having their knowledge nor their ignorance, or like them in both; and I made answer to myself and to the oracle that I was better off as I was.

This inquisition has led to my having many enemies of the worst and most dangerous kind, and has given occasion also to many calumnies. And I am called wise, for my hearers always imagine that I myself possess the wisdom which I find wanting in others: but the truth is, O men of Athens, that God only is wise; and by his answer he intends to show that the wisdom of men is worth little or nothing; he is not speaking of Socrates, he is only using my name by way of illustriaton, as if he said, He, O men, is the wisest, who, like Socrates, knows that his wisdom is in truth worth nothing. And so I go about the world, obedient to the god, and search and make enquiry into the wisdom of any one, whether citizen or stranger, who appears to be wise; and if he is not wise, then in vindication of the oracle I show him that he is not wise; and my occupation quite absorbs me, and I have no time to give either to any public matter of interest or to any concern of my own, but I am in utter poverty by reason of my devotion to the god.

There is another thing:—young men of the richer classes, who have not much to do, come about me of their own accord; they like to hear the pretenders examined, and they often imitate me, and proceed to examine others; there are plenty of persons, as they quickly discover, who think that they know something, but really know little or nothing; and then those who are examined by them instead of being angry with themselves are angry with me: This confounded Socrates, they say; this villainous misleader of youth!—and then if somebody asks them, Why, what evil does he practise or teach? they do not know, and cannot tell; but in order that they may not appear to be at a loss, they repeat the ready-made charges which are used against all philosophers about teaching things up in the clouds and under the earth, and having no gods, and making the worse appear the better cause; for they do not like to confess that their pretence of knowledge has been detected—which is the truth; and as they are numerous and ambitious and energetic, and are drawn up in battle array and have persuasive tongues, they have filled your ears with their loud and inveterate calumnies. And this is the reason why my three accusers, Meletus and Anytus and Lycon, have set upon me; Meletus, who has a quarrel with me on behalf of the poets; Anytus, on behalf of the craftsmen and politicians; Lycon, on behalf of the rhetoricians.

I have said enough in my defence against the first class of my accusers; I turn to the second class. They are headed by Meletus, that good man and true lover of his country, as he calls himself. Against these, too, I must try to make a defence:—Let their affidavit be read: it contains something of this kind: It says that Socrates is a doer of evil, who corrupts the youth; and who does not believe in the gods of the State, but has other new divinities of his own. Such is the charge; and now let us examine the particular counts. He says that I am a doer of evil, and corrupt the youth; but I say, O men of Athens, that Meletus is a doer of evil, in that he pretends to be in earnest when he is only in jest, and is so eager to bring men to trial from a pretended zeal and interest about matters in which he really never had the smallest interest. And the truth of this I will endeavour to prove to you.

Come hither, Meletus, and let me ask a question of you. You think a great deal about the improvement of youth?

Yes, I do.

Tell the judges, then, who is their improver; for you must know, as you have taken the pains to discover their corrupter, and are citing and accusing me before them. Speak, then, and tell the judges who their improver is.—Observe, Meletus, that you are silent, and have nothing to say. But is not this rather disgraceful, and a very considerable proof of what I was saying, that you have no interest in the matter? Speak up, friend, and tell us who their improver is.

The laws.

But that, my good sir, is not my meaning. I want to know who the person is, who, in the first place, knows the laws.

The judges, Socrates, who are present in court.

What, do you mean to say, Meletus, that they are able to instruct and improve youth?

Certainly they are.

What, all of them, or some only and not others?

All of them.

By the goddess Hera, that is good news! There are plenty of improvers, then. And what do you say of the audience,—do they improve them?

Yes, they do.

And the senators:

Yes, the senators improve them.

But perhaps the members of the assembly corrupt them? or do they improve them?

They improve them.

Then every Athenian improves and elevates them; all with the exception of myself; and I alone am their corrupter? Is that what you affirm?

That is what I stoutly affirm.

I am very unfortunate if you are right. But suppose I ask you a question: How about horses? does one man do them harm and all the world good? Is not the exact opposite the truth? One man is able to do them good, or at least not many;—the trainer of horses, that is to say, does them good, and others who have to do with them rather injure them? Is not that true, Meletus, of horses, or of any other animals? Most assuredly it is; whether you and Anytus say yes or no. Happy indeed would be the condition of youth if they had one corrupter only, and all the rest of the world were their improvers. But you, Meletus, have sufficiently shown that you never had a thought about the young: your carelessness is seen in your not caring about the very things which you bring against me.

And now, Meletus, I will ask you another question—by Zeus I will: Which is better, to live among bad citizens, or among good ones? Answer, friend, I say; the question is one which may be easily answered. Do not the good do their neighbours good, and the bad do them evil?

Certainly.

And is there any one who would rather be injured than benefited by those who live with him? Answer, my good friend, the law requires you to answer—does any one like to be injured?

Certainly not.

And when you accuse me of corrupting and deteriorating the youth, do you allege that I corrupt them intentionally or unintentionally?

Intentionally, I say.

But you have just admitted that the good do their neighbours good, and the evil do them evil. Now, is that a truth which your superior wisdom has recognized thus early in life, and am I, at my age, in such darkness and ignorance as not to know that if a man with whom I have to live is corrupted by me, I am very likely to be harmed by him; and yet I corrupt him, and intentionally, too—so you say, although neither I nor any other human being is ever likely to be convinced by you. But either I do not corrupt them, or I corrupt them unintentionally; and on either view of the case you lie. If my offence is unintentional, the law has no cognizance of unintentional offences: you ought to have taken me privately, and warned and admonished me; for if I had been better advised, I should have left off doing what I only did unintentionally—no doubt I should; but you would have nothing to say to me and refused to teach me. And now you bring me up in this court, which is a place not of instruction, but of punishment.

It will be very clear to you, Athenians, as I was saying, that Meletus has no care at all, great or small, about the matter. But still I should like to know, Meletus, in what I am affirmed to corrupt the young. I suppose you mean, as I infer from your indictment, that I teach them not to acknowledge the gods which the State acknowledges, but some other new divinities or spiritual agencies in their stead. These are the lessons by which I corrupt the youth, as you say.

Yes, that I say emphatically.

Then, by the gods, Meletus, of whom we are speaking, tell me and the court, in somewhat plainer terms, what you mean! For I do not as yet understand whether you affirm that I teach other men to acknowledge some gods, and therefore that I do believe in gods, and am not an entire atheist—this you do not lay to my charge,—but only you say that they are not the same gods which the city recognizes—the charge is that they are different gods. Or, do you mean that I am an atheist simply, and a teacher of atheism?

I mean the latter—that you are a complete atheist.

What an extraordinary statement! Why do you think so, Meletus? do you mean that I do not believe in the godhead of the sun or moon, like other men?

I assure you, judges, that he does not: for he says that the sun is stone, and the moon earth.

Friend Meletus, you think that you are accusing Anaxagoras: and you have but a bad opinion of the judges, if you fancy them illiterate to such a degree as not to know that these doctrines are found in the books of Anaxagoras the Clazomenian, which are full of them. And so, forsooth, the youth are said to be taught them by Socrates, when there are not infrequently exhibitions of them at the theatre (price of admission one drachma at the most); and they might pay their money, and laugh at Socrates if he pretends to father these extraordinary views. And so, Meletus, you really think that I do not believe in any god?

I swear by Zeus that you believe absolutely in none at all.

Nobody will believe you, Meletus, and I am pretty sure that you do not believe yourself. I cannot help thinking, men of Athens, that Meletus is reckless and impudent, and that he has written this indictment in a spirit of mere wantonness and youthful bravado. Has he not compounded a riddle, thinking to try me? He said to himself:—I shall see whether the wise Socrates will discover my facetious contradiction, or whether I shall be able to deceive him and the rest of them. For he certainly does appear to me to contradict himself in the indictment as much as if he said that Socrates is guilty of not believing in the gods, and yet of believing in them—but this is not like a person who is in earnest.

I should like you, O men of Athens, to join me in examing what I conceive to be his inconsistency; and do you, Meletus, answer. And I must remind the audience of my request that they would not make a disturbance if I speak in my accustomed manner:

Did ever man, Meletus, believe in the existence of human things, and not of human beings? . . . I wish, men of Athens, that he would answer, and not be always trying to get up an interruption. Did ever any man believe in horsemanship, and not in horses? or in flute-playing, and not in flute-players? No, my friend; I will answer to you and to the court, as you refuse to answer for yourself. There is no man who ever did. But now please to answer the next question: Can a man believe in spiritual and divine agencies and not in spirits or demigods?

He cannot.

How lucky I am to have extracted that answer, by the assistance of the court! But then you swear in the indictment that I teach and believe in divine or spiritual agencies (new or old, no matter for that); at any rate, I believe in spiritual agencies,—so you say and swear in the affidavit; and yet if I believe in divine beings, how can I help believing in spirits or demigods;—must I not? To be sure I must; and therefore I may assume that your silence gives consent. Now what are spirits or demigods? are they not either gods or the sons of gods?

Certainly they are.

But this is what I call the facetious riddle invented by you: the demigods or spirits are gods, and you say first that I do not believe in gods, and then again that I do believe in gods; that is, if I believe in demigods. For if the demigods are the illegitimate sons of gods, whether by the nymphs or by any other mothers, of whom they are said to be the sons—what human being will ever believe that there are no gods if they are the sons of gods? You might as well affirm the existence of mules, and deny that of horses and asses. Such nonsense, Meletus, could only have been intended by you to make trial of me. You have put this into the indictment because you had nothing real of which to accuse me. But no one who has a particle of understanding will ever be convinced by you that the same men can believe in divine and superhuman things, and yet not believe that there are gods and demigods and heroes.

I have said enough in answer to the charge of Meletus: any elaborate defence is unnecessary; but I know only too well how many are the enmities which I have incurred, and many are the enmities which I have incurred, and this is what will be my destruction if I am destroyed;—not Meletus, nor yet Anytus, but the envy and detraction of the world, which has been the death of many good men, and will probably be the death of many more; there is no danger of my being the last of them.

Some one will say: And are you not ashamed, Socrates, of a course of life which is likely to bring you to an untimely end? To him I may fairly answer: There you are mistaken: a man who is good for anything ought not to calculate the chance of living or dying; he ought only to consider whether in doing anything he is doing right or wrong—acting the part of a good man or of a bad.

. . . Strange, indeed, would be my conduct, O men of Athens, if I who, when I was ordered by the generals whom you chose to command me at Potidaea and Amphipolis and Delium, remained where they placed me, like any other man, facing death—if now, when, as I conceive and imagine, God orders me to fulfill the philosopher's mission of searching into myself and other men, I were to desert my post through fear of death, or any other fear; that would indeed be strange, and I might justly be arraigned in court for denying the existence of gods, if I disobeyed the oracle because I was afraid of death, fancying that I was wise when I was not wise. For the fear of death is indeed the pretence of wisdom, and not real wisdom, being a pretence of knowing the unknown; and no one knows whether death, which men in their fear apprehend to be the greatest evil, may not be the greatest good. Is not this ignorance of a disgraceful sort, the ignorance which is the conceit that man knows what he does not know?

. . .—If you say to me, Socrates, this time we will not mind Anytus, and you shall be let off, but upon one condition, that you are not to enquire and speculate in this way any more, and that if you are caught doing so again you shall die;—if this was the condition on which you let me go, I should reply: Men of Athens, I honour and love you; but I shall obey God rather than you, and while I have life and strength I shall never cease from the practice and teaching of philosophy, exhorting any one whom I meet and saying to him after my manner: You, my friend,—a citizen of the great and mighty and wise city of Athens,—are you not ashamed of heaping up the greatest amount of money and honour and reputation, and caring so little about wisdom and truth and the greatest improvement of the soul, which you never regard or heed at all? And if the person with whom I am arguing, says: Yes, but I do care; then I do not leave him or let him go at once; but I proceed to interrogate and examine and cross-examine him, and if I think that he has no virtue in him, but only says that he has, I reproach him with undervaluing the greater, and overvaluing the less. And I shall repeat the same words to every one whom I meet, young and old, citizen and alien, but especially to the citizens, inasmuch as they are my brethren. For know that this is the command of God; and I believe that no greater good has ever happened in the state than my service to the God. For I do nothing but go about persuading you all, old and young alike, not to take thought for your persons or your properties, but first and chiefly to care about the greatest improvement of the soul. I tell you that virtue is not given by money, but that from virtue comes money and every other good of man, public as well as private. This is my teaching, and if this is the doctrine which corrupts the youth, I am a mischievous person. But if any one says that this is not my teaching, he is speaking an untruth. Wherefore, O men of Athens, I say to you, do as Anytus bids or not as Anytus bids, and either acquit me or not; but whichever you do, understand that I shall never alter my ways, not even if I have to die many times.

Men of Athens, do not interrupt, but hear me; there was an understanding between us that you should hear me to the end: I have something more to say, at which you may be inclined to cry out; but I believe that to hear me will be good for you, and therefore I beg that you will not cry out. I would have you know, that if you kill such a one as I am, you will injure yourselves more than you will injure me. Nothing will injure me, not Meletus nor yet Anytus—they cannot, for a bad man is not permitted to injure a better than himself. I do not deny that Anytus may, perhaps, kill him, or drive him into exile, or deprive him of civil rights; and he may imagine, and others may imagine, that he is inflicting a great injury upon him: but there I do not agree. For the evil of doing as he is doing—the evil of unjustly taking away the life of another—is greater far.

And now, Athenians, I am not going to argue for my own sake, as you may think, but for yours, that you may not sin against the God by condemning me, who am his gift to you. For if you kill me you will not easily find a successor to me, who, if I may use such a ludicrous figure of speech, am a sort of gadfly, given to the state by God; and the state is a great and noble steed who is tardy in his motions owing to his very size, and requires to be stirred into life. I am that gadfly which God has attached to the state, and all day long and in all places am always fastening upon you, arousing and persuading and reproaching you. You will not easily find another like me, and therefore I would advise you to spare me. I dare say that you may feel out of temper (like a person who is suddenly awakened from sleep), and you think that you might easily strike me dead as Anytus advises, and then you would sleep on for the remainder of your lives, unless God in his care of you sent you another gadfly. When I say that I am given to you by God, the proof of my mission is this:—if I had been like other men, I should not have neglected all my own concerns or patiently seen the neglect of them during all these years, and have been doing yours, coming to you individually like a father or elder brother, exhorting you to regard virtue; such conduct, I say, would be unlike human nature. If I had gained anything, or if my exhortations had been paid, there would have been some sense in my doing so; but now, as you will perceive, not even the impudence of my accusers dares to say that I have ever exacted or sought pay of any one; of that they have no witness. And I have a sufficient witness to the truth of what I say—my poverty. . . .

But I shall be asked, Why do people delight in continually conversing with you? I have told you already, Athenians, the whole truth about this matter: they like to hear the cross-examination of the pretenders to wisdom; there is amusement in it. Now this duty of cross-examining other men has been imposed upon me by God; and has been signified to me by oracles, visions, and in every way in which the will of divine power was ever intimated to any one. . . .

The Court votes and finds him guilty, the voting being 281 for guilty, and 220 for innocent. Socrates then addresses them as to the penalty.

Some one will say: Yes, Socrates, but cannot you hold your tongue, and then you may go into a foreign city, and no one will interfere with you? Now I have great difficulty in making you understand my answer to this. For if I tell you that to do as you say would be a disobedience to the God, and therefore that I cannot hold my tongue, you will not believe that I am serious; and if I say again that daily discourse about virtue, and of those other things about which you hear me examining myself and others, is the greatest good of man, and that the unexamined life is not worth living, you are still less likely to believe me. Yet I say what is true, although a thing of which it is hard for me to persuade you. . . .

The Court then votes again, and condemns him to death.

Not much time will be gained, O Athenians, in return for the evil name which you will get from the detractors of the city, who will say that you killed Socrates, a wise man; for they will call me wise, even although I am not wise, when they want to reproach you. If you had waited a little while, your desire would have been fulfilled in the course of nature. For I am far advanced in years, as you may perceive, and not far from death. I am speaking now not to all of you, but only to those who have condemned me to death. And I have another thing to say to them: You think that I was convicted because I had no words of the sort which would have procured my acquittal—I mean, if I had thought fit to leave nothing undone or unsaid. Not so; the deficiency which led to my conviction was not of words—certainly not. But I had not the boldness or impudence or inclination to address you as you would have liked me to do, weeping and wailing and lamenting, and saying and doing many things which yu have been accustomed to hear from others, and which, as I maintain, are unworthy of me. I thought at the time that I ought not to do anything common or mean when in danger: nor do I now repent of the style of my defence; I would rather die having spoken after my manner, than speak in your manner and live. For neither in war nor yet at law ought I or any man to use every way of escaping death. Often in battle there can be no doubt that if a man will throw away his arms, and fall on his knees before his pursuers, he may escape death; and in other dangers there are other ways of escaping death, if a man is willing to say and do anything. The difficulty, my friends, is not to avoid death, but to avoid unrighteousness; for that runs faster than death. I am old and move slowly, and the slower runner has overtaken me, and my accusers are keen and quick, and the faster runner, who is unrighteousness, has overtaken them. And now I depart hence condemned by you to suffer the penalty of death,—they too go their ways condemned by the truth to suffer the penalty of villainy and wrong; and I must abide by my award—let them abide by theirs. . . .

But if death is the journey to another place, and there, as men say, all the dead abide, what good, O my friends and judges, can be greater than this? If indeed when the pilgrim arrives in the world below, he is delivered from the professors of justice in this world, and finds the true judges who are said to give judgment there, Minos and Rhadamanthus and Aeacus and Triptolemus, and other sons of God who were righteous in their own life, that pilgrimage will be worth making. What would not a man give if he might converse with Orpheus and Musaeus and Hesiod and Homer? Nay, if this be true, let me die again and again. I myself, too, shall have a wonderful interest in there meeting and conversing with Palamedes, and Ajax the son of Telamon, and any other ancient hero who has suffered death through an unjust judgment; and there will be no small pleasure, as I think, in comparing my own sufferings with theirs. Above all, I shall then be able to continue my search into true and false knowledge; as in this world, so also in the next; and I shall find out who is wise, and who pretends to be wise, and is not. What would not a man give, O judges, to be able to examine the leader of the great Trojan expedition; or Odysseus or Sisyphus, or numberless others, men and women too! What infinite delight would there be in conversing with them and asking them questions! In another world they do not put a man to death for asking questions: assuredly not. For besides being happier than we are, they will be immortal, if what is said is true.

Wherefore, O judges, be of good cheer about death, and know of a certainty, that no evil can happen to a good man, either in life or after death. He and his are not neglected by the gods; nor has my own approaching end happened by mere chance. But I see clearly that the time had arrived when it was better for me to die and be released from trouble; wherefore the oracle gave no sign. For which reason, also, I am not angry with my condemners, or with my accusers; they have done me no harm, although they did not mean to do me any good; and for this I may gently blame them.

Still I have a favour to ask of them. When my sons are grown up, I would ask you, O my friends, to punish them; and I would have you trouble them, as I have troubled you, if they seem to pretend to be something when they are really nothing,—then reprove them, as I have reproved you, for not caring about that for which they ought to care, and thinking that they are something when they are really nothing. And if you do this, both I and my sons will have received justice at your hands.

The hour of departure has arrived, and we go our ways—I to die, and you to live. Which is better God only knows.

B. SOME HISTORICAL COMMENTS ON PHILOSOPHY

The following selections are comments about philosophy by great philosophers of the past and important contemporary philosophers. They are not intended to tell you what philosophy is (this whole book is designed to do that). These selections give you some important hints about the nature of philosophy and some good advice for beginning the study of philosophy.

A CRITICISM OF SOCRATES

[Socrates, some who] occasionally hear you argue thus feel in this way. They think that owing to their inexperience in the game of question and answer they are at every question led astray a little bit by the argument, and when these bits are accumulated at the conclusion of the discussion mighty is their fall, and the apparent contradiction of what they at first said, and that just as by expert checker players the unskilled are finally shut in and cannot make a move, so they are finally blocked and have their mouths stopped by this other game of checkers played not with counters but with words; yet the truth is not affected by that outcome. I say this with reference to the present case, for this instance one might say that he is unable in words to contend against you at each question, but that when it comes to facts he sees that of those who turn to philosophy, not merely touching upon it to complete their education and dropping it while still young, but lingering too long in the study of it, the majority become cranks, not to say rascals, and those accounted the finest spirits among them are still rendered useless to society by the pursuit which you commend.

Plato, *The Republic*

PART OF SOCRATES' ANSWER

You are right in affirming that the finest spirits among the philosophers are of no service to the multitude. But bid him blame for this uselessness, not the finer spirits, but those who do not know how to make use of them. For it is not the natural course of things that the pilot should beg the sailors to be ruled by him or that wise men should go to the doors of the rich. But the true nature of things is that whether the sick man be rich or poor he must needs go to the door of the physician, and everyone who needs to be governed to the door of the man who knows how to govern, not that the ruler should implore his natural subjects to let themselves be ruled, if he is really good for anything.

Plato, *The Republic*

IDENTIFYING THE TRUE LOVER OF PHILOSOPHY

There is an experimental method for determining the truth in such cases that, far from being vulgar, is truly appropriate to those stuffed with secondhand opinions. One must point out to such men that the whole plan is possible and explain what preliminary steps and how much hard work it will require, for the hearer, if he is genuinely devoted to philosophy and is a man of God with a natural affinity and fitness for the work, sees in the course marked out a path of enchantment, which he must at once strain every nerve to follow, or die in the attempt. Thereupon he braces himself and his guide to the task and does not relax his efforts until he either crowns them with final accomplishments or acquires the faculty of tracing his own way no longer accompanied by the pathfinder. When this conviction has taken possession of him, such a man passes his life in whatever occupations he may engage in, but through it all never ceases to practice philosophy and such habits of daily life as will be most effective in making him an intelligent and retentive student, able to reason soberly by himself. Other practices than these he shuns to the end.

As for those, however, who are not genuine converts to philosophy, but have only a superficial tinge of doctrine—like the coat of tan that people get in the sun—as soon as they see how many subjects there are to study, how much hard work they involve, and how indispensable it is for the project to adopt a well-ordered scheme of living, they decide that the plan is difficult if not impossible for them, and so they really do not prove capable of practicing philosophy. Some of them too persuade themselves that they are well enough informed already on the whole subject and have no need of further application. This test then proves to be the surest and safest in dealing with those who are self-indulgent and incapable of continued hard work, since they throw the blame not on their guide but on their own inability to follow out in detail the course of training subsidiary to the project.

Plato, *Seventh Letter*

THE ORIGIN OF PHILOSOPHY

It is owing to their wonder that men both now begin and at first began to philosophize; they wondered originally at the obvious difficulties; then advanced little by little and stated difficulties about the greater matters, e.g., about the phenomena of the moon and those of the sun and of the stars, and about the genesis of the universe. And a man who is puzzled and wonders thinks himself ignorant (whence even the lover of myth is in a sense a lover of Wisdom, for the myth is composed of wonders); therefore since they philosophized in order to escape from ignorance, evidently they were pursuing science in order to know, and not for any utilitarian end. And this is confirmed by the facts; for it was when almost all the necessities of life and the things that make for comfort and recreation had been secured, that such knowledge began to be sought. Evidently then we do not seek it for the sake of any other advantage; but as the man is free, we say, who exists for his own sake and not for another's, so we pursue this as the only free science, for it alone exists for its own sake.

Aristotle, *The Metaphysics*

THE BEGINNING OF PHILOSOPHY

Observe, this is the beginning of philosophy, a perception of the disagreement of men with one another, and an inquiry into the cause of the disagreement, and a condemnation and distrust of that which only "seems" whether it "seems" rightly, and a discovery of some rule, as we have discovered a balance in the determination of weights, and a carpenter's rule in the case of straight and crooked things. This is the beginning of philosophy. Must we say that all things are right which seem so to all? And how is it possible that contradictions can be right? Not all then, but all which seem right to the Syrians? Why more than what seem right to the Egyptians? Why more than what seems right to me or to any other man? Not at all more. What then "seems" to every man is not sufficient for determining what "is"; for neither in the case of weights or measures are we satisfied with the bare appearance, but in each case we have discovered a certain rule. In this matter then is there no rule superior to what "seems"? And how is it possible that the most necessary things among men should have no sign, and be incapable of being discovered? There is then some rule. And why then do we not seek the rule and discover it, and afterward use it without varying from it, not even stretching out the finger without it? For this, I think, is that which when it is discovered cures of their madness those who use mere "seeming" as a measure, and misuse it; so that for the future proceeding from certain things known and made clear we may use it in the case of particular things the preconceptions of which are distinctly fixed.

Epictetus, *Discourses*

BEGINNING PHILOSOPHY

If a man would pursue Philosophy, his first task is to throw away conceit. For it is impossible for a man to begin to learn that he has a conceit that he already knows.

Epictetus, *Enchiridion*

TWO THEOLOGIANS ON THE LIMITS OF PHILOSOPHY

To discuss historical topics, I left the philosophers alone for a while. Now I come back to them. These men, in all their laborious investigations, seem to have had one supreme and common objective: to discover what manner of living is best suited to laying hold upon happiness. Yet, they have ended up by disagreeing—disciples with masters, and disciples with fellow disciples. Why, except that they sought the answer to their question merely in human terms, depending upon human experience and human reasoning? It is true that some of their dissensions may be explained by a less worthy factor; namely, the vainglorious desire to appear wiser and more penetrating than one's colleague, less dependent upon others' opinions, and more of a creative thinker. Nevertheless, we must be ready to allow that some at least, perhaps many, who broke with their teachers or fellow students, did so out of a pure love of the truth, determined to fight for it as they understood it (whether it was actually the truth or not). What does it all go to prove except that human unhappiness cannot get very far along the road to happiness unless divine authority shows the way?

Augustine of Hippo, *The City of God*

The philosophical sciences deal with all parts of reality, even with God; hence Aristotle refers to one department of philosophy as theology or the divine science. That being the case, no need arises for another kind of education to be admitted or entertained.

On the other hand, St. Paul says, *All Scripture inspired of God is profitable to teach, to reprove, to correct, to instruct in righteousness*. Divinely inspired Scripture, however, is no part of the branches of philosophy traced by reasoning. Accordingly it is expedient to have another body of sure knowledge inspired by God.

Reply: It should be urged that human well-being has called for schooling in what God has revealed, in addition to the philosophical researches pursued by human reasoning.

Above all because God destines us for an end beyond the grasp of reason; according to Isaiah, *Eye hath not seen, O God, without thee what thou has prepared for them that love thee*. Now we have to recognize an end before we can stretch out and exert ourselves for it. Hence the necessity for our welfare that divine truths surpassing reason should be signified to us through divine revelation.

We also stand in need of being instructed by divine revelation even in religious matters the human reason is able to investigate. For the rational truth about God would be reached only by few, and even so after a long time and mixed with many mistakes; whereas on knowing this depends our whole welfare, which is in God. In these circumstances, then, it was to prosper the salvation of human beings, and the more widely and less anxiously, that they were provided for by divine revelation about divine things.

These then are the grounds of holding the sacred doctrine which has come to us through revelation beyond the discoveries of the rational sciences.

Hence: **1.** Admittedly the reason should not pry into things too high for human knowledge, nevertheless when they are revealed by God they should be welcomed by faith: indeed the passage goes on to say, *Many things are shown thee above the understanding of men*. And on them Christian teaching rests.

2. The diversification of the sciences is brought about by the diversity of aspects under which things can be known. Both an astronomer and a physical scientist may demonstrate the same conclusion, for instance that the earth is spherical; the first, however, works in a mathematical medium prescinding from material qualities, while for the second his medium is the observation of material bodies through the senses. Accordingly there is nothing to stop the same things from being treated by the philosophical sciences when they can be looked at in the light of natural reason and by another science when they are looked at in the light of divine revelation. Consequently, the theology of holy teaching differs in kind from that theology which is ranked as a part of philosophy.

Thomas Aquinas, *Summa Theologica*

MORAL PHILOSOPHY

Moral philosophy, or the science of human nature, may be treated after two different manners; each of which has its peculiar merit, and may contribute to the entertainment, instruction, and reformation of mankind. The one considers man chiefly as born for action; and as influenced in his measures by taste and sentiment; pursuing one object, and avoiding another, according to the value which these objects seem to possess, and according to the light in which they present themselves. As virtue, of all objects, is allowed to be the most valuable, this species of philosophers paint her in the most amiable colours; borrowing all helps from poetry and eloquence, and treating their subject in an easy and obvious manner, and such as is best fitted to please the imagination, and engage the affections. They select the most striking observations and instances from common life; place opposite characters in a proper contrast; and alluring us into the paths of virtue by the views of glory and happiness, direct our steps in these paths by the soundest precepts and most illustrious examples. They make us *feel* the difference between vice and virtue; they excite and regulate our sentiments; and so they can but bend our hearts to the love of probity and true honour, they think, that they have fully attained the end of all their labours.

The other species of philosophers considers man in the light of a reasonable rather than an active being, and endeavours to form his understanding more than cultivate his manners. They regard human nature as a subject of speculation; and with a narrow scrutiny examine it, in order to find those principles, which regulate our understanding, excite our sentiments, and make us approve or blame any particular object, action, or behaviour. They think it a reproach to all literature, that philosophy should not yet have fixed, beyond controversy, the foundation of morals, reasoning, and criticism; and should for ever talk of truth and falsehood, vice and virtue, beauty and deformity without being able to determine the source of these distinctions. While they attempt this arduous task, they are deterred by no difficulties; but proceeding from particular instances to general principles, they still push on their enquiries to principles more general, and rest not satisfied till they arrive at those original principles, by which, in every science, all human curiosity must be bounded. Though their speculations seem abstract, and even unintelligible to common readers, they aim at the approbation of the learned and the wise; and think themselves sufficiently compensated for the labour of their whole lives, if they can discover some hidden truths, which may contribute to the instruction of posterity.

David Hume, *Enquiry*

THE AIM OF PHILOSOPHY

Philosophy is the system of all philosophical cognition. We must use this term in an objective sense, if we understand by it the archetype of all attempts at philosophizing, and the standard by which all subjective philosophies are to be judged. In this sense, philosophy is merely the idea of a possible science, which does not exist *in concreto*, but to which we endeavour in various ways to approximate, until we have discovered the right path to pursue—a path overgrown by the errors and illusions of sense—and the image we have hitherto tried in vain to shape has become a perfect copy of the great prototype. Until that time, we cannot learn philosophy—it does not exist; if it does, where is it, who possesses it, and how shall we know it? We can only learn to philosophize; in other words, we can only exercise our powers of reasoning in accordance with general principles, retaining at the same time, the right of investigating the sources of these principles, of testing, and even of rejecting them.

Philosophy was personified and presented to us in the ideal of a *philosopher*. In this view, philosophy is the science of the relation of all who occupies himself with conceptions—but a lawgiver, legislating for human reason. In this sense of the word, it would be in the highest degree arrogant to assume the title of philosopher, and to pretend that we had reached the perfection of the prototype which lies in the idea alone.

In view of the complete systematic unity of reason, there can only be one ultimate end of all the operations of the mind. To this all other aims are subordinate, and nothing more than means for its attainment. This ultimate end is the destination of man, and the philosophy which relates to it is termed moral philosophy. The superior position occupied by moral philosophy, above all other spheres for the operations of reason, sufficiently indicates the reason why the ancients always included the idea—and in an especial manner—of moralist in that of philosopher. Even at the present day, we call a man who appears to have the power of self-government, even although his knowledge may be very limited, by the name of philosopher.

The legislation of human reason, or philosophy, has two objects—nature and freedom—and thus contains not only the laws of nature, but also those of ethics, at first in two separate systems, which, finally, merge into one grand philosophical system of cognition. The philosophy of nature relates to that *which is*, that of ethics to that which *ought to be*.

Immanuel Kant, *Critique of Pure Reason*

A PRAGMATIST VIEW

The pragmatic method is primarily a method of settling metaphysical disputes that otherwise might be interminable. Is the world one or many?–fated or free?–material or spiritual?—here are notions either of which may or may not hold good of the world; and disputes over such notions are unending. The pragmatic method of such cases is to try to interpret each notion by tracing its respective practical consequences. What difference would it practically make to anyone if this notion, rather than that notion, were true? If no practical difference whatever can be traced, then the alternatives mean practically the same thing, and all dispute is idle. Whenever a dispute is serious, we ought to be able to show some practical diference that must follow from one side or the other's being right.

It is astonishing to see how many philosophical disputes collapse into insignificance the moment you subject them to this simple test of tracing a concrete consequence. There can *be* no difference anywhere that doesn't *make* a difference elsewhere—no difference in abstract truth that doesn't express itself in a difference in concrete fact and in conduct consequent upon that fact, imposed on somebody, will make to you and me, at definite instants of our life, if this world-formula or that world-formula be the true one.

William James, *Pragmatism*

A PHENOMENOLOGICAL VIEW

Questions, and particularly fundamental questions, do not just occur like stones and water. Questions are not found ready-made like shoes and clothes and books. Questions *are*, and are only as they are actually asked.

A leading into the asking of the fundamental questions is consequently not a going to something that lies and stands somewhere; no, this leading-to must first awaken and create the questioning. . . . It is a leading for which in the very nature of things there can be no following. When we hear of disciples, "followers," as in a school of philosophy for example, it means that the nature of questioning is misunderstood. . . . when a philosophy becomes fashionable, either it is no real philosophy or it has been misinterpreted and misused. . . . philosophy cannot be directly learned like manual and technical skills.

It [philosophy] cannot be judged by its usefulness in the manner of economic or other professional knowledge. . . . It is absolutely correct and proper to say that "You can't do anything with philosophy. It is only wrong to suppose that this is the last word on philosophy." For the rejoinder imposes itself: granted that *we* cannot do anything with philosophy, might not philosophy, if we concern ourselves with it, do something *with us?*

Martin Heidegger, "The Fundamental Question of Metaphysics"

PHILOSOPHY AND LIFE

The story is told (by Kierkegaard) of the absent-minded man so abstracted from his own life that he hardly knows he exists until, one fine morning, he wakes up to find himself dead. It is a story that has a special point today, since this civilization of ours has at last got its hands on weapons with which it could easily bring upon itself the fate of Kierkegaard's hero: we could wake up tomorrow morning dead—and without ever having touched the roots of our own existence. There is by this time widespread anxiety and even panic over the dangers of the atomic age; but the public soul-searching and stocktaking rarely, if ever, go to the heart of the matter. We do not ask ourselves what the ultimate ideas behind our civilization are that have brought us into this danger; we do not search for the human face behind the bewildering array of instruments that man has forged; in a word, we do not dare to be philosophical.

William Barrett, *Irrational Man*

AN EXISTENTIALIST VIEW

In philosophical matters almost everyone believes himself capable of judgment. Whereas it is recognized that in the sciences study, training, and method are indispensable to understanding, in philosophy men generally assume that they are competent to form an opinion without preliminary study. Our own humanity, our own destiny, our own experience strike us as a sufficient basis for philosophical opinions.

This notion that philosophy must be accessible to all is justified. The circuitous paths travelled by specialists in philosophy have meaning only if they lead man to an awareness of being and his place in it.

Second: Philosophical thought must always spring from free creation. Every man must accomplish it for himself.

A marvellous indication of man's innate disposition to philosophy is to be found in the questions asked by children. It is not uncommon to hear from the mouths of children words which penetrate to the very depths of philosophy.

Karl Jaspers, *The Way of Wisdom*

A LINGUISTIC PHILOSOPHER

[We] proceed from "ordinary language," that is, by examining *what we should say when,* and so why and what we should mean by it. Perhaps this method, at least as *one* philosophical method, scarcely requires justification at present—too evidently, there is gold in them thar hills: more opportune would be a warning about the care and thoroughness needed if it is not to fall into disrepute. I will, however, justify it very briefly.

First, words are our tools, and, as a minimum, we should use clean tools: we should know what we mean and what we do not, and we must forearm ourselves against the traps that language sets us. Secondly, words are not (except in their own little corner) facts or things: we need therefore to prise them off the world, to hold them apart from and against it, so that we can realise their inadequacies and arbitrarinesses, and can re-look at the world without blinkers. Thirdly, and more hopefully, our common stock of words embodies all the distinctions men have found worth drawing, and the connexions they have found worth marking, in the lifetimes of many generations: these surely are likely to be more numerous, more sound, since they have stood up to the long test of the survival of the fittest, and more subtle, at least in all ordinary and reasonably practical matters, than any that you or I are likely to think up in our armchairs of an afternoon— the most favored alternative method.

In view of the prevalence of the slogan "ordinary language," and of such names as "linguistic" or "analytic" philosophy or "the analysis of language," one thing needs specially emphasising to counter misunderstandings. When we examine what we should say when, what words we should use in what situations, we are looking again not *merely* at words (or "meanings," whatever they may be) but also at the realities we use the words to talk about: we are using a sharpened awareness of words to sharpen our perception of, though not as the final arbiter of, the phenomena. For this reason I think it might be better to use, for this way of doing philosophy, some less misleading name than those given above—for instance, "linguistic phenomenology," only that is rather a mouthful. What we are after [is] a good site for *field work* in philosophy. Here at last we should be able to unfreeze, to loosen up and get going on agreeing about discoveries, however small, and on agreeing about how to reach agreement.

Certainly ordinary language has no claim to be the last word, if there is such a thing. It embodies, indeed, something better than the metaphysics of the Stone Age, namely, as we said, the inherited experience and acumen of many generations of men. But then, that acumen has been concentrated primarily upon the practical business of life. If a distinction works well for practical purposes in ordinary life (no mean feat, for even ordinary life is full of hard cases), then there is sure to be something in it, it will not mark nothing: yet this is likely enough to be not the best way of arranging things if our interests are more extensive or intellectual than the ordinary. And again, that experience has been derived only from the sources available to ordinary men throughout most of civilised history: it has not been fed from the resources of the microscope and its successors. And it must be added too, that superstition and error and fantasy of all kinds do become incorporated in ordinary language and even sometimes stand up to the survival test (only, when they do, why should we not detect it?). Certainly, then, ordinary language is *not* the last word: in principle it can everywhere be supplemented and improved upon and superseded. Only remember, it is the *first* word.

John Austin, "A Plea for Excuses"

A LAST WORD

Philosophy has to be self-thought if it is to be thought at all. It is an activity, rather than a set of propositions. Each man needs to think out the problems and their solutions for himself, and although other men's philosophizing may help him in his own, he cannot accept their conclusions, or even understand their arguments, until he has already argued a lot with himself.

J. R. Lucas, *The Freedom of the Will*

C. SOME USEFUL TECHNIQUES

We have inserted here a brief discussion of logic and a selection from the chapter "How to Read Philosophy," from *How to Read a Book* by Mortimer Adler, a contemporary philosopher. These selections will help you know what to look for and what questions to ask when you read the selections from various philosophers in the remainder of the book.

A MINICOURSE IN LOGIC

Philosophers argue a lot; that is, they give *reasons* for their opinions. We can see a common form or structure in this process of reasoning, no matter what the content, no matter what we reason *about*. The structure of any argument consists in two parts: the premises (reasons, evidence) and the conclusion (the point to be proved).

In *inductive* reasoning the conclusion is only probable; *deductive* reasoning aims to be certain, to "demonstrate" with certainty that its conclusion *must* be true.

Three conditions must be met if the aim is to be achieved. First, *the argument must be valid*; that is, the conclusion must necessarily follow from the premises. Most of the science of logic consists in rules for deciding when this happens, what forms of argument are logically valid, and which are not. For instance, the first two arguments below are logically valid because the conclusion necessarily follows from the premises: *if* the premises are true, then the conclusion *must* be true. The last two arguments are *not* logically valid because the conclusion does not necessarily follow from the premises; the premises could be true without the conclusion being true.

(1) If I think, I must exist.
    I do think.
    Therefore I exist.

(2) All philosophers are insane.
    Socrates was a philosopher.
    Therefore Socrates was insane.

(3) If I die, you will be sad.
    You are sad.
    Therefore I must have died.

(4) All bodies are in space.
    All light is in space.
    Therefore light is a body.

You probably noticed that argument (2) is not as convincing as argument (1); nevertheless, the logical form is just as valid. For both, *if* the premises are true, then the conclusion must be true. What is wrong with argument (2)? The first premise is not true. Thus the second requirement for a good argument is *true premises*. (Notice that a premise is a single statement, or declarative sentence, or "proposition," not an argument. Only a single statement can be *true or false*. An argument is logically *valid or invalid*.)

Just as arguments are made of statements (propositions), so each proposition is made of *terms*: a subject term and a predicate term. Terms are neither true nor false in themselves. For instance, the term "mortal" is neither true nor false. The *sentence* "all men are mortal" is true and the sentence "numbers are mortal" is false. Terms are, however, either *clear or unclear* (ambiguous); and if they are ambiguous, they must be defined to make them clear. If we use a term ambiguously—if a term changes its meaning in the course of an argument—then the conclusion is not certain. For instance, if I argue

Whatever has a bark might be a dog.
This tree has a bark.
Therefore this tree might be a dog.

the term "bark" is used ambiguously.

Thus the three questions you should ask of your author when reading and of yourself when writing are: (1) are the terms clear or unclear? (2) are the premises true or false? and (3) are the arguments logically valid or invalid? If an argument's terms are clear, *and* the premises true, *and* the argument logically valid, then the conclusion *must* be true. So if you wish to disagree with someone's conclusion, you must show either (1) that a term has been used ambiguously, or (2) (the most usual way to disagree with an argument) that the argument has a false premise, or (3) that the argument is not logically valid: that is, that the conclusion does not necessarily follow even if the premises are granted to be true. (This applies only to deductive arguments; inductive arguements do not claim certainty, only probability.) If you cannot do any one of these three things, then you must agree with the conclusion, because it has been validly and certainly proved to be true.

HOW TO READ PHILOSOPHY

Philosophy, according to Aristotle, begins in wonder.

Adults do not lose the curiosity that seems to be a native human trait, but their curiosity deteriorates in quality. They want to know whether something is so, not why.

What happens between the nursery and college to turn the flow of questions off, or, rather, to turn it into the duller channels of adult curiosity about matters of fact? A mind not agitated by good questions cannot appreciate the significance of even the best answers. It is easy enough to learn the answers. But to develop actively inquisitive minds, alive with real questions, profound questions—that is another story.

Why should we have to try to develop such minds, when children are born with them? Somewhere along the line, adults must fail somehow to sustain the infant's curiosity at its original depth. School itself, perhaps, dulls the mind—by the dead weight of rote learning, much of which may be necessary. The failure is probably even more the parent's fault.

We have no solution for this problem; we are certainly not so brash as to think we can tell you how to answer the profound and wondrous questions that children put. But we do want you to recognize that one of the most remarkable things about the great philosophical books is that they ask the same sort of profound questions that children ask. The ability to retain the child's view of the world, with at the same time a mature understanding of what it means to retain it, is extremely rare—and a person who has these qualities is likely to be able to contribute something really important to our thinking.

We are not required to think as children in order to understand existence. (Children certainly do not, and cannot, understand it—if, indeed, anyone can.) But we must be able to see as children see, to wonder as they wonder, to ask as they ask. The complexities of adult life get in the way of the truth. The great philosophers have always been able to clear away the complexities and see simple distinctions—simple once they are stated, vastly difficult before. If we are to follow them we too must be childishly simple in our questions—and maturely wise in our replies.

The major effort of the reader, therefore, must be with respect to the terms and the initial propositions. Although the philosopher, like the scientist, has a technical terminology, the words that express his terms are usually taken from common speech, but used in a very special sense. This demands special care from the reader. If he does not overcome the tendency to use familiar words in a familiar way, he will probably make gibberish and nonsense of the book.

The basic terms of philosophical discussions are, of course, *abstract*. But so are those of science. No general knowledge is expressible except in abstract terms. There is nothing particularly difficult about abstractions. We use them every day of our lives and in every sort of conversation.

Whenever you talk generally about anything, you are using abstractions. What you perceive through your senses is always concrete and particular. What you think with your mind is always abstract and general. You cannot see or touch or even *imagine* the general aspect thus referred to. If you could, there would be no difference between the senses and the mind. People who try to *imagine* what ideas refer to befuddle themselves, and end up with a hopeless feeling about all abstractions.

There is no trouble about assumptions. Make them to see what follows, even if you yourself have contrary presuppositions. It is a good mental exercise to pretend that you believe something you really do not believe.

The method according to which you should read a philosophical book is very similar to the method according to which it is written. A philosopher, faced with a problem, can do nothing but think about it. A reader, faced with a philosophical book, can do nothing but read it—which means, as we know, thinking about it. There are no other aids except the mind itself.

But this essential loneliness of reader and book is precisely the situation that we imagined at the beginning of our long discussion of the rules of analytical reading. Thus you can see why we say that the rules of reading, as we have stated and explained them, apply more directly to the reading of philosophical books than to the reading of any other kind.

The disagreements of others are relatively unimportant. Your responsibility is only to make up your own mind.

It is, indeed, the most distinctive mark of philosophical questions that everyone must answer them for himself. Taking the opinions of others is not solving them, but evading them. And your answers must be solidly grounded, with arguments to back them up.

The questions philosophers ask are simply more important than the questions asked by anyone else. Except children.

PART ONE
WHAT CAN WE KNOW?

CHAPTER ONE
CAN WE KNOW ANYTHING? THE PROBLEM OF SCEPTICISM

A sceptic is a person who challenges claims to knowledge made by others. A sceptic in the limited sense may challenge claims to knowledge in one area while admitting that we have knowledge in other areas. For example, you might be sceptical about claims to knowledge made by astrologers, while admitting claims to knowledge made by astronomers. However ever since the beginning of philosophy there have been some thinkers who adopted, for one reason or another, a *general* scepticism. These philosophers have challenged *all* claims to knowledge and held that we do not know anything: that no claim to knowledge in *any* area can be supported.

The exact definition of knowledge has been a matter for philosophical argument ever since Socrates, but there is agreement on some points. We do not speak of knowing something unless it is *true:* if a statement turns out to be false we admit that we could not have known it, for knowing it means knowing that it is true. It also seems that to know something, we must *believe* it and have a *justification* for believing it. The idea of knowledge as *justified true belief* has been challenged, but most philosophers would agree that the general idea is correct and that the difficulties lie in working out the details: especially in saying precisely what is meant by *justified* belief.

The sceptic almost never gives arguments to show that something we claim to know is not *true*, or that we do not *believe* it. Rather the sceptic usually argues that we are not *justified* in believing the things we claim to know. A major line of argument the sceptic uses depends on the idea that if we know something we cannot be wrong about it. This sounds plausible, but it may mean no more than that we cannot know what is false. The sceptic, however, usually interprets this apparent truism as a much stronger statement, and argues that if there is any possibility that we can be wrong about a statement, then we do not really know it. Since it is possible to cast some doubt, however remote or far-fetched, on almost any statement, the sceptic concludes that we do not know anything.

Two possible answers to this line of argument are *foundationism* and *fallibilism*. The *foundationist* tries to find some statement or set of statements that cannot be doubted, about which we *cannot* be wrong. The *fallibilist* distinguishes being sure beyond all *possible* doubt and being sure beyond all *reasonable* doubt. The fallibilist usually denies that any statement is certain beyond all *possible* doubt. If a statement is certain beyond all reasonable doubt, we are fully justified in claiming to know it, says the fallibilist, even if there is a possibility that eventually we may find evidence to cause us to withdraw our claim to knowledge. The fallibilist argues that the sceptic gives us no good reason to deny that many statements are certain beyond all reasonable doubt.

Some philosophers have held a combination view, holding that some statements are certain beyond all possible doubt and others are certain beyond all reasonable doubt. Other kinds of replies to scepticism are also possible, but a great many replies to scepticism given during the history of philosophy can be classified as foundationist or fallibilist.

In this section we give two of the strongest and most historically important statements of scepticism and two important replies, one from a foundationist point of view, one from a fallibilistic position. Sextus Empiricus, who lived from about A.D. 160–210, summarizes the sceptical arguments which came down to him from five centuries or so of Greek scepticism. The general approach of the Greek sceptics was to show that in every area where we make a claim to knowledge there are opposing arguments or considerations: therefore we should suspend judgment and not claim to know anything.

As you read his arguments you might ask yourself if Sextus ever gave us good reason to support a claim he often made: that in every case the arguments or considerations are *equally* strong on *both* sides of the question. A fallibilist might make a comparison with trials of criminals. In almost every case there is *something* to be said on behalf of the defendant; that is why we have trials with defense lawyers as well as prosecutors. But it is simply not true that the evidence is always equally balanced and that we are never justified in convicting an accused criminal. Our court system requires that the defendant be proved guilty beyond a *reasonable* doubt, not beyond all possible doubt. If we had to prove the defendant guilty beyond all *possible* doubt, no one could ever be convicted, and that would be unreasonable. Similarly, the fallibilist would argue, we can often show that a statement is true beyond reasonable doubt, and we are then justified in claiming to know it.

For a classical reply to scepticism we have chosen Aristotle, who takes a foundationist position. Although he lived in the fourth century B.C., before the rise of scepticism as an organized philosophical movement and long before Sextus Empiricus, many philosophers would hold that Aristotle answered the sceptical arguments in advance. What Artistotle tried to show is that the basic principles of logic, on which all argument depends, must be beyond doubt, for if we question these basic principles we are reduced to incoherence: we cannot say anything meaningful to other people or to ourselves. Aristotle argued that once the basic principles of logic are secure, we can use arguments from our experience to be certain of many other things.

The second representative of scepticism in this section is the eighteenth-century philosopher, David Hume. He used some of the arguments found in Sextus Empiricus: both Hume and Sextus called themselves followers of *Pyrrho,* the semi-legendary founder of the sceptical school. Hume also had arguments for scepticism based on his analysis of causation and perception. However, for this book we have chosen an argument of Hume's which is both original and interesting and which does not depend on his general philosophical position. Hume argued that there is a cumulative uncertainty in all of our reasoning that reduces all of our alleged knowledge to mere probability.

Hume's arguments were discussed and answered by one of his contemporaries, Thomas Reid, who used a fallibilist approach. Since Reid discusses Hume's arguments in detail, the two selections give you a good example of debate between two able philosophers. You should try to weigh Reid's arguments against Hume's and make up your own mind as to which arguments are stronger.

The "Comment" for this section is by G.K. Chesterton and deals with the relation between scepticism and authority.

A. A CLASSICAL STATEMENT OF SCEPTICISM

Sextus Empiricus:
The Outlines of Pyrrhanism

Sextus Empiricus C. A.D. 160–210 is our main authority for the doctrines of the classical sceptics. He is known to have been a Greek physician who resided, at least for a while, in Rome, but we know very little of the details of his life. He seems to have been a compiler of the views of previous philosophers rather than an original philosopher himself. The complete text of the *Outlines* may be found in the Loeb Classical Library edition, *Sextus Empiricus,* Vol. 1 published by G.P. Putnam in 1933. The translation is by R.G. Bury.

The natural result of any investigation is that the investigators either discover the object of search or deny that it is discoverable and confess it to be inapprehensible or persist in their search. So, too, with regard to the objects investigated by philosophy, this is probably why some have claimed to have discovered the truth, others have asserted that it cannot be apprehended, while others again go on inquiring. Those who believe they have discovered it are the "'Dogmatists," specially so called—Aristotle, for example, and Epicurus and the Stoics and certain others; Cleitomachus and Carneades and other Academics treat it as inapprehensible: the Sceptics keep on searching. Hence it seems reasonable to hold that the main types of philosophy are three—the Dogmatic, the Academic, and the Sceptic. Of the other systems it will best become others to speak: our task at present is to describe in outline the Sceptic doctrine.

Scepticism is an ability, or mental attitude, which opposes appearances to judgements in any way whatsoever, with the result that, owing to the equipollence of the objects and reasons thus opposed, we are brought firstly to a state of mental suspense and next to a state of "unperturbedness" or quietude.

. . . By "appearances" we now mean the objects of sense-perception, whence we contrast them with the objects of thought or "judgements." The phrase "in any way whatsoever" can be connected . . . with the phrase "opposing appearances to judgements"; for inasmuch as we oppose these in a variety of ways—appearances to appearances, or judgements to judgements, or *alternando* appearances to judgements,—in order to ensure the inclusion of all these antitheses we employ the phrase "in any way whatsoever." . . . The phrase "opposed judgements" we do not employ in the sense of negations and affirmations only but simply as equivalent to "conflicting judgements." "Equipollence" we use of equality in respect of probability and improbability, to indicate that no one of the conflicting judgements takes precedence of any other as being more probable. "Suspense" is a state of mental rest owing to which we neither deny nor affirm anything. "Quietude" is an untroubled and tranquil condition of soul. And how quietude enters the soul along with suspension of judgement we shall explain in our chapter "Concerning the End."

The originating cause of Scepticism is, we say, the hope of attaining quietude. Men of talent, who were perturbed by the contradictions in things and in doubt as to which of the alternatives they ought to accept, were led on to inquire what is true in things and what false, hoping by the settlement of the question to attain quietude. The main basic principle of the Sceptic system is that of opposing to every proposition an equal proposition; for we believe that as a consequence of this we end by ceasing to dogmatize.

When we say that the Sceptic refrains from dogmatizing we do not use the term "dogma," as some do, in the broader sense of "approval of a thing" (for the Sceptic gives assent to the feelings which are the necessary results of sense-impressions, and he would not, for example, say when feeling hot or cold "I believe that I am not hot or cold"); but we say that "he does not dogmatize" using "dogma" in the sense, which some give it, of "assent to one of the non-evident objects of scientific inquiry"; for the Pyrrhonean philosopher assents to nothing that is non-evident. Moreover, even in the act of enunciating the Sceptic formulae concerning things non-evident—such as the formula "No more (one thing than another)," or the formula "I determine nothing," or any of the others which we shall presently mention,—he does not dogmatize. For whereas the dogmatizer posits the things about which he is said to be dogmatizing as really existent, the Sceptic does not posit these formulae in any absolute sense; for he conceives that, just as the formula "All things are false" asserts the falsity of itself as well as of everything else, as does the formula "Nothing is true," so also the formula "No more" asserts that itself, like all the rest, is "No more (this than that,") and thus cancels itself along with the rest. And of the other formulae we say the same. If then, while the dogmatizer posits the matter of his dogma as substantial truth, the Sceptic enunciates his formulae so that they are virtually cancelled by themselves, he should not be said to dogmatize in his enunciation of them. And, most important of all, in his enunciation of these formulae he states what appears to himself and announces his own impression in an undogmatic way, without making any positive assertion regarding the external realties.

Our next subject will be the End of the Sceptic system. Now an "End" is "that for which all actions or reasonings are undertaken, while it exists for the sake of none"; or, otherwise, "the ultimate object of appetency." We assert still that the Sceptic's End is quietude in respect of matters of opinion and moderate feeling in respect of things unavoidable. For the Sceptic, having set out to philosophize with the object of passing judgement on the sense-impressions and ascertaining which of them are true and which false, so as to attain quietude thereby, found himself involved in contradictions of equal weight, and being unable to decide between them suspended judgement; and as he was thus in suspense there followed, as it happened, the state of quietude in respect of matters of opinion. For the man who opines that anything is by nature good or bad is forever being disquieted: when he is without the things which he deems good he believes himself to be tormented by things naturally bad and he pursues after the things which are, as he thinks, good; which when he has obtained he keeps falling into still more perturbations because of his irrational and immoderate elation, and in his dread of a change of fortune he uses every endeavour to avoid losing the things which he deems good. On the other hand, the man who determines nothing as to what is naturally good or bad neither shuns nor pursues anything eagerly; and, in consequence, he is unperturbed.

The Sceptic, in fact, had the same experience which is said to have befallen the painter Apelles. Once, they say, when he was painting a horse and wished to represent in the painting the horse's foam, he was so unsuccessful that he gave up the attempt and flung at the picture the sponge on which he used to wipe the paints off his brush, and the mark of the sponge produced the effect of a horse's foam. So, too, the Sceptics were in hopes of gaining quietude by means of a decision regarding the disparity of the objects of sense and of thought, and being unable to effect this they suspended judgement; and they found that quietude, as if by chance, followed upon their suspense, even as a shadow follows its substance. We do not, however, suppose that the Sceptic is wholly untroubled; but we say that he is troubled by things unavoidable; for we grant that he is old at times and thirsty, and suffers various affections of that kind. But even in these cases, whereas ordinary people are afflicted by two circumstances,—namely, by the affections themselves and in no less a degree, by the belief that these conditions are evil by nature, —the belief in the natural badness of all these conditions, escapes here too with less discomfort. Hence we say that, while in regard to matters of opinion the Sceptic's End is quietude, in regard to things unavoidable it is "moderate affection." But some notable Sceptics have added the further definition "suspension of judgement in investigations."

Now that we have been saying that tranquillity follows on suspension of judgement, it will be our next task to explain how we arrive at this suspension. Speaking generally, one may say that it is the result of setting things in opposition. We oppose either appearances to appearances or objects of thought to objects of thought or *alternando*. For instance, we oppose appearances when we say "The same tower appears round from a distance, but square from close at hand"; and thoughts to thoughts, when in answer to him who argues the existence of Providence from the order of the heavenly bodies we oppose the fact that often the good fare ill and the bad fare well, and draw from this the inference that Providence does not exist. And thoughts we oppose to appearances, as when Anaxagoras countered the notion that snow is white with the argument, "Snow is frozen water, and water is black; therefore snow also is black." With a different idea we oppose things present sometimes to things present, as in the foregoing examples, and sometimes to things past or future, as, for instance, when someone propounds to us a theory which we are unable to refute, we say to him in reply, "Just as, before the birth of the founder of the School to which you belong, the theory it holds was not as yet apparent as a sound theory, although it was really in existence, so likewise it is possible that the opposite theory to that which you now propound is already really existent, though not yet apparent to us, so that we ought not as yet to yield assent to this theory which at the moment seems to be valid."

But in order that we may have a more exact understanding of these antitheses I will describe the Modes by which suspension of judgement is brought about, but without making any positive assertion regarding either their number or their validity; for it is possible that they may be unsound or there may be more of them than I shall enumerate.

The later Sceptics hand down Five Modes leading to suspension, namely these: the first based on discrepancy, the second on regress *ad infinitum*, the third on relativity, the fourth on hypothesis, the fifth on circular reasoning. That based on discrepancy leads us to find that with regard to the object presented there has arisen both amongst ordinary people and amongst the philosophers an interminable conflict because of which we are unable either to choose a thing or reject it, and so fall back on suspension. The Mode based upon regress *ad infinitum* is that whereby we assert that the thing adduced as a proof of the matter proposed needs a further proof, and this again another, and so on *ad infinitum*, so that the consequence is suspension, as we possess no starting-point for our argument. The Mode based upon relativity, as we have already said, is that whereby the object has such or such an appearance in relation to the subject judging and to the concomitant percepts, but as to its real nature we suspend judgement. We have the Mode based on hypothesis when the Dogmatists, being forced to recede *ad infinitum*, take as their starting-point something which they do not establish by argument but claim to assume as granted simply and without demonstration. The Mode of circular reasoning is the form used when the proof itself which ought to establish the matter of inquiry requires confirmation derived from that matter; in this case, being unable to assume either in order to establish the other, we suspend judgement about both.

That every matter of inquiry admits of being brought under these Modes we shall show briefly in this way. The matter proposed is either a sense-object or a thought-object, but whichever it is, it is an object of controversy; for some say that only sensibles are true, others only intelligibles, others that some sensible and some intelligible objects are true. Will they then assert that the controversy can or cannot be decided? If they say it cannot, we have it granted that we must suspend judgement; for concerning matters of dispute which admit of no decision it is impossible to make an assertion. But if they say that it can be decided, we ask by what is it to be decided. For example, in the case of the sense-object (for we shall base our argument on it first), is it to be decided by a sense-object or a thought-object? For if they say by a sense-object, since we are inquiring about sensibles that object itself also will require another to confirm it; and if that too is to be a sense-object, it likewise will require another for its confirmation, and so on *ad infinitum*. And if the sense-object shall have to be decided by a thought-object, then, since thought-objects also are controverted, this being an object of thought will need examination and confirmation. Whence then will it gain confirmation? If from an intelligible object, it will suffer a similar regress *ad infinitum;* and if from a sensible object, since an intelligible was adduced to establish the sensible and a sensible to establish the intelligible, the Mode of circular reasoning is brought in.

If, however, our disputant, by way of escape from this conclusion, should claim to assume as granted and without demonstration some postulate for the demonstration of the next steps of his argument, then the Mode of hypothesis will be brought in, which allows no escape. For if the author of the hypothesis is worthy of credence, we shall be no less worthy of credence every time that we make the opposite hypothesis. Moreover, if the author of the hypothesis assumes what is true he causes it to be suspected by assuming it by hypothesis rather than after proof; while if it is false, the foundation of his argument will be rotten. Further, if hypothesis conduces at all to proof, let the subject of inquiry itself be assumed and not some other thing which is merely a means to establish the actual subject of the argument; but if it is absurd to assume the subject of inquiry, it will also be absurd to assume that upon which it depends.

It is also plain that all sensibles are relative; for they are relative to those who have the sensations. Therefore it is apparent that whatever sensible object is presented can easily be referred to one of the Five Modes. And concerning the intelligible object we argue similarly. For if it should be said that it is a matter of unsettled controversy, the necessity of our suspending judgement will be granted. And if, on the other hand, the controversy admits of decision, then if the decision rests on an intelligible object we shall be driven to the regress *ad infinitum,* and to circular reasoning if it rests on a sensible; for since the sensible again is controverted and cannot be decided by means of itself because of the regress *ad infinitum,* it will require the intelligible object, just as also the intelligible will require the sensible. For these reasons, again, he who assumes anything by hypothesis will be acting illogically. Moreoever, objects of thought, or intelligibles, are relative; for they are so named on account of their relation to the person thinking, and if they had really possessed the nature they are said to possess, there would have been no controversy about them. Thus the intelligible also is referred to the Five Modes, so that in all cases we are compelled to suspend judgement concerning the object presented.

Such then are the Five Modes handed down amongst the later Sceptics; but they propound these . . . in order to expose the rashness of the Dogmatists with more variety and completeness. . . .

Discussion Questions

1. Read the *Apology* of Plato on page 2. According to the definition of scepticism given by Sextus, is Socrates a sceptic? Why or why not?

2. Sextus claims that "no one of the conflicting arguments takes precedence of any other as being more probable." Does he ever support this claim? Can it be supported?

3. Sextus says that the sceptic "enunciates his formulas so that they are virtually cancelled out by themselevs." Does this avoid the "dogmatist's" challenge that the sceptic must either say something positive (and thus not be completely sceptical) or else not really be saying anything? Why or why not?

4. Sextus says that the sceptic will not pursue anything "eagerly," but will the sceptic have any reason for pursuing *any* course of action? Why or why not?

5. Consider the examples of opposed appearances or judgments give by Sextus, e.g., the tower that appears round and square, the snow example, etc. Are these really cases of opposition? See if you can show in one case that there is no real opposition and therefore no grounds for a sceptical conclusion.

6. Take one of the Five Modes. Explain the alleged opposition briefly, and give an example of an argument which falls under this Mode. Discuss whether the argument is a good one.

B. A CLASSICAL ANSWER TO SCEPTICISM

Aristotle:
The Metaphysics, Book IV, Chapters 4-6

Aristotle (384–322 B.C.) was a Greek philosopher and logician, founder of one of the first schools of philosophy, a pupil of Plato, and tutor to Alexander the Great. The first and one of the greatest of the builders of philosophical systems, Aristotle held connected and coherent views in almost every area of philosophy. Aristotle's view is frequently the "common-sense" or "ordinary man's" view raised to a considerable degree of technical sophistication. Despite subsequent developments and changes in points of view, Aristotle's arguments and conclusions still have to be reckoned with, especially in ethics and metaphysics. Because his surviving works are essentially his lecture notes, Aristotle is not easy to read. Some of Aristotle's major works are *The Metaphysics,* the *Nichomachean Ethics,* the *Prior Analytics,* and the *Posterior Analytics.*

Anyone who claims thoroughly to understand a given genus must be able to state the best established principles thereof. So the philosopher, whose subject is being *qua* being, must have an equal grasp of the best established of all principles; i.e., those about which it is impossible to be mistaken, which are best known and rest on no hypothesis, and which indeed *must* be known if one is to know anything at all.

Now the best established of all principles may be stated as follows: The same attribute cannot at the same time belong and not belong to the same subject in the same respect. . . . It is impossible for anyone to believe—though some say Heraclitus did—that the same thing can *be* and *not be*. If contrary attributes cannot at the same time belong to the same subject . . . and if any belief is (as an attribute of the thinker) contrary to the contradictory belief, then obviously no one can at same time believe the same thing to be and not to be. Otherwise he would hold two contrary opinions at the same time. Therefore everyone in argument relies upon this ultimate law, on which all others rest. (Bk. 11, ch. 4)

There are some who maintain (a) that the same thing can be and not be, and (b) that it is possible so to judge. . . . Now we have just assumed that a thing cannot both be and not be, and have also shown this to be the most indubitable of all principles. The demand that we should prove the law argues a defective education in logic—a science which enables one to recognize what requires proof and what does not. It is absolutely impossible to have proof of *everything;* the process would continue indefinitely, and the result would be no proof of anything whatsoever. Granted, on the other hand, that there are some things which do not call for proof, what principle, I ask, is more self-evident than the law of contradiction?

We can, however, adduce *negative* proof even of this law by refuting our opponent, *provided only that he will make some positive statement.* For it is quite hopeless to argue with a man who will not produce evidence in support of his own theory; in so far as he declines to reason he is no better than a vegetable. I have distinguished negative proof from demonstration properly so called. If we employ the latter we may be accused of begging the question; whereas, if the discussion is precipitated by someone else, we may proceed rather by way of refutation. . . .

If all contradictory statements are true of the same thing at the same time, clearly all things will be one. If we can indifferently either assert or deny a predicate of any subject, the same thing will be a warship, a wall, and a man . . . in which case all things are indistinguishable, and all statements are both true and untrue. It is clearly hopeless to argue with a man who says nothing definite, answering neither 'yes' nor 'no,' but only 'yes and no.'

. . . anyone who maintains that all judgments are alike false and true can neither say nor even *mean* anything; for he is at the same time both affirming and denying. Again, if he makes no judgment, but 'thinks' and 'thinks not' indifferently, what difference is there between him and a plant?

Hence it is obvious that no thinker, to whatever school he may belong, holds this view with any degree of sincerity. Why does he walk to Megara, and not rather stay at home, when he thinks he ought to go? Why does he not walk early one morning into a well or over the nearest precipice, instead of taking care not to do so and thereby showing that he does not consider it equally good and not-good to step over the edge? Why? Clearly because he believes one course to be better than the other. . . .

. . . if his assertion, that the same thing can at the same time be and not be, were true, even it itself would not be true. (Bk. 4, ch. 4)

The doctrine of Protagoras (that 'Man is the measure of all things'; i.e., what *seems* to each man *is* so) is the logical result of denying the law of contradiction, and must stand or fall with it.

1. If all opinions and all appearances are true, every statement must be at once true and false. For many people reach contradictory conclusions, and each believes the other to be wrong; so that the same thing must at the same time *be* and *not be*.

2. Conversely, if everything *is* and at the same time *is not,* all opinions must be true. . . .

[Some] have concluded that contradictories or contraries are compatible from their observation of the sensible world. Seeing contraries generated from the same thing, they infer that since nothing can come into existence from what is not, an existing thing must previously have possessed both contrary qualities. . . . To this we shall reply as follows. We shall admit that in one sense they are right, but wrong in another. For since 'being' has two meanings (i.e., potential and actual being), there is a sense in which a thing cannot come into existence from what is not but there is another sense in which it can; and to this extent one may truthfully say that the same thing 'is and is not.' It cannot, however, be and not be *in the same respect;* for it may have contrary qualities *potentially* but not *actually*. . . .

In general, it is because they identify knowledge with sensation, and the latter with physical impression, that our opponents claim that the impressions derived through sense-perception are necessarily true. It was, in fact, upon these very grounds that Empedocles, Democritus, and indeed most other thinkers, became entangled in such theories. . . . Now this . . . leads to serious consequences; for if the most eminent thinkers, who have the clearest vision of such truth as we can attain, openly express such opinions about truth, what wonder if beginners lose heart? The pursuit of truth will seem to them a mere wild-goose chase.

The conclusions reached by these men are rooted in the fact that, while professing to study the nature of reality, they identified reality with the sensible world. . . . They also observed that the whole sensible world of nature is constantly changing, and they concluded that no true statement can be made about something which is always and everywhere in a state of flux. It was this latter belief which blossomed into the extreme theory of those who claimed to represent the doctrine of Heraclitus. Cratylus, for example, ended by refusing to commit himself to any statement whatever, and would only move his finger. He criticized Heraclitus for saying that one cannot enter the same river twice; his own view was that it is impossible to do so even once.

Now our reply to these arguments is as follows:

1. . . . What is in process of losing an attribute still has something of what it is losing, and something of that which is coming to be must already exist . . .

2. Qualitative change is not the same as quantitative change. A thing may have nothing permanent about it as far as quantity is concerned, but it is by their form, or quality, that we know things.

3. Our opponents are open to criticism for basing their view of the whole material universe upon what they have observed in a minority of sensible objects . . .

4. We must try to convince our opponents . . . that there is an unchanging reality. . . .

We may fairly express surprise when our opponents ask questions like these: Are magnitudes and colours such as they appear at a distance or close at hand; as they are seen by the healthy or by the diseased? Are those things heavy which appear so to the weak or to the strong? Is truth as it appears to the sleeping or to the waking? Surely they do not believe that these are open questions. At any rate, (a) if a man dreams that he is in Athens when he is really in Africa, he does not set out for the Odeum as soon as he wakes up. (b) Regarding the future, as Plato says, the opinion of the doctor and that of the layman are presumably not equally valid, e.g., as to whether or not a patient will recover. (c) As to the senses themselves, the informaion with which a given sense furnishes us about its proper object is more reliable than that which it suggests regarding the object of another (even a kindred) sense. No; in the case of colours, sight is more reliable than taste; and vice versa in the case of flavour. No sense contradicts itself at the same moment about the same object, nor at different moments with regard to that object's quality, but only with regard to the object itself. Take a wine: you may, in consequence of its own change or of some change in your own physical condition, find it at one time sweet and not so at another; but sweetness itself is always the same definite and unmistakable quality which everything must *necessarily* have in order to be sweet. (Bk. 4, ch. 5)

Some of our opponents, whether genuinely convinced or merely professing to hold these views, ask who is to be judge of a healthy man, and in general who is to decide the issue in any given dispute. Now this is like wondering whether we are here and now asleep or awake. All problems of this kind are alike in that they imply that we must needs prove everything. . . . Their mistake, as I have already explained, is that they require a reason for things which have no reason, since the starting-point of demonstration is not a matter of demonstration.

Our 'genuine' opponents, then, can easily be convinced of this truth, because it is not difficult to grasp. Those, on the other hand, who invite us to refute them by a knock-down argument ask for the impossible; for they claim the privilege of self-contradiction—a claim which of course contradicts itself from the outset. (Bk. 4, ch. 6)

Discussion Questions

1. Aristotle says that "the same attribute cannot at the same time belong and not belong to the same subject in the same respect." Do the qualifications "at the same time . . . in the same respect" take care of all of the examples of "opposition" given by Sextus (the tower, the snow, etc.)? Why or why not?

2. Artistotle argues that "law of contradiction" does not need proof because it is "self-evident." Does this avoid the sceptic's dilemma "either infinite regress or arbitrary hypothesis" (Second and Fourth Modes)? Why or why not?

3. Does Aristotle's argument that the law of contradiction is presupposed by any meaningful statement show that the sceptic cannot logically make meaningful statements? Why or why not?

4. How could the sceptic answer Aristotle's argument that scepticism removes all reasons for acting in one way rather than another?

5. Do Aristotle's arguments deal with all of the cases advanced by Sextus? If not, which sceptical arguments remain? Show in detail how one sceptical argument *is* answered.

C. HUME'S SCEPTICISM

David Hume:
Treatise of Human Nature, Book I, Part IV

The Scottish philosopher David Hume (1711-1776), a major figure in modern philosophy, began with an empiricist position that all knowledge is confined to what we can learn from our senses and arrived at a position of complete scepticism in every department of human thought. While some philosophers accept Hume's sceptical conclusions in one or more areas (e.g., his religious scepticism) a great part of Hume's importance for modern philosophy is the formidable challenge he offers, a challenge which must be taken up by any nonsceptical philosophical theory. Two of Hume's most important works are the *Treatise of Human Nature* and the *Enquiry Concerning Human Understanding.*

OF SKEPTICISM WITH REGARD TO REASON

In all demonstrative sciences the rules are certain and infallible, but when we apply them our fallible and uncertain faculties are very apt to depart from them and fall into error. We must, therefore, in every reasoning form a new judgment, as a check or control on our first judgment or belief, and must enlarge our view to comprehend a kind of history of all the instances wherein our understanding has deceived us, compared with those wherein its testimony was just and true. Our reason must be considered as a kind of cause of which truth is the natural effect, but such-a-one as by the irruption of other causes, and by the inconstancy of our mental powers, may frequently be prevented. By this means all knowledge degenerates into probability, and this probability is greater or less, according to our experience of the veracity or deceitfulness of our understanding, and according to the simplicity or intricacy of the question.

There is no algebraist nor mathematician so expert in his science as to place entire confidence in any truth immediately upon his discovery of it, or regard it as anything but a mere probability. Every time he runs over his proofs his confidence increases, but still more by the approbation of his friends, and is raised to its utmost perfection by the universal assent and applauses of the learned world. Now it is evident that this gradual increase of assurance is nothing but the addition of new probabilities, and is derived from the constant union of causes and effects, according to past experience and observation.

In accounts of any length or importance, merchants seldom trust to the infallible certainty of numbers for their security, but by the artificial structure of the accounts produce a probability beyond what is derived from the skill and experience of the accountant. For that is plainly of itself some degree of probability, though uncertain and variable, according to the degrees of his experience and length of the account. Now as none will maintain that our assurance in a long numeration exceeds probability, I may safely affirm that there scarce is any proposition concerning numbers of which we can have a fuller security. For it is easily possible, by gradually diminishing the numbers, to reduce the longest series of addition to the most simple question which can be formed, to an addition of two single numbers; and upon this supposition we shall find it impracticable to show the precise limits of knowledge and of probability, or discover that particular number at which the one ends and the other begins. But knolwedge and probability are of such contrary and disagreeing natures that they cannot well run insensibly into each other, and that because they will not divide, but must be either entirely present or entirely absent. Besides, if any single addition were certain every one would be so, and consequently the whole or total sum, unless the whole can be different from all its parts. I had almost said that this was certain, but I reflect that it must reduce *itself*, as well as every other reasoning, and from knowledge degenerate into probability.

Since therefore all knowledge resolves itself into probability and becomes at last of the same nature with that evidence which we employ in common life, we must now examine this latter species of reasoning, and see on what foundation it stands.

In every judgment which we can form concerning probability, as well as concerning knowledge, we ought always to correct the first judgment, derived from the nature of the object, by another judgment, derived from the nature of the understanding. It is certain a man of solid sense and long experience ought to have, and usually has, a greater assurance in his opinions than one that is foolish and ignorant, and that our sentiments have different degrees of authority, even with ourselves, in proportion to the degrees of our reason and experience. In the man of the best sense and longest experience, this authority is never entire, since even such-a-one must be conscious of many errors in the past, and must still dread the like for the future. Here then arises a new species of probability to correct and regulate the first, and fix its just standard and proportion. As demonstration is subject to the control of probability, so is probability liable to a new correction by a reflex act of the mind, wherein the nature of our understanding and our reasoning from the first probability become our objects.

Having thus found in every probability, beside the original uncertainty inherent in the subject, a new uncertainty derived from the weakness of that faculty which judges, and having adjusted these two together, we are obliged by our reason to add a new doubt derived from the possibility of error in the estimation we make of the truth and fidelity of our faculties. This is a doubt which immediately occurs to us and of which, if we would closely pursue our reason, we cannot avoid giving a decision. But this decision, though it should be favorable to our preceding judgment, being founded only on probability, must weaken still further our first evidence, and must itself be weakened by a fourth doubt of the same kind, and so on *in infinitum,* till at last there remain nothing of the original probability, however great we may suppose it to have been and however small the diminution by every new uncertainty. No finite object can subsist under a decrease repeated *in infinitum,* and even the vastest quantity which can enter into human imagination must in this manner be reduced to nothing. Let our first belief be ever so strong, it must infallibly perish by passing through so many new examinations, of which each diminishes somewhat of its force and vigor. When I reflect on the natural fallibility of my judgment, I have less confidence in my opinions than when I only consider the objects concerning which I reason; and when I proceed still further, to turn the scrutiny against every successive estimation I make of my faculties, all the rules of logic require a continual diminution, and at last a total extinction of belief and evidence.

Should it here be asked me whether I sincerely assent to this argument, which I seem to take such pains to inculcate, and whether I be really one of those skeptics who hold that all is uncertain and that our judgment is not in *anything* possessed of *any* measures of truth and falsehood, I should reply that this question is entirely superfluous, and that neither I nor any other person was ever sincerely and constantly of that opinion. Nature, by an absolute and uncontrollable necessity, has determined us to judge as well as to breathe and feel, nor can we any more forbear viewing certain objects in a stronger and fuller light, upon account of their customary connection with a present impression, than we can hinder ourselves from thinking as long as we are awake, or seeing the surrounding bodies when we turn our eyes towards them in broad sunshine. Whoever has taken the pains to refute the cavils of this *total* skepticism has really disputed without an antagonist, and endeavored by arguments to establish a faculty which nature has antecedently implanted in the mind and rendered unavoidable.

My intention then in displaying so carefully the arguments of that fantastic sect is only to make the reader sensible of the truth of my hypothesis, *that all our reasonings concerning causes and effects are derived from nothing but custom, and that belief is more properly an act of the sensitive than of the cogitative part of our natures.* I have here proved that the very same principles which make us form a decision upon any subject, and correct that decision by the consideration of our genius and capacity and of the situation of our mind when we examined that subject; I say, I have proved that these same principles, when carried further and applied to every new reflex judgment, must, by continually diminishing the original evidence, at last reduce it to nothing, and utterly subvert all belief and opinion. If belief, therefore, were a simple act of the thought, without any peculiar manner of conception or the addition of a force and vivacity, it must infallibly destroy itself, and in every case terminate in a total suspense of judgment. But as experience will sufficiently convince anyone who thinks it worthwhile to try, that though he can find no error in the foregoing arguments, yet he still continues to believe and think and reason as usual, he may safely conclude that his reasoning and belief is some sensation or peculiar manner of conception, which it is impossible for mere ideas and reflections to destroy.

But here, perhaps, it may be demanded how it happens, even upon my hypothesis, that these arguments above explained produce not a total suspense of judgment, and after what manner the mind ever retains a degree of assurance in any subject? For as these new probabilities, which by their repetition perpetually diminish the original evidence, are founded on the very same principles, whether of thought or sensation, as the primary judgment, it may seem unavoidable that in either case they must equally subvert it, and by the opposition, either of contrary thoughts or sensations, reduce the mind to a total uncertainty. I suppose there is some question proposed to me, and that after revolving over the impressions of my memory and senses and carrying my thoughts from them to such objects as are commonly conjoined with them, I feel a stronger and more forcible conception on the one side than on the other. This strong conception forms my first decision. I suppose that afterwards I examine my judgment itself, and observing from experience that it is sometimes just and sometimes erroneous, I consider it as regulated by contrary principles or causes, of which some lead to truth and some to error; and in balancing these contrary causes I diminish by a new probability the assurance of my first decision. This new probability is liable to the same diminution as the foregoing, and so on, *in infinitum.* It is therefore demanded, *how it happens that even after all we retain a degree of belief which is sufficient for our purpose, either in philosophy or common life.*

I answer that after the first and second decision, as the action of the mind becomes forced and unnatural and the ideas faint and obscure, though the principles of judgment and the balancing of opposite causes be the same as at the very beginning, yet their influence on the imagination and the vigor they add to or diminish from the thought is by no means equal. Where the mind reaches not its objects with easiness and facility, the same principles have not the same effect as in a more natural conception of the ideas, nor does the imagination feel a sensation which holds any proportion with that which arises from its common judgments and opinions. The attention is on the stretch; the posture of the mind is uneasy; and the spirits, being diverted from their natural course, are not governed in their movements by the same laws, at least not to the same degree, as when they flow in their usual channel.

If we desire similar instances, it will not be very difficult to find them. The present subject of metaphysics will supply us abundantly. The same argument which would have been esteemed convincing in a reasoning concerning history or politics has little or no influence in these abstruser subjects, even though it be perfectly comprehended, and that because there is required a study and an effort of thought in order to its being comprehended, and this effort of thought disturbs the operation of our sentiments on which the belief depends. The case is the same in other subjects. The straining of the imagination always hinders the regular flowing of the passions and sentiments. A tragic poet that would represent his heroes as very ingenious and witty in their misfortunes would never touch the passions. As the emotions of the soul prevent any subtle reasoning and reflection, so these latter actions of the mind are equally prejudicial to the former. The mind, as well as the body, seems to be endowed with a certain precise degree of force and activity, which it never employs in one action but at the expense of all the rest. This is more evidently true where the actions are of quite different natures, since in that case the force of the mind is not only diverted, but even the disposition changed, so as to render us incapable of a sudden transition from one action to the other, and still more of performing both at once. No wonder, then, the conviction which arises from a subtle reasoning diminishes in proportion to the efforts which the imagination makes to enter into the reasoning, and to conceive it in all its parts. Belief, being a lively conception, can never be entire where it is not founded on something natural and easy.

This I take to be the true state of the question, and cannot approve of that expeditious way which some take with the skeptics, to reject at once all their arguments without inquiry or examination. If the skeptical reasonings be strong, say they, it is a proof that reason may have some force and authority; if weak, they can never be sufficient to invalidate all the conclusions of our understanding. This argument is not just, because the skeptical reasonings, were it possible for them to exist and were they not destroyed by their subtlety, would be successively both strong and weak, according to the successive dispositions of the mind. Reason first appears in possession of the throne, prescribing laws and imposing maxims, with an absolute sway and authority. Her enemy, therefore, is obliged to take shelter under her protection, and by making use of rational arguments to prove the fallaciousness and imbecility of reason, produces, in a manner, a patent under her hand and seal. This patent has at first an authority proportioned to the present and immediate authority of reason, from which it is derived. But as it is supposed to be contradictory to reason, it gradually diminishes the force of that governing power, and its own at the same time, till at last they both vanish away into nothing, by a regular and just diminution. The skeptical and dogmatical reasons are of the same kind, though contrary in their operation and tendency, so that where the latter is strong, it has an enemy of equal force in the former to encounter, and as their forces were at first equal, they still continue so as long as either of them subsists, nor does one of them lose any force in the contest without taking as much from its antagonist. It is happy, therefore, that nature breaks the force of all skeptical arguments in time, and keeps them from having any considerable influence on the understanding. Were we to trust entirely to their self-destruction, that can never take place till they have first subverted all conviction, and have totally destroyed human reason.

Discussion Questions

1. Hume says that a mathematician is not entirely confident of a proof or an accountant of a calculation until they have repeatedly checked the result and had others check it. Is this true? If it were true, would the doubt involved be a reasonable one? On what might such a doubt be based?

2. Hume says that knowledge and probability are mutually exclusive: that if one is present the other is absent. He argues that if all the small parts of a long calculation were certain, the whole would be certain. He says that the whole is not certain, therefore the parts are not. Criticize Hume's argument. Are his assumptions correct? Is his reasoning valid?

3. Hume states that since there is some uncertainty involved each time we check a calculation or proof, these uncertainties accumulate and destroy any certainty we had originally. Yet, as Hume himself admits, repeated checking *increases* our confidence. Can Hume explain this apparent contradiction? How?

4. Hume seems to argue as follows: If we are 90 percent certain that we are right in our original calculation and 90 percent certain we are right when we check out the calculation, we should be less than 90 percent certain that *both* the calculation and the check of the calculation are correct. Is Hume right or has he made a mistake? If he has, what is the mistake? If you think he is right, give an argument in support of Hume.

5. Hume says that his sceptical arguments will not cause trouble in practical life because habit or custom will inevitably cause us to act as if we do know. Would this be true of someone really convinced by Hume's arguments? Even if it were, would this be an adequate solution to the problem raised by Hume? What difficulties can you see, and how might Hume answer them?

D. REID'S ANSWER TO HUME

Thomas Reid:
Essay on the Intellectual Powers of Man

Thomas Reid (1710-1796) is another Scottish philosopher. A contemporary and fellow countryman of David Hume, Reid rigorously rejected Hume's sceptical conclusions. A professor of philosophy at King's College in Aberdeen and at the University of Glasgow, Reid was the founder of the "common-sense" school of philosophy, which attempted to refute Humean scepticism and establish ordinary certainties on the basis of common-sense and reason.

OF MR. HUME'S SCEPTICISM
WITII REGARD TO REASON

In the *Treatise of Human Nature*, Bk. I. Part IV. §I, the author undertakes to prove two points: *First,* That all that is called human knowledge (meaning demonstrative knowledge) is only probability; and *secondly,* That this probability, when duly examined, vanishes by degrees, and leaves at last no evidence at all: so that, in the issue, there is no ground to believe any one proposition rather than its contrary; and "all those are certainly fools who reason or believe anything."

According to this account, reason that boasted prerogative of man, and the light of his mind, is an *ignis fatuus* which misleads the wandering travellers and leaves him at last in absolute darkness.

How unhappy is the condition of man, born under a necessity of believing contradictions and of trusting to a guide who confesses himself to be a false one!

It is some comfort that this doctrine can never be seriously adopted by any man in his senses. And after this author had shown that "all the rules of logic require a total extinction of all belief and evidence," he himself, and all men that are not insane, must have believed many things, and yielded assent to the evidence which he had extinguished.

This indeed he is so candid as to acknowledge. "He finds himself absolutely and necessarily determined to live and talk and act like other people in the common affairs of life. And since reason is incapable of dispelling these clouds, most fortunately it happens that nature herself suffices to that purpose, and cures him of this philosophical melancholy and delirium." See § 7.

This was surely a very kind and friendly interposition of nature, for the effects of this philosophical delirium, if carried into life, must have been very melancholy.

It may, however, not be improper to inquire whether, as the author thinks, it was produced by a just application of the rules of logic or, as others may be apt to think, by the misapplication and abuse of them.

First, Because we are fallible, the author infers that all knowledge degenerates into probability.

That man, and probably every created being, is fallible; and that a fallible being cannot have that perfect comprehension and assurance of truth which an infallible being has—I think ought to be granted. It becomes a fallible being to be modest, open to new light, and sensible that, by some false bias or by rash judging, he may be misled. If this be called a degree of scepticism, I cannot help approving of it, being persuaded that the man who makes the best use he can of the faculties which God has given him, without thinking them more perfect that they really are, may have all the belief that is necessary in the conduct of life, and all that is necessary to his acceptance with his Maker.

It is granted, then, that human judgments ought always to be formed with a humble sense of our fallibility in judging.

This is all that can be inferred by the rules of logic from our being fallible. And if this be all that is meant by our knowledge degenerating into probability, I know no person of a different opinion.

But it may be observed that the author here uses the word probability in a sense for which I know no authority but his own. Philosophers understand probability as opposed to demonstration, the vulgar as opposed to certainty; but this author understands it as opposed to infallibility, which no man claims.

One who believes himself to be fallible may still hold it to be certain that two and two make four, and that two contradictory propositions cannot both be true. He may believe some things to be probable only, and other things to be demonstrable, without making any pretence to infallibility.

If we use words in their proper meaning, it is impossible that demonstration should degenerate into probability from the imperfection of our faculties. Our judgment cannot change the nature of the things about which we judge. What is really demonstration will still be so, whatever judgment we form concerning it. It may likewise be observed that, when we mistake that for demonstration which really is not, the consequence of this mistake is not that demonstration degenerates into probability, but that what we took to be demonstration is no proof at all; for one false step in a demonstration destroys the whole, but cannot turn it into another kind of proof.

Upon the whole, then, this first conclusion of our author, that the fallibility of human judgment turns all knowledge into probability, if understood literally, is absurd; but if it be only a figure of speech, and means no more but that in all our judgments we ought to be sensible of our fallibility, and ought to hold our opinions with that modesty that becomes fallible creatures—which I take to be what the author meant—this I think nobody denies, nor was it necessary to enter into a laborious proof of it.

One is never in greater danger of transgressing against the rules of logic than in attempting to prove what needs no proof. Of this we have an instance in this very case, for the author begins his proof that all human judgments are fallible with affirming that some are infallible.

"In all demonstrative sciences," says he, "the rules are certain and infallible; but when we apply them, our fallible and uncertain faculties are very apt to depart from them, and fall into error."

He had forgot, surely, that the rules of demonstrative sciences are discovered by our fallible and uncertain faculties, and have no authority but that of human judgment. If they be infallible, some human judgments are infallible; and there are many in various branches of human knowledge which have as good a claim to infallibility as the rules of the demonstrative sciences.

We have reason here to find fault with our author for not being sceptical enough, as well as for a mistake in reasoning, when he claims infallibility to certain decisions of the human faculties in order to prove that all their decisions are fallible.

The *second* point which he attempts to prove is, That this probability, when duly examined, suffers a continual diminution and at last a total extinction.

I examine the proof of a theorem of Euclid. It appears to me to be strict demonstration. But I may have overlooked some fallacy, therefore I examine it again and again, but can find no flaw in it. I find all that have examined it agree with me. I have now that evidence of the truth of the proposition which I and all men call demonstration, and that belief of it which we call certainty.

Here my sceptical friend interposes and assures me that the rules of logic reduce this demonstration to no evidence at all. I am willing to hear what step in it he thinks fallacious, and why. He makes no objection to any part of the demonstration, but pleads my fallibility in judging. I have made the proper allowance for this already, by being open to conviction. But, says he, there are two uncertainties, the first inherent in the subject, which I have already shown to have only probable evidence; the second arising from the weakness of the faculty that judges. I answer, it is the weakness of the faculty only that reduces this demonstration to what you call probability. You must not therefore make it a second uncertainty, for it is the same with the first. To take credit twice in an account for the same article is not agreeable to the rules of logic. Hitherto, therefore, there is but one uncertainty—to wit, my fallibility in judging.

But, says my friend, you are obliged by reason to add a new uncertainty, derived from the possibility of error in the estimation you make of the truth and fidelity of your faculties. I answer—

This estimation is ambiguously expressed; it may either mean an estimation of my liableness to err by the misapplication and abuse of my faculties, or it may mean an estimation of my liableness to err by conceiving my faculties to be true and faithful, while they may be false and fallacious in themselves, even when applied in the best manner. I shall consider this estimation in each of these senses.

If the first be the estimation meant, it is true that reason directs us, as fallible creatures to carry along with us in all our judgment a sense of our fallibility. It is true also that we are in greater danger of erring in some cases and less in others, and that this danger of erring may, according to the circumstances of the case, admit of an estimation which we ought likewise to carry along with us in every judgment we form.

When a demonstration is short and plain; when the point to be proved does not touch our interest or our passions; when the faculty of judging, in such cases, has acquired strength by much exercise—there is less danger of erring; when the contrary circumstances take place, there is more.

In the present case every circumstance is favourable to the judgment I have formed. There cannot be less danger of erring in any case, excepting perhaps when I judge of a self-evident axiom.

The sceptic further urges that this decision, though favourable to my first judgment, being founded only on probability, must still weaken the evidence of that judgment.

Here I cannot help being of a quite contrary opinion; nor can I imagine how an ingenious author could impose upon himself so grossly, for surely he did not intend to impose upon his reader.

After repeated examination of a proposition of Euclid, I judge it to be strictly demonstrated; this is my first judgment. But as I am liable to err from various causes, I consider how far I may have been misled by any of these causes in this judgment. My decision upon this second point is favourable to my first judgment, and therefore, as I apprehend, must strengthen it. To say that this decision, because it is only probable, must weaken the first evidence seems to me contrary to all rules of logic and to common sense.

The first judgment may be compared to the testimony of a credible witness; the second, after a scrutiny into the character of the witness, wipes off every objection that can be made to it, and therefore surely must confirm and not weaken his testimony.

But let us suppose that in another case I examine my first judgment upon some point, and find that it was attended with unfavourable circumstances, what, in reason, and according to the rules of logic, ought to be the effect of this discovery?

The effect surely will be, and ought to be, to make me less confident in my first judgment, until I examine the point anew in more favourable circumstances. If it be a matter of importance, I return to weigh the evidence of my first judgment. If it was precipitate before, it must now be deliberate in every point. If at first I was in passion, I must now be cool. If I had an interest in the decision, I must place the interest on the other side.

It is evident that this review of the subject may confirm my first judgment notwithstanding the suspicious circumstances that attended it. Though the judge was biassed or corrupted, it does not follow that the sentence was unjust. The rectitude of the decision does not depend upon the character of the judge but upon the nature of the case. From that only it must be determined whether the decision be just. The circumstances that rendered it suspicious are mere presumptions which have no force against direct evidence.

Thus, I have considered the effect of this estimation of our liableness to err in our first judgment, and have allowed to it all the effect that reason and the rules of logic permit. In the case I first supposed, and in every case where we can discover no cause of error, it affords a presumption in favour of the first judgment. In other cases it may afford a presumption against it. But the rules of logic require that we should not judge by presumption where we have direct evidence. The effect of an unfavourable presumption should only be to make us examine the evidence with the greater care.

The sceptic urges, in the last place, that this estimation must be subjected to another estimation, that to another, and so on *in infinitum;* and as every new estimation takes away from the evidence of the first judgment, it must at last be totally annihilated.

I answer, *first,* It has been shown above that the first estimation, supposing it unfavourable, can only afford a presumption against the first judgment; the second, upon the same supposition, will be only the presumption of a presumption; and the third, the presumption that there is a presumption of a presumption. This infinite series of presumptions resembles an infinite series of quantities, decreasing in geometrical proportion, which amounts only to a finite sum.

Secondly, I have shown that the estimation of our first judgment may strengthen it; and the same thing may be said of all the subsequent estimations. It would, therefore, be as reasonable to conclude that the first judgment will be brought to infallible certainty when this series of estimations is wholly in its favour, as that its evidence will be brought to nothing by such a series supposed to be wholly unfavourable to it. But in reality one serious and cool re-examination of the evidence by which our first judgment is supported, has, and in reason ought to have, more force to strengthen or weaken it than an infinite series of such estimations as our author requires.

Thirdly, I know no reason nor rule in logic that requires that such a series of estimations should follow every particular judgment.

A wise man who has practised reasoning knows that he is fallible and carries this conviction along with him in every judgment he forms. He knows likewise that he is more liable to err in some case than in others. He has a scale in his mind by which he estimates his liableness to err, and by this he regulates the degree of his assent in his first judgment upon any point.

The author's reasoning supposes that a man, when he forms his first judgment, conceives himself to be infallible; that by a second and subsequent judgment he discovers that he is not infallible; and that by a third judgment, subsequent to the second, he estimates his liableness to err in such a case as the present.

If the man proceeds in this order, I grant that his second judgment will with good reason bring down the first from supposed infallibility to fallibility, and that his third judgment will in some degree either strengthen or weaken the first, as it is corrected by the second.

But every man of understanding proceeds in a contrary order. When about to judge in any particular point, he knows already that he is not infallible. He knows what are the cases in which he is most or least liable to err. The conviction of these things is always present to his mind, and influences the degree of his assent in his first judgment, as far as to him appears reasonable.

If he should afterwards find reason to suspect his first judgment, and desires to have all the satisfaction his faculties can give, reason will direct him not to form such a series of estimations upon estimations, as this author requires, but to examine the evidence of his first judgment carefully and coolly; and this review may very reasonably, according to its result, either strengthen or weaken, or totally overturn his first judgment.

This infinite series of estimations, therefore, is not the method that reason directs, in order to form our judgment in any case. It is introduced without necessity, without any use but to puzzle the understanding, and to make us think that to judge, even in the simplest and plainest cases, is a matter of insurmountable difficulty and endless labour; just as the ancient sceptic, to make a journey of two thousand paces appear endless, divided it into an infinite number of stages.

But we observed that the estimation which our author requires may admit of another meaning which indeed is more agreeable to the expression, but inconsistent with what he advanced before.

By the possibility of error in the estimation of the truth and fidelity of our faculties may be meant that we may err by esteeming our faculties true and faithful while they may be false and fallacious, even when used according to the rules of reason and logic.

If this be meant, I answer, *first,* That the truth and fidelity of our faculty of judging is, and must be, taken for granted in every judgment and in every estimation.

If the sceptic can seriously doubt of the truth and fidelity of his faculty of judging when properly used, and suspend his judgment upon that point till he finds proof his scepticism admits of no cure by reasoning, and he must even continue in it until he have new faculties given him which shall have authority to sit in judgment upon the old. Nor is there any need of an endless succession of doubts upon this subject, for the first puts an end to all judgment and reasoning and to the possibility of conviction by that means. The sceptic has here got possession of a stronghold which is impregnable to reasoning, and we must leave him in possession of it till nature, by other means, makes him give it up.

Secondly, I observe that this ground of scepticism from the supposed infidelity of our faculties contradicts what the author before advanced in this very argument—to wit, that "the rules of the demonstrative sciences are certain and infallible, and that truth is the natural effect of reason, and that error arises from the irruption of other causes."

But perhaps he made these concessions unwarily. He is therefore at liberty to retract them, and to rest his scepticism upon this sole foundation, That no reasoning can prove the truth and fidelity of our faculties. Here he stands upon firm ground, for it is evident that every argument offered to prove the truth and fidelity of our faculties takes for granted the thing in question, and is therefore that kind of sophism which logicians call *petitio principii.*

All we would ask of this kind of sceptic is that he would be uniform and consistent, and that his practice in life does not belie his profession of scepticism with regard to the fidelity of his faculties; for the want of faith, as well as faith itself, is best shown by works. If a sceptic avoid the fire as much as those who believe it dangerous to go into it, we can hardly avoid thinking his scepticism to be feigned, and not real.

Upon the whole, I see only two conclusions that can be fairly drawn from this profound and intricate reasoning against reason. The first is, That we are fallible in all our judgments and in all our reasonings. The second, That the truth and fidelity of our faculties can never be proved by reasoning, and therefore our belief of it cannot be founded on reasoning. If the last be what the author calls his hypothesis, I subscribe to it, and think it not an hypothesis but a manifest truth; though I conceive it to be very improperly expressed, by saying that belief is more properly an act of the sensitive than of the cogitative part of our nature.

Discussion Questions

1. Does Reid give a fair statement of Hume's arguments? Are there any cases where Hume says something different from what Reid represents him as saying? Has Reid ignored any of Hume's points?

2. Reid argues that Hume's doctrine "can never be seriously adopted by any man in his senses." Has Hume's appeal to the force of custom and habit disarmed this objection? Why or why not?

3. Reid argues that Hume has assumed that the only alternative to probability is infallibility: that if we do not know without any possibililty of a doubt, we have only probability. Is this what Hume is really saying? Is this an important objection to Hume's position? If so, state the objection in your own words. If you think Hume could answer this objection, state how he could do so.

4. Reid argues that whether something is demonstrably true is a matter of fact and does not depend on our abilities. How might Hume reply to this?

5. Reid states that Hume begins his proof that all human judgments are fallible by assuming that some are infallible and, if these are infallible, not all human judgments are fallible. Has Reid misrepresented Hume's view? Criticize Reid's argument.

Comment: G.K. Chesterton
"The Suicide of Thought" from *Orthodoxy*

The modern world is not evil; in some ways the modern world is far too good. It is full of wild and wasted virtues. When a religious scheme is shattered (as Christianity was shattered at the Reformation), it is not merely the vices that are let loose. The vices are, indeed, let loose, and they wander and do damage. But the virtues are let loose also; and the virtues wander more wildly, and the virtues do more terrible damage. The modern world is full of the old Christian virtues gone mad. The virtues have gone mad because they have been isolated from each other and are wandering alone. Thus some scientists care for truth; and their truth is pitiless. Thus some humanitarians only care for pity; and their pity (I am sorry to say) is often untruthful. As the other extreme, we may take the acrid realist, who has deliberately killed in himself all human pleasure in happy tales or in the healing of the heart. Torquemada tortured people physically for the sake of moral truth. Zola tortured people morally for the sake of physical truth. But in Torquemada's time there was at least a system that could to some extent make righteousness and peace kiss each other. Now they do not even bow. But a much stronger case than these two of truth and pity can be found in the remarkable case of the dislocation of humility.

It is only with one aspect of humility that we are here concerned. Humility was largely meant as a restraint upon the arrogance and infinity of the appetite of man. He was always outstripping his mercies with his own newly invented needs. His very power of enjoyment destroyed half his joys. By asking for pleasure, he lost the chief pleasure; for the chief pleasure is surprise. Hence it became evident that if a man would make his world large, he must be always making himself small. Even the haughty visions, the tall cities, and the toppling pinnacles are the creations of humility. Giants that tread down forests like grass are the creations of humility. Towers that vanish upwards above the loneliest star are the creations of humility. For towers are not tall unless we look up at them; and giants are not giants unless they are larger than we. All this gigantesque imagination, which is, perhaps, the mightiest of the pleasures of man, is at bottom entirely humble. It is impossible without humility to enjoy anything—even pride.

But what we suffer from today is humility in the wrong place. Modesty has moved from the organ of ambition. Modesty has settled upon the organ of conviction; where it was never meant to be. A man was meant to be doubtful about himself, but undoubting about the truth; this has been exactly reversed. Nowadays the part of a man that a man does assert is exactly the part he ought not to assert—himself. The part he doubts is exactly the part he ought not to doubt—the Divine Reason. Huxley preached a humility content to learn from Nature. But the new sceptic is so humble that he doubts if he can even learn. Thus we should be wrong if we had said hastily that there is no humility typical of our time. The truth is that there is a real humility typical of our time; but it so happens that it is practically a more poisonous humility than the wildest prostrations of the ascetic. The old humility was a spur that prevented a man from stopping; not a nail in his boot that prevented him from going on. For the old humility made a man doubtful about his efforts, which might make him work harder. But the new humility makes a man doubtful about his aims, which will make him stop working altogether.

At any street corner we may meet a man who utters the frantic and blasphemous statement that he may be wrong. Every day one comes across somebody who says that of course his view may not be the right one. Of course his view must be the right one, or it is not his view. We are on the road to producing a race of men too mentally modest to believe in the multiplication table. We are in danger of seeing philosophers who doubt the law of gravity as being a mere fancy of their own. Scoffers of old time were too proud to be convinced; but these are too humble to be convinced. The meek do inherit the earth; but the modern sceptics are too meek even to claim their inheritance. It is exactly this intellectual helplessness which is our second problem.

The last chapter has been concerned only with a fact of observation: that what peril of morbidity there is for man comes rather from his reason than his imagination. It was not meant to attack the authority of reason; rather it is the ultimate purpose to defend it. For it needs defence. The whole modern world is at war with reason; and the tower already reels.

The sages, it is often said, can see no answer to the riddle of religion. But the trouble with our sages is not that they cannot see the answer; it is that they cannot even see the riddle. They are like children so stupid as to notice nothing paradoxical in the playful assertion that a door is not a door. The modern latitudinarians speak, for instance, about authority in religion not only as if there were no reason in it, but as if there had never been any reason for it. Apart from seeing its philosophical basis, they cannot even see its historical cause. Religious authority has often, doubtless, been oppressive or unreasonable; just as every legal system (and especially our present one) has been callous and full of a cruel apathy. It is rational to attack the police; nay, it is glorious. But the modern critics of religious authority are like men who should attack the police without ever having heard of burglars. For there is a great and possible peril to the human mind: a peril as practical as burglary. Against it religious authority was reared, rightly or wrongly, as a barrier. And against it something certainly must be reared as a barrier, if our race is to avoid ruin.

That peril is that the human intellect is free to destroy itself. Just as one generation could prevent the very existence of the next generation, by all entering a monastery or jumping into the sea, so one set of thinkers can in some degree prevent further thinking by teaching the next generation that there is no validity in any human thought. It is idle to talk always of the alternative of reason and faith. Reason is itself a matter of faith. It is an act of faith to assert that our thoughts have any relation to reality at all. If you are merely a sceptic, you must sooner or later ask yourself the question, "Why should *anything* go right; even observation and deduction? Why should not good logic be as misleading as bad logic? They are both movements in the brain of a bewildered ape?" The young sceptic says, "I have a right to think for myself." But the old sceptic, the complete sceptic, says, "I have no right to think for myself. I have no right to think at all."

There is a thought that stops thought. That is the only thought that ought to be stopped. That is the ultimate evil against which all religious authority was aimed. It only appears at the end of decadent ages like our own: and already Mr. H.G. Wells has raised its ruinous banner; he has written a delicate piece of scepticism called "Doubts of the Instrument." In this he questions the brain itself, and endeavours to remove all reality from all his own assertions, past, present, and to come. But it was against this remote ruin that all the military systems in religion were originally ranked and ruled. The creeds and the crusades, the hierarchies and the horrible persecutions were not organized, as is ignorantly said, for the suppression of reason. They were organized for the difficult defence of reason. Man, by a blind instinct, knew that if once things were wildly questioned, reason could be questioned first. The authority of priests to absolve, the authority of popes to define the authority, even of inquisitors to terrify: these were all only dark defences erected round one central authority, more undemonstrable, more supernatural than all—the authority of a man to think. We know now that this is so; we have no excuse for not knowing it. For we can hear scepticism crashing through the old ring of authorities, and at the same moment we can see reason swaying upon her throne. In so far as religion is gone, reason is going. For they are both of the same primary and authoritative kind. They are both methods of proof which cannot themselves be proved. And in the act of destroying the idea of Divine authority we have largely destroyed the idea of that human authority by which we do a long-division sum. With a long and sustained tug we have attempted to pull the mitre off pontifical man; and his head has come off with it.

CHAPTER TWO
WHAT IS REAL?
THE PROBLEM OF
METAPHYSICS

Metaphysics addresses the basic questions about the nature of reality. What is ultimately real? What are the general characteristics of that which exists? One of the philosopher's most difficult tasks is to analyze a two-letter word we use many times every day: "is."

Any theory of the nature of reality is necessarily related to our beliefs about how we know that reality exists. Conversely, an assumption about the nature of reality can lead a person to adopt a particular theory of knowledge. Philosophy, insofar as it is considered to be the search for *first principles* or the basic assumptions implicit in any question, is metaphysics. Every philosopher is a metaphysician insofar as he or she pays critical attention to first principles.

Being and *Nonbeing* occupy an important place in metaphysics. Aristotle defined the task of metaphysics as the consideration of "being *qua* being." Many sciences and disciplines focus on some special area (for example chemistry, psychology, sociology), but Aristotle thought there should be a discipline to consider the nature of things as a whole. In this respect every metaphysics concerns *Being*, since every metaphysics attempts to present the most general description of the structure of things, i.e., a description which characterizes and applies to all that does or will or could exist.

Philosophy in the western world had, so far as we know, its origin with a Greek named Thales, who lived in Asia Minor in the sixth century B.C. Thales offered an answer to a central metaphysical question: what is the natural world composed of? According to Thales, water is the single elementary cosmic material at the base of the transformations of nature. This is the first attempt on record in which a thinker attempted to reduce the seemingly endless variety of the world to a singular element. The thinkers who followed Thales offered other explanations of things. Fire, earth, and air were also identified as the ultimate substance of which all else is composed.

By the fifth century B.C. philosophers began to recognize that, if they were to succeed in accounting for the diversity of things, they would have to produce a more general theory of substance. The result was atomism, which has ever since remained a highly recognized explanation of the physical world, being held, in a somewhat altered form, by many scientists right down to our own time. Atomism is both general and simple. Three eternal entities are emphasized: 1) atoms or matter; 2) motion; and 3) empty space. In addition to being eternal, these atoms are also indestructible, have no qualities like color or smell, and are too small to be observed.

Materialism: A "materialist," in today's speech, refers to a person who measures success in terms of money and worldly goods. Materialism, when used to refer to a world view, is very different. A metaphysical materialist holds that matter or substance is the stuff of the universe and that which is ultimately real. A strict materialist today argues that life is nothing more than a complicated physical-chemical process. He maintains that the mind and consciousness are nothing but the electrochemical activities of the brain.

The metaphysical materialist as we have defined him must reject God and the existence of a supernatural Being. For him, there is no controlling or directing intelligence or Being anywhere in the universe; human beings and the world are the products of nonintelligent forces. And while a materialist does not find it necessary to deny the "self," he must insist that a physical substratum is primary and is the sufficient cause of all mental phenomena.

Idealism: In popular language today idealism, too, has a different meaning from its philosophical use. In its popular meaning, an idealist refers to a person motivated by high standards. However, the philosophical meaning stresses *idea* and *mind* more than *ideal*. Idealism asserts that ultimate reality is of a nature more like ideas, thought, or mind. Idealism places emphasis on mind as in some way prior to matter. A materialist will point to matter as real and mind as the byproduct. Conversely, for the idealist, mind is real and the material world is secondary.

Several types of idealism will be introduced in this section. Pluralistic or subjective idealism is probably best represented by George Berkeley (1685—1753). For Berkeley, minds and ideas are all that exist. *Esse est percipi,* "to be is to be perceived," is the center of his philosophy. Berkeley holds that there can be no object without a knower; that the knower in some way creates its object (matter, or thing known). Berkeley believed the world consists of many minds, one of which is God.

Other idealists, like Plato and Hegel, reject the view that all that is real must either be a conscious mind or a perception by such a mind. When they maintain that the ultimate nature of the universe is mind, they mean that the universe is essentially spiritual in character. Plato (427-347 B.C.) concluded that in addition to the empirical world of becoming and change, which we feel and see, there is an ideal world of eternal essences, forms, or "Ideas." In a very real sense it was Plato's desire for a greater degree of certainty than our changing and uncertain world allows that led him to accept the necessity for a world of Forms (or Ideas), different in kind from the things of our empirical world.

Aristotle, like Plato, has a special place in the history of metaphysics. The term metaphysics itself is derived from the title given to those of his considerations which were "beyond physics" (meta = beyond), and it is to Aristotle that we must attribute the beginning of a technical vocabulary for metaphysics. Other terms have been introduced subsequently, the stress is different in places, and significant revisions have been made in Aristotle's work, yet a discussion of metaphysics still today rebuilds upon the technical terminology established by Aristotle.

Aristotle agrees with Plato in giving form a central place in reality. Moreover, he gives it many of the same properties. Form is universal and separable from the individual; form is unchanging in itself, and the source through which sense-objects are to be understood. But as has often been noted, Aristotle's main disagreement with Plato comes over the existence of and the status assigned to forms. In Aristotle's view, forms do not exist separated from the objects of the physical world. Forms exist only in these objects, and are extracted from them by human intelligence for the purpose of understanding.

Another contrast between Plato and Aristotle points up two main ways of doing metaphysics. Plato is less formal in his arguments. He is less interested in giving finished definitions and technical proofs. His intent is to raise issues and to offer a suggestive framework for their consideration. In contrast, Aristotle introduces and defines technical terminology, and thus outlines his arguments more formally.

A. AN IDEALIST VIEW

George Berkeley:
Three Dialogues Between Hylas and Philonous (Dialogue I)

George Berkeley (1685-1753) was a native of Ireland. He studied at Trinity College, Dublin, and subsequently taught there. Berkeley was an Anglican bishop and philosopher, a deeply religious man who tried to reconcile the science of his day with the doctrines of Christianity. Berkeley believed he could demonstrate that "matter" does not exist and yet the laws of physics are true. The arguments by which he tried to prove this are the most important part of his philosophy. He held that "to exist" means "to be perceived." Nothing exists unless it is perceived by some mind. Although Berkeley held that things are mind-dependent, he did not maintain that things are dependent on human minds for their existence. Things exist even when nobody is perceiving them because they are being thought about by God.

... HYLAS: You were represented in last night's conversation as one who maintained the most extravagant opinion that ever entered into the mind of man, to wit, that there is no such thing as *material substance* in the world.

PHILONOUS: That there is no such thing as what philosophers call *material substance,* I am seriously persuaded: but if I were made to see anything absurd or sceptical in this, I should then have the same reason to renounce this, that I imagine I have now to reject the contrary opinion.

HYLAS: What! can anything be more fantastical, more repugnant to common sense, or a more manifest piece of scepticism, than to believe there is no such thing as *matter?*

PHILONOUS: Softly, good Hylas. What if it should prove that you, who hold there is, are by virtue of that option a greater *sceptic,* and maintan more paradoxes and repugnancies to common sense, than I who believe no such thing?

* * *

PHILONOUS: How cometh it to pass then, Hylas, that you pronounce me a *sceptic,* because I deny what you affirm, to wit, the existence of matter? Since, for aught you can tell, I am as peremptory in my denial, as you in your affirmation.

HYLAS: Hold. Philonous ... I said indeed, that a *sceptic* was one who doubted of everything; but I should have added, or who denies the reality and truth of things.

PHILONOUS: What things? Do you mean the principles and theorems of sciences? But these you know are universal intellectual notions, and consequently independent of matter; the denial therefore of this doth not imply the denying them.

HYLAS: I grant it. But are there no other things? What think you of dis-
              trusting the senses, of denying the real existence of sensible things,
              or pretending to know nothing of them. Is not this sufficient to
              denominate a man a *sceptic?*

PHILONOUS: Shall we therefore examine which of us it is that denies the reality
              of sensible things, or professes the greatest ignorance of them;
              since, if I take you rightly, he is to be esteemed the greatest *sceptic?*

HYLAS: That is what I desire.

PHILONOUS: What do you mean by sensible things?

HYLAS: Those things which are perceived by the senses. Can you imagine
              that I mean anything else?

PHILONOUS: Pardon me, Hylas, if I am desirous clearly to apprehend your
              notions, since this may much shorten our inquiry. Suffer me then
              to ask you this farther question. Are those things only perceived by
              the senses which are perceived immediately? Or may those things
              properly be said to be *sensible,* which are perceived mediately, or
              not without the intervention of others?

HYLAS: I do not sufficiently understand you.

PHILONOUS: In reading a book, what I immediately perceive are the letters, but
              mediately, or by means of these, are suggested to my mind the
              notions of God, virtue, truth, etc. Now, that the letters are truly
              sensible things, or perceived by sense, there is no doubt: but I
              would know whether you take the things suggested by them to be
              so too.

HYLAS: No certainly, it were absurd to think *God* or *virtue* sensible things,
              though they may be signified and suggested to the mind by sensi-
              ble marks, with which they have an arbitrary connexion.

PHILONOUS: It seems then, that by *sensible things* you mean those only which can
              be perceived immediately by sense.

HYLAS: Right.

PHILONOUS: Doth it not follow from this, that though I see one part of the sky
              red, and another blue, and that my reason doth thence evidently
              conclude there must be some cause of that diversity of colours, yet
              that cause cannot be said to be a sensible thing, or perceived by the
              sense of seeing?

HYLAS: It doth.

PHILONOUS: In like manner, though I hear variety of sounds, yet I cannot be
              said to hear the causes of those sounds.

HYLAS: You cannot.

PHILONOUS: And when by my touch I perceive a thing to be hot and heavy, I
              cannot say with any truth or propriety, that I feel the cause of its
              heat or weight.

HYLAS: To prevent any more questions of this kind, I tell you once for all,
              that by *sensible things* I mean those only which are perceived by
              sense, and that in truth the senses perceive nothing which they do
              not perceive immediately: for they make no inferences. The
              deducing therefore of causes or occasions from effects and

appearances, which alone are perceived by sense, entirely relates to reason.

PHILONOUS: This point then is agreed between us, that *sensible things are those only which are immediately perceived by sense.* You will farther inform me, whether we immediately perceive by sight anything beside light, and colours, and figures: or by hearing, anything but sounds: by the palate, anything beside tastes: by the smell, beside odours: or by touch, more than tangible qualities.

HYLAS: We do not.

PHILONOUS: It seems, therefore, that if you take away all sensible qualities, there remains nothing sensible.

HYLAS: I grant it.

PHILONOUS: Sensible things therefore are nothing else but so many sensible qualities, or combinations of sensible qualities.

HYLAS: Nothing else.

PHILONOUS: Heat then is a sensible thing.

HYLAS: Certainly.

PHILONOUS: Doth the reality of sensible things consist in being perceived? or, is it something distinct from their being perceived, and that bears no relation to the mind?

HYLAS: To *exist* is one thing, and to be *perceived* is another.

PHILONOUS: I speak with regard to sensible things only: and of these I ask, whether by their real existence you mean a subsistence exterior to the mind, and distinct from their being perceived?

HYLAS: I mean a real absolute being, distinct from, and without any relation to their being perceived.

PHILONOUS: Heat therefore, if it be allowed a real being, must exist without the mind.

HYLAS: It must.

* * *

HYLAS: I frankly own, Philonous, that it is in vain to stand out any longer. Colours, sounds, tastes, in a word, all those termed *secondary qualities,* have certainly no existence without the mind. But by this acknowledgment I must not be supposed to derogate anything from the reality of matter or external objects, seeing it is no more than several philosophers maintain, who nevertheless are the farthest imaginable from denying matter. For the clearer understanding of this, you must know sensible qualities are by philosophers divided into *primary* and *secondary.* The former are extension, figure, solidity, gravity, motion, and rest. And these they hold exist really in bodies. The latter are those above enumerated; or briefly, all sensible qualities beside the primary, which they assert are only so many sensations or ideas existing nowhere but in the mind. But all this, I doubt not, you are already apprised of. For my part, I have been a long time sensible there was such an opinion current among philosophers, but was never thoroughly convinced of its truth till now.

PHILONOUS: You are still then of opinion that extension and figures are inherent in external unthinking substances.

HYLAS: I am.

PHILONOUS: But what if the same arguments which are brought against secondary qualities, will hold good against these also?

HYLAS: Why then I shall be obliged to think, they too exist only in the mind.

* * *

PHILONOUS: To help you out, do but consider, that if extension be once acknowledged to have no existence without the mind, the same must necessarily be granted of motion, solidity, and gravity, since they all evidently suppose extension. It is therefore superfluous to inquire particularly concerning each of them. In denying extension, you have denied them all to have any real existence.

* * *

HYLAS: One great oversight I take to be this: that I did not sufficiently distinguish the *object* from the *sensation*. Now though this latter may not exist without the mind, yet it will not thence follow that the former cannot.

PHILONOUS: What object do you mean? The object of the senses?

HYLAS: The same.

PHILONOUS: It is then immediately perceived.

HYLAS: Right.

PHILONOUS: Make me to understand the difference between what is immediately perceived, and a sensation.

HYLAS: The sensation I take to be an act of the mind perceiving; beside which, there is something perceived; and this I call the *object*. For example, there is red and yellow on that tulip. But then the act of perceiving those colours is in me only, and not in the tulip.

PHILONOUS: What tulip do you speak of? Is it that which you see?

HYLAS: The same.

PHILONOUS: And what do you see beside colour, figure, and extension?

HYLAS: Nothing.

PHILONOUS: What would you say then is, that the red and yellow are coexistent with the extension; is it not?

HYLAS: That is not all; I would say, they have a real existence without the mind, in some unthinking substance.

PHILONOUS: That the colours are really in the tulip which I see, is manifest. Neither can it be denied that this tulip may exist independent of your mind or mine; but that any immediate object of the senses, that is, any idea, or combination of ideas, should exist in an unthinking substance, or exterior to all minds, is in itself an evident contradiction. Nor can I imagine how this follows from what you said just now, to wit that the red and yellow were on the tulip *you saw*, since you do not pretend to *see* that unthinking substance.

HYLAS: You have an artful way, Philonous, of diverting our inquiry from the subject.

PHILONOUS: I see you have no mind to be pressed that way. To return then to your distinction between *sensation* and *object;* if I take you right, you distinguish in every perception two things, the one an action of the mind, the other not.

HYLAS: True.

PHILONOUS: And this action cannot exist in, or belong to any unthinking thing; but whatever beside is implied in a perception, may.

HYLAS: That is my meaning.

PHILONOUS: So that if there was a perception without any act of the mind, it were possible such a perception should exist in an unthinking substance.

HYLAS: I grant it. But it is impossible there should be such a perception.

PHILONOUS: When is the mind said to be active?

HYLAS: When it produces, puts an end to, or changes anything.

PHILONOUS: Can the mind produce, discontinue, or change anything but by an act of the will?

HYLAS: It cannot.

PHILONOUS: The mind therefore is to be accounted active in its perceptions, so far forth as volition is included in them.

* * *

HYLAS: I acknowledge, Philonous, that upon a fair observation of what passes in my mind, I can discover nothing else, but that I am a thinking being, affected with variety of sensations; neither is it possible to conceive how a sensation should exist in an unperceiving substance. But then on the other hand, when I look on sensible things in a different view, considering them as so many modes and qualities, I find it necessary to suppose a material *substratum*, without which they cannot be conceived to exist.

PHILONOUS: *Material substratum* call you it? Pray, by which of your senses came you acquainted with that being?

HYLAS: It is not itself sensible; its modes and qualities only being perceived by the senses.

PHILONOUS: I presume then, it was by reflexion and reason you obtained the idea of it.

HYLAS: I do not pretend to any proper positive idea of it. However, I conclude it exists, because qualities cannot be conceived to exist without a support.

PHILONOUS: It seems then you have only a relative notion of it, or that you conceive it not otherwise than by conceiving the relation it bears to sensible qualities.

HYLAS: Right.

PHILONOUS: Be pleased therefore to let me know wherein that relation consists.

HYLAS: Is it not sufficiently expressed in the term *substratum,* or *substance?*

PHILONOUS: If so, the word *substratum* should import that it is spread under the sensible qualities or accidents.

HYLAS: True.

PHILONOUS: And consequently under extension.

HYLAS:	I own it.
PHILONOUS:	It is therefore somewhat in its own nature entirely distinct from extension.
HYLAS:	I tell you, extension is only a mode, and matter is something that supports modes. And is it not evident the thing supported is different from the thing supporting?
PHILONOUS:	So that something distinct from, and exclusive of extension, is supposed to be the *substratum* of extension.
HYLAS:	Just so.
PHILONOUS:	Answer me, Hylas. Can a thing be spread without extension? Or is not the idea of extension necessarily included in *spreading?*
HYLAS:	It is.
PHILONOUS:	Whatsoever therefore you suppose spread under anything, must have in itself an extension distinct from the extension of that thing under which it is spread.
HYLAS:	It must.
PHILONOUS:	Consequently every corporeal substance being the *substratum* of extension, must have in itself another extension by which it is qualified to be a *substratum:* and so on to infinity. And I ask whether this be not absurd in itself, and repugnant to what you granted just now, to wit, that the *substratum* was something distinct from, and exclusive of extension.
HYLAS:	Ay but, Philonous, you take me wrong. I do not mean that matter is *spread* in a gross literal sense under extension. The word *substratum* is used only to express in general the same thing with *substance.*
PHILONOUS:	Well then, let us examine the relation implied in the term *substance.* Is it not that it stands under accidents?
HYLAS:	The very same.
PHILONOUS:	But that one thing may stand under or support another, must it not be extended?
HYLAS:	It must.
PHILONOUS:	Is not therefore this supposition liable to the same absurdity with the former?
HYLAS:	You still take things in a strict literal sense: that is not fair, Philonous.
PHILONOUS:	I am not for imposing any sense on your words: you are at liberty to explain them as you please. Only I beseech you, make me understand something by them. You tell me, matter supports or stands under accidents. How! is it as your legs support your body?
HYLAS:	No; that is the literal sense.
PHILONOUS:	Pray let me know any sense, literal or not literal, that you understand it in.—How long must I wait for an answer, Hylas?
HYLAS:	I declare I know not what to say. I once thought I understood well enough what was meant by matter's supporting accidents. But now the more I think on it, the less can I comprehend it; in short, I find that I know nothing of it.
PHILONOUS:	It seems then you have no idea at all, neither relative nor positive,

of matter; you know neither what is is in itself, nor what relation it bears to accidents.

HYLAS: I acknowledge it.

* * *

HYLAS: To speak the truth, Philonous, I think there are two kinds of objects, the one perceived immediately, which are likewise called *ideas;* the other are real things or external objects perceived by the mediation of ideas, which are their images and representations. Now I own, ideas do not exist without the mind; but the latter sort of objects do. I am sorry I did not think of this distinction sooner; it would probably have cut short your discourse.

PHILONOUS: Are those external objects perceived by sense, or by some other faculty?

HYLAS: They are perceived by sense.

PHILONOUS: How! is there anything perceived by sense, which is not immediately perceived?

HYLAS: Yes, Philonous, in some sort there is. For example, when I look on a picture or statue of Julius Caesar, I may be said after a manner to perceive him (though not immediately) by my senses.

PHILONOUS: It seems then, you will have our ideas, which alone are immediately perceived, to be pictures of external things: and that these also are perceived by sense, inasmuch as they have a conformity or resemblance to our ideas.

HYLAS: That is my meaning.

PHILONOUS: And in the same way that Julius Caesar, in himself invisible, is nevertheless perceived by sight; real things in themselves imperceptible are perceived by sense.

HYLAS: In the very same.

PHILONOUS: Tell me, Hylas, when you behold the picture of Julius Caesar, do you see with your eyes any more than some colours and figures with a certain symmetry and composition of the whole?

HYLAS: Nothing else.

PHILONOUS: And would not a man, who had never known anything of Julius Caesar, see as much?

HYLAS: He would.

PHILONOUS: Consequently he hath his sight, and the use of it, in as perfect a degree as you.

HYLAS: I agree with you.

* * *

PHILONOUS: My aim is only to learn from you the way to come at the knowledge of *material beings.* Whatever we perceive, is perceived either immediately or mediately: by sense, or by reason and reflexion. But as you have excluded sense, pray show me what reason you have to believe their existence; or what *medium* you can possibly make use of, to prove it either to mine or your own understanding.

HYLAS: To deal ingenuously, Philonous, now I consider the point, I do not find I can give you any good reason for it. But thus much seems pretty plain, that it is at least possible such things may really exist. And as long as there is no absurdity in supposing them, I am resolved to believe as I did, till you bring good reasons to the contrary.

PHILONOUS: What! is it come to this, that you only believe the existence of material objects, and that your belief is founded barely on the possibility of its being true? Then you will have me bring reasons against it: though another would think it reasonable, the proof should lie on him who holds the affirmative. And after all, this very point which you are now resolved to maintain without any reason, is in effect what you have more than once during this discourse seen good reason to give up. But to pass over all this; if I understand you rightly, you say our ideas do not exist without the mind; but that they are copies, images, or representations of certain originals that do.

HYLAS: You take me right.

PHILONOUS: They are then like external things.

HYLAS: They are.

PHILONOUS: Have those things a stable and permanent nature independent of our senses; or are they in a perpetual change, upon our producing any motions in our bodies, suspending, exerting, or altering our faculties or organs of sense?

HYLAS: Real things, it is plain, have a fixed and real nature, which remains the same, notwithstanding any change in our senses, or in the posture and motion of our bodies; which indeed may affect the ideas in our minds, but it were absurd to think they had the same effect on things existing without the mind.

PHILONOUS: How then is it possible, that things perpetually fleeting and variable as our ideas, should be copies or images of anything fixed and constant? Or in other words, since all sensible qualities, as size, figure, colour, etc., that is, our ideas, are continually changing upon every alteration in the distance, medium, or instruments of sensation; how can any determinate material objects be properly represented or painted forth by several distinct things, each of which is so different from and unlike the rest? Or if you say it resembles some one only of our ideas, how shall we be able to distinguish the true copy from all the false ones?

HYLAS: I profess, Philonous, I am at a loss. I know not what to say to this.

PHILONOUS: But neither is this all. Which are material objects in themselves, perceptible or imperceptible?

HYLAS: Properly and immediately nothing can be perceived but ideas. All material things therefore are in themselves insensible, and to be perceived only by their ideas.

PHILONOUS: Ideas then are sensible, and their archetypes or originals insensible.

HYLAS: Right.

PHILONOUS: But how can that which is sensible be like that which is insensible? Can a real thing in itself *invisible* be like a *colour;* or a real thing which is not *audible*, be like a *sound?* In a word, can anything be like a sensation or idea, but another sensation or idea?

HYLAS: I must own, I think not.

PHILONOUS: Is it possible there should be any doubt in the point? Do you not perfectly know your own ideas?

HYLAS: I know them perfectly; since what I do not perceive or know, can be no part of my idea.

PHILONOUS: Consider therefore, and examine them, and then tell me if there be anything in them which can exist without the mind: or if you can conceive anything like them existing without the mind.

HYLAS: Upon inquiry, I find it is impossible for me to conceive or understand how anything but an idea can be like an idea. And it is most evident that *no idea can exist without the mind.*

PHILONOUS: You are therefore by your principles forced to deny the reality of sensible things, since you made it to consist in an absolute existence exterior to the mind. That is to say, you are a downright *sceptic.* So I have gained my point, which was to show your principles led to scepticism.

HYLAS: For the present I am, if not entirely convinced, at least silenced.
. . .

Discussion Questions

1. Philonous believes that a belief in the existence of matter leads to scepticism. What does he mean? What are his reasons for saying this?

2. What, according to Philonous, is perceived by the senses? Do you agree? Why or why not?

3. Hylas maintains that to exist is one thing, and to be perceived is another? Do you agree? Why or why not?

4. Philonous argues that what philosophers call material substance does not exist. What steps does he go through? Do you agree with him? Why or why not?

5. Hylas distinguishes between primary and secondary qualities. Explain this distinction in your own words.

6. If you were convinced that Philonous is right in his denial of the existence of matter, would you change the way you lived? If yes, how? If no, why not?

B. A MATERIALIST VIEW

Lucretius: *De Rerum Natura*

Lucretius (94?–55 B.C.) was a Roman philosophical poet whose chief work, *De Rerum Natura* (*On the Nature of Things*), is both a great poem and a statement of a major metaphysical thesis. Lucretius' full name was Titus Lucretius Carus. He was born in Rome. Very little is known of his life.

Lucretius' book is based on the philosophy of Epicurus, which taught that the world is without divine design or rule. *De Rerum Natura* is concerned with how all the objects and events that make up the world we live in can be explained through an appeal to matter (atoms) in motion. Moreover, Lucretius seeks to show the consequences of the materialist view of reality for human life. He stresses that much of the suffering human beings endure results from religious superstition. Lucretius explained his arguments with vivid word pictures which, he said, were like honey on the rim of a cup of bitter medicine.

BOOK I

O bountiful Venus, mother of the race of Aeneas, delight of gods and men, who, beneath the gliding constellations of heaven, fillest with life the ship-bearing sea and the fruit-producing earth; since by thy influence every kind of living creature is conceived, and springing forth, hails the light of the sun. Thee, O goddess, thee the winds flee; before thee, and thy approach, the clouds of heaven disperse; for thee the variegated earth puts forth her fragrant flowers; on thee the waters of ocean smile, and the calmed heaven beams with effulgent light. For, as soon as the vernal face of day is unveiled, and the genial gale of Favonius exerts its power unconfined, the birds of the air first, O goddess, testify of thee and thy coming, smitten in heart by thy influence. Next, the wild herds bound over the joyous pastures, and swim across the rapid streams. So all kinds of living creatures, captivated by thy charms and thy allurements, eagerly follow thee whithersoever thou proceedest to lead them. In fine, throughout seas, and mountains, and whelming rivers, and the leafy abodes of birds, and verdant plains, thou, infusing balmy love into the breasts of all, causest them eagerly to propagate their races after their kind.

Since thou alone dost govern all things in nature, neither does any thing without thee spring into the ethereal realms of light, nor any thing become gladsome or lovely; I desire thee to be my associate in this my song, which I am essaying to compose on the NATURE OF THINGS, for the instruction of my friend Memmius. . . .

* * *

Wherefore with reason then, not only an inquiry concerning celestial affairs is to be accurately made by us, (as by what means the courses of the sun and moon are affected, and by what influence all things individually are directed upon the earth,) but especially also we must consider, with scrutinizing examination, of what the soul and the nature of the mind consist, and what it is, which, haunting us, sometimes when awake, and sometimes when overcome by disease or buried in sleep, terrifies the mind;

so that we seem to behold and to hear speaking before us, those whose bones, after death is passed, the earth embraces.

* * *

This terror and darkness of the mind, therefore, it is not the rays of the sun, or the bright shafts of day, that must dispel, but the reason and the contemplation of nature; of which our first principle shall hence take its commencement, THAT NOTHING IS EVER DIVINELY GENERATED FROM NOTHING. For thus it is that fear restraints all men, because they observe many things effected on the earth, and in heaven, of which effects they can by no means see the causes, and therefore think that they are wrought by a divine power. For which reasons, when we shall have clearly seen that NOTHING CAN BE PRODUCED FROM NOTHING, we shall then have a more accurate perception of that of which we are in search, and shall understand whence each individual thing is generated, and how all things are done without the agency of the gods.

For if things came forth from nothing, every kind of thing might be produced from all things; nothing would require seed. In the first place, men might spring from the sea; the scaly tribe, and birds, might spring from the earth; herds and other cattle might burst from the sky; the cultivated fields, as well as the deserts, might contain every kind of wild animal without any settled law of production: nor would the same fruits be constant to the same trees, but would be changed; and all trees might bear all kinds of fruit. Since, when there should not be generative elements for each production, how could a certain parent-producer remain invariable for all individual things? But now, because all things are severally produced from certain seeds, each is produced, and comes forth into the regions of light, from that spot in which the matter, and first elements of each, subsist. And for this cause all things cannot be produced from all, inasmuch as there are distinct and peculiar faculties in certain substances.

Besides, why do we see the rose put forth in spring, corn in summer heat, and vines under the influence of autumn, if it be not because, when the determinate seeds of things have united together at their proper time, whatever is produced appears while the seasons are favourable, and while the vigorous earth securely brings forth her tender productions into the regions of light. But if these were generated from nothing, they might arise suddenly at indefinite periods, and at unsuitable seasons of the year, inasmuch as there would be no original elements, which might be restrained from a generative combination at any season, however inconvenient.

* * *

Add, too, that nature resolves each thing into its own constituent elements, and DOES NOT REDUCE ANY THING TO NOTHING.

For if any thing were perishable in all its parts, every thing might then dissolve, being snatched suddenly from before our eyes; for there would be no need of force to produce a separation of its parts, and break their connexion. Whereas now, since all things individually consist of eternal seed, nature does not suffer the destruction of any thing to be seen, until such power assail them as to sever them with a blow, or penetrate inwardly through the vacant spaces, and dissolve the parts.

Besides, if time utterly destroys whatever things it removes through length of age, consuming all their constituent matter, whence does Venus restore to the light of life the race of animals according to their kinds? Whence does the variegated earth nourish and develop them, when restored, affording them sustenances according to their kinds? Whence do pure fountains, and eternal rivers flowing from afar, supply the sea? Whence does the aether feed the stars? For infinite time already past, and length of days, ought to have consumed all things which are of mortal consistence: but if those elements, of which this sum of things consists and is renewed, have existed through that long space, and that past duration of time, they are assuredly endowed with an immortal nature. Things therefore cannot return to nothing.

Further, the same force and cause might destroy all things indiscriminately, unless an eternal matter held them more or less bound by mutual connexion. For a mere touch, indeed, would be a sufficient cause of destruction, supposing that there were no parts of eternal consistence, but all perishable, the union of which any force might dissolve. But now, because various connexions of elements unite together, and matter is eternal, things continue of unimpaired consistence, until some force of sufficient strength be found to assail them, proportioned to the texture of each. No thing, therefore, relapses into nonexistence, but all things at dissolution return to the first principles of matter.

Lastly, you may say, perhaps, the showers of rain perish, when Father Aether has poured them down into the lap of Mother Earth. But it is not so; for hence the smiling fruits arise, and the branches become verdant on the trees; the trees themselves increase, and are weighed down with produce. Hence, moreover, is nourished the race of man, and that of beasts; hence we see joyous cities abound with youth, and the leafy woods resound on every side with newly-fledged birds; hence the weary cattle, sleek in the rich pastures, repose their bodies, and the white milky liquor flows from their distended udders; hence the new offspring gambol sportive, with tottering limbs, over the tender grass, their youthful hearts exhilarated with pure milk. Things, therefore, do not utterly perish, which seem to do so, since Nature recruits one thing from another, nor suffers any thing to be produced, unless its production be furthered by the death of another.

Attend, now, further: since I have shown that things cannot be produced from nothing, and also that, when produced, they cannot return to nothing, yet, lest haply thou shouldst begin to distrust my words, because the primary particles of things cannot be discerned by the eye, hear, in addition, what substances thou thyself must necessarily confess to exist, although impossible to be seen.

In the first place, the force of the wind, when excited, lashes the sea, agitates the tall ships, and scatters the clouds; at times, sweeping over the earth with an impetuous hurricane, it strews the plains with huge trees, and harasses the mountain-tops with forest-rending blasts; so violently does the deep chafe with fierce roar and rage with menacing murmur. The winds, then, are invisible bodies, which sweep the sea, the land, the clouds of heaven, and, agitating them, carry them along with a sudden tornado.

* * *

Moreover we perceive various odours of objects, and yet never see them approaching our nostrils. Nor do we behold violent heat, or distinguish cold with our eyes; nor are we in the habit of viewing sounds; all which things, however, must of necessity consist of a corporeal nature, since they have the power of striking the senses: FOR NOTHING, EXCEPT BODILY SUBSTANCE, CAN TOUCH OR BE TOUCHED.

Further, garments, when suspended upon a shore on which waves are broken, grow moist; the same, when spread out in the sun, become dry; yet neither has it been observed how the moisture of the water settled in them, nor, on the other hand, how it escaped under the influences of the heat. The moisture, therefore, is dispersed into minute particles, which our eyes can by no means perceive.

* * *

Lastly, whatever substances time and nature add little by little to objects, obliging them to increase gradually, those substances no acuteness of vision, however earnestly exerted, can perceive; nor, moreover, whatever substances waste away through age and decay; nor can you discern what the rocks, which overhang the sea, and are eaten by the corroding salt of the ocean, lose every time that they are washed by the waves. Nature, therefore, carries on her operations by imperceptible particles.

Nor, however, are all things held enclosed by corporeal substance; for there is a void in things; a truth which it will be useful for you, in reference to many points, to know; and which will prevent you from wandering in doubt, and from perpetually inquiring about the entire of things, and from being distrustful of my words. Wherefore, I say, there is space INTANGIBLE, EMPTY, and VACANT. If this were not the case, things could by no means be moved; for that which is the quality of body, namely, to obstruct and to oppose, would be present at all times, and would be exerted against all bodies; nothing, therefore, would be able to move forward, since nothing would begin to give way. But now, throughout the sea and land and heights of heaven, we see many things moved before our eyes in various ways and by various means, which, if there were no void, would not so much want their active motion, as being deprived of it, as they would, properly speaking, never by any means have been produced at all; since matter, crowded together on all sides, would have remained at rest, and have been unable to act.

Besides, although some things may be regarded as solid, yet you may, for the following reasons, perceive them to be of a porous consistence. In rocks and caves, the liquid moisture of the waters penetrates their substance, and all parts weep, as it were, with abundant drops; food distributes itself through the whole of the body in animals; the groves increase, and yield their fruits in their season, because nourishment is diffused through the whole of the trees, even from the lowest roots, over all the trunks and branches; voices pass through the walls, and fly across the closed apartments of houses; keen frost penetrates to the very marrow of our bones; which kind of effects, unless there were void spaces in bodies, where the several particles might pass, you would never by any means observe to take place.

* * *

All that exists . . . is bounded in no direction; for, if it were bounded, it must have some extremity; but it appears that there cannot be an extremity of anything, unless there be something beyond which may limit it; so that there may appear to be some line farther than which this faculty of our senses cannot extend. Now, since it must be confessed that there is nothing beyond the WHOLE, the whole has no extremity; nor does it matter at what part of it you stand, with a view to being distant from its boundary; inasmuch as, whatever place any one occupies, he leaves the WHOLE just as much boundless in every direction.

Besides, if all space which is, be supposed to be bounded, and if any one should go forward as far as possible, even to what he thinks its extreme limits, and should throw, or attempt to throw, a flying dart, whether would you have that dart, hurled with vigorous strength, go on in the direction in which it may have been propelled, and fly far forwards, or do you rather prefer to think that something would have power to hinder and stop it? For one of the two alternatives you must of necessity admit and adopt; of which alternatives either cuts off escape from you, and compels you to grant that the WHOLE extends without limit. Since whether there is anything to stop the javelin, and to cause that it may not go on in the direction in which it was aimed, and fix itself at the destined termination of its flight, or whether it is borne onwards beyond the supposed limit, it evidently did not begin its flight from a boundary of the WHOLE. In this manner I will go on with you, and wheresoever you shall fix the extreme margin of space, I will ask you what then would be the case with the javelin. The case will be, that a limit can no where exist; and that room for the flight of the javelin will still extend its flight.

BOOK II

Attend now, therefore, and I will explain to thee by what motions the generative bodies of matter produce various things, and resolve them when produced; and by what force they are thus compelled to act, and what activity has been communicated to them for passing through the mighty void of space. Do thou remember to give thyself wholly to my words.

For, assuredly, matter does not constantly cohere as being closely condensed in itself, since we see every object diminished, and perceive that all things flow away, as it were, through length of time, and that age withdraws them from our eyes; while, nevertheless, the sum of all seems to remain undecayed. And this happens for this reason, that the particles of matter which depart from each object, lessen the object from which they depart, and endow with increase the object or objects to which they have transferred themselves; and oblige the former to decay, but the latter, on the contrary, to flourish. Nor do they continue always in the place to which they have gone; and thus the sum of things is perpetually renewed, and the races of mortal men subsist by change and transference from one to the other. Some nations increase, others are diminished, and, in a short space of time, the tribes of living creatures are changed by successive generations, and, like the racers, deliver the torch of life from hand to hand.

If you think that the elemental atoms of things can remain at rest, and can, by remaining at rest, generate fresh motions of things, you stray with a wide deviation from true reason. For, since the primary-particles of all things wander through the void of space, they must necessarily be all carried forward by their own gravity, or, as it may chance, by the force of another body; for when, being often moved, they, meeting, have struck against one another, it happens that they suddenly start asunder in different directions; since neither is it to be wondered at that bodies should do so, which are of the utmost hardness, and of solid weight; nor, it is to be observed, does any thing behind oppose their motion. And that you may the more clearly understand that all the atoms of matter are tossed about and kept in motion, remember that in the sum of the whole, or in the entire universe, there is no lowest place; nor has it any point where the primary atoms may make a stand; since space is without bound and limit, and shows of itself, by many indications, that it extends around infinite in every direction. And this has been proved by indisputable argument.

* * *

And many atoms besides wander through the great void, which are rejected by combination of bodies, and have nowhere been able, admitted into union, to associate their motions with other atoms. Of which circumstance, as I conceive, an example and image is, from time to time, moving and present before our eyes. For, behold, whensoever the beams of the sun pour themselves through a chink into the dark parts of houses, you will see, in the light of the rays, many minute particles throughout the open space, mingled together in many ways, and, as it were, in perpetual conflict, exhibiting battles and fights, contending in companies, nor allowing any pause to their strife, being agitated by frequent concussions and separations; so that you may conjecture, from this spectacle, what it is for the primary-particles of things to be perpetually tossed about in the great void. Assuredly a small thing may give an example, and traces leading to the knowledge of great things. On this account it is more fitting that you should give your attention to these motes which seem to confuse one another in the rays of the sun; because such disorders signify that there secretly exist tendencies to motion also in the principles of matter, though latent and unapparent to our senses. For you will see there, among those atoms in the sun-beam, many, struck with imperceptible forces, change their course, and turn back, being repelled sometimes this way, and sometimes that, everywhere, and all directions. And doubtless this errant-motion in all these atoms proceeds from the primary elements of matter; for the first primordial atoms of things are moved of themselves; and then those bodies which are of light texture, and are, as it were, nearest to the nature of the primary elements, being urged by secret impulses of those elements, are put into motion, and these latter themselves, moreover, agitate others which are somewhat larger. Thus motion ascends from the first principles, and spreads forth by degrees so as to be apparent to our senses, and so that those atoms are moved before us, which we can see in the light of the sun; though it is not clearly evident by what impulses they are thus moved.

* * *

BOOK III

And since I have shown of what kind the primordial atoms of all things are, and how, differing in their various forms, and actuated by motion from all eternity, they fly through the void of space of their own accord; and since I have also demonstrated by what means all individual things may be produced from them; the nature of the mind and of the soul now seems, next to these subjects, proper to be illustrated in my verses; and there must be driven utterly from our minds that fear of Acheron, which disturbs human life from its very foundation, suffusing all things with the blackness of death, nor allows any pleasure to be pure and uncontaminated.

* * *

This same course of reasoning teaches us that the nature or substance of the mind and soul is corporeal; for when this nature or substance is seen to impel the limbs, to rouse the body from sleep, and to change the countenance, and to guide and turn about the whole man;—of which effects we see that none can be produced without touch, and that touch, moreover, cannot take place without body;—must we not admit that the mind and soul are of a corporeal nature?

* * *

I shall now proceed to give you a demonstration, in plain words, of what substance this mind is, and of what it consists.

In the first place, I say that it is extremely subtle, and is formed of very minute atoms. And you may, if you please, give me your attention, in order that you may understand clearly that this is so, from the following arguments. Nothing is seen to be done in so swift a way, as if the mind proposes it to be done, and itself undertakes it. The mind, therefore, impels itself more speedily than any thing, among all those of which the nature is manifestly seen before our eyes. But that which is so exceedingly active, must consist of atoms exquisitely round and exquisitely minute; that they may be moved, when acted on, by a slight impulse. For water is moved, and flows, with so trifling a force as we see act upon it, inasmuch as it is composed of voluble and small particles. But the substance of honey, on the other hand, is more dense, and its fluid is sluggish, and its movement more tardy; for its whole mass of material-particles clings more closely together; because, as is evident, it consists of atoms neither so smooth, nor so small and round.

* * *

Since, therefore, the nature of the mind has been found preeminently active, it must of necessity consist of particles exceedingly diminutive, and smooth and round. Which point, being thus known to you, my excellent friend, will be found useful, and be of advantage, in many of your future inquiries.

This fact also indicates the nature of the soul, and shows of how subtle a texture it consists, and in how small a space it would contain itself, if it could be condensed; because, when the tranquil repose of death has taken possession of a man, and the substance of the mind and the soul has departed, you can there perceive nothing detracted as to appearance, nothing as to weight, from the whole body. Death leaves all things entire, except vital sense and quickening heat.

It must therefore necessarily be the case, that the whole soul consists of extremely small seminal atoms, connected and diffused throughout the veins, the viscera, and the nerves; inasmuch as, when the whole of the body, the extreme outline of the members still shows itself unaltered, nor is an atom of weight withdrawn; just as is the case when the aroma of wine has flown off, or when the sweet odour of ointment has passed away into the air, or when the flavour has departed from any savoury substance; for still the substance itself does not, on that account, appear diminished to the eye, nor does anything seem to have been deducted from the weight;

evidently because many and minute atoms compose the flavour and odour throughout the whole constitution of bodies.

* * *

Again, neither can a tree exist in the sky, nor clouds in the deep sea; nor can fish live in the fields; nor blood be in wood, nor liquid in stones. It is fixed and arranged where everything may grow and subsist; thus the nature or substance of the mind cannot spring up alone without the body, or exist apart from the nerves and the blood. Whereas if this could happen, the power of the mind might at time rather arise in the head or the shoulders, or the bottom of the heels, and might rather accustom itself to grow in any place, than to remain in the same man and in the same receptacle. But since it seems fixed and appointed also in our own body, where the soul and the mind may subsist and grow up by themselves, it is so much the more to be denied that they can endure and be produced out of the entire body. For which reason, when the body has perished, you must necessarily admit that the soul, which is diffused throughout the body, has perished with it.

Besides, to join the mortal to the immortal, and to suppose that they can sympathize together, and perform mutual operations, is to think absurdly; for what can be conceived more at variance with reason, or more inconsistent and irreconcilable in itself, than that which is mortal, joined to that which is imperishable and eternal, should submit to endure violent storms and troubles in combination with it?

Further, whatsoever bodies remain eternal, must either, as being of a solid consistence, repel blows, and suffer nothing to penetrate them, that can disunite their compact parts within (such as are primary-articles of matter, the nature of which we have shown above); or they must be able to endure throughout all time, because they are free from blows, or unsusceptible of them (as is a vacuum, which remains intangible, and suffers nothing from a stroke); or they must be indestructible for this reason, that there is no sufficiency of space round about, into which their constituent substances may, as it were, separate and be dissolved (as the entire universe is eternal, inasmuch as there is neither any space without it into which its parts may disperse; nor are there any bodies which may fall upon it, and break it to pieces by a violent concussion): but, as I have shown, neither is the nature of the soul of a solid consistence, since with all compound bodies vacuum is mixed; nor is it like a vacuum itself; nor, again, are bodies wanting, which, rising fortuitously from the infinite of things, may overturn this frame of the mind with a violent tempest, or bring upon it some other kind of disaster and danger; nor, moreover, is vastness and profundity of space wanting, into which the substance of the soul may be dispersed, or may otherwise perish and be overwhelmed by any other kind of force. The gate of death, therefore, is not shut against the mind and soul.

* * *

Death, therefore, is nothing, nor at all concerns us, since the nature or substance of the soul is to be accounted mortal.

* * *

And even if the substance of the mind, and the powers of the soul, after they have been separated from our body, still retain their faculties, it is nothing to us, who subsist only as being conjointly constituted by an arrangement and union of body and soul together. Nor, if time should collect our material atoms after death, and restore them again as they are now placed, and the light of life should be given back to us, would it yet at all concern us that this were done, when the recollection of our existence has once been interrupted.

* * *

Yet we cannot revive that time in our memory; for a pause of life has been thrown between, and all the motions of our atoms have wandered hither and thither, far away from sentient movements. For he, among men now living, to whom misery and pain are to happen after his death, must himself exist again, in his own identity, at that very time on which the evil which he is to suffer may have power to fall; but since death, which interrupts all consciousness, and prevents all memory of the past, precludes the possibility of this; and since the circumstance of having previously existed, prohibits him who lived before, and with whom these calamities which we suffer might be associated, from existing a second time (with any recollection of his other life), as the same combination of atoms of which we now consist, we may be assured that in death there is nothing to be dreaded by us; that he who does not exist, cannot become miserable; and that it makes not the least difference to a man, when immortal death has ended his mortal life, that he was ever born at all.

Discussion Questions

1. *De Rerum Natura* is both a great poem and a major metaphysical statement. Is the style of writing different from the style of other philosophers you have read? If yes, how is it differenct?

2. Lucretius argues that nothing can be generated from nothing. Do you think his argument is convincing? Explain.

3. What does Lucretius believe is (are) eternal? How does he account for the destruction of physical substances?

4. How does Lucretius explain the movement of physical substances?

5. Do you find persuasive Lucretius' argument to prove that the universe is infinite? Why or why not?

6. Analogy is an inference that if two or more things agree with one another in some respects they will probably agree in others. Can you find an example where Lucretius argues by analogy? Explain.

7. How does Lucretius describe "mind" and "soul"?

8. In general, Lucretius denies personal immortality. Can you find any sense in which he acknowledges the possibility of immortality?

9. Are you in essential agreement with Lucretius' explanation of "the general nature of things"? Explain.

C. REALITY IS MORE THAN APPEARANCE

Plato: *Phaedo*

Plato (428/7–348/7 B.C.), a Greek philosopoher, was founder of the first school of philosophy (the Academy), pupil of Socrates, and teacher of Aristotle. Plato had a powerful, though not systematic, philosophical intellect, which he combined with literary gifts of the very highest order. His surviving philosophical works are in the form of dialogues, usually with a fictionalized Socrates as the major figure. These dialogues have been so influential among professional philosophers and educated people in general that it is not entirely absurd to describe subsequent philosophy as a series of commentaries on Plato. One important Platonic idea was the contrast between a nonmaterial world of pure ideals or forms and the changing world of matter and appearance.

Plato is looking for stability. He finds it in form rather than in matter. Forms are the reality behind the appearances; forms are stability in change. Particulars (body, matter) are a "shadow" of deeper reality. Plato asserts in *The Republic* that nonphilosophers are unconcerned with true being, which is stable and abiding. Nonphilosophers are concerned with fleeting phenomena or appearances, objects which are in a state of becoming, constantly coming to be and passing away.

Do we believe that there is such a thing as death?

Most certainly, said Simmias, taking up the role of answering.

Is it simply the release of the soul from the body? Is death nothing more or less than this, the separate condition of the body by itself when it is released from the soul and the separate condition by itself of the soul when released from the body? Is death anything else than this?

No, just that.

Well then, my boy, see whether you agree with me. I fancy that this will help us to find out the answer to our problem. Do you think that it is right for a philosopher to concern himself with the so-called pleasures connected with food and drink?

Certainly not, Socrates, said Simmias.

What about sexual pleasures?

No, not at all.

And what about the other attentions that we pay to our bodies? Do you think that a philosopher attaches any importance to them? I mean things like providing himself with smart clothes and shoes and other bodily ornaments; do you think that he values them or despises them—insofar as there is no real necessity for him to go in for that sort of thing?

I think the true philosopher despises them, he said.

Then it is your opinion in general that a man of this kind is not concerned with the body, but keeps this attention directed as much as he can away from it and toward the soul?

Yes, it is.

So it is clear first of all in the case of physical pleasures that the philosopher frees his soul from association with the body, so far as is possible, to a greater extent than other men?

It seems so.

* * *

Here are some more questions, Simmias. Do we recognize such a thing as absolute uprightness?

Indeed we do.

And absolute beauty and goodness too?

Of course.

Have you ever seen any of these things with your eyes?

Certainly not, said he.

Well, have you ever apprehended them with any other bodily sense? By 'them' I mean not only absolute tallness or health or strength, but the real nature of any given thing—what it actually is. Is it through the body that we get the truest perception of them? Isn't it true that in any inquiry you are likely to attain more nearly to knowledge of your object in proportion to the care and accuracy with which you have prepared yourself to understand that object in itself?

Certainly.

Don't you think that the person who is likely to succeed in this attempt most perfectly is the one who approaches each object, as far as possible, with the unaided intellect, without taking account of any sense of sight in his thinking, or dragging any other sense into his reckoning—the man who pursues the truth by applying his pure and unadulterated thought to the pure and unadulterated object, cutting himself off as much as possible from his eyes and ears and virtually all the rest of his body, as an impediment which by its presence prevents the soul from attaining to truth and clear thinking? Is not this the person, Simmias, who will reach the goal of reality, if anybody can?

What you say is absolutely true, Socrates, said Simmias.

All these considerations, said Socrates, must surely prompt serious philosophers to review the position in some such way as this. It looks as though this were a bypath leading to the right track. So long as we keep to the body and our soul is contaminated with this imperfection, there is no chance of our ever attaining satisfactorily to our object, which we assert to be truth. In the first place, the body provides us with innumerable distractions in the pursuit of our necessary sustenance, and any diseases which attack us hinder our quest for reality. Besides, the body fills us with loves and desires and fears and all sorts of fancies and a great deal of nonsense, with the result that we literally never get an opportunity to think at all about anything. Wars and revolutions and battles are due simply and solely to the body and its desires. All wars are undertaken for the acquisition of wealth, and the reason why we have to acquire wealth is the body, because we are slaves in its service. That is why, on all these accounts, we have so little time for philosophy. Worst of all, if we do obtain any leisure from the body's claims and turn to some line of inquiry, the body intrudes once more into our investigations, interrupting, disturbing, distracting, and preventing us from getting a glimpse of the truth. We are in fact convinced that if we are ever to have pure knowledge of anything, we must get rid of the body and contemplate things by themselves with the soul by itself.

. . . We admit, I suppose, that there is such a thing as equality—not the equality of stick to stick and stone to stone, and so on, but something beyond all that and distinct from it—absolute equality. Are we to admit this or not?

Yes indeed, said Simmias, most emphatically.

And do we know what it is?

Certainly.

Where did we get our knowledge? Was it not from the particular examples that we mentioned just now? Was it not from seeing equal sticks or stones or other equal objects that we got the notion of equality, although it is something quite distinct from them? Look at it in this way. Is it not true that equal stones and sticks sometimes, without changing in themselves, appear equal to one person and unequal to another?

Certainly.

Well, now, have you ever thought that things which were absolutely equal were unequal, or that equality was inequality?

No, never, Socrates.

Then these equal things are not the same as absolute equality.

Not in the least, as I see it, Socrates.

And yet it is these equal things that have suggested and conveyed to you your knowledge of absolute equality, although they are distinct from it?

Perfectly true.

Whether it is similar to them or dissimilar?

Certainly.

It makes no difference, said Socrates. So long as the sight of one thing suggests another to you, it must be a cause of recollection, whether the two things are alike or not.

Quite so.

Well, now, he said, what do we find in the case of the equal sticks and other things of which we were speaking just now? Do they seem to us to be equal in the sense of absolute equality, or do they fall short of it insofar as they only approximate to equality? Or don't they fall short at all?

They do, said Simmias, a long way.

Suppose that when you see something you say to yourself, This thing which I can see has a tendency to be like something else, but it falls short and cannot be really like it, only a poor imitation. Don't you agree with me that anyone who receives that impression must in fact have previous knowledge of that thing which he says that the other resembles, but inadequately?

Certainly he must.

Very well, then. Is that our position with regard to equal things and absolute equality?

Exactly.

Then we must have had some previous knowledge of equality before the time when we first saw equal things and realized that they were striving after equality, but fell short of it.

That is so.

And at the same time we are agreed also upon this point, that we have not and could not have acquired this notion of equality except by sight or touch or one of the other senses. I am treating them as being all the same.

They are the same, Socrates, for the purpose of our argument.

So it must be through the senses that we obtained the notion that all sensible equals are striving after absolute equality but falling short of it. Is that correct?

Yes, it is.

So before we began to see and hear and use our other senses we must somewhere have acquired the knowledge that there is such a thing as absolute equality. Otherwise we could never have realized, by using it as a standard for comparison, that all equal objects of sense are desirous of being like it, but are only imperfect copies.

That is the logical conclusion, Socrates.

Did we not begin to see and hear and possess our other senses from the moment of birth?

Certainly.

But we admitted that we must have obtained our knowledge of equality before we obtained them.

Yes.

So we must have obtained it before birth.

So it seems.

Then if we obtained it before our birth, and possessed it when we were born, we had knowledge, both before and at the moment of birth, not only of equality and relative magnitudes, but of all absolute standards. Our present argument applies no more to equality than it does to absolute beauty, goodness, uprightness, holiness, and, as I maintain, all those characteristics which we designate in our discussions by the term 'absolute.' So we must have obtained knowledge of all these characteristics before our birth.

That is so.

And unless we invariably forget it after obtaining it we must always be born *knowing* and continue to *know* all through our lives, because 'to know' means simply to retain the knowledge which one has acquired, and not to lose it. Is not what we call 'forgetting' simply the loss of knowledge, Simmias?

Most certainly, Socrates.

And if it is true that we acquired our knowledge before our birth, and lost it at the moment of birth, but afterward, by the exercise of our senses upon sensible objects, recover the knowledge which we had once before, I suppose that what we call learning will be the recovery of our own knowledge, and surely we should be right in calling this recollection.

Quite so.

Yes, because we saw that it is possible for the perception of an object by sight or hearing or any of the other senses to suggest to the percipient, through association, whether there is any similarity or not, another object which he has forgotten. So, as I maintain, there are two alternatives. Either we are all born with knowledge of these standards, and retain it throughout our lives, or else, when we speak of people learning, they are simply recollecting what they knew before. In other words, learning is recollection.

Yes, that must be so, Socrates. . . .

If all these absolute realities, such as beauty and goodness, which we are always talking about, really exist, if it is to them, as we rediscover our own former knowledge of them, that we refer, as copies to their patterns, all the objects of our physical perception—if these realities exist, does it not follow that our souls must exist too even before our birth, whereas if they do not exist, our discussion would seem to be a waste of time? Is this the position, that it is logically just as certain that our souls exist before our birth as it is that these realities exist, and that if the one is impossible, so is the other?

It is perfectly obvious to me, Socrates, said Simmias, that the same logical necessity applies to both. It suits me very well that your argument should rely upon the point that our soul's existence before our birth stands or falls with the existence of your grade of reality. I cannot imagine anything more self-evident than the fact that absolute beauty and goodness and all the rest that you mentioned just now exist in the fullest possible sense. In my opinion the proof is quite satisfactory . . .

Then let us return to the same examples which we were discussing before. Does that absolute reality which we define in our discussions remain always constant and invariable, or not? Does absolute equality or beauty or any other independent entity which really exists ever admit change of any kind? Or does each one of these uniform and independent entities remain always constant and invariable, never admitting any alteration in any respect or in any sense?

They must be constant and invariable, Socrates, said Cebes.

Well, what about the concrete instances of beauty—such as men, horses, clothes, and so on—or of equality, or any other members of a class corresponding to an absolute entity? Are they constant, or are they, on the contrary, scarcely ever in the same relation in any sense either to themselves or to one another?

With them, Socrates, it is just the opposite: they are never free from variation.

And these concrete objects you can touch and see and perceive by your other senses, but those constant entities you cannot possibly apprehend except by thinking; they are invisible to our sight.

That is perfectly true, said Cebes.

So you think that we should assume two classes of things, one visible and the other invisible?

Yes, we should.

The invisible being invariable, and the visible never being the same?

Yes, we should assume that too.

Well, now, said Socrates, are we not part body, part soul?

Certainly.

Then to which class do we say that the body would have the closer resemblance and relation?

Quite obviously to the visible.

And the soul, is it visible or invisible?

Invisible to men, at any rate, Socrates, he said.

But surely we have been speaking of things visible or invisible to our human nature. Do you think that we had some other nature in view?

No, human nature.

What do we say about the soul, then? Is it visible or invisible?

Not visible.

Invisible, then?

Yes.

So soul is more like the invisible, and body more like the visible?

That follows inevitably, Socrates.

Did we not say some time ago that when the soul uses the instrumentality of the body for any inquiry, whether through sight or hearing or any other sense—because using the body implies using the senses—it is drawn away by the body into the realm of the variable, and loses its way and becomes confused and dizzy, as though it were fuddled, through contact with things of a similar nature?

Certainly.

But when it investigates by itself, it passes into the realm of the pure and everlasting and immortal and changeless, and being of a kindred nature, when it is once independent and free from interference, consorts with it always and strays no longer, but remains, in that realm of the absolute, constant and invariable, through contact with beings of a similar nature. And this condition of the soul we call wisdom.

An excellent description and perfectly true, Socrates.

Very well, then, in the light of all that we have said, both now and before, to which class do you think that the soul bears the closer resemblance and relation?

I think, Socrates, said Cebes, that even the dullest person would agree, from this line of reasoning, that the soul is in every possible way more like the invariable than the variable.

And the body?

To the other.

Look at it in this way too. When soul and body are both in the same place, nature teaches the one to serve and be subject, the other to rule and govern. In this relation which do you think resembles the divine and which the mortal part? Don't you think that it is the nature of the divine to rule and direct, and that of the mortal to be subject and serve?

I do.

Then which does the soul resemble?

Obviously, Socrates, soul resembles the divine, and body the mortal.

Now, Cebes, he said, see whether this is our conclusion from all that we have said. The soul is most like that which is divine, immortal, intelligible, uniform, indissoluble, and ever self-consistent and invariable, whereas body is most like that which is human, mortal, multiform, unintelligible, dissoluble, and never self-consistent. Can we adduce any conflicting argument, my dear Cebes, to show that this is not so?

No, we cannot.

Very well, then, in that case is it not natural for body to disintegrate rapidly, but for soul to be quite or very nearly indissoluble?

Certainly.

Of course you know that when a person dies, although it is natural for the visible and physical part of him, which lies here in the visible world and which we call his corpse, to decay and fall to pieces and be dissipated, none of this happens to it immediately. It remains as it was for quite a long time, even if death takes place when the body is well nourished and in the warm season. Indeed, when the body is dried and embalmed, as in Egypt, it remains almost intact for an incredible time, and even if the rest of the body decays, some parts of it—the bones and sinews and anything else like them—are practically everlasting. That is so, is it not?

Yes.

But the soul, the invisible part which goes away to a place that is like itself, glorious, pure, and invisible—the true Hades or unseen world—into the presence of the good and wise God where, if God so wills, my soul must shortly go—will it, if its very nature is such as I have described, be dispersed and destroyed at the moment of its release from the body, as is the popular view? Far from it, my dear Simmias and Cebes. The truth is much more like this. If at its release the soul is pure and carries with it no contamination of the body, because it has never willingly associated with it in life, but has shunned it and kept itself separate as its regular practice—in other words, if it has pursued philosophy in the right way and really practiced how to face death easily—this is what 'practicing death' means, isn't it?

Most decidedly.

Very well, if this is its condition, then it departs to that place which is like itself, invisible, divine, immortal, and wise, where, on its arrival, happiness awaits it, and release from uncertainty and folly, from fears and uncontrolled desires, and all other human evils, and where, as they say of the initiates in the Mysteries, it really spends the rest of time with God. Shall we adopt this view, Cebes, or some other?

This one, by all means, said Cebes.

But, I suppose, if at the time of its release the soul is tainted and impure, because it has always associated with the body and cared for it and loved it, and has been so beguiled by the body and its passions and pleasures that nothing seems real to it but those physical things which can be touched and seen and eaten and drunk and used for sexual enjoyment, and if it is accustomed to hate and fear and avoid what is invisible and hidden from our eyes, but intelligible and comprehensible by philosophy—if the soul is in this state, do you think that it will escape independent and uncontaminated?

That would be quite impossible, he said.

On the contrary, it will, I imagine, be permeated by the corporeal, which fellowship and intercourse with the body will have ingrained in its very nature through constant association and long practice.

Certainly.

And we must suppose, my dear fellow, that the corporeal is heavy, oppressive, earthly, and visible. So the soul which is tainted by its presence is weighed down and dragged back into the visible world, through fear, as they say, of Hades or the invisible, and hovers about tombs and graveyards. The shadowy apparitions which have actually been seen there are the ghosts of those souls which have not got clear away, but still retain some portion of the visible, which is why they can be seen.

That seems likely enough, Socrates.

Yes, it does, Cebes. Of course these are not the souls of the good, but of the wicked, and they are compelled to wander about these places as a punishment for their bad conduct in the past. They continue wandering until at last, through craving for the corporeal, which unceasingly pursues them, they are imprisoned once more in a body. And as you might expect, they are attached to the same sort of character or nature which they have developed during life.

What sort do you mean, Socrates?

Well, those who have cultivated gluttony or selfishness or drunkenness, instead of taking pains to avoid them, are likely to assume the form of donkeys and other perverse animals. Don't you think so?

Yes, that is very likely.

And those who have deliberately preferred a life of irresponsible lawlessness and violence become wolves and hawks and kites, unless we can suggest any other more likely animals.

No, the ones which you mention are exactly right.

So it is easy to imagine into what sort of animals all the other kinds of soul will go, in accordance with their conduct during life.

Yes, certainly.

I suppose that the happiest people, and those who reach the best destination, are the ones who have cultivated the goodness of an ordinary citizen—what is called self-control and integrity—which is acquired by habit and practice, without the help of philosophy and reason.

How are these the happiest?

Because they will probably pass into some other kind of social and disciplined creature like bees, wasps and ants, or even back into the human race again, becoming decent citizens.

Very likely.

But no soul which has not practiced philosophy, and is not absolutely pure when it leaves the body, may attain to the divine nature; that is only for the lover of wisdom. This is the reason, my dear Simmias and Cebes, why true philosophers abstain from all bodily desires and withstand them and do not yield to them. It is not because they are afraid of financial loss or poverty, like the average man who thinks of money first, nor because they shrink from dishonor and a bad reputation, like those who are ambitious for distinction and authority.

No, those would be unworthy motives, Socrates, said Cebes.

They would indeed, he agreed. And so, Cebes, those who care about their souls and do not subordinate them to the body dissociate themselves firmly from these others and refuse to accompany them on their haphazard journey, and, believing that it is wrong to oppose philosophy with her offer of liberation and purification, they turn and follow her wherever she leads.

What do you mean, Socrates?

I will explain, he said. Every seeker after wisdom knows that up to the time when philosophy takes it over his soul is a helpless prisoner, chained hand and foot in the body, compelled to view reality not directly but only through its prison bars, and wallowing in utter ignorance. And philosophy can see that the imprisonment is ingeniously effected by the prisoner's own active desire,which makes him first accessory to his own confinement. Well, philosophy takes over the soul in this condition and by gentle persuasion tries to set it free. She points out that observation by means of the eyes and ears and all the other senses is entirely deceptive, and she urges the soul to refrain from using them unless it is necessary to do so, and encourages it to collect and concentrate itself by itself, trusting nothing but its own independent judgment upon objects considered in themselves, and attributing no truth to anything which it views indirectly as being subject to variation, because such objects are sensible and visible but what the soul itself sees is intelligible and invisible. Now the soul of the true philosopher feels that it must not reject this opportunity for release, and so it abstains as far as possible from pleasures and desires and griefs, because it reflects that the result of giving way to pleasure or fear or desire is not as might be supposed the trivial misfortune of becoming ill or wasting money through self-indulgence, but the last and worst calamity of all, which the sufferer does not recognize.

What is that, Socrates? asked Cebes.

When anyone's soul feels a keen pleasure or pain it cannot help supposing that whatever causes the most violent emotion is the plainest and truest reality, which it is not. It is chiefly visible things that have this effect, isn't it?

Quite so.

Is it not on this sort of occasion that soul passes most completely into the bondage of body?

How do you make that out?

Because every pleasure or pain has a sort of rivet with which it fastens the soul to the body and pins it down and makes it corporeal, accepting as true whatever the body certifies. The result of agreeing with the body and finding pleasure in the same things is, I imagine, that it cannot help becoming like it in character and training, so that it can never get entirely away to the unseen world, but is always saturated with the body when it sets out, and so soon falls back again into another body where it takes root and grows. Consequently it is excluded from all fellowship with the pure and uniform and divine.

Discussion Questions

1. Does Plato make a strong case for being cheerful in the face of death? Do you agree with him? Why?

2. What does Plato value more, the body or the soul? Why?

3. How does Plato distinguish between the soul and the body?

4. Plato refers to "uprightness" and "equality." Why does he think they exist? Does he experience them through the senses?

5. What are the other ideas or forms which Plato refers to in this section? Do you think Plato's arguments apply equally well to these? Why or why not?

6. How does Plato characterize "absolute reality"? Is it the soul or the body which most resembles this "absolute reality"?

7. What does Plato mean by a "lover of wisdom"? How does that relate to the study of philosophy?

D. REALITY IS MATTER AND FORM

Aristotle: *Metaphysics* (Book I)

Aristotle (384–322 B.C.), Greek philosopher and logician, founded one of the first schools of philosophy, and was a pupil of Plato and tutor of Alexander the Great. The first and one of the greatest of the builders of philosophical systems, Aristotle held connected and coherent views in almost every area of philosophy. Aristotle's view is frequently the "common-sense" or "ordinary man's" view raised to a considerable degree of technical sophisticatio... Despite subsequent developments and changes in points of view, Aristotle's arguments and conclusions have still to be reckoned with, especially in ethics and metaphysics. Because his surviving works are essentially his lecture notes, Aristotle is not easy to read.

Now we recognize four kinds of cause: (1) the definition, essence, or essential nature of the thing; (2) its matter or substratum; (3) its source of motion; and (4) opposite to the third, the 'end' or 'good,' which is the goal in all generation and movement.

I have dealt with these four kinds of causes—essential (formal), material, efficient, and final—in the *Physics* (II: 3,7). What I want to do here is to examine the evidence afforded by those of my predecessors who undertook the investigation of reality, who studied the intimate nature of things, and who refer to a variety of causes. A survey of their teaching will be useful at this point, for it will either discover some other kind of cause or else confirm the accuracy of my own list.

Most of the early philosophers recognize only material principles underlying everything. That of which they believed all things to consist, from which they believed all things to be generated, and into which they believed all things to be resolved when destroyed, they called an 'element' or 'principle'. . . . They disagreed, however, as to the number and nature of these substances. Thales, who was the first to seek the material cause of all things, says that it is water. Presumably he derived this view from observing (1) that the nutriment of everything is moist and . . . (2) that the seeds of everything have a moist character. . . .

Anaximines and Diogenes considered air prior to water, and recognized it as the primary substance of all bodies. . . . Heraclitus of Ephesus held the same of fire. Empedocles, on the other hand, maintained that there are four primary substances; he added earth to the other three, and affirmed that all four are eternal except that they become few or many by being aggregated into or segregated out of one whole by love and strife respectively.

Anaxagoras . . . taught an infinity of first principles. He says that nearly all things are homogeneous. . . .

Leucippus and his associate Democritus held that 'the Full' and 'the Void' are material elements. They likewise spoke of the 'Existent' and the 'Non-existent,' and identified the Full (or solid) with the Existent, the Void (or rare) with the Non-existent. These they posited as the material causes of things. . . . (Ch. 3)

* * *

The foregoing chapter might suggest that the only kind of cause is the one we call material. Further reflection, however, brought men up against another question: if generation and destruction really proceed from one source, or even from more than one, why does this happen—what sets the process going? After all, the substratum does not cause *itself* to change: wood, for example, or bronze does not change of its own accord. I mean, wood does not make a bed, nor bronze a statue. No, some other agency is at work, and to ask what it is, is to inquire into the second kind of cause, the source of motion or efficient cause.

The early monists, whose investigations led them to recognize only one substratum of all things, were not conscious of any such problem. . . . It is easier to detect the idea of an efficient cause in the thought of a pluralist like Empedocles, who affirmed that the primary sustance is hot and cold, i.e., fire and earth. For he treated fire as a source of movement; water and earth, etc., as passive elements. Once again, however, the fact that none of these material or material-efficient causes is sufficient to generate the world, obliged later philosophers to look for a purely efficient cause. Common sense, for example, forbids us to assign fire or earth or any such element as the cause of beauty and order in the universe, either existing or coming into being; nor, indeed, would it be less absurd to imagine that those thinkers really held such views. Equally, one cannot attribute the goodness of things to spontaneity or chance.

When, therefore, Anaxagoras affirmed that Mind is present in nature, just as in animals, and is the cause of order and all arrangement therein, he appeared like a sober man among a crowd of drunkards, compared with the futile theorists who preceded him. . . . those who held it assumed a principle which was at once the cause of goodness in things and that by which motion is communicated to them.

One might suspect that the first person to look for something which was at once the cause of goodness in things and of their movement was Hesiod, or Parmenides, or whoever it was that first spoke of Love or Desire as a principle. Parmenides, describing the origin of the world, says: 'Love she created first of all the gods.' Hesiod's words are: 'First there was Chaos; next, broad-bosomed Earth; . . . then Love, chief among all the immortals.' Their idea seems to have been that there must exist in nature some principle imparting movement and holding things together. We must postpone the discussion as to which of them was actually the first to treat Love as an efficient cause.

Now it is evident that there is bad in nature as well as good, disorder as well as order, ugliness as well as beauty. And it is no less clear that the bad and commonplace outweigh the good and noble. Empedocles therefore introduced Love (concord) and Strife (discord) to account for good and evil respectively. . . .

* * *

It is clear, from what I have said, that philosophers down to the time of Empedocles recognized two of the causes defined in my *Physics:* the material and the efficient. But they did so vaguely, inadequately, and rather like untrained troops in action, who run about all over the field and may often get in some good blows, though not as the result of any skill. In the same way, these philosophers appear to have misunderstood the efficient causes which they posited; for on the whole one must confess that they seldom if ever apply them. Anaxagoras, for instance, uses Mind as a sort of *deus ex machina* to produce order, and only drags it in when he is at a loss to explain a necessary result. Otherwise he makes anything rather than Mind the cause of what happens. . . . (Ch. 4)

* * *

So far we have been discussing material and efficient causes as understood by the early philosophers. Contemporary with them and even prior to them were the so-called Pythagoreans, who led the field in mathematics. . . . the Pythagoreans thought they saw in numbers, rather than in fire or earth or water, many resemblances to things which exist and which come into being. They also realized that the properties and ratios of musical scales depend on numbers. In a word, they saw that other things, in respect of the whole of their natures, resemble numbers, and that numbers are the primary elements of the whole of nature. Hence they considered the principles of numbers as the principles of all things, and the whole universe as a harmony or number. Moreover, they collected and systematized all the instances they could find of correspondence between (1) numbers or harmonies and (2) the properties and relations of the heavens and the whole universal order. If anything was lacking to complete their theories, they quickly supplied it. They held, for instance, that 10 is a perfect number and embraces all the powers of number. On this view they asserted that there must be ten heavenly bodies; and as only nine were visible they invented the 'counter-earth' to make a tenth. . . . (Ch. 5)

* * *

Having dealt with earlier . . . systems, we come not to that of Plato. . . . From his early years Plato was familiar with the Heraclitean doctrine of Cratylus, that all sensible things are in a constant state of flux and that we can have no knowledge of them. To the end of his life Plato remained loyal to those tenets, so much so that when Socrates, who ignored the material world and looked for universals in the moral sphere, began to build his system of ethics and for the first time directed man's attention to definition, Plato accepted his method and argued that definition is properly concerned with something other than sensibles; for he realized that there can be no permanent definition of sensibles if they are always changing. He described these non-sensibles as 'Ideas' or 'Forms,' with reference to and in respect of which sensibles exist. In other words, he affirmed that sensibles exist only by *participation* in the Forms after which they are called. . . . (Ch. 6)

* * *

I have now briefly summarized the teaching of my predecessors about causes and the ultimate nature of things, from which it appears that none of them mentioned any kind of cause or principle other than those listed in the *Physics*. It is certainly towards these types that they were feeling their way, however tentatively.

Some of them describe the first principle as material, and regard it as one or many. . . . Though none of these thinkers recognizes an efficient cause, others do so in the shape of Love and Strife, Mind, or Desire. Not one of them clearly enunciates a formal cause. The Platonists come nearest to doing so when they treat the Forms . . . not as the matter of sensibles . . . but as imparting to them their essence. [Finally,] the ancient philosophers refer vaguely to an end towards which actions, changes and motions tend, but not directly to a final cause as such. Those who speak of Mind or Love treat them, indeed, as a good, but rather as the source of motion than as the object. . . .

It appears, therefore, from their failure to discover a fifth kind (1) that earlier thinkers confirm my account of the number and nature of the causes (2) and that all principles must be sought for along some such lines. (Ch. 7)

Discussion Questions

1. Do you think that Aristotle's four kinds of causes relate to our discussion of materialism and idealism in the introductory section? Why or why not?

2. Aristotle refers to "early" explanations regarding causality. What principles do they emphasize? What are some of their examples?

3. What does Aristotle mean by "the substratum does not cause *itself* to change"?

4. Who "appeared like a sober man among a crowd of drunkards"? What did he maintain?

5. What is Aristotle's evaluation of his predecessors? Do you agree? Why or why not?

E. REALITY IS SPIRIT DEVELOPING IN MATTER

Hegel: *Lectures on the Philosophy of History*

Georg Friedrich Wilhelm Hegel (1770–1831) was a German philosopher and one of the most influential thinkers of recent times. Like Aristotle and Aquinas before him, Hegel tried to develop a system of philosophy in which the major contributions of his predecessors were integrated. Hegel considered the historical sequence of philosophical ideas as crucial. He believed that various systems represent successive phases in the development of the human spirit. More than any other philosopher, Hegel established the history of philosophy as an important field of study. The thirteen years of Hegel's professorship at the University of Berlin (1818–1831) brought him to the summit of his career and made him the recognized leader of philosophic thought in Germany.

The only Thought which Philosophy brings with it to the contemplation of History, is the simple conception of *Reason;* that Reason is the Sovereign of the World; that the history of the world, therefore, presents us with a rational process. This conviction and intuition is a hypothesis in the domain of history as such. In that of Philosophy it is no hypothesis. It is there proved by speculative cognition, that Reason—and this term may here suffice us, without investigating the relation sustained by the Universe to the Divine Being,—is *Substance,* as well as *Infinite Power;* its own *Infinite Material* underlying all the natural and spiritual life which it originates, as also the *Infinite Form,*—that which sets this Material in motion. On the one hand, Reason is the *substance* of the Universe; viz. that by which and in which all reality has its being and subsistence. On the other hand, it is the *Infinite Energy* of the Universe; since Reason is not so powerless as to be incapable of producing anything but a mere ideal, a mere intention—having its place outside reality, nobody knows where; something separate and abstract, in the heads of certain human beings. It is *the infinite complex of things,* their entire Essence and Truth. It is its own material which it commits to its own Active Energy to work up; not needing, as finite action does, the conditions of an external material of given means from which it may obtain its support, and the objects of its activity. It supplies its own nourishment, and is the object of its own operations. While it is exclusively its own basis of existence, and absolute final aim, it is also the energising power realising this aim; developing it not only in the phenomena of the Natural, but also of the Spiritual Universe—the History of the World. That this "Idea" or "Reason" is the *True,* the *Eternal,* the absolutely *powerful* essence; that it reveals itself in the World, and that in that World nothing else is revealed but this and its honour and glory—is the thesis which, as we have said, has been proved in Philosophy, and is there regarded as demonstrated.

Shorter Logic

C.—THE IDEA.

213.] The Idea is truth in itself and for itself,—the absolute unity of the notion and objectivity. Its 'ideal' content is nothing but the notion in its detailed terms: its 'real' content is only the exhibition which the notion gives itself in the form of external existence, whilst yet, by enclosing this shape in its ideality, it keeps it in its power, and so keeps itself in it.

The definition, which declares the Absolute to be the Idea, is itself absolute. All former definitions come back to this. The Idea is the Truth: for Truth is the correspondence of objectivity with the notion:—not of course the correspondence of external things with my conceptions,—for these are only *correct* conceptions held by *me,* the individual person. In the idea we have nothing to do with the individual, nor with figurate conceptions, nor with external things. And yet, again, everything actual, insofar as it is true, is the Idea, and has its truth by and in virtue of the Idea alone. Every individual being is some one aspect of the Idea: for which, therefore, yet other actualities are needed, which in their turn appear to have a self-subsistence of their own. It is only in them altogether and in their relation that the notion is realised. The individual by itself does not correspond to its notion. It is this limitation of its existence which constitutes the finitude and the ruin of the individual.

The Idea itself is not to be taken as an idea of something or other, any more than the notion is to be taken as merely a specific notion. The Absolute is the universal and one idea, which, by an act of 'judgment,' particularises itself to the system of specific ideas; which after all are constrained by their nature to come back to the one idea where their truth lies.

As issued out of this 'judgment' the Idea is *in the first place* only the one universal *substance:* but its developed and genuine actuality is to be as a *subject* and in that way as mind.

Because it has no *existence* for starting-point and *point d'appui,* the Idea is frequently treated as a mere logical form. Such a view must be abandoned to those theories, which ascribe so-called reality and genuine actuality to the existent thing and all the other categories which have not yet penetrated as far as the Idea. It is no less false to imagine the Idea to be mere abstraction. It is abstract certainly, insofar as everything untrue is consumed in it: but in its own self it is essentially concrete, because it is the free notion giving character to itself, and that character, reality. It would be an abstract form, only if the notion, which is its principle, were taken as an abstract unity, and not as the negative return of it into self and as the subjectivity which it really is.

* * *

214.] The Idea may be described in many ways. It may be called reason (and this is the proper philosophical signification of reason); subject-object; the unity of the ideal and the real, of the finite and the infinite, of soul and body; the possibility which has its actuality in its own self; that of which the nature can be thought only as existent, &c. All these descriptions apply, because the Idea contains all the relations of understanding, but contains them in their infinite self-return and self-identity.

* * *

. . . The Idea itself is the dialectic which forever divides and distinguishes the self-identical from the differentiated, the subjective from the objective, the finite from the infinite, soul from body. Only on these terms is it an eternal creation, eternal vitality, and eternal spirit. But while it thus passes or rather translates itself into the abstract understanding, it forever remains reason. The Idea is the dialectic which again makes this mass of understanding and diversity understand its finite nature and the pseudo-independence in its productions, and which brings the diversity back to unity. Since this double movement is not separate or distinct in time, nor indeed in any other way—otherwise it would be only a repetition of the abstract understanding—the Idea is the eternal vision of itself in the other,—notion which in its objectivity *has* carried out *itself,*—object which is inward design, essential subjectivity.

* * *

215.] The Idea is essentially a process, because its identity is the absolute and free identity of the notion, only insofar as it is absolute negativity and for that reason dialectical. It is the round of movement, in which the notion, in the capacity of universality which is individuality, gives itself the character of objectivity and of the antithesis thereto; and this externality which has the notion for its substance, finds its way back to subjectivity through its imminent dialectic.

As the idea is (*a*) a process, it follows that such an expression for the Absolute as *unity* of thought and being, of finite and infinite, &c. is false; for unity expresses an abstract and merely quiescent identity. As the idea is (*b*) subjectivity, it follows that the expression is equally false on another account. That unity of which it speaks expresses a merely virtual or underlying presence of the genuine unity. The infinite would thus seem to be merely *neutralised* by the finite, the subjective by the objective, thought by being. But in the negative unity of the Idea, the infinite overlaps and includes the finite, thought overlaps being, subjectivity overlaps objectivity. The unity of the Idea is thought, infinity, and subjectivity, and is in consequence to be essentially distinguished from the Idea as *substance*, just as this overlapping subjectivity, thought, or infinity is to be distinguished from the one-sided subjectivity, one-sided thought, one-sided infinity to which it descends in judging and defining.

The idea as a process runs through three stages in its development. The first form of the idea is Life: that is, the idea in the form of immediacy. The second form is that of mediation or differentiation; and this is the idea in the form of Knowledge, which appears under the double aspect of the Theoretical and Practical idea. The process of knowledge eventuates in the restoration of the unity enriched by difference. This gives the third form of the idea, the Absolute Idea: which last stage of the logical idea envinces itself to be at the same time the true first, and to have a being due to itself alone.

Discussion Questions

1. Hegel asserts that the only thought which philosophy brings to the study of history is Reason. What does he mean by Reason?

2. Is Hegel more akin to Lucretius or Plato? Why?

3. Are you drawn to Hegel's thesis? Why or why not?

COMMENT: Guy de Maupassant
Was it a Dream?

I had loved her madly!

"Why does one love? Why does one love? How queer it is to see only one being in the world, to have only one thought in one's mind, only one desire in the heart, and only one name on the lips—a name which comes up continually, rising, like the water in a spring, from the depths of the soul to the lips, a name which one repeats over and over again, which one whispers ceaselessly, everywhere, like a prayer.

"I am going to tell you our story, for love only has one, which is always the same. I met her and loved her; that is all. And for a whole year I have lived on her tenderness, on her caresses, in her arms, in her dresses, on her words, so completely wrapped up, bound, and absorbed in everything which came from her, that I no longer cared whether it was day or night, or whether I was dead or alive, on this old earth of ours.

"And then she died. How? I do not know; I no longer know anything. But one evening she came home wet, for it was raining heavily, and the next day she coughed, and she coughed for about a week, and took to her bed. What happened I do not remember now, but doctors came, wrote, and went away. Medicines were brought, and some women made her drink them. Her hands were hot, her forehead was burning, and her eyes bright and sad. When I spoke to her, she answered me, but I do not remember what we said. I have forgotten everything, everything, everything! She died, and I very well remember her slight, feeble sigh. The nurse said: 'Ah!' and I understood, I understood!

"I knew nothing more, nothing. I saw a priest, who said: 'Your mistress?' and it seemed to me as if he were insulting her. As she was dead, nobody had the right to say that any longer, and I turned him out. Another came who was very kind and tender, and I shed tears when he spoke to me about her.

"They consulted me about the funeral, but I do not remember anything that they said, though I recollected the coffin, and the sound of the hammer when they nailed her down in it. Oh! God, God!

"She was buried! Buried! She! In that hole! Some people came—female friends. I made my escape and ran away. I ran, and then walked through the streets, went home, and the next day started on a journey.

"Yesterday I returned to Paris, and when I saw my room again—our room, our bed, our furniture, everything that remains of the life of a human being after death—I was seized by such a violent attack of fresh grief, that I felt like opening the window and throwing myself out into the street. I could not remain any longer among these things, between these walls which had inclosed and sheltered her, which retained a thousand atoms of her, of her skin and of her breath, in their imperceptible crevices. I took up my hat to make my escape, and just as I reached the door, I passed the large glass in the hall, which she had put there so that she might look at herself every day from head to foot as she went out, to see if her toilette looked well, and was correct and pretty, from her little boots to her bonnet.

"I stopped short in front of that looking-glass in which she had so often been reflected—so often, so often, that it must have retained her reflection. I was standing there, trembling, with my eyes fixed on the glass—on that flat, profound, empty glass—which had contained her entirely, and had possessed her as much as I, as my passionate looks had. I felt as if I loved that glass. I touched it; it was cold. Oh! the recollection!

sorrowful minor, burning mirror, horrible mirror, to make men suffer such torments! Happy is the man whose heart forgets everything that it has contained, everything that has passed before it, everything that has looked at itself in it, or has been reflected in its affection, in its love! How I suffer!

"I went out without knowing it, without wishing it, and toward the cemetery. I found her simple grave, a white marble cross, with these few words:

"'*She loved, was loved, and died.*'

"She is there, below, decayed! How horrible! I sobbed with my forehead on the ground, and I stopped there for a long time, a long time. Then I saw that it was getting dark, and a strange, mad wish, the wish of a despairing lover, seized me. I wished to pass the night, the last night, in weeping on her grave. But I should be seen and driven out. How was I to manage? I was cunning, and got up and began to roam about in that city of the dead. I walked and walked. How small this city is, in comparison with the other, the city in which we live. And yet, how much more numerous the dead are than the living. We want high houses, wide streets, and much room for the four generations who see the daylight at the same time, drink water from the spring, and wine from the vines, and eat bread from the plains.

"And for all the generations of the dead, for all that ladder of humanity that has descended down to us, there is scarcely anything, scarcely anything! The earth takes them back, and oblivion effaces them. Adieu!

"At the end of the cemetery, I suddenly perceived that I was in its oldest part, where those who had been dead a long time are mingling with the soil, where the crosses themselves are decayed, where possibly newcomers will be put to-morrow. It is full of untended roses, of strong and dark cypress-trees, a sad and beautiful garden, nourished on human flesh.

"I was alone, perfectly alone. So I crouched in a green tree and hid myself there completely amid the thick and somber branches. I waited, clinging to the stem, like a shipwrecked man does to a plank.

"When it was quite dark, I left my refuge and began to walk softly, slowly, inaudibly, through that ground full of dead people. I wandered about for a long time, but could not find her tomb again. I went on with extended arms, knocking against the tombs with my hands, my feet, my knees, my chest, even with my head, without being able to find her. I groped about like a blind man finding his way, I felt the stones, the crosses, the iron railings, the metal wreaths, and the wreaths of faded flowers! I read the names with my fingers, by passing them over the letters. What a night! What a night! I could not find her again!

"There was no moon. What a night! I was frightened, horribly frightened in these narrow paths, between two rows of graves. Graves! graves!

graves! nothing but graves! On my right, on my left, in front of me, around me, everywhere there were graves! I sat down on one of them, for I could not walk any longer, my knees were so weak. I could hear my heart beat! And I heard something else as well. What? A confused, nameless noise. Was the noise in my head, in the impenetrable night, or beneath the mysterious earth, the earth sown with human corpses? I looked all around me, but I cannot say how long I remained there; I was paralyzed with terror, cold with fright, ready to shout out, ready to die.

"Suddenly, it seemed to me that the slab of marble on which I was sitting, was moving. Certainly it was moving, as if it were being raised. With a bound, I sprang on to the neighboring tomb, and I saw, yes, I distinctly saw the stone which I had just quitted rise upright. Then the dead person appeared, a naked skeleton, pushing the stone back with its bent back. I saw it quite clearly, although the night was so dark. On the cross I could read:

> "*Here lies Jacques Olivant, who died at the age of fifty-one. He loved his family, was kind and honorable, and died in the grace of the Lord.*'

"The dead man also read what was inscribed on his tombstone; then he picked up a stone off the path, a little, pointed stone, and began to scrape the letters carefully. He slowly effaced them, and with the hollows of his eyes he looked at the places where they had been engraved. Then with the tip of the bone that had been his forefinger, he wrote in luminous letters, like those lines which boys trace on walls with the tip of a lucifer match:

> "*Here reposes Jacques Olivant, who died at the age of fifty-one. He hastened his father's death by his unkindness, as he wished to inherit his fortune, he tortured his wife, tormented his children, deceived his neighbors, robbed everyone he could, and died wretched.*'

"When he had finished writing, the dead man stood motionless, looking at his work. On turning round I saw that all the graves were open, that all the dead bodies had emerged from them, and that all had effaced the lies inscribed on the gravestones by their relations, substituting the truth instead. And I saw that all had been the tormentors of their neighbors—malicious, dishonest, hypocrites, liars, rogues, calumniators, envious; that they had stolen, deceived, performed every disgraceful, every abominable action, these good fathers, these faithful wives, these devoted sons, these chaste daughters, these honest tradesmen, these men and women who were called irreprochable. They were all writing at the same time, on the threshold of their eternal abode, the truth, the terrible and the holy truth of which everybody was ignorant, or pretended to be ignorant, while they were alive.

"I thought that *she* also must have written something on her tombstone, and now running without any fear among the half-open coffins, among the corpses and skeletons, I went toward her, sure that I should find her immediately. I recognized her at once, without seeing her face, which was covered by the winding-sheet, and on the marble cross, where shortly before I had read:

"*'She loved, was loved, and died.'*

I now saw:

"*'Having gone out in the rain one day, in order to deceive her lover, she caught cold and died.'*

"It appears that they found me at daybreak, lying on the grave unconscious."

CHAPTER THREE
HOW CAN WE KNOW?
THE PROBLEM OF
EPISTEMOLOGY

"Epistemology," or theory of knowledge, is the division of philosophy that investigates human knowing. *What*ever we know, we are knowing; epistemology turns from the "what" to the act of knowing itself. It wants to know what knowing is.

This is a distinctively human question, for whether or not *knowledge* is distinctively human and not shared with other animals, *the knowledge of knowledge* certainly seems to be. Animals may "know" the world, but they do not know knowing, as we do.

We are curious about this question because it concerns our human distinctiveness and thus our dignity. As Pascal put it, "all our dignity consists in thought. In space, the universe engulfs me and swallows me up; in thought I engulf the universe."

The three main questions within this field are (1) the origin, (2) the nature, and (3) the extent of human knowledge.

The two poles of our knowledge are our reason (intellect) and our senses. At the two poles of answers to the question of the origin of knowledge we find Rationalism and Empiricism. Neither position denies the existence of the other pole of knowledge, but Rationalism insists that all certain knowledge is rational, not empirical, and Empiricism insists that all knowledge is derived from empirical knowledge: "there is nothing in the mind that was not first in the senses."

There is a difference between ancient and modern Rationalism. To Plato, an ancient Rationalist, "reason" means not primarily logical calculation as it does to Descartes, "the father of modern philosophy," but intuitive wisdom, philosophical insight into the essences or natures of things. Both Plato and Descartes try to build philosophical systems by rational, not empirical, knowledge. Locke and Hume, as Empiricists, argue that such a system is impossible because, as we can see by reflection on our own process of knowing, there is no nonempirical knowledge of reality; reason knows only its own ideas, or relations of ideas, not matters of fact.

Our other two philosophers, Aquinas and Kant, are neither Rationalists nor Empiricists, but midway between these two positions. In different ways they try to join what Rationalism and Empiricism separate. Aquinas, following Aristotle, teaches that (a) real things are composed of both "matter" and "form" (essence), and that (b) the mind knows a thing by "abstracting" its form from its matter; but (c) in order to do this, the thing must first be presented to the mind by the senses. Kant blends mind and senses too, but differently; instead of receiving form from things via sensation and abstraction, the mind imposes form on things; things conform to mind rather than mind to things. This is what Kant calls his "Copernican Revolution in philosophy."

This brings us to our second question, that of the nature of knowledge. For Kant, knowing is making or constructing the object rather than discovering it, rather like forming cookie dough with cookie cutters. This is his "Copernican Revolution." Pre-Kantian thinkers taught that mind conformed or corresponded to its object rather than vice versa.

The third question concerns the *extent* of our knowledge: how *much* can we know? Here five possible answers can be distinguished:

1. Scepticism: we can know nothing, at least nothing with certainty (see pages 29–57).

2. Kantian Idealism: we can know only phenomena, or appearances, not "things in themselves," not objective reality. We know what we mentally construct.

3. Empiricism: we can know whatever is given to us in sense experience: the material world and also our minds' operations in knowing that world, by reflection (a kind of inner sensation).

4. Realism: we can know real things by abstracting their forms.

5. Rationalism: we can know beyond experience by a direct intuition into essences (Plato) or deduction from innate clear and distinct ideas (Descartes).

Plato

In the passage of *The Republic* immediately preceding the one excerpted in this chapter, Plato distinguished four kinds or levels of knowledge and four corresponding kinds of reality, or objects of knowledge in his famous metaphor of the "Divided Line," as follows:

Plato's Epistemology: 4 Kinds of Knowing	Plato's Metaphysics: 4 Kinds of Being

4. wisdom,
   true philosophy,
   intellectual insight
	4. forms, essences,
	   objective ideas and ideals,
	   especially "The Good"

3. deductive reasoning,
   logical and mathematical
      knowledge
	3. logical and mathematical
	      truths

2. first-hand sense experience	2. concrete material things

1. second-hand experience of
      things through images
	1. images or reflections (or
	      pictures) of material things

In our excerpted passage, probably the most famous passage in the entire history of philosophy, the "Allegory of the Cave," Plato dramatizes the educational progress of the philosopher (who is to rule the ideal state) through the four levels of knowledge, from the "cave" of subjective opinion (1) to the "enlightenment" of reason (4). Plato's point is that there is much *more*, both to knowledge and to reality, than we usually think.

Aquinas

Aristotle, the philosopher of "the golden mean" between extremes, took a middle position between two of his Greek predecessors, Democritus the empiricist and Plato the rationalist. Aquinas follows this lead in our first excerpted "article" (question) in explaining how the immaterial soul knows material bodies (things): 84,1. It is by intellect and senses working together (84,6), like two blades of a scissors; not by turning away from the senses to "innate ideas," as Plato taught (84,3) nor by a purely material impression made on the senses, as taught by Democritus and later Lucretius (see pages 70–79).

The way in which intellect and senses cooperate centers on the intellect "abstracting" the universal form of the individual thing (e.g., the "treeness" of this tree) from the "phantasm," or sense image, which is particular. Aquinas calls these knowable forms "species" or "ideas"; the word does not mean subjective ideas in our mind but objective ideas or essences. (85,1)

The last article (85,2) argues that ideas are only the *means* of knowing, not the objects known. Real things are the objects known. This puts Aquinas in disagreement with Locke, who says that ideas (Aquinas' "intelligible species abstracted from the phantasm") are the *objects* understood, and also with Kant, who says we can know only phenomena (appearances, how things appear to us after we have formed them in our knowledge), not noumena (things in themselves, objective reality).

Descartes

We have included a longer passage and more questions for Descartes because, next to Socrates and Plato, Descartes probably has changed the nature of philosophy more than any other person. His *Discourse on the Method* (1637) quickly became popular because it seemed to be the application to philosophy of the method which had proved so spectacularly successful in other fields, viz. the scientific method.

To justify the use of the scientific method in philosophy, Descartes first had to redefine and democratize reason itself. No longer the "wisdom" of the few (the fourth level of Plato's "Divided Line"; see page 104), it now became the logical, analytical reasoning common to everyone (Plato's third level). From this equality of reason in everyone it follows that the only reason for differences of opinion is that we use different methods, not that we have different degrees of wisdom. Use of the same method by all, therefore, should resolve all differences, thus ending ideological warfare. (Note Descartes' reference to the wars he had gone to see.)

Descartes' autobiographical description of his dissatisfaction with his study of past philosophy and his sudden discovery "alone in a warm room" (like his own mind) of the new method is really the beginning of the so-called "Enlightenment" or "Age of Reason." Perhaps it should be called the age of *faith* in Reason, in Reason's ability to solve all problems if only we use *the* right method (Discours de *la* methode): see the paragraph following the four rules of the method (page 124).

Beginning with no assumptions (is this possible?), with a "universal methodic doubt," Descartes tries to prove everything by reason alone. Reason conjures the rabbit of reality out of the empty hat of doubt if only we have the magic wand of the method. His starting point is the famous "I think therefore I am," which he believes is self-evident, or self-proving. It seems to need no premises; it is self-contradictory to deny it; and it is a "clear and distinct idea" evident to everyone.

With this fulcrum Descartes seeks to move the world of thought with his deductive lever. He next proves God's existence, not from the world of nature, which he has not yet proved, but from his thought alone. Finally, he proves the reality of the material world by reason, not sense experience, deducing it from God's veracity. Thus he returns to the common-sense triad of self, God, and world which he began by doubting, but returning to it through purely rational, not empirical means. It is not the conclusions but the method that is new; not the metaphysics but the epistemology. This way of doing philosophy, by logical analysis of pure ideas without dependence on sensation, will be criticized by the Empiricists as untrue to the real human situation in the world, where all our ideas come from experience.

Locke

Locke's fundamental points are clearly outlined. Note especially the first premise, which contrasts with the position of Aquinas (85,2). From the premise that we know ideas first (though these ideas are copies of sensations) and the world only secondarily, the consequence of scepticism seems logically to follow; for if we never know the real world directly, there is no way to check the truth of our ideas by the real standard or criterion of the world. Hume draws this sceptical conclusion which Locke, common-sensical and nonradical thinker that he was, did not draw.

Notice also Locke's criticism of Descartes' Rationalism: behind Descartes' rationalistic *method* is implied the rationalistic *doctrine* that at least some ideas are innate in our minds, not derived from sense experience. Locke and Hume both deny this rationalistic assumption of "innate ideas" (Locke's "baby in the dark room" argument).

Hume

Like Locke, Hume begins by locating the object of thought not in reality but in ideas and impressions (sense images). And like Locke he denies innate ideas. These are two very serious limitations on our knowledge. The whole tendency of Empiricism is not to extend but to limit our knowledge; there are not "*more* things in heaven and earth than are dreamed of in your philosophy," but fewer.

From his Empiricist premises Hume deduces the conclusion that we cannot be sure of the validity of causal reasoning, i.e., reasoning from cause to effect. (Does his argument also impugn reasoning from effect to cause?) This is the basic kind of reasoning about all matters of fact, including science and common sense; so that the two things Empiricism begins by exalting are in the end just as much subjected to its sceptical critique as is traditional philosophy. The philosophical arguments of Hume would have to be consigned to the flames too, by the standard of his own last paragraph. The scepticism of the Empiricist, like any form of scepticism, seems self-contradictory.

Kant

Kant seeks to mediate the dispute between Rationalism and Empiricism by finding a place for both rational and empirical knowledge, i.e., both "*a priori* knowledge" (knowledge prior to sense experience) and "*a posteriori* knowledge" (knowledge after sense experience). His justification of *a priori* knowledge is "The Copernican Revolution in philosophy," the hypothesis that knowing constructs rather than discovers the forms of its objects. This subjectivism, even though it is the same for everyone, limits our knowledge even more than Empiricism does in a way, for it cuts off the possibility of knowing the real world ("things in themselves") by reason *or* the senses; we know only the appearances that our knowing makes. (In that case, how can we know there *is* anything beyond these appearances? asked Kant's successors.)

The three most important *a priori* truths not derived from experience are (according to Kant) God, freedom, and immortality, the three presuppositions of moral meaningfulness. Kant loved to say that two things made him wonder (and what philosophers wonder at is a key to their deepest concerns), "the starry sky above and the moral law within." Morality, argued Kant, demands God as ideal, free will as power to choose responsibly, and immortality for ultimate justice.

But how can we justify these three metaphysical ideas? How is metaphysics possible? This is the question of Kant's *Critique of Pure Reason*, and "the Copernican Revolution" is his essential answer. It is a critique of reason's ability to do objective metaphysics. But if we call Kant's metaphysics "subjective," we must remember that it is not private or arbitrary. It is not *my* reason that knows *a priori*, but Reason itself, Reason as such, Reason as universal (the same for all) and necessary. It is this "Reason" that Hegel talks about in the passage on pages 94–95.

The problem in Kant's teaching that the subject determines the object in knowing, rather than vice versa, is that it seems, like simple scepticism, self-contradictory. Is this "truth" also a construction of knowledge rather than an objective fact discovered? Does Kant announce as a discovered truth that truth is not discovered but constructed? Is the subjectivity of truth itself an objective truth? If so, it seems self-contradictory; if not, how can Kant avoid Solipsism?

Solipsism

The short story in the "Comment" section illustrates a fifth epistemological position, called Solipsism (from *sole*, only, and *ipse*, self): the view that nothing but the knowing self itself can be known to be real. No one *wants* to be a Solipsist, but the problem of overcoming Solipsism has plagued modern philosphers ever since Descartes began by doubting everything and proving only himself to begin with. *Can* anything else be proved? The three major modern epistemologies begin with the self and try to build three different bridges from self to reality. If they are all unsuccessful, the only alternative to Solipsism seems to be the "uncritical" premodern epistemology, which begins with reality rather than with knowing, with metaphysics rather than with epistemology. In that case, the question philosophers from Descartes to Kant have struggled with, reason's critique of itself, cannot be the starting point; just as the eye cannot see its own act of seeing, reason cannot prove its own validity.

A. ANCIENT RATIONALISM

Plato: *The Republic*

Plato (428–348 B.C.) is the first systematic philosopher. No one knows how much in his 30 dialogues comes from his master, Socrates, who wrote nothing, and how much from Plato himself, who used Socrates as his literary mouthpiece, but in these dialogues, nearly every major question in the next 2400 years of Western philosophy is raised. Thus Ralph Waldo Emerson says that "Plato is philosophy and philosophy is Plato," and Alfred North Whitehead calls the whole history of Western philosophy "a series of footnotes to Plato."

BOOK VII

And now, I said, let me show in a figure how far our nature is enlightened or unenlightened:—Behold! human beings living in an underground den, which has a mouth open towards the light and reaching all along the den; here they have been from their childhood, and have their legs and necks chained so that they cannot move, and can only see before them, being prevented by the chains from turning round their heads. Above and behind them a fire is blazing at a distance, and between the fire and the prisoners there is a raised way; and you will see, if you look, a low wall built along the way, like the screen which marionette players have in front of them, over which they show the puppets.

I see.

And do you see, I said, men passing along the wall carrying all sorts of vessels, and statues and figures of animals made of wood and stone and various materials, which appear over the wall? Some of them are talking, others silent.

You have shown me a strange image, and they are strange prisoners.

Like ourselves, I replied; and they see only their own shadows, or the shadows of one another, which the fire throws on the opposite wall of the cave?

True, he said; how could they see anything but the shadows if they were never allowed to move their heads?

And of the objects which are being carried in like manner they would only see the shadows?

Yes, he said.

And if they were able to converse with one another, would they not suppose that they were naming what was actually before them?

Very true.

And suppose further that the prison had an echo which came from the other side, would they not be sure to fancy when one of the passers-by spoke that the voice which they heard came from the passing shadow?

No question, he replied.

To them, I said, the truth would be literally nothing but the shadows of the images.

That is certain.

And now look again, and see what will naturally follow if the prisoners are released and disabused of their error. At first, when any of them is liberated and compelled suddenly to stand up and turn his neck round and walk and look towards the light, he will suffer sharp pains; the glare will distress him, and he will be unable to see the realities of which in his former state he had seen the shadows; and then conceive some one saying to him, that what he saw before was an illusion, but that now, when he is approaching nearer to being and his eye is turned towards more real existence, he has a clearer vision,—what will be his reply? And you may further imagine that his instructor is pointing to the objects as they pass and requiring him to name them,—will he not be perplexed? Will he not fancy that the shadows which he formerly saw are truer than the objects which are now shown to him?

Far truer.

And if he is compelled to look straight at the light, will he not have a pain in his eyes which will make him turn away to take refuge in the objects of vision which he can see, and which he will conceive to be in reality clearer than the things which are now being shown to him?

True, he said.

And suppose once more, that he is reluctantly dragged up a steep and rugged ascent, and held fast until he is forced into the presence of the sun himself, is he not likely to be pained and irritated? When he approaches the light his eyes will be dazzled, and he will not be able to see anythng at all of what are now called realities.

Not all in a moment, he said.

He will require to grow accustomed to the sight of the upper world. And first he will see the shadows best, next the reflections of men and other objects in the water, and then the objects themselves; then he will gaze upon the light of the moon and the stars and the spangled heaven; and he will see the sky and the stars by night better than the sun or the light of the sun by day?

Certainly.

Last of all he will be able to see the sun, and not mere reflections of him in the water, but he will see him in his own proper place, and not in another; and he will contemplate him as he is.

Certainly.

He will then proceed to argue that this is he who gives the season and the years, and is the guardian of all that is in the visible world, and in a certain way the cause of all things which he and his fellows have been accustomed to behold?

Clearly, he said, he would first see the sun and then reason about him.

And when he remembered his old habitation, and the wisdom of the den and his fellow-prisoners, do you not suppose that he would felicitate himself on the change, and pity them?

Certainly, he would.

And if they were in the habit of conferring honours among themselves on those who were quickest to observe the passing shadows and to remark which of them went before, and which followed after, and which were together; and who were therefore best able to draw conclusions as to the future, do you think that he would care for such honours and glories, or envy the possessors of them? Would he not say with Homer,

'Better to be the poor servant of a poor master,'

and to endure anything, rather than think as they do and live after their manner?

Yes, he said, I think that he would rather suffer anything than entertain these false notions and live in this miserable manner.

Imagine once more, I said, such an one coming suddenly out of the sun to be replaced in his old situation; would he not be certain to have his eyes full of darkness?

To be sure, he said.

And if there were a contest, and he had to compete in measuring the shadows with the prisoners who had never moved out of the den, while his sight was still weak, and before his eyes had become steady (and the time which would be needed to acquire this new habit of sight might be very considerable), would he not be ridiculous? Men would say of him that up he went and down he came without his eyes; and that it was better not even to think of ascending; and if any one tried to lose another and lead him up to the light, let them only catch the offender, and they would put him to death.

No question, he said.

This entire allegory, I said, you may now append, dear Glaucon, to the previous argument; the prison-house is the world of sight, the light of the fire is the sun, and you will not misapprehend me if you interpret the journey upwards to be the ascent of the soul into the intellectual world according to my poor belief, which, at your desire, I have expressed— whether rightly or wrongly God knows. But, whether true or false, my opinion is that in the world of knowledge the idea of good appears last of all, and is seen only with an effort; and, when seen is also inferred to be the universal author of all things beautiful and right, parent of light and of the lord of light in this visible world, and the immediate source of reason and truth in the intellectual; and that this is the power upon which he who would act rationally either in public or private life must have his eye fixed.

I agree, he said, as far as I am able to understand you.

Moreover, I said, you must not wonder that those who attain to this beatific vision are unwilling to descend to human affairs; for their souls are ever hastening into the upper world where they desire to dwell; which desire of theirs is very natural, if our allegory may be trusted.

Yes, very natural.

And is there anything surprising in one who passes from divine contemplations to the evil state of man, misbehaving himself in a ridiculous manner; if, while his eyes are blinking and before he has become accustomed to the surrounding darkness, he is compelled to fight in courts of law, or in other places, about the images or the shadows of images of justice, and is endeavouring to meet the conceptions of those who have never yet seen absolute justice?

Anything but surprising, he replied.

Any one who has common sense will remember that the bewilderments of the eyes are of two kinds, and arise from two causes, either from coming out of the light or from going into the light, which is true of the mind's eye, quite as much as of the bodily eye; and he who remembers this when he sees any one whose vision is perplexed and weak, will not be too ready to laugh; he will first ask whether that soul of man has come out of the brighter life, and is unable to see because unaccustomed to the dark, or having turned from darkness to the day is dazzled by excess of light. And he will count the one happy in his condition and state of being, and he will pity the other; or, if he have a mind to laugh at the soul which comes from below into the light, there will be more reason in this than in the laugh which greets him who returns from above out of the light, into the den.

That, he said, is a very just distinction.

But then, if I am right, certain professors of education must be wrong when they say that they can put a knowledge into the soul which was not there before, like sight into blind eyes.

They undoubtedly say this, he replied.

Whereas, our argument shows that the power and capacity of learning exists in the soul already; and that just as the eye was unable to turn from darkness to light without the whole body, so too the instrument of knowledge can only by the movement of the whole soul be turned from the world of becoming into that of being, and learn by degrees to endure the sight of being, and of the brightest and best of being, or in other words, of the good.

Very true.

And must there not be some art which will effect conversion in the easiest and quickest manner; not implanting the faculty of sight, for that exists already, but has been turned in the wrong direction, and is looking away from the truth?

Yes, he said, such an art may be presumed.

And whereas the other so-called virtues of the soul seem to be akin to bodily qualities, for even when they are not originally innate they can be implanted later by habit and exercise, the virtue of wisdom more than anything else contains a divine element which always remains, and by this conversion is rendered useful and profitable; or, on the other hand, hurtful and useless. Did you never observe the narrow intelligence flashing from the keen eye of a clever rogue—how eager he is, how clearly his paltry soul sees the way to his end; he is the reverse of blind, but his keen eye-sight is forced into the service of evil, and he is mischievous in proportion to his cleverness?

Very true, he said.

But what if there had been a circumcision of such natures in the days of their youth; and they had been severed from those sensual pleasures, such as eating and drinking, which, like leaden weights, were attached to them at their birth, and which drag them down and turn the vision of their souls upon the things that are below—if, I say, they had been released from these impediments and turned in the opposite direction, the very same faculty in them would have seen the truth as keenly as they see what their eyes are turned to now.

Very likely.

Yes, I said; and there is another thing which is likely, or rather a necessary inference from what has preceded, that neither the uneducated and uninformed of the truth, nor yet those who never make an end of their education, will be able ministers of State; not the former, because they have no single aim of duty which is the rule of all their actions, private as well as public; nor the latter, because they will not act at all except upon compulsion, fancying that they are already dwelling apart in the islands of the blest.

Very true, he replied.

Then, I said, the business of us who are the founders of the State will be to compel the best minds to attain that knowledge which we have already shown to be the greatest of all—they must continue to ascend until they arrive at the good; but when they have ascended and seen enough we must not allow them to do as they do now.

What do you mean?

I mean that they remain in the upper world: but this must not be allowed; they must be made to descend again among the prisoners in the den, and partake of their labours and honours, whether they are worth having or not.

But is not this unjust? he said; ought we to give them a worse life, when they might have a better?

You have again forgotten, my friend, I said, the intention of the legislator, who did not aim at making any one class in the State happy above the rest; the happiness was to be in the whole State, and he held the citizens together by persuasion and necessity, making them benefactors of the

State, and therefore benefactors of one another; to this end he created them, not to please themselves, but to be his instruments in binding up the State.

True, he said, I had forgotten.

Observe, Glaucon, that there will be no injustice in compelling our philosophers to have a care and providence of others; we shall explain to them that in other States, men of their class are not obliged to share in the toils of politics: and this is reasonable, for they grow up at their own sweet will, and the government would rather not have them. Being self-taught, they cannot be expected to show any gratitude for a culture which they have never received. But we have brought you into the world to be rulers of the hive, kings of yourselves and of the other citizens, and have educated you far better and more perfectly than they have been educated and you are better able to share in the double duty. Wherefore each of you, when his turn comes, must go down to the general undergound abode, and get the habit of seeing in the dark. When you have acquired the habit, you will see ten thousand times better than the inhabitants of the den, and you will know what the several images are, and what they represent, because you have seen the beautiful and just and good in their truth. And thus our State which is also yours will be a reality, and not a dream only, and will be administered in a spirit unlike that of other States, in which men fight with one another about shadows only and are distracted in the struggle for power, which in their eyes is a great good. Whereas the truth is that the State in which the rulers are most reluctant to govern is always the best and most quietly governed, and the State in which they are most eager, the worst.

Quite true, he replied.

And will our pupils, when they hear this, refuse to take their turn at the toils of State, when they are allowed to spend the greater part of their time with one another in the heavenly light?

Impossible, he answered; for they are just men, and the commands which we impose upon them are just; there can be no doubt that every one of them will take office as a stern necessity, and not after the fashion of our present rulers of State.

Yes, my friend, I said; and there lies the point. You must contrive for your future rulers another and a better life than that of a ruler, and then you may have a well-ordered State; for only in the State which offers this, will they rule who are truly rich, not in silver and gold, but in virtue and wisdom, which are the true blessings of life. Whereas if they go to the administration of public affairs, poor and hungering after their own private advantage, thinking that hence they are to snatch the chief good, order there can never be; for they will be fighting about office, and the civil and domestic broils which thus arise will be the ruin of the rulers themselves and of the whole State.

Most true, he replied.

And the only life which looks down upon the life of political ambition is that of true philosophy. Do you know of any other?

Indeed, I do not, he said.

And those who govern ought not to be lovers of the task? For, if they are, there will be rival lovers, and they will fight.

No question.

Who then are those whom we shall compel to be guardians? Surely they will be the men who are wisest about affairs of State, and by whom the State is best administered, and who at the same time have other honours and another and a better life than that of politics?

They are the men, and I will choose them, he replied.

Discussion Questions

1. In the passage of the *Republic* immediately preceding this one, Plato distinguishes four kinds or levels of knowledge and four corresponding levels of reality, or objects of knowledge, in his famous metaphor of the "Divided Line" (see page 104).

In the Allegory of the Cave, Plato symbolically dramatizes the educational progress of the philosopher (who is to rule the ideal state) through these four levels. Can you find their symbols in the passage excerpted here?

2. What are some of the things Plato's cave suggests or symbolizes to you, both in general and in particular?

3. Do you agree with Plato that most people live most or all of the time in this cave? Do you? If so, how can you know there is another world outside the cave?

4. By what power do the prisoners escape? Can they unbind themselves? If not, and if we are all born into this cave, who unbound the first prisoner? If Socrates was the first enlightened philosopher, who enlightened him? See pages 3–5 for Socrates' answer to this question; evaluate it.

5. Why must the ascent be steep, rugged and difficult?

6. Plato believed that learning is really remembering (*anamnésis*) innate ideas we have forgotten. How does the Socratic method of questioning the student rather than lecturing follow from this theory of knowledge?

7. Find at least three political applications on pages 112–114. Do you think they necessarily follow from what preceded? Why or why not?

B. REALISM

St. Thomas Aquinas: *Summa Theologiae*

St. Thomas Aquinas (A.D. 1225–1274), exemplified the medieval ideal of a rational synthesis of Christian theology and Greek philosophy (especially

Aristotle) in voluminous works of tightly and carefully defined arguments, notably his enormous *Summa Theologiae* (summary of theology). About 6000 ordinary-length pages written "for beginners," it remains unfinished because shortly before his death an experience of God's immediate presence left him unwilling to write another word: "Compared with what I have seen, all I have written seems to be straw." This "straw" is only the most ambitious and complete philosophical and theological system ever constructed.

ST. THOMAS AQUINAS, SUMMA THEOLOGIAE I

Question 84, "How the Soul While United to the Body Understands Corporeal [Material] Things Beneath It

First Article: Whether the Soul Knows Bodies Through the Intellect?

Science is in the intellect. If, therefore, the intellect does not know bodies, it follows that there is no science of bodies; and thus perishes natural science, which treats of mobile bodies.

It should be said in order to elucidate this question, that the early [pre-Socratic] philosophers, who inquired into the natures of things, thought there was nothing in the world save bodies. And because they observed that all bodies are mobile, and considered them to be ever in a state of flux, they were of the opinion that we can have no certain knowledge of the true nature of things. For what is in a continual state of flux, cannot be grasped with any degree of certitude, for it passes away before the mind can form a judgment thereon: according to the saying of Heraclitus, that "it is not possible twice to touch a drop of water in a passing torrent," as the Philosopher relates (*Metaphysics* 4,3,5).

After these came Plato, who, wishing to save the certitude of our knowledge of truth through the intellect, maintained that, besides these things corporeal, there is another genus of beings, separate from matter and movement, which beings he called *species* or *ideas* [not subjective thoughts but objective essences], by participation of [sharing in] which each of these singular and sensible things is said to be either a man, or a horse, or the like. Wherefore he said that sciences and definitions, and whatever appertains to the act of the intellect, are not referred to [about] these sensible bodies, but to those beings immaterial and separate: so that according to this the soul does not understand these corporeal things, but the separate species thereof.

Now this may be shown to be false for two reasons. First, because since those species are immaterial and immovable, knowledge of movement and matter would be excluded from science (which knowledge is proper to natural science), and likewise all demonstration through moving and material causes. Secondly, because it seems ridiculous, when we seek for knowledge of things which are to us manifest [viz. bodies] to introduce other beings [viz. separate species or ideas of those things], since they differ from them essentially: so that granted that we have a knowledge of those separate substances, we cannot for that reason claim to form a judgment concerning these sensible things.

* * *

Third Article: Whether the Soul Understands All Things Through Innate Species [Ideas]?

The Philosopher, speaking of the intellect, says (*De Anima* 3,4) that it is like "a tablet on which nothing is written."

. . . We observe that man sometimes is only a potential knower, both as to sense and as to intellect. And he is reduced [changed] from such potentiality to act [actuality] through the action of sensible objects on his senses, to the act of sensation; by instruction or discovery, to the act of understanding. Wherefore we must say that the cognitive soul is in potentiality both to the images which are the principles [sources] of sensing, and to those which are the principles of understanding. For this reason Aristotle held that the intellect by which the soul understands has no innate species, but is at first in potentiality to all such species.

. . . Plato held that man's intellect is naturally filled with all intelligible species, but that by being united to the body it is hindered from the realization of its act. But this seems to be unreasonable. First, because if the soul has a natural [innate] knowledge of all things, it seems impossible for the soul so far to forget the existence of such knowledge as not to know itself to be possessed thereof, for no man forgets what he knows naturally: for instance, that the whole is larger than the part, and such like. And especially unreasonable does this seem if we suppose that it is natural for the soul to be united to the body, as we have established above (Question 76, Article 1); for it is unreasonable that the natural operation of a thing be totally hindered by that which belongs to it naturally. Secondly, the falseness of this opinion [of Plato] is clearly proved from the fact that if a sense be wanting, the knowledge of what is apprehended through that sense is wanting also: for instance, a man who is born blind can have no knowledge of colors. This would not be the case if the soul had innate images of all intelligible things. We must therefore conclude that the soul does not know corporeal things through innate species.

* * *

Sixth Article: Whether Intellectual Knowledge Is Derived from Sensible Things?

On this point the Philosopher says (*Metaphysics* 1,1) that the principle [source] of knowledge is in the senses.

On this point the philosophers held three opinions. For Democritus [and Lucretius] held that "all knowledge is caused by images issuing from the bodies we think of and entering into our souls," as Augustine says in his letter to Dioscorus (118,4). And Aristotle says (*De Somn. et Vigil.*) that Democritus held that knowledge is caused by a "discharge of images." And the reason for this opinion was that both Democritus and the other early [pre-Socratic] philosophers did not distinguish between intellect and sense, as Aristotle relates (*De Anima* 3,3). Consequently, since the sense is affected by the sensible, they thought that all our knowledge is affected by this mere impression brought about by sensible things, which impression Democritus held to be caused by a discharge of images.

Plato, on the other hand, held that the intellect is distinct from the senses, and that it is an immaterial power not making use of a corporeal organ for its action. And since the incorporeal cannot be affected by the corporeal, he held that intellectual knowledge is not brought about by sensible things affecting the intellect, but by separate intelligible forms being participated [shared in] by the intellect, as we have said above (Articles 4,5). Moreover, he held that sense is a power operating of itself. Consequently neither is sense, since it is a spiritual power, affected by the sensible [objects], but the sensible organs are affected by the sensible [objects], the result being that the soul is in a way roused to form within itself the species of the sensible. Augustine seems to touch on this opinion (Gen. ad lit. 12,24) where he says that the "body feels not, but the soul through the body, which it makes use of as a kind of messenger, for reproducing within itself what is announced from without." Thus according to Plato, neither does intellectual knowledge proceed from sensible knowledge, nor sensible knowledge exclusively from sensible things; but these rouse the sensible soul to sentient act, while the senses rouse the intellect to the act of understanding.

Aristotle chose a middle course. For with Plato he agreed that intellect and sense are different. But he held that the sense has not its proper operation without the cooperation of the body; so that to feel is not an act of the soul alone, but of the *composite*. And he held the same in regard to all the operations of the sensitive part. Since, therefore, it is not unreasonable that the sensible objects which are outside the soul should produce some effect in the *composite*, Aristotle agreed with Democritus in this, that the operations of the sensitive part are caused by the impression of the sensible [object] on the senses; not by a discharge, as Democritus said, but by some kind of operation. For Democritus maintained that every operation is by way of a discharge of atoms, as we gather from *De Gener.* 1,8. But Aristotle held that the intellect has an operation which is independent of the body's cooperation. Now nothing corporeal can make an impression on the incorporeal. And therefore in order to cause the intellectual operation, according to Aristotle, the impression caused by the sensible [object] does not suffice, but something more noble is required, for "the agent is more noble than the patient," as he says (*ibid.* 5). Not, indeed, in the sense that the intellectual operation is effected in us by the mere impression of some superior beings, as Plato held; but that the higher and more noble agent which he calls the active intellect, of which we have spoken above (Q. 79, art. 3,4) causes the phantasms received from the senses to be actually intelligible by a process of abstraction.

According to this opinion, then, on the part of the phantasms intellectual knowledge is caused by the senses. But since the phantasms cannot of themselves affect the passive intellect, and require to be made actually intelligible by the active intellect, it cannot be said that sensible knowledge is the total and perfect cause of intellectual knowledge, but rather that it is in a way the material cause.

Question 85: The Mode and Order of Understanding

First Article: Whether Our Intellect Understands Corporeal and Material Things by Abstraction from Phantasms?

As stated above (Q. 84, a. 7), the object of knowledge is proportionate to the power of knowledge. Now there are three grades of the cognitive powers. For one cognitive power, namely the senses, is the act of a corporeal organ. And therefore the object of every sensitive power is a form as existing in corporeal matter. And since such matter is the principle of individuality, therefore every power of the sensitive part can only have knowledge of the individual.

There is another grade of cognitive power which is neither the act of a corporeal organ nor in any way connected with corporeal matter. Such is the angelic intellect, the object of whose cognitive power is therefore a form existing apart from matter. For though angels know material things, yet they do not know them save in something immaterial, namely either in themselves or in God.

But the human intellect holds a middle place, for it is not the act of an organ, yet it is a power of the soul which is the form of the body, as is clear from what we have said above (Q. 76, a.1). And therefore it is proper for it to know a form existing individually in corporeal matter, but not *as* existing in this individual matter. But to know what *is* in individual matter, not *as* existing in such matter, is to abstract the form from individual matter which is represented by the phantasms. Therefore we must say that our intellect understands material things by abstracting from the phantasms; and through material things thus considered we acquire some knowledge of immaterial things, just as, on the contrary, angels know material things through the immaterial.

But Plato, considering only the immateriality of the human intellect, and not its being in a way united to the body, held that the objects of the intellect are separate ideas, and that we understand not by *abstraction* [of abstract universal forms from concrete individual material things] but by *participating in* things abstract [the separate Forms or Ideas], as stated above (Q. 84, a. 1).

Second Article: Whether the Intelligible Species Abstracted from the Phantasm Is Related to Our intellect as That Which Is Understood?

The intelligible species is to the intellect what the sensible image is to the sense. But the sensible image is not what is perceived, but rather that by which sense perceives. Therefore the intelligible species is not what is actually understood, but that by which the intellect understands.

Some have asserted that our intellectual faculties know only the impression made on them; as, for example, that sense is cognizant only of the impression made on its own organ. According to this theory, the intellect understands only its own impression, namely, the intelligible species which it has received, so that this species is what is understood.

This is, however, manifestly false for two reasons. First, because the things we understand are the objects of science; therefore if what we understand is merely the intelligible species in the soul, it would follow that every science would not be concerned with objects outside the soul, but only with the intelligible species within the soul. . . .

Secondly, it is untrue, because it would lead to the opinion of those ancients who maintained that "whatever seems, is true," and that consequently contradictories are true simultaneously. For if the faculty knows its own impression only, it can judge of that only. Now a thing *seems* according to the impression made on the cognitive faculty. Consequently the cognitive faculty will always judge of its own impression as such, and so every judgment will be true. For instance, if taste perceived only its own impression, when anyone with a healthy taste perceives that honey is sweet, he would judge truly, and if anyone with a corrupt taste perceives that honey is bitter, this would be equally true; for each would judge according to the impression on his taste. Thus every opinion would be equally true; in fact, every sort of apprehension.

Therefore it must be said that the intellectual species is related to the intellect as that *by* which it understands.

Discussion Questions

1. Aquinas attempts to combine rational and empirical elements in his epistemology. Why do you think not all philosophers agree with this attempt (if not with the particular way Aquinas does it)? That is, why are Rationalism and Empiricism plausible? What suspicion would a Rationalist have against empirical knowledge and what suspicion would an Empiricist have against purely rational knowledge?

2. Which of the following concepts are examples of what Aquinas means by abstractions of universal forms from particular matter? (a) philosophy, (b) philosopher, (c) Plato, (d) green, (e) mud, (f) mind, (g) body, (h) my body, (i) my mind.

3. Why does Aquinas think that materialism in metaphysics necessarily results in scepticism in epistemology (see 84,1, paragraph 2). How would Lucretius reply to this?

4. State in your own words Aquinas' two arguments against Plato in 84,1. How do you think Plato might answer them?

5. In 84,3, put in your own words (a) Plato's theory of innate ideas and (b) Aquinas' arguments against it. How do you think Plato might reply to these arguments?

6. Which ingredients of Democritus' materialistic theory does Aquinas agree with and which does he disagree with (84,6, paragraph 1)? Which ingredients of Plato's immaterialism does he agree with and which does he disagree with (paragraph 2)?

7. Why does Aquinas think "active intellect" necessary? Why can't the intellect just receive forms passively? (85,6, last two paragraphs)

8. In the light of 85,1, explain the following images from Chesterton: for Democritus, the human knower is like a mole burrowing in the earth; for Plato, like a balloon flying free in the sky; for Aquinas, like a tree with its roots planted firmly in the earth but with its branches reaching into the heavens.

9. Put in your own words and evaluate Aquinas' two arguments in 85,2. What is the importance of this issue? What are the *consequences* of taking each side in this issue?

C. MODERN RATIONALISM

René Descartes: *Discourse on the Method*

René Descartes (1596–1650), "the father of modern philosophy," was a mathematical, scientific, and philosophical genius, like his antagonist and fellow Frenchman Pascal, the anti-Rationalist and proto-Existentialist. Surrounded by dead medieval scholasticism, irrational occultisms and nature-mysticisms, and popular scepticism (notably that of Montaigne, whose essays impressed Descartes), he hoped to rehabilitate philosophy and reconstruct the sciences by his analytical method, which he had already used to invent a new science, analytic geometry. He was most interested in medicine, but soon abandoned hopes of reducing it to the exactitude of mathematics. Ironically, his death was due to the unhealthy, cold, damp climate of

Sweden, where he was invited by the Queen to teach philosophy to her during the wee hours of the morning.

---

(1) Good sense is mankind's most equitably divided endowment, for everyone thinks that he is so abundantly provided with it that even those with the most insatiable appetites and most difficult to please in other ways do not usually want more than they have of this. As it is not likely that everyone is mistaken, this evidence shows that the ability to judge correctly, and to distinguish the true from the false—which is really what is meant by good sense or reason—is the same by innate nature in all men; and that differences of opinion are not due to differences in intelligence, but merely to the fact that we use different approaches. . . .

(2) . . . Reason . . . is the only thing which makes us men and distinguishes us from the animals, and I am therefore satisfied that it is fully present in each one of us. In this I follow the general opinion of philosophers, who say that there are differences in degree only in the *accidental* qualities, and not in the *essential* qualities or natures of individuals of the same species. . . .

(3) As for myself, I have never supposed that my mind was above the ordinary. . . . But I do not hesitate to claim the good fortune of having stumbled, in my youth, upon certain paths which led me without difficulty to certain considerations and maxims from which I formed a method of gradually increasing my knowledge and of improving my abilities as much as the mediocrity of my talents and the shortness of my life will permit. For I have already had such results that although in self-judgment I try to lean toward undervaluation rather than to presumption, I cannot escape a feeling of extreme satisfaction with the progress I believe I have already made in the search for truth. . . .

(4) So it is not my intention to present a method which every one ought to follow in order to think well, but only to show how I have made the attempt myself. . . . I only propose this writing as an autobiography, or, if you prefer, as a story in which you may possibly find some examples of conduct which you might see fit to imitate. . . .

(5) From my childhood I lived in a world of books, and since I was taught that by their help I could gain a clear and assured knowledge of everything useful in life, I was eager to learn from them. But as soon as I had finished the course of studies which usually admits one to the ranks of the learned, I changed my opinion completely. For I found myself saddled with so many doubts and errors that I seemed to have gained nothing in trying to educate myself unless it was to discover more and more fully how ignorant I was.

(6) Nevertheless I had been in one of the most celebrated schools in all of Europe, where I thought there whould be wise men if wise men existed anywhere on earth. I had learned there everything that others

learned. . . . I knew . . . that treatises on morals contain very useful teachings and exhortations to virtue; that theology teaches us how to go to heaven; that philosophy teaches us to talk with an appearance of truth about all things and to make ourselves admired by the less learned. . . .

(7) I was especially pleased with mathematics, because of the certainty and self-evidence of its proofs; but I did not yet see its true usefulness, and, thinking that it was good only for the mechanical arts, I was astonished that nothing more noble had been built on so firm and solid a foundation. On the other hand, I compared the ethical writings of the ancient pagans to very superb and magnificent palaces built only on mud and sand: they laud the virtues and rightly make them appear more desirable than anything else in the world; but they give no adequate criterion of virtue. . . .

(8) I revered our theology and hoped as much as anyone else to get to heaven, but having learned on great authority that the road was just as open to the most ignorant as to the most learned, and that the truths of revelation which lead thereto are beyond our understanding, I would not have dared to submit them to the weakness of my reasonings. I thought that to succeed in their examination it wold be necessary to have some extraordinary assistance from heaven, and to be more than a man.

(9) I will say nothing of philosophy except that it has been studied for many centuries by the most outstanding minds without having produced anything which is not in dispute and consequently doubtful and uncertain. I did not have enough presumption to hope to succeed better than the others; and when I noticed how may different opinions learned men may hold on the same subject, despite the fact that no more than one of them can ever be right, I resolved to consider almost as false any opinion which was merely plausible.

(10) Finally, when it came to the other branches of learning, since they took their cardinal principles from philosophy, I judged that nothing solid could have been built on so insecure a foundation. . . .

(11) This is why I gave up my studies entirely as soon as I reached the age when I was no longer under the control of my teachers. I resolved to seek no other knowledge than that which I might find within myself, or perhaps in the great book of nature. . . . But after spending several years in thus studying the book of nature and acquiring experience, I eventually reached the decision to study my own self. . . .

(12) I was then in Germany, where I had gone because of the desire to see the wars which are still not ended; and while I was returning to the army from the coronation of the Emperor, I was caught by the onset of winter. There was no conversation to occupy me, and being untroubled by any cares or passions, I remained all day alone in a warm room. There I had plenty of leisure to examine my ideas. One of the first that occurred to me was that frequently there is less perfection in a work produced by several persons than in one produced by a single hand. Thus we notice that

buildings conceived and completed by a single architect are usually more beautiful and better planned than those remodeled by several persons using ancient walls of various vintages that had originally been built for quite other purposes along with new ones. Similarly, those ancient towns which were originally nothing but hamlets, and in the course of time have become great cities, are ordinarily very badly arranged compared to one of the symmetrical metropolitan districts which a city planner has laid out on an open plain according to his own designs. . . . And similarly I thought that the sciences found in books, at least those whose reasons were only probable and which had no proofs, have grown up little by little by the accumulation of the opinions of many different persons, and are therefore by no means as near to the truth as the simple and natural reasonings of a man of good sense, laboring under no prejudice concerning the things which he experiences. . . .

(13) I cannot approve those mischievous spirits who, not being called either by birth or by attainments to a position of political power, are nevertheless constantly proposing some new reform. If I thought the slightest basis could be found in this *Discourse* for a suspicion that I was guilty of this folly, I would be loath to permit it to be published. Never has my intention been more than to try to reform my own ideas, and rebuild them on foundations that would be wholly mine. If my building has pleased me sufficiently to display a model of it to the public, it is not because I advise anyone to copy it . . . the decision to abandon all one's preconceived notions is not an example for all to follow, and the world is largely composed of two sorts of individuals who should not try to follow it. First, there are those who think themselves more able than they really are, and so make precipitate judgments. . . . Secondly, there are those who have enough sense or modesty to realize that they are less wise and less able to distinguish the true from the false than are others, and so should rather be satisfied to follow the opinions of these others than to search for better ones themselves. . . .

(14) I had discovered in college that one cannot imagine anything so strange and unbelievable but that it has been upheld by some philosopher; and in my travels I had found that those who held opinions contrary to ours were neither barbarians nor savages, but that many of them were at least as reasonable as ourselves. I had considered how the same man, with the same capacity for reason, becomes different as a result of being brought up among Frenchmen or Germans than he would be if he had been brought up among Chinese or Americans or cannibals; and how, in our fashions, the thing which pleased us ten years ago and perhaps will please us again ten years in the future, now seems extravagant and ridiculous; and felt that in all these ways we are much more greatly influenced by custom and example than by any certain knowledge. Faced with this divergence of opinion, I could not accept the testimony of the majority,

for I thought it worthless as a proof of anything somewhat difficult to discover, since it is much more likely that a single man will have discovered it than a whole people. . . .

(15) . . . Just as . . . a state is much better governed with a few laws which are strictly adhered to, so I thought that instead of the great number of precepts of which logic is composed, I would have enough with the four following ones, provided that I made a firm and unalterable resolution not to violate them even in a single instance.

(16) The first rule was never to accept anything as true unless I recognized it to be certainly and evidently such; that is, carefully to avoid all precipitation and prejudgment, and to include nothing in my conclusions unless it presented itself so clearly and distinctly to my mind that there was no reason or occasion to doubt it.

(17) The second was to divide each of the difficulties which I encountered into as many parts as possible, and as might be required for an easier solution.

(18) The third was to think in an orderly fashion when concerned with the search for truth, beginning with the things which were simplest and easiest to understand, and gradually and by degrees reaching toward more complex knowledge, even treating as though ordered materials which were not necessarily so.

(19) The last was, both in the process of searching and in reviewing when in difficulty, always to make enumerations so complete, and reviews so general, that I would be certain that nothing was omitted.

(20) The long chains of reasoning, so simple and easy, which enabled the geometricians to reach the most difficult demonstrations, had made me wonder whether all things knowable to men might not fall into a similar logical sequence. If so, we need only refrain from accepting as true that which is not true, and carefully follow the order necessary to deduce each one from the others, and there cannot be any propositions so abstruse that we cannot prove them, or so recondite that we cannot discover them . . . there is only one true solution to a given problem, and whoever finds it knows all that anyone can know about it. . . .

* * *

(21) I had noticed for a long time that in practice it is sometimes necessary to follow opinions which we know to be very uncertain, just as though they were indubitable, as I stated before; but inasmuch as I desired to devote myself wholly to the search for truth, I thought that I should take a course precisely contrary, and reject as absolutely false anything of which I could have the least doubt, in order to see whether anything would be left after this procedure which could be called wholly certain. Thus, as our senses deceive us at times, I was ready to suppose that nothing was at all the way our senses represented them to be. As there are men who make mistakes in reasoning even on the simplest topics in geometry, I judged that I

was as liable to error as any other, and rejected as false all the reasoning which I had previously accepted as valid demonstration. Finally, as the same precepts which we have when awake may come to us when asleep without their being true, I decided to suppose that nothing that had ever entered my mind was more real than the illusions of my dreams.

(22) [From *Meditations* I:] I feel sure that I cannot overdo this distrust, since it is not now a question of acting, but only of meditating and learning. I will therefore suppose that, not a true God who is very good and who is the supreme source of truth, but a certain evil spirit, not less clever and deceitful than powerful, has bent all his efforts to deceiving me. I will suppose that the sky, the air, the earth, colors, shapes, sounds, and all other objective things that we see are nothing but illusions and dreams that he has used to trick my credulity. I will consider myself as having no hands, no eyes, no flesh, no blood, nor any senses, yet falsely believing that I have all these things. I will remain resolutely attached to this hypothesis; and if I cannot attain the knowledge of any truth by this method, at any rate it is in my power to suspend my judgment. That is why I shall take great care not to accept any falsity among my beliefs and shall prepare my mind so well for all the ruses of this great deceiver that, however powerful and artful he may be, he will never be able to mislead me in anything. . . .

(23) I have just convinced myself that nothing whatsoever existed in the world, that there was no sky, no earth, no minds, and no bodies; have I not thereby convinced myself that I did not exist? Not at all; without doubt I existed if I was convinced or even if I thought anything. Even though there may be a deceiver of some sort, very powerful and very tricky, who bends all his efforts to keep me perpetually deceived, there can be no slightest doubt that I exist, since he deceives me; and let him deceive me as much as he will, he can never make me be nothing as long as I think that I am something. Thus, after having thought well on this matter, and after examining all things with care, I must finally conclude and maintain that this proposition: *I am, I exist,* is necessarily true every time that I pronounce it or conceive it in my mind.

(24) [From the *Discourse on the Method:*] Since this truth, *I think, therefore I am, or exist,* was so firm and assured that all the most extravagant suppositions of the sceptics were unable to shake it, I judged that I could safely accept it as the first principle of the philosophy I was seeking.

(25) I then examined closely what I was, and saw that I could imagine that I had no body, and that there was no world nor any place that I occupied, but that I could not imagine for a moment that I did not exist. On the contrary, from the very fact that I doubted the truth of other things, or had any other thought, it followed very evidently and very certainly that I existed. On the other hand, if I had ceased to think while my body and the world and all the rest of what I had ever imagined remained true, I would have had no reason to believe that I existed during that time;

therefore I concluded that I was a thing or substance whose whole essence or nature was only to think, and which, to exist, has no need of space nor of any material thing or body. Thus it follows that this ego, this mind, this soul, by which I am what I am, is entirely distinct from the body and is easier to know than the latter, and that even if the body were not, the soul would not cease to be all that it now is.

(26) Next, I considered in general what is required of a proposition for it to be true and certain, for since I had just discovered one to be such, I thought I ought also to know of what that certitude consisted. I saw that there was nothing at all in this statement, "I think, therefore I am," to assure me that I was saying the truth, unless it was that I saw very clearly that to think one must exist. So I judged that I could accept as a general rule that the things which we conceive very clearly and very distinctly are always true, but that there may well be some difficulty in deciding which are those which we conceive distinctly.

(27) After that I reflected upon the fact that I doubted many things, and that, in consequence, my spirit was not wholly perfect, for I saw clearly that it was a greater perfection to know than to doubt. I decided to ascertain from what source I had learned to think of something more perfect than myself, and it appeared evident that it must have been from some nature which was in fact more perfect . . . To derive it from nothingness was manifestly impossible, and it is no less repugnant to good sense to assume what is more perfect comes from and depends on the less perfect than it is to assume that something comes from nothing, so that I could not assume that it came from myself. Thus the only hypothesis left was that this idea was put in my mind by a nature that was really more perfect than I was, which had all the perfections that I could imagine, and which was, in a word, God. . . .

(28) To know the nature of God, whose existence has been proved, following the reasoning which I have just explained, as far as I was capable of such knowledge, I had only to consider each quality of which I had an idea, and decide whether it was or was not a perfection to possess that quality. I would then be certain that none of those which had some imperfection were in him, but that all the others were. . . .

(29) What makes many people feel that it is difficult to know of the existence of God, or even of the nature of their own souls, is that they never withdraw their minds from their senses and consider things higher than corporeal objects. They are so accustomed never to think of anything without picturing it, that is, without picturing in their imagination some image, as though of a corporeal thing—a method of thinking suitable only for material objects—that everything which is not picturable seems to them unintelligible. This is also manifest in the fact that even philosophers hold it as a maxim in the schools that there is nothing in the understanding

which was not first in the senses, a location where it is clearly evident that the ideas of God and of the soul have never been. . . .

(30) How could one know that the thoughts which come to us in dreams are false rather than the others which we have when awake, since they are often no less vivid and detailed? Let the best minds study this question as long as they wish; I do not believe they can find any reason good enough to remove this doubt unless they presuppose the existence of God. The very principle which I took as a rule to start with, namely, that all those things which we conceived very clearly and very distinctly are true, is known to be true only because God exists, and because he is a supreme and perfect Being, and because everything in us necessarily comes from Him. From this it follows that our ideas or notions, being real things which come from God insofar as they are clear and distinct, cannot to that extent fail to be true. Consequently, though we often have ideas which contain falsity, they can only be those ideas which contain some confusions and obscurity, in which respect they do not come from the supreme Being. . . .

Discussion Questions

1. Descartes' *Discourse on the Method* (1637) quickly became popular because it applied to philosophy the scientific method. Do you think the experiment of doing philosophy by the scientific method is a good one? Why or why not?

2. Descartes' philosophy is a deductive system: everything depends on the starting point, which is the redefinition of reason in paragraph 1.

    (a) How would Plato evaluate this paragraph? (Remember the difference between levels 3 and 4 of his Divided Line in answering.)

    (b) How does Descartes try to prove this first thesis? Evaluate his two arguments, one in paragraph 1 and one in paragraph 2.

    (c) What is the cause (paragraph 1) and cure (paragraph 3) of differences of opinion, according to Descartes? Evaluate. Has this cure in fact worked in the history of philosophy? the history of science?

3. What was Descartes' youthful search? (paragraphs 5,6, and 14) Why didn't philosophy help him in his search? (paragraph 5) Are his descriptions of philosophy (paragraphs 6,9) and theology (paragraph 8) fair and accurate?

4. Given Descartes' problem in paragraph 9, is his method of suspended judgment or universal methodic doubt (paragraph 16) reasonable? necessary? possible? (*Can* anyone doubt *everything*?) Give reasons for your answers.

5. (a) Why does Descartes trust "the simple and natural reasonings of a man of good sense laboring under no prejudice"? (paragraph 12)

(b) What alternative does he reject? (Cf. also paragraph 11)

(c) Evaluate Descartes' choice: which trust seems more naive to you? Why?

(d) Do you agree that philosophy is best done individually, not communally? (paragraph 12) Why or why not?

(e) Is it *reason* or *faith* in reason that is Descartes' starting point? (Cf. also paragraph 20.)

6. Do you see any apparent contradiction between paragraphs 1 and 13? Explain.

7. Have you ever worried about the problem in paragraph 14? How do you solve it?

8. Rule 2 (paragraph 17) calls for analytic, not synthetic, thinking. How would Plato evaluate this? Do you see any limitations of analytical thinking, any real and knowable thing that cannot be known in this way? If so, *why* can't it?

9. Why does Descartes introduce his "evil spirit"? (paragraph 22)

10. Why couldn't anything else besides "I think, therefore I am" answer the "evil spirit" doubt (paragraph 22) or the "dream" doubt (paragraph 21)?

11. Evaluate the argument "I think, therefore I am."

12. Does Descartes' next step logically follow, as he claims in the last sentence of paragraph 25? If so, from what premises does it follow?

13. State in your own words and evaluate Descartes' argument for God's existence in paragraph 27.

14. Paragraph 29 is an attack on Empiricism. Evaluate, especially the argument in the last sentence.

15. Do you have any better answer to Descartes' question in paragraph 30?

D. AN EMPIRICIST VIEW

John Locke: *An Essay on Human Understanding*

John Locke (1632–1704), an English physician, tried to do for the mappings of human knowledge what Newton, the intellectual idol of the Age of the Enlightenment, did for the physical world. (Thus ideas are like Newtonian particles, bouncing around in mental space by the gravity of association.) Alexander Pope had expressed Newton's dominance in the couplet, "Nature and Nature's laws lay hid in night; God said, 'Let Newton be!'—and all was

light." **Locke** is not, however, the first Empiricist; in fact, most British philosophers, from John of Salisbury and Roger Bacon in the Middle Ages,
through Frances Bacon (1561–1626) and up to the twentieth-century "analytic philosophers," have tended toward Empiricism: not of a gutty and materialistic sort, but cool, rational, clear, and even arranged in a deductive
system as logical as any Rationalist.

CHAPTER I: OF IDEAS IN GENERAL, AND THEIR ORIGIN

1. *Idea is the object of thinking.*—Every man being conscious to himself that
he thinks, and that which his mind is applied about whilst thinking being
the ideas that are there, it is past doubt that men have in their minds several
ideas, such as those expressed by the words whiteness, hardness, sweetness,
thinking, motion, man, elephant, army, drunkenness, and others. It is in
the first place then to be inquired, How he comes by them? I know it is a
received doctrine, that men have native ideas and original characters
stamped upon their minds in their very first being. This opinion I have at
large examined already; and, I suppose, what I have said in the foregoing
book will be much more easily admitted, when I have shown whence the
understanding may get all the ideas it has, and by what ways and degrees
they may come into the mind; for which I shall appeal to everyone's own
observation and experience.

2. *All ideas come from sensation or reflection.*—Let us then suppose the mind
to be, as we say, white paper, void of all characters, without any ideas; how
comes it by that vast store, which the busy and boundless fancy of man has
painted on it with an almost endless variety? Whence has it all the materials
of reason and knowledge? To this I answer, in one word, from experience.
In that all our knowledge is founded, and from that it ultimately derives
itself. Our observation, employed either about external sensible objects, or
about the internal operations of our minds, perceived and reflected on by
ourselves, is that which supplies our understandings with all the materials
of thinking. These two are the fountains of knowledge, from whence all the
ideas we have, or can naturally have, do spring.

3. *The object of sensation one source of ideas.*—First, our senses, conversant
about particular sensible objects, do convey into the mind several distinct
perceptions of things, according to those various ways wherein those
objects do affect them; and thus we come by those ideas we have of yellow,
white, heat, cold, soft, hard, bitter, sweet, and all those which we call sensible qualities; which when I say the senses convey into the mind, I mean,
they from external objects convey into the mind what produces there those
perceptions. This great source of most of the ideas we have, depending

wholly upon our senses, and derived by them to the understanding, I call *sensation*.

4. *The operations of our minds the other source of them.*—Secondly, the other fountain, from which experience furnisheth the understanding with ideas, is the perception of the operations of our own mind within us, as it is employed about the ideas it has got; which operations when the soul comes to reflect on and consider, do furnish the understanding with another set of ideas which could not be had from things without; and such are perception, thinking, doubting, believing, reasoning, knowing, willing, and all the different actings of our own minds; which we, being conscious of, and observing in ourselves, do from these receive into our understandings as distinct ideas, as we do from bodies affecting our senses. This source of ideas every man has wholly in himself; and though it be not sense as having nothing to do with external objects, yet it is very like it, and might properly enough be called *internal sense*. But as I call the other sensation, so I call this *reflection*, the ideas it affords being such only as the mind gets by reflecting on its own operations within itself. By reflection, then, in the following part of this discourse, I would be understood to mean that notice which the mind takes of its own operations, and the manner of them, by reason whereof there come to be ideas of these operations in the understanding. These two, I say, viz., external material things as the object of sensation, and the operations of our own minds within as the objects of reflection, are, to me, the only originals from whence all our ideas take their beginnings. The term *operations* here, I use in a large sense, as comprehending not barely the actions of the mind about its ideas, but some sort of passions arising sometimes from them, such as is the satisfaction or uneasiness arising from any thought.

5. *All our ideas are of the one or the other of these.*—The understanding seems to me not to have the least glimmering of any ideas which it doth not receive from one of these two. *External objects* furnish the mind with the ideas of sensible qualities, which are all those different perceptions they produce in us; and *the mind* furnishes the understanding with ideas of its own operations.

These, when we have taken a full survey of them, and their several modes, combinations, and relations, we shall find to contain all our whole stock of ideas; and that we have nothing in our minds which did not come in one of these two ways. Let anyone examine his own thoughts, and thoroughly search into his understanding, and then let him tell me, whether all the original ideas he has there, are any other than of the objects of his senses, or of the operations of his mind considered as objects of his reflection; and how great a mass of knowledge soever he imagines to be lodged there, he will, upon taking a strict view, see that he has not any idea in his mind but what one of these two have imprinted, though perhaps with infinite variety compounded and enlarged by the understanding, as we shall see hereafter.

6. *Observable in children.*—He that attentively considers the state of a child at his first coming into the world, will have little reason to think him stored with plenty of ideas that are to be the matter of his future knowledge. It is by degrees he comes to be furnished with them; and though the ideas of obvious and familiar qualities imprint themselves before the memory begins to keep a register of time or order, yet it is often so late before some unusual qualities come in the way, that there are few men that cannot recollect the beginning of their acquaintance with them; and, if it were worth while, no doubt a child might be so ordered as to have but a very few even of the ordinary ideas till he were grown up to a man. But all that are born into the world being surrounded with bodies that perpetually and diversely affect them, variety of ideas, whether care be taken about it or not, are imprinted on the minds of children. Light and colors are busy at hand everywhere when the eye is but open; sounds and some tangible qualities fail not to solicit their proper senses, and force an entrance to the mind; but yet I think it will be granted easily, that if a child were kept in a place where he never saw any other but black and white till he were a man, he would have no more ideas of scarlet or green than he that from his childhood never tasted an oyster or a pineapple has of those particular relishes.

Discussion Questions

1. Compare Locke's first statement (I,1) with Aquinas, *Summa* I,85,2 (page 119). Who do you think is right? Why?

2. What does Locke include in the term "experience" (paragraph 2)? Why is the term not broad enough to include "innate ideas"?

3. If the operations of the mind are a separate source of ideas, as Locke says in paragraph 4, how is he an Empiricist? Distinguish "reflection" from innate ideas."

4. Do you have any answer to Locke's argument in paragraph 5, especially the last sentence?

6. Evaluate the argument in paragraph 6. (What is he trying to prove? i.e., What is his conclusion?)

E. ANOTHER EMPIRICIST VIEW

David Hume:
Enquiry Concerning Human Understanding

David Hume (1711–1776) carried the argument begun by Locke and continued by Berkeley to its conclusion; thus the English Locke, Irish Berkeley, and Scotch Hume form the classic triad of British Empiricism. In his *Dialogs on Natural Religion* Hume had leaned toward agnosticism in religion as well as in epistemology. He found it difficult to live his sceptical conclusions, however, and confessed that to keep his sanity and return to the real world after a few hours' immersion in his philosophy, he had to go into another room and play backgammon. Unlike Locke, Hume was a tortured and unhappy soul who exemplified the difficulties of a sceptic in joining thought and life together: one can think scepticism, but one can scarcely live it.

SECTION II: OF THE ORIGIN OF IDEAS

(1) . . . We may divide all the perceptions of the mind into two classes or species, which are distinguished by their different degrees of force and vivacity. The less forcible and lively are commonly denominated *Thoughts* or *Ideas*. The other species want a name in our language, and in most others; I suppose, because it was not requisite for any but philosophical purposes to rank them under a general term or appellation. Let us, therefore, use a little freedom, and call them *Impressions*; employing that word in a sense somewhat different from the usual. By the term *impression*, then, I mean all our more lively perceptions, when we hear, or see, or feel, or love, or hate, or desire, or will. And impressions are distinguished from ideas, which are the less lively perceptions, of which we are conscious, when we reflect on any of those sensations or movements above mentioned.

(2) Nothing, at first view, may seem more unbounded than the thought of man, which not only escapes all human power and authority, but is not even restrained within the limits of nature and reality. To form monsters, and join incongruous shapes and appearances, costs the imagination no more trouble than to conceive the most natural and familiar objects. And while the body is confined to one planet, along which it creeps with pain and difficulty; the thought can in an instant transport us into the most distant regions of the universe; or even beyond the universe, into the unbounded chaos, where nature is supposed to lie in total confusion. What never was seen, or heard of, may yet be conceived; nor is any thing beyond the power of thought, except what implies an absolute contradiction.

(3) But though our thought seems to possess this unbounded liberty, we shall find, upon a nearer examination, that it is really confined within very narrow limits, and that all this creative power of the mind amounts to no more than the faculty of compounding, transposing, augmenting, or diminishing the materials afforded us by the senses and experience. When we think of a golden mountain, we only join two consistent ideas, *gold* and *mountain*, with which we were formerly acquainted. A virtuous horse we can conceive; because, from our own feeling, we can conceive virtue; and this we may unite to the figure and shape of a horse, which is an animal familiar to us. In short, all the materials of thinking are derived either from

our outward or inward sentiment: the mixture and composition of these belongs alone to the mind and will. Or, to express myself in philosophical language, all our ideas or more feeble perceptions are copies of our impressions or more lively ones.

(4) To prove this, the two following arguments will, I hope, be sufficient. First, when we analyze our thoughts or ideas, however compounded or sublime, we always find that they resolve themselves into such simple ideas as were copied from a precedent feeling or sentiment. Even those ideas which, at first view, seem the most wide of this origin, are found, upon a nearer scrutiny, to be derived from it. The idea of God, as meaning an infinitely intelligent, wise, and good Being, arises from reflecting on the operations of our own mind, and augmenting, without limit, those qualities of goodness and wisdom. We may prosecute this enquiry to what length we please; where we shall always find that every idea which we examine is copied from a similar impression. Those who would assert that this position is not universally true, have only one, and that an easy method of refuting it: by producing that idea which, in their opinion, is not derived from this source. It will then be incumbent on us, if we would maintain our doctrine, to produce the impression, or lively perception, which corresponds to it.

(5) Secondly. If it happen, from a defect of the organ, that a man is not susceptible of any species of sensation, we always find that he is as little susceptible of the correspondent ideas. A blind man can form no notion of colours; a deaf man of sounds. Restore either of them that sense in which he is deficient; by opening this new inlet for his sensations, you also open an inlet for the ideas, and he finds no difficulty in conceiving these objects.

SECTION IV: SCEPTICAL DOUBTS CONCERNING THE OPERATIONS OF THE UNDERSTANDING

(6) All the operations of human reason or enquiry may naturally be divided into two kinds, to wit, *Relations of Ideas*, and *Matters of Fact*. Of the first kind are the sciences of Geometry, Algebra, and Arithmetic; and in short, every affirmation which is either intuitively or demonstratively certain. *That the square of the hypotenuse is equal to the squares of the two sides*, is a proposition which expresses a relation between these figures. *That three times five is equal to the half of thirty*, expresses a relation between these numbers. Propositions of this kind are discoverable by the mere operation of thought, without dependence on what is anywhere existent in the universe. Though there never were a circle or triangle in nature, the truths demonstrated by Euclid would for ever retain their certainty and evidence.

(7) Matters of fact, which are the second objects of human reason, are not ascertained in the same manner; nor is our evidence of their truth, however great, of a like nature with the foregoing. The contrary of every matter of fact is still possible, because it can never imply a contradiction,

and is conceived by the mind with the same facility and distinctness as if ever so conformable to reality. *That the sun will not rise to-morrow* is no less intelligible a proposition, and implies no more contradiction than the affirmation, *that it will rise.* We should in vain, therefore, attempt to demonstrate its falsehood. Were it demonstratively false, it would imply a contradiction, and could never be distinctly conceived by the mind.

(8) It may, therefore, be a subject worthy of curiosity, to enquire what is the nature of that evidence which assures us of any real existence and matter of fact, beyond the present testimony of our senses, or the records of our memory. This part of philosophy, it is observable, has been little cultivated, either by the ancients or moderns; and therefore our doubts and errors, in the prosecution of so important an enquiry, may be the more excusable; while we march through such difficult paths without any guide or direction. They may even prove useful, by exciting curiosity, and destroying that implicit faith and security, which is the bane of all reasoning and free inquiry. The discovery of defects in the common philosophy, if any such there be, will not, I presume, be a discouragement, but rather an incitement, as is usual, to attempt something more full and satisfactory than has yet been proposed to the public.

(9) All reasonings concerning matter of fact seem to be founded on the relation of *Cause and Effect.* By means of that relation alone we can go beyond the evidence of our memory and senses. If you were to ask a man, why he believes any matter of fact, which is absent; for instance, that his friend is in the country, or in France; he would give you a reason; and this reason would be some other fact; as a letter received from him, or the knowledge of his former resolutions and promises. A man finding a watch or any other machine in a desert island, would conclude that there had once been men in that island. All our reasonings concerning fact are of the same nature. And here it is constantly supposed that there is a connexion between the present fact and that which is inferred from it. Were there nothing to bind them together, the inference would be entirely precarious. The hearing of an articulate voice and rational discourse in the dark assures us of the presence of some person: Why? because these are the effects of the human make and fabric, and closely connected with it. If we anatomize all the other reasonings of this nature, we shall find that they are founded on the relation of cause and effect, and that this relation is either near or remote, direct or collateral. Heat and light are collateral effects of fire, and the one effect may justly be inferred from the other.

(10) If we would satisfy ourselves, therefore, concerning the nature of that evidence which assures us of matters of fact, we must enquire how we arrive at the knowledge of cause and effect.

(11) I shall venture to affirm, as a general proposition, which admits of no exception, that the knowledge of this relation is not, in any instance, attained by reasonings *a priori*; but arises entirely from experience, when

we find that any particular objects are constantly conjoined with each other. Let an object be presented to a man of ever so strong natural reason and abilities; if that object be entirely new to him, he will not be able, by the most accurate examination of its sensible qualities, to discover any of its causes or effects. Adam, though his rational faculties be supposed, at the very first, entirely perfect, could not have inferred from the fluidity and transparency of water that it would suffocate him, or from the light and warmth of fire that it would consume him. No object ever discovers, by the qualities which appear to the senses, either the causes which produced it, or the effects which will arise from it; nor can our reason, unassisted by experience, ever draw any inference concerning real existence and matter of fact. . . .

(12) The mind can never possibly find the effect in the supposed cause, by the most accurate scrutiny and examination. For the effect is totally different from the cause, and consequently can never be discovered in it. Motion in the second Billiard-ball is a quite distinct event from motion in the first; nor is there anything in the one to suggest the smallest hint of the other. A stone or piece of metal raised into the air, and left without any support, immediately falls, but to consider the matter *a priori*, is there anything we discover in this situation which can beget the idea of a downward, rather than an upward, or any other motion, in the stone or metal?

(13) And as the first imagination or invention of a particular effect, in all natural operations is arbitrary, where we consult not experience; so must we also esteem the supposed tie or connexion between the cause and effect, which binds them together, and renders it impossible that any other effect could result from the operation of that cause. When I see, for instance, a Billiard-ball moving in a straight line towards another, even suppose motion in the second ball should by accident be suggested to me, as the result of their contact or impulse; may I not conceive, that a hundred different events might as well follow from that cause? May not both these balls remain at absolute rest? May not the first ball return in a straight line, or leap off from the second in any line or direction? All these suppositions are consistent and conceivable. Why then should we give the preference to one, which is no more consistent or conceivable than the rest? All our reasonings *a priori* will never be able to show us any foundation for this preference.

(14) In a word, then, every effect is a distinct event from its cause. It could not, therefore, be discovered in the cause, and the first invention or conception of it, *a priori*, must be entirely arbitrary. And even after it is suggested, the conjunction of it with the cause must appear equally arbitrary; since there are always many other effects which, to reason, must seem fully as consistent and natural. In vain, therefore, should we pretend to determine any single event, or infer any cause or effect, without the assistance of observation and experience.

(15) Hence we may discover the reason why no philosopher, who is rational and modest, has ever pretended to assign the ultimate cause of any natural operation, or to show distinctly the action of that power, which produces any single effect in the universe. It is confessed, that the utmost effort of human reason is to reduce the principles, productive of natural phenomena, to a greater simplicity, and to resolve the many particular effects into a few general causes, by means of reasonings from analogy, experience, and observation. But as to the cause of these general causes, we should in vain attempt their discovery; nor shall we ever be able to satisfy ourselves, by any particular explication of them. These ultimate springs and principles are totally shut up from human curiosity and enquiry. Elasticity, gravity, cohesion of parts, communication of motion by impulse, these are probably the ultimate causes and principles which we ever discover in nature; and we may esteem ourselves sufficiently happy if, by accurate inquiry and reasoning, we can trace up the particular phenomena to, or near to, these general principles. The most perfect philosophy of the natural kind only staves off our ignorance a little longer; as perhaps the most perfect philosophy of the moral or metaphysical kind serves only to discover larger portions of it. Thus the observation of human blindness and weakness is the result of all philosophy, and meets us at every turn in spite of our endeavours to elude or avoid it. . . .

(16) These two propositions are far from being the same; *I have found that such an object has always been attended with such an effect,* and *I foresee that other objects, which are, in appearance similar, will be attended with similar effects.* I shall allow, if you please, that the one proposition may justly be inferred from the other; I know, in fact, that it always is inferred. But if you insist that the inference is made by a chain of reasoning, I desire you to produce that reasoning. The connexion between these propositions is not intuitive. There is required a medium, which may enable the mind to draw such an inference, if indeed it be drawn by reasoning and argument. What that medium is, I must confess, passes my comprehension; and it is incumbent on those to produce it who assert that it really exists and is the origin of all our conclusions concerning matter of fact. . . .

* * *

(17) [Conclusion:] When we run over libraries, persuaded of these principles, what havoc must we make? If we take in our hand any volume; of divinity or school metaphysics, for instance; let us ask, *Does it contain any abstract reasoning concerning quantity or number?* No. *Does it contain any experimental reasoning concerning matter of fact and existence?* No. Commit it then to the flames: for it can contain nothing but sophistry and illusion.

Discussion Questions

1. Compare Hume's division of knowledge (paragraph 1) with Locke's.

Does Hume share Locke's doctrine of ideas as the *objects* of knowledge? Give evidence from the text for your answer.

2. How does Hume explain the apparently unbounded reach of thought beyond "impressions and ideas" (paragraphs 2 and 3)?

3. Plato expanded our ordinary view of the reaches of knowledge in his Allegory of the Cave (pages 108–114); Hume contracts it (see especially paragraph 3). Which is more likely to be right, do you think? Why?

4. Summarize and evaluate Hume's two arguments in paragraphs 4 and 5.

5. Into which of his two categories, "relations of ideas" or "matters of fact", would Hume place each of the following? How would (a) Plato, (b) Aristotle or Aquinas, (c) Descartes, and (d) Hume try to prove each one?

(1) Pyramids can be found in Egypt.	(8) All men are mortal.
(2) Pyramids are triangular.	(9) The sun will rise tomorrow.
(3) Triangles have three sides.	(10) Every event has a cause.
(4) God exists.	(11) There are no animals on Mars.
(5) God does not exist.	(12) There are no square circles.
(6) I think.	(13) Nothing is not itself.
(7) I exist.	(14) I am good and trustable.

6. Concerning causality,

(a) Do you agree that all our reasoning about matters of fact is founded on the cause-effect relation? Can you think of any exception?

(b) How does Hume account for our knowledge of causal relations? Do you agree? Can you think of any exceptions to his answer?

(c) Does Hume's account of causality apply equally to reasoning from cause to effect *and* from effect to cause? Give examples.

(d) Do you agree that the causal connection in general ("every event has a cause") is just as unknowable *a priori* (before sense experience) as a particular causal connection (e.g., "eggs come from birds")? Why or why not?

(e) Do you *sense* the causal connection itself, or only the things thus connected? If you do not sense it, where do you think the idea comes from?

7. Apply Hume's paragraph 15 to Aquinas' arguments for the existence of God (pages 276–279). How might Aquinas reply to Hume's criticism?

8. What *is* the "medium" Hume asks for in paragraph 16, if there is one?

9. Hume's last paragraph gives the consequences of having no answer to the challenges above.

(a) Do you think these consequences necessarily follow? Why or why not?

(b) How much of the history of philosophy would be "consigned to the flames" by Hume? (Does he mean it literally?) Would any discussion of ethics or values survive? Why or why not?

(c) Is this radical consequence a *refutation* of Hume? If so, how? Formulate it as an argument. If not, what *is* a refutation of Hume, if there is one?

F. IDEALISM

Immanuel Kant: *Critique of Pure Reason*

Immanuel Kant (1724–1804) lived an unspectacular professorial life in Königsberg, Germany. He was so punctual that citizens set their clocks by his regular walks. Yet this quiet professor was a philosophical revolutionary, whose *Critique of Pure Reason* laid to rest the ghost of objective metaphysics. (Actually, the ghost returned with a vengeance with Kant's idealist successors, Fichte, Schelling, and Hegel.) Kant himself always considered his ethical work, especially his *Critique of Practical Reason*, much more important, and regarded his epistemology as mere ground clearing or foundation laying for it. His third great critique, the *Critique of Judgment*, dealt with aesthetics.

PREFACE TO THE SECOND EDITION

(1) Hitherto it has been assumed that all our knowledge must conform to objects. But all attempts to extend our knowledge of objects by establishing something in regard to them *a priori*, by means of concepts, have, on this assumption, ended in failure. We must therefore make trial whether we may not have more success in the tasks of metaphysics if we suppose that objects must conform to our knowledge. This would agree better with what is desired, namely, that it should be possible to have knowledge of objects *a priori*, determining something in regard to them prior to their being given. We should then be proceeding precisely on the lines of Copernicus' primary hypothesis. Failing of satisfactory progress in explaining the movements of the heavenly bodies on the supposition that they all revolved round the spectator, he tried whether he might not have better success if he made the spectator to revolve and the stars to remain at rest. A similar experiment can be tried in metaphysics, as regards the *intuition* of objects. If intuition must conform to the constitution of objects, I do not see how we could know anything of the latter *a priori*; but if the object . . . must conform to the constitution of our faculty of intuition, I have no difficulty in conceiving such a possibility. . . .

(2) But this deduction of our power of knowing *a priori* . . . has a consequence which is startling, and which has the appearance of being highly prejudicial to the whole purpose of metaphysics. . . . For we are

brought to the conclusion that we can never transcend the limits of possible experience . . . our *a priori* knowledge of reason . . . has only to do with appearances, and must leave the thing in itself as indeed real *per se*, but as not known by us . . . all progress in the field of the supersensible has thus been denied to speculative reason. . . .

(3) But, it will be asked, what sort of a treasure is this that we propose to bequeath to posterity? What is the value of the metaphysics that is alleged to be thus purified by criticism and established once for all? On a cursory view of the present work it may seem that its results are merely *negative*, warning us that we must never venture with speculative reason beyond the limits of experience. Such is in fact its primary use. But such teaching at once acquires a *positive* value when we recognize that the principles with which speculative reason ventures out beyond its proper limits do not in effect extend the employment of reason. . . . To deny that the service which the Critique renders is positive in character would thus be like saying that the police are of no positive benefit, inasmuch as their main business is merely to prevent the violence of which citizens stand in mutual fear, in order that each may pursue his vocation in peace and security. That space and time are only forms of sensible intuition, and so only conditions of the existence of things as appearances . . . and that we can therefore have no knowledge of any object as thing in itself, but only in so far as it is an . . . appearance—all this is proved in the analytical part of the Critique. Thus it does indeed follow that all possible speculative knowledge of reason is limited to mere objects of *experience*. But our further contention must also be duly borne in mind, namely, that though we cannot *know* these objects as things in themselves, we must yet be in position at least to *think* them as things in themselves; otherwise we should be landed in the absurd conclusion that there can be appearances without anything that appears. . . .

INTRODUCTION

I. Distinction Between Pure and Empirical Knowledge

(4) There can be no doubt that all our knowledge begins with experience. For how should our faculty of knowledge be awakened into action; did not objects affecting our senses partly of themselves produce representations, partly arouse the activity of our understanding to compare these representations? . . . In the order of time, therefore, we have no knowledge antecedent to experience, and with experience all our knowledge begins.

(5) But though all our knowledge begins with experience, it does not follow that it all arises out of experience. For it may well be that even our empirical knowledge is made up of what we receive through impressions and of what our own faculty of knowledge (sensible impressions serving merely as the occasion) supplies from itself. If our faculty of knowledge

makes any such addition, it may be that we are not in a position to distinguish it from the raw material until with long practice of attention we have become skilled in separating it.

(6) This, then, is a question which at least calls for closer examination, and does not allow of any off-hand answer:—whether there is any knowledge that is thus independent of experience and even of all impressions of the senses. Such knowledge is entitled *a priori*, and distinguished from the *empirical*, which has its sources *a posteriori*, that is, in experience. . . .

II. We Are in Possession of Certain Modes of *A Priori* Knowledge, and Even the Common Understanding Is Never Without Them

(7) What we here require is a criterion by which to distinguish with certainty between pure and empirical knowledge. Experience teaches us that a thing is so and so, but not that it cannot be otherwise. First, then, if we have a proposition which in being thought is thought as *necessary*, it is an *a priori* judgment. . . . Secondly, experience never confers on its judgments true or strict . . . *universality*. . . . We can properly only say . . . that so far as we have hitherto observed, there is no exception to this or that rule. When, on the other hand, strict universality is essential to a judgment, this indicates a special source of knowledge, namely, a faculty of *a priori* knowledge. Necessity and strict universality are thus sure criteria of *a priori* knowledge, and are inseparable from one another.

(8) Now it is easy to show that there actually are in human knowledge judgments which are necessary and in the strictest sense universal, and which are therefore pure *a priori* judgments. If an example from the sciences be desired, we have only to look to any of the propositions of mathematics; if we seek an example from the understanding in its quite ordinary employment, the proposition 'Every alternation must have a cause' will serve our purpose. . . .

III. Philosophy Stands in Need of a Science Which Shall Determine the Possibility, the Principles, and the Extent of All *A Priori* Knowledge

(9) But what is still more extraordinary than all the preceding is this, that certain modes of knowledge leave the field of all possible experiences and have the appearance of extending the scope of our judgments beyond all limits of experience, and this by means of concepts to which no corresponding object can ever be given in experience.

(10) It is precisely by means of the latter modes of knowledge, in a realm beyond the world of the senses, where experience can yield neither guidance nor correction, that our reason carries on those enquiries which owing to their importance we consider to be far more excellent, and in the purpose far more lofty, than all the understanding can learn in the field of

appearances. . . . These unavoidable problems set by pure reason itself are *God, freedom,* and *immortality.* The science which, with all its preparations, is in its final intention directed solely to their solution is metaphysics; and its procedure is at first dogmatic, that is, it confidently sets itself to this task without any previous examination of the capacity or incapacity of reason for so great an undertaking.

(11) Now it does indeed seem natural that . . . we should, through careful enquiries assure ourselves as to the foundations of any building that we propose to erect, not making use of any knowledge that we possess without first determining whence it has come, and not trusting to principles without knowing their origin. It is natural, that is to say, that the question should first be considered, how the understanding can arrive at all this knowledge *a priori,* and what extent, validity, and worth it may have. Nothing, indeed, could be more natural if by the term 'natural' we signify what fittingly and reasonably ought to happen. But if we mean by 'natural' what ordinarily happens, then on the contrary nothing is more natural and more intelligible than the fact that this enquiry has been so long neglected. . . . It was thus that Plato left the world of the senses, as setting too narrow limits to the understanding, and ventured out beyond it on the wings of the Ideas, in the empty space of the pure understanding. He did not observe that with all his efforts he made no advance—meeting no resistance that might, as it were, serve as a support upon which he could take a stand, to which he could apply his powers, and so set his understanding in motion. It is, indeed, the common fate of human reason to complete its speculative structures as speedily as may be, and only afterwards to enquire whether the foundations are reliable.

Discussion Questions

1. Explain in your own words the problem Kant refers to in the second sentence. How does Hume highlight this problem? (Kant said Hume "woke me from my dogmatic slumber.")

2. Put the overall argument of the first paragraph into a syllogism and evaluate it. (The last sentence summarizes the argument.)

3. Why does Kant believe there *are* "things in themselves" if he thought no one could know them? (Cf. the last sentence of paragraph 3; evaluate this argument.) Do you agree with the criticism that to draw a limit to thought, as Kant does, is to think both sides of that limit, which is self-contradictory? If so, does that mean thought is necessarily unlimited? If not, how would Kant answer the criticism?

4. How does Kant answer the question what *good* it does to be so negative, limiting, and sceptical? Evaluate his answer.

5. Kant mentions in paragraph 3 that space and time, as forms of our sensible intuition, are subjective, not objective, not forms of "things in themselves." Does this mean you didn't *really* eat your lunch *after* you ate your breakfast?

6. What does Kant mean by "universality" and "necessity" as criteria of *a priori* knowledge (paragraph 7)? (By the way, what is "*a priori* knowledge"?) Give examples.

7. Would Aquinas agree with Kant (paragraphs 9 and 10) that knowledge of God, free will, and immortality extend beyond all experience and that no object corresponding to these concepts can ever be given in experience? If so, how can we know them? Does experience play any role?

8. Kant would insist that all metaphysics not based on epistemology is dogmatic and uncritical, for we must examine the capacity of the knowing instrument before we build a house of ideas with it (paragraph 11). How would a pre-Kantian (Plato or Aquinas) answer this charge?

9. Put Kant's critique of Plato in paragraph 11 into your own words. How would Plato answer it? Does it apply equally to Aristotle or Aquinas?

COMMENT: Frederick Brown
"Solipsist" from *Star Shine*

Walter B. Jehovah, for whose name I make no apology since it really *was* his name, had been a solipsist all his life. A solipsist, in case you don't happen to know the word, is one who believes that he himself is the only thing that really exists, that other people and the universe in general exist only in his imagination, and that if he quit imagining them they would cease to exist.

One day Walter B. Jehovah became a practicing solipsist. Within a week his wife had run away with another man, he'd lost his job as a shipping clerk and he had broken his leg chasing a black cat to keep it from crossing his path.

He decided, in his bed at the hospital, to end it all.

Looking out the window, staring up at the stars, he wished them out of existence, and they weren't there any more. Then he wished all other people out of existence and the hospital became strangely quiet even for a hospital. Next, the world, and he found himself suspended in a void. He got rid of his body quite as easily and then he took the final step of willing *himself* out of existence.

Nothing happened.

Strange, he thought, can there be a limit to solipsism?

"Yes," a voice said.

"Who are you?" Walter B. Jehovah asked.

"I am the one who created the universe you have now just willed out of existence. And now that you have taken my place—" There was a deep sigh. "—I can finally cease my own existence, find oblivion, and let you take over."

"But—how can *I* cease to exist? That's what I'm trying to do, you know."

"Yes, I know," said the voice. "You must do it the same way *I* did. Create a universe. Wait till someone in it really believes what you believed and wills it out of existence. Then you can retire and let him take over. Goodby now."

And the voice was gone.

Walter B. Jehovah was alone in the void and there was only one thing he could do. He created the heaven and the earth.

It took him seven days.

PART TWO
WHAT SHOULD WE DO?

CHAPTER FOUR
ARE WE FREE
TO CHOOSE?
THE PROBLEM
OF FREE WILL

The question of whether we are free to choose has to be discussed before the questions related to morality and the good life, since if we are not free to choose there is no point in discussing whether to pick one course of action rather than another. The problem of free choice can be stated in this way: There are three statements, each of which seem to have some claim to be true, yet which cannot all be true. The statements are:

1. We are responsible for our actions.
2. If every event has causes beyond our control we are not responsible for our actions.
3. Every event has causes that are beyond our control.

Statements 1 and 2 could both be true, but if they were it would follow that every event does not have causes beyond our control, so statement 3 would be false. Statements 2 and 3 could both be true, but if they were it would follow that we are not responsible for our actions, and so statement 1 would have to be false. Finally, statements 1 and 3 might both be true, but if they were 2 would have to be false, since if 1 and 2 were true, 3 would be false, and if 2 and 3 were true, 1 would have to be false.

There are three main positions on the question of free will. Defenders of the *free will view,* the view that we are free to choose, accept statements 1 and 2, but deny statement 3. This does not mean that they deny that any events have causes, only that they hold that at least some events have at least some causes that *are* within our control.

Strict determinists accept statements 2 and 3 and deny statement 1; they hold that we are not responsible for our actions and that, therefore, moral praise and blame are out of place in evaluating human actions. On this view we cannot help doing what we do and therefore planning or deliberating about the future is useless. Strict determinists take the same attitude to the future as most people take to the past: It can't be changed, so it is no use trying.

Finally, *compatibilists,* sometimes called "soft determinists," accept statements 1 and 3 and deny statement 2. They hold that even though every event has causes beyond our control, we are still responsible for our actions. In fact, compatibilists often take the position that responsibility is not only compatible with causal determinism but actually requires it.

Some of the arguments for or against these three positions attack the issues directly. For example, proponents of the free will view argue from our experience that we are in fact responsible for our actions, or argue against the idea that every event has causes beyond our control. Strict determinists often use arguments based on science to argue for the idea that every event has causes beyond our control. Compatibilists, as we have mentioned, often try to show that responsibility requires determinism, instead of being incompatible with it.

However, a great many arguments between the three points of view involve confusions that weaken or destroy the force of the argument. One of the key confusions is between *necessary* causes and *sufficient* causes. A necessary cause is a fact which must be present if a certain effect is to occur. For example, oxygen must be present if a fire is to burn. A necessary cause *enables* its effect to occur but does not *make* it occur. A *sufficient* cause, on the other hand, is a factor or set of factors such that if it occurs a certain effect *must* occur. If, for example, I were crushed absolutely flat by a steamroller, it would be a sufficient cause of death; once that event occurred my death would be inevitable.

The problem about sufficient causes is this: If *every* event has a sufficient cause then every event has causes beyond our control. Take some action of mine, say, drinking coffee at breakfast this morning. If every event has a sufficient cause then this action of mine has a sufficient cause. But that cause itself would have a sufficient cause, and that cause too would have a sufficient cause, and so on. Obviously if we go on tracing base causes back into the past we will eventually reach some event or a set of events which occurred before I was even born. And, clearly, events which happened before I was born are beyond my control. Yet once this event or set of events had occurred it was inevitable that I would drink coffee this morning. So whether or not I drank coffee this morning, or any other morning, is beyond my control.

The same argument could be applied to any action of mine whether it be a crime or an act of kindness or heroism. Whether I perform any action, good or bad, would be beyond my control, on this view.

Now very often defenders of determinism will argue that every event has a "cause" without specifying whether they mean a necessary cause or a sufficient cause. It may or may not be true that every event has a necessary cause, but whether or not it is true it would not mean that every event is beyond our control. However, if every event has a sufficient cause then, as we have just seen, every event is beyond our control. Thus it is crucial which claim is being made, and often arguments that every event has a cause are really only arguments that every event has a *necessary* cause.

A confusion that sometimes arises on the part of the defenders of free will is the confusion between thinking or feeling that some events are within our control and knowing this to be true. Probably most people believe that at least some of their actions are within their control, but of course they *might* be mistaken about that, just as we are sometimes mistaken in thinking that we are healthy when we are actually ill.

The solutions that follow present some of the strongest arguments for and against free will. Fichte presents an argument for strict determinism, based on the idea that nature is a vast interconnected system any part of which would be impossible to change without changing the whole system. David Hume gives arguments for compatibilism, including the argument mentioned above, that responsibility requires determinism. John Lucas replies to this argument, which he considers to be a fallacy, and gives arguments for the free-will view. James Jordan argues that determinism is self-defeating.

In reading these selections, keep in mind the distinctions made in this introduction. Is Fichte or Hume confusing necessary causes and sufficient causes? Is Jordan's argument a workable refutation of determinism? Is Lucas right in considering the compatibilist's argument to be a fallacy?

In reading these selections ask yourself what claims are being made by each philosopher and what arguments are being given to back up these claims. Then ask yourself whether the arguments are sufficient to establish the claims being made. The introduction to each selection will give some help in this but they will not do all the work for you. The final decision as to which position has the strongest arguments is one which you should work out for yourself. One argument you will have to consider is one given by Lucas, that the very process of arguing and making up our minds already presupposes that we are forced to choose. If Lucas is correct, not only this argument but all arguments would be useless if determinism were true.

The *Comment* is from Feodor Dostoevsky's *Notes from Underground*. Dostoevsky's character explores the moral and emotional effects of accepting determinism and gives his own view of human unpredictability. What light does this selection shed on the philosophical arguments in the earlier selections?

A. STRICT DETERMINISM

Johann Gottlieb Fichte:
The Vocation of Man, Book I

Johann Gottlieb Fichte (1762–1814) is one of the most important of the post-Kantian German philosophers whose ideas developed in response to, and sometimes in opposition to, the theories of Immanuel Kant. He had a major influence on Hegel and Schopenhauer. Fichte was a professor at the University of Jena from 1793 to 1799 and was involved in a number of the political and religious controversies of his time. His work, *The Vocation of Man,* is probably the most understandable to someone not familiar with post-Kantian German philosophy. It should be noted that the view that Fichte expresses in this selection is not one that he accepts himself; in Book I of *The Vocation of Man,* which is entitled "Doubt," he is setting forth the conflicting claims of freedom and determinism.

I seize on Nature in its rapid flight, detain it for an instant and hold the present moment steadily in view; I reflect upon this Nature within which my thinking powers have hitherto been developed and trained to those researches that belong to her domain.

I am surrounded by objects which I am compelled to regard as separate, independent, self-subsisting wholes. I behold plants, trees, animals. To each individual I ascribe certain properties and attributes by which I distinguish it from others; to this plant, such a form; to that plant, another; to this tree, leaves of one shape; to that tree, leaves of another.

Every object has its appointed number of attributes, neither more nor less. To every question, whether it is this or that, there is, for anyone who is thoroughly acquainted with it, a decisive Yes possible, or a decisive No—so that there is an end of all doubt of hesitation on the subject. Everything that exists *is* something, or it *is not* this something; is colored, or is not colored; has a certain color, or has it not, may be tasted, or may not; is tangible, or is not; and so on, *ad infinitum.*

Every object possesses each of these attributes in a definite degree. Let a measure be given for any of its attributes; then we may discover the exact extent of that attribute, which it neither exceeds nor falls short of. I measure the height of this tree; it is defined, and it is not a single line higher or lower than it is. I consider the green of its leaves; it is a definite green, not the smallest shade darker or lighter, fresher or more faded than it is; although I may have neither measure nor expression for these qualities. I turn my eye to this plant; it is at a definite stage of growth between its budding and its maturity, not in the smallest degree nearer or more remote from either than it is. *Everything that exists is determined throughout; it is what it is, and nothing else.*

Not that I am unable to conceive of an object as floating unattached between opposite determinations. I do certainly conceive of indefinite objects; for more than half of my thoughts consist of such conceptions. I think of a tree *in general*. Has this tree fruit or not, leaves or not; if it has, what is their number? What kind of a tree is it? How large is it? And so on. All these questions remain unanswered, and my thought is undetermined in these respects; for I did not propose to myself the thought of any particular tree, but of a tree generally. But in leaving the tree thus undetermined, I deprive it of any possibility of existing. Everything that actually exists has its determinate number of all the possible attributes of actual existence, and each of these in a determinate measure, as surely as it actually exists, even though I may not be able to exhaust the properties of any one object, or to apply to them any standard of measurement.

But Nature pursues its course of ceaseless change, and, while I speak, the moment I sought to hold before me is gone, and all is changed; before I could lay hold of it, everything was different. It had not always been as it was when I observed it; it had *become* so.

Why then, and from what cause, had it become so? Why had Nature, amid the infinite variety of possible forms, assumed in this moment precisely these and no others?

For this reason: that they were preceded precisely by those conditions which did precede them, and by no others; and because the present could arise out of those and out of no other possible conditions. Had anything in the preceding moment been in the smallest degree different from what it was, then in the present moment something would have been different from what it is. And from what cause were all things in that preceding moment precisely such as they were? For this reason: that in the moment preceding that, they were such as they were then. And this moment again was dependent on its predecessor, and that on another, and so on into the past without limit. In like manner will Nature, in the next moment, be necessarily determined to the particular forms which it will then assume— for this reason, that in the present moment it is determined exactly as it is; and were anything in the present moment in the smallest degree different from what it is, then in the succeeding moment something would necessarily be different from what it will be. And in the moment following that, all things will be precisely as they will be, because in the immediately previous moment they will be as they will be; and so will *its* successor proceed forth from it, and another from that, and so on into the future without limit.

Nature proceeds throughout the whole infinite series of her possible determinations without pause; and the succession of these changes is not arbitrary, but follows strict and unalterable laws. Whatever exists in Nature, necessarily exists as it does exist, and it is absolutely impossible that it should be otherwise. I enter within an unbroken chain of phenomena in which every link is determined by that which has preceded it, and in its turn determines the next; so that, were I able to trace into the past the causes through which alone any given moment could have come into actual existence, and to follow out in the future the consequences which must necessarily flow from it, then, at that moment, and by means of thought alone, I could discover all possible conditions of the universe, both past and future—past, by explaining the given moment; future, by predicting its consequences. In every point I experience the whole, for *only* through the whole is each part what it is; but through this it is *necessarily* what it is.

When I contemplate all things as one whole, one Nature, there is but one power. When I regard them as separate existences, there are many powers which develop themselves according to their inward laws and pass through all the possible forms of which they are capable; all objects in Nature are but those powers under certain determinate forms. The manifestations of each individual power of Nature become what they are—are determined—partly by the essential character of the power itself, and partly through the manifestations of all the other powers of Nature with which it is connected; but it is connected with them all, for Nature is one connected whole. The individual powers of Nature, therefore, are unalterably determined; while the essential character of each power remains what it is, and while the power continues to manifest itself under these particular circumstances, its manifestations must necessarily be what they are; it is absolutely impossible that they should be in the smallest degree different from what they are.

In every moment of her duration Nature is one connected whole; in every moment each individual part must be what it is, because all the others are what they are; and you could not remove a single grain of sand from its place without thereby (although perhaps imperceptibly to you) changing something throughout all parts of the immeasurable whole. But *every moment of this duration is determined by all past moments, and will determine every future moment;* and you cannot conceive even the position of a grain of sand other than as it is in the *present,* without being compelled to conceive the whole indefinite *past* to have been other than what it has been, and the whole indefinite *future* to be other than what it will be. Make the experiment, for instance, with this grain of sand. Suppose it to lie some few paces further inland than it does—then the stormwind that drove it in from the sea must have been stronger than it actually was; then the preceding state of the weather, by which this wind was occasioned and its degree of strength determined must have been different from what it actually was; and the previous state by which this particular weather was determined, and so on; and thus you have, without stay or limit, a wholly different temperature of the air from that which really existed, and a different constitution of the bodies which possess an influence over this temperature, and over which, on the other hand, it exercises such an influence. On the fruitfulness or unfruitfulness of countries, and through that, or even directly, on the duration of human life, this temperature exercises a most decided influence. How can you know—since it is not permitted us to penetrate the arcana of Nature, and it is therefore allowable to speak of possibilities—how can you know that in such a state of weather as may have been necessary to carry this grain of sand a few paces further inland, some one of your forefathers might not have perished from hunger, or cold, or heat, before begetting that son from whom you are descended; and that thus you might never have been at all, and all that you have ever done, and all that you ever hope to do in this world, must have been obstructed in order that a grain of sand might lie in a different place?

I myself, with all that I call mine, am a link in this chain of the rigid necessity of Nature. There was a time—so others tell me who were then alive, and I am compelled by reasoning to admit such a time of which I am not immediately conscious—there was a time in which I am not immediately conscious—there was a time in which I was not, and a moment in which I began to be. I then existed only for others, and not yet for myself. Since then, my self, my self-consciousness, has gradually unfolded itself, and I have discovered in myself certain capacities and faculties, wants, and natural desires. I am a definite creature, which came into being at a certain time.

I have not come into being by my own power. It would be the highest absurdity to suppose that I existed before I came into existence, in order to bring myself into existence. I have, then, been called into being by another power beyond myself. And by what power but the universal power of Nature, since I too am a part of Nature? The time at which my existence began, and the attributes with which I came into being, were determined by this universal power of Nature; and all the forms under which these inborn attributes have since manifested themselves, and will manifest themselves as long as I have a being, are determined by the same power. It was impossible that, instead of me, another should have come into existence; it is impossible that this being, once here, should at any moment of its existence be other than what it is and will be.

. . . no combination of circumstances can perfectly resemble those through which I came into existence, unless the universe could divide itself into two perfectly similar but independent worlds. It is impossible that two perfectly similar individuals can come into actual existence at the same time. It is thus determined what I, this definite person, must be; and the general law by which I am what I am is discovered. Nature's power of forming a human person having been what it was, being what it is, and standing in this particular relation to the other opposing powers of Nature, I am that which this power *could become;* and—there being no ground of limitation within itself—since it *could* become, necessarily *must become.* I am that which I am, because in the particular position of the great system of Nature only such a person, and absolutely no other, was possible. A spirit who could look through the innermost secrets of Nature would, from knowing one single man, be able distinctly to declare what men had formerly existed, and what men would exist at any future moment; in one individual he would discern *all* individuals. It is this, my interconnection with the whole system of Nature, which determines what I have been, what I am, and what I shall be. From any possible moment of my existence the same spirit could deduce infallibly what I had previously been, and what I was afterwards to become. All that, at any time, I am and shall be, I am and shall be of absolute necessity; and it is impossible that I should be anything else.

I am, indeed, conscious of myself as an independent and, in many occurrences of my life, a free being; but this consciousness may easily be explained on the principles already laid down, and may be thoroughly reconciled with the conclusions which have been drawn. My immediate consciousness, my proper perception, cannot go beyond myself and the modes of my own being. I have immediate knowledge of myself alone: whatever I may know more than this, I know only by inference, in the same way in which I have inferred the existence of original powers of Nature, which yet do not lie within the circle of my perceptions. But I myself—that which I call *me,* my personality—am not the same as Nature's power of producing a human being; I am only one of the manifestations of this power. And in being conscious of myself, I am conscious only of this manifestation and not of that power whose existence I infer when I try to explain my own. This manifestation, however, in its true nature, is really the product of an original and independent power, and must appear as such in consciousness. On this account I recognize myself generally as an independent being. For this reason I appear to myself *as free* in certain occurrences of my life, when these occurrences are the manifestations of the independent power which falls to my share as an individual; *as restrained and limited,* when, by any combination of outward circumstances, which may arise in time, but do not lie within the original limitations of my personality, I cannot do what my individual power would naturally, if unobstructed, be capable of doing; *as compelled,* when this individual power, by the superiority of antagonistic powers, is constrained to manifest itself even in opposition to the laws of its own nature.

Bestow consciousness on a tree, and let it grow, spread out its branches, and bring forth leaves and buds, blossoms and fruits, after its kind, without hindrance or obstruction—it will perceive no limitation to its existence in being only a tree, a tree of this particular species, and this particular individual of the species; it will feel itself perfectly *free*, because, in all those manifestations, it will do nothing but what its nature requires; and it will desire to do nothing else, because it can desire only what that nature requires. But let its growth be hindered by unfavorable weather, want of nourishment, or other causes, and it will feel itself *limited and restrained*, because an impulse which actually belongs to its nature is not satisfied. Bind its free-waving boughs to a wall, force foreign branches on it by ingrafting, and it will feel itself *compelled* to one course of action; its branches will grow, but not in the direction they would have taken if left to themselves; it will produce fruits, but not those which belong to its original nature. In immediate consciousness, I appear to myself as free; by reflection on the whole of Nature, I discover that freedom is absolutely impossible; the former must be subordinate to the latter, for it can be explained only by means of it.

. . . The vice or crime of each individual is irrevocably determined. Let Nature, once again, determine the path of a muscle, or the turn of a hair, in any particular individual; if Nature had the power of thinking upon the whole and could reply to your questions, it could tell you of all the good and evil deeds of this man's life from the beginning to the end of it. Nevertheless, virtue does not cease to be virtue, nor vice to be vice. The virtuous man is a noble product of Nature; the vicious, an ignoble and contemptible one: yet both are necessary results of the connected system of the universe.

Repentance is the consciousness of the continued effort of humanity within me, even after it has been overcome, associated with the disagreeable sense of having been subdued—a disquieting but still precious pledge of our nobler nature. From this consciousness of the fundamental impulse of our nature arises the sense which has been called "conscience," and its greater or less degree of strictness and susceptibility, down to the absolute want of it in many individuals. The ignoble man is incapable of repentance, for in him humanity has at no time sufficient strength to contend with the lower impulses. Reward and punishment are the natural consequences of virtue and vice for the production of new virtue and new vice. By frequent and important victories, our peculiar power is extended and strengthened; by inaction or frequent defeat, it becomes ever weaker. The ideas of guilt and accountability have no meaning outside of external legislation. Man incurs guilt, and must render an account of his crime only if he compels society to use artificial, external force to restrain those of his impulses which are injurious to the general welfare.

. . . I do not truly act at all: Nature acts in me. To make myself anything other than that which Nature has intended is something I cannot even propose to myself. I am not the author of my own being; Nature has made me what I am and everything that I am going to be. I may repent and rejoice and form good resolutions—although, strictly speaking, I cannot even do this, for all these things come to me of themselves when it is appointed for them to come. But it is certain that, with all my repentance and all my resolutions, I cannot produce the smallest change in that which I must inevitably become. I stand under the inexorable power of rigid necessity: if this necessity has destined me to become a fool and a profligate, a fool and a profligate without doubt I shall become; if it has destined me to be wise and good, wise and good I shall doubtless be. Blame and merit do not apply to necessity, nor do they apply to me. Necessity stands under its own laws. I stand under them as well. I see this and feel that my tranquillity would be best ensured if I could make my wishes accord with that necessity to which my being is wholly subject.

But, oh, these conflicting wishes! For why should I any longer hide from myself the sadness, the horror, the amazement with which I was filled when I saw how my inquiry must end? I had solemnly promised myself that my inclinations should have no influence in the direction of my thoughts; and I have not knowingly allowed them any such influence. But now, at the end, may I not confess that this result contradicts the profoundest aspirations, wishes, and wants of my being? And, despite the accuracy and the decisive strictness of proofs, how can I truly believe in a theory of my being which strikes at the very root of that being, which so distinctly contradicts all the purposes for which alone I live, and without which I should loathe my existence?

Why must my heart grieve over, and be torn by, that which so perfectly satisfies my understanding? Since nothing in Nature contradicts itself, is man alone a contradiction? Or perhaps not man in general, but only myself and those who resemble me? Had I but remained amid the pleasant delusions that surrounded me, satisfied with the immediate consciousness of my existence, and had never raised those questions concerning its foundation! But if the answer—which has caused me this misery—be true, then I *must* of necessity have raised these questions: or, rather, the thinking nature within me—and not I myself—raised them. I was destined to this misery, and it is in vain that I mourn the lost innocence of soul which can never return.

That I should be destined to be wise and good, or to be foolish and profligate, without power to change this destiny in the least—in the former case having no merit, and in the latter having no guilt: this it was that filled me with amazement and horror. That my very being and all of its characteristics should be determined by something external to me, 1 and that this thing in turn should be determined by something external to it: it was this from which I so violently recoiled. That whatever freedom there may be in the world be freedom which is not my own but that of some power other than myself—and even then only a limited half-freedom: it was this which did not satisfy me. What I had desired was this: that I myself, that of which I am conscious as my own being and person, but which in this system appears as only the manifestation of a higher existence, that this "I" would be independent, would be something which exists not by another or through another, but of myself, and, as such, would be the final root of all my own determinations. The rank which in this system is assumed by an original power of Nature I would myself assume; with this difference, that my nature would not be determined by any foreign power. I desire to possess an inward and peculiar power of manifestation, infinitely manifold like those powers of Nature; and this power shall manifest itself in the particular way in which it does manifest itself, for no other reason than because it does so manifest itself; not, like these powers of Nature, because it is placed under such or such outward conditions.

What then, according to my wish, shall be the especial seat and center of this peculiar inward power? Evidently not my body, for that I willingly allow to pass for a manifestation of the powers of Nature—at least in its existence, if not with regard to its further determinations; not my sensuous inclinations, for these I regard as a relation of those powers to my consciousness. Hence it must be my thought and will. I would exercise my voluntary power freely, for the accomplishment of aims which I shall have freely adopted; and this will, as its ultimate ground can be determined by no higher, shall move and mold, first my own body, and through it the surrounding world. My active powers shall be under the control of my will alone, and shall be set in motion by nothing else than by it. Thus it shall be. There shall be a Supreme Good in the spiritual world; I shall have the power to seek this with freedom until I find it, to acknowledge it as such when found, and it shall be my fault if I do not find it. This Supreme Good I shall will to know, merely because I will it; and if I will anything else instead of it, the fault shall be mine. My actions shall be the result of this will; without it I shall not act at all, since there shall be no other power over my actions but this will. Then my powers, determined by and subject to the dominion of, my will, will affect the external world. I will be the lord of Nature, and she shall be my servant. I will influence her according to the measure of my capacity, but she shall have no influence on me.

This, then, is the substance of my wishes and aspirations. But the system, which has satisfied my understanding, has wholly repudiated these.

Discussion Questions

1. Fichte seems to argue that since everything has definite attributes, everything is determined. Is he equivocating on two different senses of "determined" here? What would the two senses be? Can something be determined in one sense and not the other?

2. Fichte claims that the present state of affairs can arise only out of those conditions which did in fact precede it: "Had anything in the preceding moment been in the smallest degree different from what it was then in the present moment, something would have been different from what it was." Does this mean that the preceding conditions were a *sufficient* cause of the present conditions or only that they were a *necessary* cause? How would this affect the argument that the past determines the future?

3. Fichte claims that nature follows "fixed and unalterable laws" and that "whatever exists in Nature, necessarily exists as it does exist." Does the second claim follow from the first? Could something follow fixed and unalterable laws and yet not be necessary? Why or why not?

4. Fichte says that to account for change we need an "active power" which "produces by its own energy . . . this definite effect and no other." Could there be an "active power" which sometimes produces one effect and sometimes even in the same circumstances produces another effect? Can you give an example of such an "active power"?

5. Fichte says that the same "nature" in the same circumstances will always produce the same effect, so that a different effect is always due to a change in nature or circumstances. Does Fichte give any evidence for this? Can you give any evidence to show that this claim is or is not true?

6. Fichte gives an explanation of why we believe we are free. What is this explanation? Is it convincing? Does the fact that such an explanation can be given show that our belief that we are free is mistaken?

7. Fichte concludes that since what we are is determined by Nature, "Blame and merit . . . do not apply to me." Could someone accept Fichte's views about universal causation and still hold that it is reasonable to praise or blame people for their actions? Why or why not?

8. Fichte claims that the picture of our situation which he gives goes against our deep desire for freedom and independence. He claims that we wish to be completely independent of any outside influence. Is this possible? Is complete independence even desirable? Would it satisfy our "deep desires" if we had some independence and were not totally determined by Nature?

9. Does Fichte give any arguments for his view or merely present the view as if it were self-evident? If he gives arguments, what are they? If he does not give arguments, what reason do we have to accept his view?

10. State whether you agree or disagree with Fichte's views and give your reasons for agreeing or disagreeing.

B. COMPATIBILISM

David Hume:
A Treatise of Human Nature, Book II, Part 3

David Hume (1711–1776), a Scottish philosopher, is a major figure in modern philosophy. Hume began with the empiricist position that all knowledge is confined to what we can learn from our senses and arrived at a position of complete scepticism in every department of human thought. While some philosophers accept Hume's sceptical conclusions in one or more areas (e.g., his religious scepticism) a great part of Hume's importance for modern philosophy is the formidable challenge he offers, a challenge which must be taken up by any nonsceptical philosophical theory. Two of Hume's most important works are *An Enquiry Concerning Human Reason* and *A Treatise of Human Nature.*

Of all the immediate effects of pain and pleasure, there is none more remarkable than the *will;* . . . by the *will,* I mean nothing but *the internal impression we feel, and are conscious of, when we knowingly give rise to any new motion of our body, or new perception of our mind.* This impression, like the ones of pride and humility, love and hatred, it is impossible to define, and needless to describe any further; for which reason we shall cut off all those definitions and distinctions with which philosophers . . . perplex rather than clear up this question; and entering at first upon the subject, shall examine that long-disputed question concerning *liberty and necessity,* which occurs so naturally in treating of the will.

. . . Every object is determined by an absolute fate to a certain degree and direction of its motion, and can no more depart from that precise line in which it moves, than it can convert itself into an angel, or spirit, or any superior substance. The actions, therefore, of matter, are to be regarded as instances of necessary actions; and whatever is, in this respect, on the same footing with matter, must be acknowledged to be necessary. That we may know whether this be the case with the actions of the mind, we shall begin with examining matter, and considering on what the idea of a necessity in its operations are founded, and why we conclude one body or action to be the infallible cause of another.

It has been observed that in no single instance the ultimate connection of any objects is discoverable either by our senses or reason, and that we can never penetrate so far into the essence and construction of bodies, as to perceive the principle on which their mutual influence depends. It is their constant union alone with which we are acquainted; and it is from the constant union that the necessity arises. If objects had not a uniform and regular conjunction with each other, we should never arrive at any idea of cause and effect; and even after all, the necessity which enters into that idea, is nothing but a determination of the mind to pass from one object to its usual attendant, and infer the existence of one from that of the other. Here then are two particulars which we are to consider as essential to necessity, viz. the constant *union* and the *inference* of the mind; and wherever we discover these, we must acknowledge a necessity. As the actions of matter have no necessity but what is derived from these circumstances, and it is not by any insight into the essence of bodies we discover their connection, the absence of this insight, while the union and inference remain, will never, in any case, remove the necessity. It is the observation of the union which produces the inference; for which reason it might be thought sufficient, if we prove a constant union in the actions of the mind, in order to establish the inference along with the necessity of these actions. But that I may bestow a greater force on my reasoning, I shall . . . first prove from experience that our actions have a constant union with our motives, tempers, and circumstances, before I consider the inferences we draw from it.

To this end a very . . . general view of the common course of human affairs will be sufficient. There is no light in which we can take them that does not confirm this principle. Whether we consider mankind according to the difference of sexes, ages, governments, conditions, or methods of education; the same uniformity and regular operation of natural principles are discernible. Like causes still produce like effects; in the same manner as in the mutual action of the elements and powers of nature.

There are different trees which regularly produce fruit, whose taste is different from each other; and this regularity will be admitted as an instance of necessity and causes in external bodies. But are the products of Guienne and of Champagne more regularly different than the sentiments, actions, and passions of the two sexes, of which the one are distinguished by their force and maturity, the other by their delicacy and softness?

Are the changes of our body from infancy to old age more regular and certain than those of our mind and conduct? And would a man be more ridiculous, who would expect that an infant of four years old will raise a weight of three hundred pounds, than one who, from a person of the same age, would look for a philosophical reasoning, or a prudent and well concerted action? . . .

The skin, pores, muscles, and nerves of a day-labourer, are different from those of a man of quality: so are his sentiments, actions, and manners. The different stations of life influence the whole fabric, external and internal; and these different stations arise necessarily, because uniformly, from the necessary and uniform principles of human nature. Men cannot live without society, and cannot be associated without government. Government makes a distinction of property, and establishes the different ranks of men. This produces industry, traffic, manufacturers, lawsuits, war, leagues, alliances, voyages, travels, cities, fleets, ports, and all those other actions and objects which cause such a diversity, and at the same time maintain such an uniformity in human life.

Should a traveller, returning from a far country, tell us, that he had seen a climate in the fiftieth degree of northern latitude, where all the fruits ripen and come to perfection in the winter, and decay in the summer, after the same manner as in England they are produced and decay in the contrary seasons, he would find few so credulous as to believe him. I am apt to think a traveller would meet with as little credit, who should inform us of people exactly of the same character with those in Plato's republic on the one hand, or those in Hobbes's *Leviathan* on the other. There is a general course of nature in human actions, as well as in the operations of the sun and the climate. There are also characters peculiar to different nations and particular persons, as well as common to mankind. The knowledge of these characters is founded on the observation of an uniformity in the actions that flow from them; and this uniformity forms the very essence of necessity.

I can imagine only one way of eluding this argument, which is by denying that uniformity of human actions, on which it is founded. As long as actions have a constant union and connection with the situation and temper of the agent, however, we may in words refuse to acknowledge the necessity, we really allow the thing. Now, some may perhaps find a pretext to deny this regular union and connection. For what is more capricious than human actions? What more inconstant than the desires of man? And what creature departs more widely, not only from right reason, but from his own character and disposition? An hour, a moment is sufficient to make him change from one extreme to another, and overturn what cost the greatest pain and labour to establish. Necessity is regular and certain. Human conduct is irregular and uncertain. The one therefore proceeds not from the other.

To this I reply, that in judging of the actions of men we must proceed upon the same maxims, as when we reason concerning external objects. When any phenomena are constantly and invariably conjoined together, they acquire such a connection in the imagination, that it passes from one to the other without any doubt or hesitation. But below this there are many inferior degrees of evidence and probability, nor does one single contrariety of experiment entirely destroy all our reasoning. The mind balances the contrary experiments, and, deducting the inferior from the superior, proceeds with that degree of assurance or evidence, which remains. Even when these contrary experiments are entirely equal, we remove not the notion of causes and necessity; but, supposing that the usual contrariety proceeds from the operation of contrary and concealed causes, we conclude, that the chance or indifference lies only in our judgment on account of our imperfect knowledge, not in the things themselves, which are in every case equally necessary, though, to appearance, not equally constant or certain. No union can be more constant and certain than that of some actions with some motives and characters; and if, in other cases, the union is uncertain, it is no more than what happens in the operations of body; nor can we conclude anything from the one irregularity which will not follow equally from the other.

It is commonly allowed that madmen have no liberty. But, were we to judge by their actions, these have less regularity and constancy than the actions of wise men, and consequently are further removed from necessity. Our way of thinking in this particular is, therefore, absolutely inconsistent; but is a natural consequence of these confused ideas and undefined terms, which we so commonly make use of in our reasonings, especially on the present subject.

We must now show that as the *union* between motives and actions has the same constancy as that in any natural operations, so its influence on the understanding is also the same in *determining* us to infer the existence of one from that of another. If this shall appear, there is no known circumstance that enters into the connection and production of the actions of matter that is not to be found in all the operations of the mind; and consequently we cannot, without a manifest absurdity, attribute necessity to the one, and refuse it to the other.

There is no philosopher, whose judgment is so riveted to this fantastical system of liberty, as not to acknowledge the force of *moral evidence,* and both in speculation and practice proceed upon it as upon a reasonable foundation. Now, moral evidence is nothing but a conclusion concerning the actions of men, derived from the consideration of their motives, temper, and situation. Thus, when we see certain characters or figures described upon paper, we infer that the person who produced them would affirm such facts, the death of Caesar, the success of Augustus, the cruelty of Nero; and, remembering many other concurrent testimonies, we conclude that those facts were once really existent, and that so many men, without any interest, would never conspire to deceive us; especially since they must, in the attempt, expose themselves to the derision of all their contemporaries, when these facts were asserted to be recently and universally known. The same kind of reasoning runs through politics, war, commerce, economy, and indeed mixes itself so entirely in human life, that it is impossible to act or subsist a moment without having recourse to it. A prince, who imposes a tax upon his subjects, expects their compliance. A general, who conducts an army, makes account of a certain degree of courage. A merchant looks for fidelity and skill in his factor or supercargo. A man, who gives orders for his dinner, doubts not of the obedience of his servants. In short, as nothing more nearly interests us than our own actions and those of others, the greatest part of our reasonings is employed in judgments concerning them. Now I assert that whoever reasons after this manner does *ipso facto* believe the actions of the will to arise from necessity, and that he knows not what he means when he denies it.

All those objects, of which we call the one *cause* and the other *effect,* considered in themselves, are as distinct and separate from each other as any two things in nature; nor can we ever, by the most accurate survey of them, infer the existence of the one from that of the other. It is only from experience and the observation of their constant union, that we are able to form this inference; and even after all, the inference is nothing but the effects of custom on the imagination. We must not here be content with saying that the idea of cause and effect arises from objects constantly united; but must affirm that it is the very same with the idea of these objects, and that the *necessary connection* is not discovered by a conclusion of the understanding, but is merely a perception of the mind. Wherever, therefore, we observe the same union, and wherever the union operates in the same manner upon the belief and opinion, we have the idea of cause and necessity, though perhaps we may avoid those expressions. Motion in one body, in all past instances that have fallen under our observation, is followed upon impulse by motion in another. It is impossible for the mind to penetrate further. From this constant union it *forms* the idea of cause and effect, and by its influence *feels* the necessity. As there is the same constancy, and the same influence, in what we call moral evidence, I ask no more. What remains can only be a dispute of words.

And indeed, when we consider how aptly *natural* and *moral* evidence cement together, and form only one chain of argument betwixt them, we shall make no scruple to allow, that they are of the same nature, and derived from the same principles. A prisoner who has neither money nor interest discovers the impossibility of his escape, as well from the obstinacy of the gaoler, as from the walls and bars with which he is surrounded; and in all attempts for his freedom, chooses rather to work upon the stone and iron of the one, than upon the inflexible nature of the other. The same prisoner, when conducted to the scaffold, foresees his death as certainly from the constancy and fidelity of his guards, as from the operation of the axe or wheel. His mind runs along a certain train of ideas: the refusal of the soldiers to consent to his escape; the action of the executioner; the separation of the head and body, bleeding, convulsive motions, and death. Here is a connected chain of natural causes and voluntary actions; but the mind feels no difference betwixt them in passing from one link to another; nor is less certain of the future event than if it were connected with the present impressions of the memory and senses by a train of causes cemented together by what we are pleased to call a *physical necessity*. The same experienced union has the same effect on the mind, whether the united objects be motives, volitions, and actions, or figure and motion. We may change the names of things, but their nature and their operation on the understanding never change.

I dare be positive no one will ever endeavour to refute these reasonings otherwise than by altering my definitions, and assigning a different meaning to the terms of *cause, and effect, and necessity, and liberty, and chance.* According to my definitions, necessity makes an essential part of causation; and consequently liberty, by removing necessity, removes all causes, and is the very same thing with chance. As chance is commonly thought to imply a contradiction, and is at least directly contrary to experience, there are always the same arguments against liberty or free-will. If any one alters the definitions, I cannot pretend to argue with him till I know the meaning he assigns to these terms.

I believe we may assign the three following reasons for the prevalence of the doctrine of liberty, however absurd it may be in one sense, and unintelligible in any other. First, after we have performed any action, though we confess we were influenced by particular views and motives, it is difficult for us to persuade ourselves we were governed by necessity, and that it was utterly impossible for us to have acted otherwise, the idea of necessity seeming to imply something of force, and violence, and constraint, of which we are not sensible. Few are capable of distinguishing betwixt the liberty of *spontaneity,* as it is called in the schools, and the liberty of *indifference;* betwixt that which is opposed to violence, and that which means a negation of necessity and causes. The first is even the most common sense of the word; and as it is only that species of liberty which it concerns us to preserve, our thoughts have been principally turned towards it, and have almost universally confounded it with the other.

Secondly, there is a *false sensation or experience* even of the liberty of indifference, which is regarded as an argument for its real existence. The necessity of any action, whether of matter or of mind, is not properly a quality in the agent, but in any thinking or intelligent being who may consider the action, and consists in the determination of his thought to infer its existence from some preceding objects: as liberty or chance, on the other hand, is nothing but the want of that determination, and a certain looseness, which we feel in passing or not passing from the idea of one to that of the other. Now, we may observe, that though in reflecting on human actions, we seldom feel such a looseness or indifference, yet it very commonly happens that, in performing the actions themselves, we are sensible of something like it: and as all related or resembling objects are readily taken for each other, this has been employed as a demonstrative, or even an intuitive proof of human liberty. We feel that our actions are subject to our will on most occasions, and imagine we feel that the will itself is subject to nothing; because when, by a denial of it, we are provoked to try, we feel that it moves easily every way, and produces an image of itself even on that side on which it did not settle. This image or faint motion, we persuade ourselves, could have been completed into the thing itself; because, should that be denied, we find, upon a second trial, that it can. But these efforts are all in vain; and whatever capricious and irregular actions we may perform, as the desire of showing our liberty is the sole motive of our actions, we can never free ourselves from the bonds of necessity. We may imagine we feel a liberty within ourselves, but a spectator can commonly infer our actions from our motives and character; and even where he cannot, he concludes in general that he might, were he perfectly acquainted with every circumstance of our situation and temper, and the most secret springs of our complexion and disposition. Now, this is the very essence of necessity, according to the foregoing doctrine.

A third reason why the doctrine of liberty has generally been better received in the world than its antagonist, proceeds from *religion*, which has been very unnecessarily interested in this question. There is no method of reasoning more common, and yet none more blamable, than in philosophical debates to endeavour to refute any hypothesis by a pretext of its dangerous consequences to religion and morality. When any opinion leads us into absurdities, it is certainly false; but it is not certain an opinion is false because it is of dangerous consequence. Such topics, therefore, ought entirely to be forborne, as serving nothing to the discovery of truth, but only to make the person of an antagonist odious. This I observe in general, without pretending to draw any advantage from it. I submit myself frankly to an examination of this kind, and dare venture to affirm that the doctrine of necessity, according to my explication of it, is not only innocent, but even advantageous to religion and morality.

I define necessity two ways, conformable to the two definitions of *cause*, of which it makes an essential part. I place it either in the constant union and conjunction of like objects, or in the inference of the mind from the one to the other. Now, necessity, in both these senses, has universally, though tacitly, in the schools, in the pulpit, and in common life, been allowed to belong to the will of man; and no one has ever pretended to deny that we can draw inferences concerning human actions, and that those inferences are founded on the experienced union of like actions with like motives and circumstances. The only particular in which any one can differ from me is, either that perhaps he will refuse to call this necessity; but as long as the meaning is understood, I hope the word can do no harm; or, that he will maintain there is something else in the operations of matter. Now, whether it be so or not is of no consequence to religion, whatever it may be to natural philosophy. I may be mistaken in asserting that we have no idea of any other connection in the actions of body, and shall be glad to be further instructed on that head: but sure I am, I ascribe nothing to the actions of the mind, but what must readily be allowed of. Let no one, therefore, put an invidious construction on my words, by saying simply, that I assert the necessity of human actions, and place them on the same footing with the operations of senseless matter. I do not ascribe to the will that unintelligible necessity, which is supposed to lie in matter. But I ascribe to matter that intelligible quality, call it necessity or not, which the most rigorous orthodoxy does or must allow to belong to the will. I change, therefore, nothing in the received systems, with regard to the will, but only with regard to material objects.

Nay, I shall go further, and assert that this kind of necessity is so essential to religion and morality, that without it there must ensue an absolute subversion of both, and that every other supposition is entirely destructive to all laws, both *divine* and *human*. It is indeed certain, that as all human laws are founded on rewards and punishments, it is supposed as a fundamental principle that these motives have an influence on the mind, and both produce the good and prevent the evil actions. We may give to this influence what name we please; but as it is usually conjoined with the action, common sense requires it should be esteemed a cause, and be looked upon as an instance of that necessity, which I would establish.

This reasoning is equally solid, when applied to *divine* laws, so far as the Deity is considered as a legislator, and is supposed to inflict punishment and bestow rewards with a design to produce obedience. But I also maintain that even where he acts not in his magisterial capacity, but is regarded as the avenger of crimes merely on account of their odiousness and deformity, not only it is impossible, without the necessary connection of cause and effect in human actions, that punishments could be inflicted compatible with justice and moral equity; but also that it could ever enter into the thoughts of any reasonable being to inflict them. The constant and universal object of hatred or anger is a person or creature endowed with thought and consciousness; and when any criminal or injurious actions excite that passion, it is only by their relation to the person or connection with him. But according to the doctrine of liberty or chance, this connection is reduced to nothing, nor are men more accountable for those actions, which are designed and premeditated, than for such as are the most casual and accidental. Actions are, by their very nature, temporary and perishing; and where they proceed not from some cause in the characters and dispositions of the person who performed them, they infix not themselves upon him, and can neither redound to his honour, if good, nor infamy, if evil. The action itself may be blamable; it may be contrary to all the rules of morality and religion: but the person is not responsible for it; and as it proceeded from nothing in him that is durable or constant, and leaves nothing of that nature behind it, it is impossible he can, upon its account, become the object of punishment or vengeance. According to the hypothesis of liberty, therefore, a man is as pure and untainted, after having committed the most horrid crimes, as at the first moment of his birth, nor is his character any way concerned in his actions, since they are derived from it, and the wickedness of the one can never be used as a proof of the depravity of the other. It is only upon the principles of necessity that a person acquires any merit or demerit from his actions, however the common opinion may incline to the contrary.

But so inconsistent are men with themselves, that though they often assert that necessity utterly destroys all merit and demerit either towards mankind or superior powers, yet they continue still to reason upon these very principles of necessity in all their judgments concerning this matter. Men are not blamed for such evil actions as they perform ignorantly and casually, whatever may be their consequences. Why? but because the causes of these actions are only momentary, and terminate in them alone. Men are less blamed for such evil actions as they perform hastily and unpremeditatedly, than for such as proceed from thought and deliberation. For what reason? but because a hasty temper, though a constant cause in the mind, operates only by intervals, and infects not the whole character. Again, repentance wipes off every crime, especially if attended with an evident reformation of life and manners. How is this to be accounted for? but by asserting that actions render a person criminal, merely as they are proofs of criminal passions or principles in the mind; and when, by any alteration of these principles, they cease to be just proofs, they likewise cease to be criminal. But according to the doctrine of *liberty or chance*, they never were just proofs, and consequently never were criminal.

Here then I turn to my adversary, and desire him to free his own system from these odious consequences before he charges them upon others. Or, if he rather chooses that this question should be decided by fair arguments before philosophers, than by declamations before the people, let him return to what I have advanced to prove that liberty and chance are synonymous; and concerning the nature of moral evidence and the regularity of human actions. Upon a review of these reasonings, I cannot doubt of an entire victory . . .

Discussion Questions

1. How does Hume's idea of causation differ from Fichte's? If their ideas of causation are very different, does this mean that even though they often use very similar language they mean very different things by it? What would Fichte mean by saying, "Every event has a cause"? What would Hume mean by saying the same thing?

2. Hume seems to say as Fichte does, that everything, including human beings, is "determined" and "necessary." But Hume does not draw the conclusion that Fichte does, that we are not responsible for our actions. What accounts for the difference between Fichte and Hume on this point?

3. For Hume to say that A causes B is to say that A is always followed by B and that we have a mental disposition to expect B when we observe A. Does this "Humean cause" seem more like a necessary cause or a sufficient cause (as defined in the introduction to this section)? Even if all of our actions were caused in the Humean sense, would this mean that we were not free? Why or why not?

4. Hume makes certain remarks about men and women that many people today would regard as sexist and makes statements about "common people" that seem to be undemocratic or elitist. Is there any connection between these views and his deterministic views? Why or why not?

5. Hume argues that, far from being a threat to freedom, causation is necessary to freedom. State his argument in your own words. What objections can you see to this argument?

C. THE FREE WILL VIEW

John Lucas:
The Freedom of the Will

John R. Lucas (b. 1929), English philosopher, Fellow of Merton College, Oxford, since 1960, is the author of *The Principles of Politics* (Oxford: Oxford University Press, 1970), *The Concept of Probability* (Oxford: Oxford University Press, 1970), *A Treatise on Space and Time* (London: Methuen, 1973), and a number of papers in philosophical journals. Lucas resembles Aristotle, both in the breadth of his interests and in the occasional compression and difficulty of his arguments. His valuable and original work in diverse fields has not yet been fully understood or appreciated.

The chief general arguments for determinism turn on ideas, often confused, of explicability. Provided we take reasonable care to distinguish the different senses of 'explanation', 'cause' and 'causal', we see that the arguments do not really hold at all.

Historians are sometimes determinists, because they confuse partial and complete explanations. They are committed to explaining historical events, and explanation, they feel, involves determination. If a historian can explain why an event took place, he is explaining why it must have taken place. For he is explaining why the event in question took place, and not any other. And if no other event could have taken place, then the event that did take place must have taken place, and determinism is true. An explanation which does not have deterministic implications is less than complete, and therefore less than satisfactory. The only libertarian history is incomplete history. Only the idle or incompetent historian can avoid aspiring to be a determinist.

Historical determinism takes many forms. The Marxist claims that economic factors alone determine the course of history, and are themselves governed by the definite laws of dialectical materialism. Even those historians who reject the crudities of Marxism are liable to the feeling that some set of factors, not necessarily economic, determines the course of history, and that the decisions of the individual play no real part. It may be just a feeling of impotence and the recalcitrance of human affairs. "I pondered," said William Morris ". . . how men fight and lose the battle, and the thing they fought for comes about in spite of their defeat, and when it comes turns out to be not what they meant, and other men have to fight for what they meant under another name": often this feeling is cast in metaphysical form, and a theory of historical determinism propounded.

The argument turns on the nature of historical explanation. It assumes that a satisfactory explanation must not only show why the event in question took place, but why no other event could have taken place. But actual explanations offered by historians seldom do this. Often they are not of the "Why necessarily" form, but of the "How possibly"? Even those explanations which explain why, do not reveal a necessity that precludes freedom. In explaining why a man did something we may give, or reconstruct, his reasons. But reasons are seldom all one way. Usually there are arguments on both sides, some for the proposed action, some against: if not, the action hardly needs explaining. Where there are arguments on both sides, we can explain the man's decision by recounting the arguments on that side: but if he had decided against the action, we could have then explained his decision to the contrary, by recounting the arguments on the other side. Either way we could have given an explanation. In each case the explanation would have explained why the alternative action was not undertaken. But in neither case would it have shown that the agent had to act the way he did, and was unable to act otherwise. We give his reasons in each case, and his reasons show why he should have acted as he did; but not that, in the relevant sense of 'could', he could not have acted otherwise. Historical explicability fails to yield determinism, because a characteristic historical explanation is not a complete one, and the reasons adduced are not outside the agent's control. It is up to him whether he regards them as cogent, or some factor on the other side as decisive. We may ask the further question, why did such and such a person regard such and such reasons as good ones; but that is a different question and one that historians do not normally seek to answer. It is difficult enough to tell us how things happened and show us the reasons why people acted as they did, without presuming to prove that nothing could have happened otherwise than it did.

Besides confusing partial with complete explanations, people often confuse explanations of different types. Many thinkers affirm a principle of universal causation, that Every Event has a Cause. If we take the word 'cause' to mean 'causal cause' (*i.e.* regularity cause) as seems reasonable, then granted certain conditions, the principle is a determinist one. But when pressed to justify the principle of universal causation, its proponents interpret it to mean that every event has an explanation. This is a different principle, and a much easier one to maintain. If the word 'cause' means simply 'explanation', then it may well be true that every event has a cause, but it carries no determinist implications: if it means cause in the strict regularity sense, then it is far from self-evident that every event has a cause.

The argument is particularly seductive when applied to human actions. For it is characteristic of actions that the agent can say why he did them. If we think of our actions, we can usually remember why we did them, and assign as "causes" (*i.e.* partial explanations) some antecedent condition; and then interpret these causes as causal causes, as parts of complete regularity explanations. Sir Francis Galton, "kept account in a notebook of occasions on which he made important choices with a full measures of [the] feeling of freedom; then shortly after each choice he turned his eye backward in search of constraints that might have been acting on him stealthily. He found it so easy to bring such constraining factors to light that he surrendered to the determinist view." "You are too much preoccupied," he tells the reader ". . . to give any attention to the causes of which your choice may be an effect. But that is no reason for thinking that if you did preoccupy yourself you would not find them at work."

Many besides Sir Francis Galton have been convinced of the truth of determinism by this line of reasoning. But once we distinguish different types of explanation, the spring of the argument is broken. From the fact that an action is explicable, it does not follow that it is determined, in the sense in which we are using the word 'determined'. I refuse an invitation. You ask me to think why I refused. On reflection I say that it was because the last time I went to a party, I found it very boring. The boringness of the previous party was, if you like, the cause of my refusing now. But it did not necessitate a refusal on my part. I could perfectly well have accepted—I might have decided it was my duty to put up with being bored for the sake of sociability. I had a reason for refusing, but my refusing was not inevitable, ineluctable, necessitated or determined.

Some philosophers, however, do use the word 'determined' in a wider sense, in which it is more or less equivalent to 'explained'. So far as ordinary usage goes, it is perfectly permissible: we do speak of a man's decision being "determined by the need to preserve his reputation": a musician composing a piece or a logician making a deduction. But although we use these locutions in common parlance, it only generates confusion to use them in philosophy. For the reasons which "determine" a composer to add a particular bar to his composition are parts of some sort of rational explanation, not a regularity one; they do not enable us to make predictions in advance, but only to see how right it was *ex post facto*. It is the mark of creative genius that it is original and unpredictable; although after it has manifested itself, its *rationale* is manifest also. There is no question of denying the artist's freedom, or of explaining away his stroke of genius as not being his but the inevitable result of circumstance. To explain his achievement is to explain it as *his*. Therefore it is not the sort of determinism with which we need to be concerned. The only relevance it has to the freedom of the will is that it provides one *route* whereby philosophers are led from possibly true and certainly innocuous premises to dangerously false and disastrous conclusions. It is easy to accept "determinism" in some dilute sense, in which all that is being claimed is that there is some reason for every action, and then believe that one is committed to determinism in a strong sense, in which all our actions are causally determined by conditions outside our control because occurring before our birth. Having agreed that there is a *rationale* to everything, we allow that each thing is rationally necessary—morally necessary, artistically necessary, aesthetically necessary—and then drop the adverb that qualifies the systematically ambiguous term 'necessary' and assume that they are all necessary, pure and simple, that is to say, physically necessary. But the shift is illegitimate. Our starting-point was the principle that every event has an explanation; which is not the same as, and does not imply, the contention that every event has a regularity explanation.

The shift from the wide, unspecified, sense of 'explanation' to the narrow causal one is made less glaring and more plausible in virtue of three considerations. First, there is a corresponding shift between *methodological* and *ontological* interpretations of the principle of universal causation. Second, the argument is often made to proceed through the negative concepts 'random' or 'chance'. Third, an explicit metaphysical doctrine that regularity explanations are the only real explanations is sometimes invoked. "Nothing," according to Leucippus, "occurs by chance, but there is a reason and a necessity for everything." He seems to be talking ontologically about the nature of things, how things are. But the appeal to reason is more methodological—how we are to think of the world, and how conduct our enquiries—in tone. Chrysippus is more explicitly ontological. He says

> Everything that happens is followed by something else which depends on it by causal necessity. Likewise, everything that happens is preceded by something with which it is causally connected. For nothing exists or has come into being in the cosmos without a cause. There is nothing in it that is completely divorced from all that went before. The Universe will be disrupted and disintegrate into pieces and cease to be a unity functioning as a single system, if any uncaused movement is introduced into it. Such a movement will be introduced, unless everything that exists and happens has a previous cause from which it of necessity follows. In their view, the lack of cause resembles a *creatio ex nihilo* and is just as possible.

It would be unreasonable to criticize severely the confusion between ontological and methodological interpretations of the Principle of Universal Causation: indeed the distinction is a difficult one to sustain absolutely. We are all inclined to construe our fundamental principles as being ones about Reality. Many modern scientsts would feel that Chrysippus expressed exactly what they felt. If pressed, we should allow that the principle that Every Event has a Cause may be taken as an ontological principle, about the nature of things; but then we should be very much on our guard against unconsciously supposing that since 'every event has a cause (*i.e.* an explanation)' is a statement about Reality, about the nature of things, therefore the cause must be a thingly cause (*i.e.* an explanation in terms of things, a regularity explanation). Subject to an important qualification, I shall argue that we can say 'Every event has an explanation', and this is a statement about the universe. But the explanations are not all causal or regularity ones, and carry no determinist implications.

With the advent of quantum mechanics, the Leucippus fallacy has been revived, so that even if the human body is subject to quantum indeterminism, it still may be argued that it does not give the libertarian what he wants. Undetermined actions are random actions. But a man's random actions are not those we can usefully ask him his reasons for undertaking, or hold him responsible for.

Since the two definitions are jointly exhaustive, it follows that all actions for which we can be held responsible are determined. We can briefly represent his argument thus. All, or almost all, actions can be explained. Often the spectator can give one or two explanations, and the agent nearly always can give his reasons. On the few occasions where a person acts for apparently no reason at all, we stigmatize his action as random, and wonder whether it should really be called *his* action, or even *an action.* Certainly we do not want to say that all our moral actions are random, and therefore . . . they must be determined.

All these arguments turn on an equivocation in the use of the terms 'random' or 'uncaused', or the phrase 'by pure chance'. These concepts are *negative* concepts. 'Random' means *in*explicable. But since the concepts of explanation, cause and prediction are themselves equivocal, the concepts 'random', 'uncaused' and 'by pure chance' are so too. The randomness of quantum mechanics is opposed to *physical* explanation. It says nothing about whether there is any *human* or *rational* explanation to be offered. An action not altogether caused by antecedent physical conditions is in one sense uncaused, but not in the same sense as an action uncaused by the agent, which therefore is really not an action of his at all. There is a simple fallacy implicit in describing actions as geninely uncaused, absolutely random or occurring by pure chance; for uncausedness, randomness and chance, are not qualities, which are either present or absent, and if present are always the same. They are, instead, chameleon words, which take their colour from their context, and cannot be transferred from one context to another, and still carry the same significance. We can reconstruct Leucippus' argument thus

Everything has *an* explanation (λόγοφ)
∴ Nothing is inexplicable
∴ Nothing occurs at random (μάτην)
Nothing is inexplicable

or

Nothing occurs for which there is no explanation
∴ Everything has a regularity explanation
∴ There is a (regularity) necessity for everything

and the fallacy is obvious.

The argument from explicability is usually a muddle. Occasionally, however, it is advanced respectably, on the explicit claim that all explanation must be, really, regularity explanation. Although we cannot say that explanations as we know them in ordinary life are all regularity explanations, it can be maintained as an explicit metaphysical thesis that they must be. Materialists believe it. They regard things as the fundamental entities, and therefore regard thing-like explanation as the fundamental category of explanation. They were wrong, as I hope to show, to believe in things rather than in persons, but they are respectably wrong.

It is sometimes argued that every event must have a cause, because only so can we manipulate events. The argument fails; because, when it comes to other people, we neither think that we can, nor that we ought to be able to, manipulate them. All that the argument from manipulability shows is that things must be fairly reliable and persons sometimes reasonable. Life would be impossible, as Nowell-Smith argues, if the fish I have just decided to eat "is liable to turn into a stone or to disintegrate in mid-air or to behave in any other utterly unpredictable manner". But to exclude this radical unpredictability is not to embrace complete inevitability. For practical purposes, we do not require strongly quantified universal laws, that under certain conditions a specific event will absolutely always happen, but only weakly quantified universal laws, that the event will usually happen. Indeed, so far as our actual knowledge of material objects goes, we reckon ourselves lucky when we can go even as far as that. So far as other people are concerned, it is enough that we can sometimes influence them, either by argument and reason, or by virtue of our having under our control some factor which would be for them a reason for acting in the way we wish. You want my car. You offer me money for it. Being offered money is a perfectly good reason for my selling you my car. But it does not make it inevitable that I should sell it. I am perfectly free not to.

The argument from manipulation does not support determinism. Indeed, it argues against it, and shows that the whole notion of cause does not imply the truth of determinism, but, on the contrary, presupposes its falsity. For the notion of cause is based not, as Hume thought, on our *observing* constant conjunctions of events, but on our being able *to make things happen*. I can, if I want to, bring about a certain result, and afterwards, if I do so, say "I did it", or, more grandly, "I caused it". I discover that I can achieve some of my ends only by accomplishing certain means first, whereupon the end ensues. Construing 'cause' as a transitive relation, I say "I caused the means and the means caused the end and that is how I caused the end". In this way we obtain the third-personal use of 'cause'. It is a back-formation from the first-personal use which is the primary one and gave the original sense. The conceptual environment in which 'I cause', 'I do' and 'I make things happen' flourish is our normal untutored one in which men are the initiators of chains of events and I can cause things without myself having been caused: and although the third personal use is now much the more extensive, it is unlikely that even the third-personal meaning would survive being transplanted into a conceptual environment in which the root meaning could not survive.

This turns out to be the case. Even when reformulated so as to fit the third-personal use only, the notion of cause still requires that of the freedom of the will. Constant conjunction by itself does not rule out the possibility of pre-arranged harmony or of both events being consequences of some third event rather than being directly related to each other. Two college clocks always chime, the one shortly after the other; it may be that they are electrically connected, but other explanations are possible. The decisive test would be for the observer to introduce an arbitrary alteration in the earlier-chiming clock, and see whether this has any effect on the other. More generally, we discover causal relations not by merely observing passively but by experimenting as well. We have to be agents, not just spectators. And the reason is this: we believe that as free agents we can introduce an arbitrary disturbance into the universe and thus destroy any pre-arranged harmony: under the transformations that our arbitary interventions produçe, only real regularities will be preserved, and coincidental and pre-arranged ones will be destroyed. This argument is valid if we really are free agents. Unless we are, the argument is invalid, because we still have not ruled out the possibility of the agent's intervention and the occurrence of the second event both being consequences of some earlier determining factor. We just do not know, supposing the determinist thesis is to be true, what are the causal antecedents of my "deciding" to introduce an "arbitrary" alteration in the universe. It might be that the only occasions on which an experimenter could or would do this were occasions in which the occurrences of the second event were already going to be disturbed. Thus in this case, as in others, man can only have a true view of the universe and the laws of nature by excepting himself from their sway, and considering himself over against the universe, not as part of it, but independent of it, and not subject to its laws.

A second general argument against determinism stems not from intervention in natural phenomena but communication with other sentient beings. Communication is not manipulation. When I tell somebody something, I am not making him believe it or do anything: I am giving him a reason which he is free to accept or reject. It is a presupposition of communication that each party believes the other to have been, or to be, able to act otherwise. A linguistic utterance is one which the speaker could have not uttered, and which the hearer believes he need not have uttered, and which is intended, and known to be intended, to be taken in a particular way, but to which the response is not, and is not supposed to be, automatic. There are important differences between our responses to linguistic utterances and conditioned reflexes. Conversation is not a series of parade-ground commands.

* * *

Man is not God. Although men may sometimes take a God's eye view of the universe, they cannot consistently think of themselves as not being covered by any universal account they give of the world or of humanity. For they are men, and live in the world. It is a fair criticism of many philosophies, and not only determinism, that they are hoist with their own petard. The Marxist who says that all ideologies have no independent valildity and merely reflect the class interests of those who hold them can be told that in that case his Marxist views merely express the economic interests of his class, and have no more claim to be adjudged true or valid than any other views. So too the Freudian, if he makes out that everybody else's philosophy is merely the consequence of childhood experiences, is, by parity of reasoning, revealing merely his delayed response to what happened to him when he was a child. So too the determinist. If what he says is true, he says it merely as the result of his heredity and environment, and of nothing else. He does not hold his determinist views because they are true, but because he has such-and-such a genetic make-up, and has received such-and-such stimuli; that is, not because the *structure* of the universe is such-and-such but only because the configuration of only part of the universe, together with the structure of the determinist's brain, is such as to produce that result. Voltaire was contradicting himself when he wrote "I necessarily have the passion for writing this, and you have the passion for condemning me; both of us are equally fools, equally the playthings of destiny. Your nature is to do harm, mine is to love truth, and to make it public in spite of you." For if equally the playthings of destiny, then no distinction between doing harm and loving truth; nor any point in making true views public if their acceptance by men is determined by physical factors only, and not by the rational appeal of truth. In maintaining that his own views are true, Voltaire is denying that he is, along with all false believers, equally the plaything of destiny. He excepts himself. He, at least, is not determined by antecedent physical factors: he is open-minded towards the truth, and can be moved by new arguments that may occur to him. And, in publishing his views, he thinks that others too are likewise rational, and are open to rational argument, and hence not completely determined by purely physical factors.

Voltaire's successors today find their intellectual attitudes belying their determinist beliefs. They are committed to the view that whether or not determinism is true, they will believe that it is, as a result of certain physical variables having had certain values at a certain antecedent time. Even if determinism is false, they will, according to them, still say that it is true, and therefore their saying that it is true affords us no reason whatever for supposing that it really is true, but is to be construed solely as the end-product of some physical process. Yet this they are unwilling to accept. They want to be considered as rational agents arguing with other rational agents; they want their beliefs to be construed as beliefs, and subjected to rational assessment; and they want to secure the rational assent of those they argue with, not a brainwashed repetition of acquiescent patter. Consistent determinists should regard it as all one whether they induce conformity to their doctrines by auditory stimuli or a suitable injection of hallucinogens: but in practice they show a welcome reluctance to get out their syringes, which does equal credit to their humanity and discredit to their views.

Determinism, therefore, cannot be true, because if it was, we should not take the determinists' arguments as being really arguments, but as being only conditioned reflexes. Their statements should not be regarded as really claiming to be true, but only as seeking to cause us to respond in some way desired by them. And equally, if I myself come to believe in determinism, it would be because I had been subject to certain pressures or counter-pressures, not because the arguments were valid or the conclusion true. And therefore I cannot take determinism, whether in the mouth of another or believed by myself, seriously; for if it were true, it would destroy the possibility of its being rationally considered and recognised as such. Only a free agent can be a rational one. Reasoning, and hence truth, presupposes freedom just as much as deliberation and moral choice do.

Discussion Questions

1. Lucas says that historians assume that complete explanations must be deterministic but in fact are able to give only nondeterministic explanations. How might a historical determinist reply to this?

2. Lucas argues that some philosophers are led to accept determinism by confusing different senses of such words as "explained," "determined" or "necessary." Take one of these words and discuss in your own words the different senses of the word and how the confusing of these senses might lead to deterministic conclusions.

3. Compare the view expressed in Lucas's quotation from Chrysippus and the view expressed by Fichte.

4. Express in your own words Lucas's objections to the argument which he attributes to Leucippus. How could a determinist reply to this objection?

5. Give in your own words Lucas's argument that "the argument from manipulation does not favor determinism but argues against it." How might a determinist reply to this argument?

6. Do Lucas's arguments give a basis for refuting Hume's deterministic view? Why or why not?

7. What is Lucas's argument that reasoning presupposes freedom? State it in your own words and give a possible objection to it.

D. AN ARGUMENT FOR FREE WILL

James N. Jordan:
"Determinism's Dilemma"

James N. Jordan (b. 1938), American philosopher, is the author of a number of articles in philosophical journals. Professor Jordan is currently Dean of Social Sciences at Queen's College of the City University of New York.

Among *a priori* arguments against the justifiability of believing that determinism is true, there is one of which nearly everyone seems to have heard, but about which little has been written. This is the line of argument professing to show that any argument for determinism is "self-defeating" in the sense that, if it were sound, the soundness of no argument whatever could be established. Something at least very much like it occurs in the Third Section of Kant's *Foundations of the Metaphysics of Morals*. All that is claimed here is that the argument advanced in this paper is sound and that it was suggested by certain statements [by Kant and other philosophers].

There are many ways in which the thesis of determinism can be stated. The one taken here is perhaps the most common, viz., that every event, including in particular every event in the life of each person, has sufficient—not only necessary—spatio-temporal or temporal antecedent or concomitant conditions ("causes"). To say that an event of type A is a sufficient condition of an event of type X is, as usual, understood to mean that, at least as a matter of fact, whenever an event of type A happens, an event of type X happens, either simultaneously or shortly afterwards. And to say that an event of type B is a necessary condition of an event of type X is, as usual, understood to mean that events of type X never, at least as a matter of fact, occur without being accompanied or preceded by events of type *B*.

From the deterministic thesis as so formulated, it follows not only that the particular events in a person's life have sufficient causes, but also that they have sufficient causes that antedate his birth. If every event has a sufficient cause, then the sufficient cause-events that occur during one's lifetime are members of one or more series of sufficient causes which commenced long before he was born. Such is the view that is of concern here. There is no need to elaborate it further. For it is a matter of indifference to the determinism-is-self-defeating argument how exactly the thesis is explicated, whether in terms of "heredity and environment," "brain and nervous system," "character and circumstances," or any of the other factors that determinists have adduced to indicate the sort of sufficient causes in question.

Determinism is not construed here as *predictability* for the reason that, while it may be logically impossible to predict some events—e.g., each prediction, advances in human knowledge—every event still might be "determined" in the sense of having sufficient and necessary causal conditions. And that there can be no justification for believing that all events are so determined, if they are, is the stronger conclusion which the argument advanced here is held to establish.

There are many ways in which the thesis of determinism, however stated, may be taken. One may take it as a presupposition of empirical inquiry, as a valuable regulative principle or methodological rule, as a constitutive principle of human experience, as a statement of metaphysics, and so on. But the argument to be presented here is indifferent to the ways in which the deterministic thesis might be taken. If the argument is sound, it establishes that there can be no recognizably good reason to take the thesis in any light or for any purpose unless it is false. Of course, a view whose usefulness could be defended only if it were false may still have its uses. The argument given here has nothing to say about this. It does not imply that no one has the right to entertain the deterministic thesis as, say, a falsehood that provides needed encouragement to behavioral scientists. And inasmuch as the argument does not demonstrate that determinism is false, it has nothing to say against even those who, knowing that the arguments for determinism are self-defeating, knowing that the soundness of no argument could be established if any argument for determinism were sound, accept the deterministic thesis anyway, on the chance that their reasons for doing so are good. The argument does not deny that their reasons might be good. It denies only that they could have ascertainably good reasons to think so. It seems to me that [there are] two arguments, one narrower, the other wider. The first appears clearly defective as a general criticism of deterministic views, but the second can be developed into a powerful argument of considerable application. Each will be considered in turn.

(1) First, there is an attempt to show that rational activity cannot be accurately described in terms of conscious responses to external causes, foreign influences, compulsive mental associations, etc. A rational being is, by definition, one who recognizes his ability to judge in accordance with principles that are "his own," of which he is somehow the "author," in light of which he is able to assess arguments and arrive at tested judgments. If he were aware that his conclusions and principles of judgment were determined "from without," he would not be aware of them as *his;* his "assent" to an argument's conclusion would be a passive reaction to states of affairs "outside" himself and so less assent than capitulation; his "rational activity" would only be one way in which his "character" knowingly responded to his "circumstances." To say "we cannot conceive of a reason which consciously responds to a bidding from the outside" therefore amounts to this: it is contradictory to say of one who recognizes his ability to judge in accordance with his own principles both that he recognizes this and that his judgments or reasoned assessments are solely and *consciously* prompted by "foreign" stimuli. There could be no such thing as reason, that is, no one capable of regarding himself as reasoning, if the sort of determinism in question were true. In that case, there could be no one capable of regarding himself as reasoning for determinism, and so "determinism itself could not be accepted as true, nor could the arguments in its defence be accepted as valid." In fact, "there could be no difference between valid and invalid inference . . . and ultimately there can be no truth." So if the sort of determinism in question were true, no one could be capable of ascertaining that any argument for it is sound, and in this way determinism is self-defeating.

This argument does effectively indicate a profitable line of criticism against any deterministic view which entails that one is more or less conscious that all his judgments are responses to sufficient and necessary "biddings from the outside." It seems clear that one who would be conscious of this could not also be conscious that his conclusions have been adopted by him on their merits. He would be aware that his adoption of them was compulsive, in the nature of biases that frustrated his clear-headedness, etc. But the argument is compatible with deterministic theories which deny that the sufficient and necessary conditions of rational judgment are conscious or need be felt as compulsive intrusions. It has been argued that, far from denying one's experience of rational self-determination, a deterministic theory of this "softer" type is necessary to an understanding of it. It is held that, if our rational assessments do not have sufficient and necessary causal conditions, they could only be random occurrences, which is absurd; but the sufficient conditions of rationality are certainly not felt as intrusive influences, warring with one's "inner self" and inhibiting its self-determination. Our experience of autonomy in rational judgment, it may be said, is incompatible with only a grossly inadequate deterministic theory. What is required is a *better* theory, and against that the argument in question has nothing to say.

The argument has other defects as well. Supposing that the sort of determinism against which the argument is directed were true, would it follow that "there can be no difference between valid and invalid inference . . . and ultimately there can be no truth"? In fact, would either of these things follow from the truth of *any* deterministic theory? Surely, it would not follow from the *truth* of a deterministic theory that there is no *truth*. If the argument that determinism is self-defeating is sound, it would follow that, if determinism is true, no one would ever be able to discover the truth or falsity, rational defensibility or indefensibility, of any of his beliefs. But this is another matter. For all such an argument would tell us, some deterministic theory may be true. Nor would it follow from the truth of any deterministic theory that there is no difference between valid and invalid arguments. What does follow from the argument above is that, if the sort of determinism against which it is directed is true, no one is able rationally to assess an argument for validity. This, too, is another matter, but one of great importance for determinism-is-self-defeating arguments, as will be shown in some detail.

(2) Approaching [the] argument . . . from another perspective, one finds the suggestion of an argument much wider in scope and more compelling than the one just considered. Suppose that our assessments of arguments are the results of sufficient causal conditions whose complete statement involves no reference to "rational insight into a nexus between premises and conclusion," no mention of judgment "in accordance with objective laws or principles." Would it not be merely fortuitous if our assessments were in accord with what "objective laws or principles" prescribe as conditions for sound argumentation? Let us admit that the sufficient conditions of rational judgment need not be felt as compulsive foreign intrusions. Would there not still be a problem about knowing when, if ever, our assessments are reliable, if their sufficient conditions are logically indifferent to criteria of truth and validity?

Suppose we are asked to accept the proposition that all our rational assessments have sufficient—not just necessary—causal conditions. In order to show that we ought to believe this, someone would need to produce evidence which is seen to conform to criteria of reasonable trustworthiness and which is recognized to confer, by virtue of some principle of deductive or probable inference, certainty or sufficient probability upon it. But if the proposition is true, this could never happen, for it implies that whether anyone believes it and what he considers trustworthy evidence and acceptable principles of inference are determined altogether by conditions that have no assured congruence with the proposition's own merits or with criteria of sound argumentation whose validity consists of more than that we accept them. Whether we believe the proposition and what considerations we undertake before making a decision depend simply on sufficient and necessary causal conditions that logically need not be, and quite probably are not, relevant to the issues involved in assessing propositions for truth and arguments for validity. If our rational assessments are conditioned solely by factors whose exhaustive statement would omit mention of the recognized accordance of our deliberations with criteria of trustworthy evidence and correct inference, then the recognition of the relevance of these criteria is either inefficacious or absent. Of course, one still might occasionally believe what is true, but this would always be the outcome of happy circumstances, never of reasoned investigation. And if this is true of our rational assessment of any argument, it is true of our attempts to determine the strengths and weaknesses of any argument for the proposition in question. If the latter is true, any argument for it is self-defeating, for it entails that no argument can be known to be sound. The result was tersely expressed by A.E. Taylor: "Each of us, if we are to push the 'determinist' theory to its logical conclusion, thinks what he does think, and that is all there is to be said on the matter; which of us thinks *truly* is a question which, even if it has an intelligible meaning, is, and eternally must remain, without an answer."

. . . One may accept a proposition as logically true because he recognizes its logical truth. Alternatively, one may affirm that a proposition is logically true simply because that is what "heredity and environment" strongly or softly suggest that he affirm. But if determinism is true, recognizing a proposition's logical truth is always also a matter of what, and only what, "heredity and environment" may happen to suggest. Now it is possible that "heredity and environment" are so beneficent as always to suggest the right things, and it is possible that, even if they do not, they should sometimes or always contrive that we fail to affirm their false suggestions; but neither of these is in the least likely, and even if either were likely, we could not have any reason to think so, beyond what "heredity and environment" themselves suggest. Therefore, if all events have sufficient causal conditions, such as "heredity and environment," any warrantable acceptance of logical truths and of arguments as valid is impossible, and there can be no justifiable argument for any thesis, including determinism.

Now, of course, the argument is capable of wider deployment than this. It need not be viewed as applying to the recognition of logical truths only, or to arguments as abiding by them. Its essential point is that, if determinism is true, we can have no reasonable assurance that any of our various criteria of truth or warranted assertability are cogent. Only an unbelievable pre-established harmony could insure that what "character and circumstances" give us to believe is in accord with what ought to be believed if we are to believe truly. This holds for any theory of truth that does not make truth a function of "subjective passion." If there is to be a distinction, knowledgeably applicable by us, between justifiable belief and baseless opinion, we must be in a position to assess our judgments independently of "foreign influences," felt or unfelt, and to do this in recognized consonance with criteria that we do not just happen to have, but for which we can offer justification itself free from irrelevant, or not assurably relevant, causal conditions.

* * *

There are at least two major types of criticism to which the determinism-is-self-defeating argument may appear to be open. Both of them agree with the argument in holding that, in order to justify one's belief in the conclusion of an argument, it is irrelevant to appeal to the causes as such of one's belief; both insist that one should instead appeal to those formal and material characteristics of an argument that constitute its soundness, to relevant criteria of truth and validity and to the argument's fulfillment of them. But both maintain that the argument that determinism is self-defeating makes too much of this. The first criticism claims that such rational actions as assessments of arguments would simply be random occurrences, mere chance events, if they did not have sufficient causal conditions, if the reasons which govern and justify our conclusions were not themselves a species of cause. On this view, causal determination is a prerequisite of reason-guided activity, and to show that this is the case is to demonstrate the fallaciousness of arguments that assume or imply the contrary. The second criticism does not deny that reasons and causes are different in kind, but it claims that the determinism-is-self-defeating argument wrongly supposes that there is an incompatibility between explaining the adoption of a belief in terms of sufficient causes and justifying it in terms of reasons. To show that the two are compatible would then demonstrate the fallaciousness of arguments that assume or imply the contrary

At least two questions may pertinently be asked of this: (a) can we have any reason to believe that we are "programmed" *if we are,* and (b) is "free will" unintelligible apart from some such view of ourselves? If a negative answer to the first question is established, this will have decisive results for our approach to the second question. Something more will be said about this later. But it is the chief task of the determinism-is-self-defeating argument to establish negative answers to questions like (a), . . .

Suppose, then, that we are "programmed" by "our genetic endowment, together with certain environmental influences both when we were embryos and ever since." There would be no one to check the operations of computers, but worse yet, there would be no one able to discover whether we, who are also "programmed," are so constructed as even occasionally to come up with reliable answers. Let us admit that there is no incompatibility between something's operations being governed by causal laws and those operations being logically and informationally impeccable. By and large, computers are splendid instances of this. Nevertheless, we must also admit that, as delinquent computers themselves make abundantly clear, there is also no incompatibility between something's operations being governed by causal laws and those operations being sometimes or always wrong. And if we are indeed "programmed," would it not be impossible for us to discover whether we are not always wrong, or, if we are sometimes right, *when* we are not wrong? Some of us may take it upon ourselves to check the thoughts of others, but this is wasted effort if everyone's "circuitry" is more or less improperly wired, and no one is able to find out. Who would be in a position to claim with reason that he was properly wired? Could not anyone who sincerely believed and said that he was rightly wired be wrongly wired? Thus if we are asked, "are we not ourselves 'programmed'?" we can only reply that we certainly *may* be—the thing is possible, perhaps likely—but if such is the case, we are in the sad position of being unable to justify our confidence in any argument to that effect or to any other effect.

[A reply might make] the following principal points: (1) The argument is fallacious because it wrongly assumes that acting for a reason is incompatible with acting from a cause. (2) That there are necessary and sufficient causal conditions for one's acceptance of a view does not imply that one does not really accept it or that he does so for *reasons* other than those he cites. (3) That there are necessary and sufficient causal conditions for one's acceptance of a view is a matter logically distinct from the question whether the reasons one cites in defense of his acceptance are good or bad. . . .

It can be shown, however, that the argument does not make the assumption under (1), that it does not deny (2), and that it emphatically insists upon the truth of (3), but draws a different conclusion from it.

(1) The argument does not assume that acting for a reason is incompatible with acting from a cause. What it maintains is rather that, if our rational assessments are governed by causal laws, then whether we believe a proposition and what we consider relevant to supporting our belief are governed by conditions that have no assurable accordance with the proposition's own merits or with criteria of justified belief whose worth consists of more than that we happen to accept and employ them. "It might indeed happen that the belief which so resulted was true, but this would be the fruit of one's good fortune, not of one's rational judgment." This at no stage involves the assertion that our acts of rational assessment are not governed by causal laws, much less that they could not be. All that is claimed is that, if our judgments are so governed, then while they may sometimes, even always, be correct, one cannot know or reasonably believe that any judgment whatever is correct. To say this is not inconsistent with saying that one's acting for a reason in every case has necessary and sufficient causal conditions. What the argument, not assumes, but argues for is that the following two statements are incompatible: all one's actions are governed by causal laws; and there are recognizably good reasons to believe that this is so.

(2) The argument does not deny that, even if determinism is true, one can adopt beliefs and do so for the reasons one cites. Its point is rather that, if determinism is true, what one considers relevant to ascertaining the cogency of a belief is governed by conditions whose conformity to criteria of what ought to be believed would be merely fortuitous. A rightly-constructed calculating machine really does come out with reliable answers; these answers are produced in conformity with criteria of what ought to be believed in the realm of mathematics. We know that this is so because that is how we constructed the machine. Now suppose that persons are analogously deterministic mechanisms: a rightly-constructed person really does come out with reliable answers; these answers are produced in conformity with criteria of what ought to be believed. We know that this is so because of . . . what? Clearly, we could not know this. At best it may just happen to be true.

Men often make errors of judgment. Thus there is a notable difference between men and rightly-constructed calculating machines. If men are at all analogous to deterministic machines, they are analogous to faulty ones. But then how could they know that they are faulty? Sometimes it happens that they are right; sometimes it happens that they are wrong. In either case, however, their beliefs occur because of the presence of antecedent and concomitant conditions without whose accordance with, or departure from what is right, they can determine nothing. If they make mistakes, they cannot recognize them; if they believe themselves mistaken in any instance, their belief is fortuitously correct if correct at all. So if determinism is true, one cannot recognize errors of judgment. Still, one's errors would be one's errors; one's belief that he is in some instance mistaken would be his belief, and he may well hold his belief for precisely the reasons he cites in its behalf. But if his belief is right, and his reasons cogent, he is lucky.

(3) Far from denying, the argument explicitly insists that, even if our rational assessments do have necessary and sufficient causal conditions, this has no bearing on the question whether the reasons given in support of any belief are good or bad, relevant or irrelevant, sufficient or insufficient. When discussing criteria for determining what counts as a good reason for believing any type of proposition, the issue of the appropriateness of those criteria to that type of proposition is a logically separate issue from the question of what sufficient causes might have prompted someone to accept those criteria as appropriate; it is crucial to the success of the argument that this difference be recognized. This premise is required by the *reductio ad absurdum* which is the kernel of the argument: if determinism is true, it is impossible for us justifiably to claim that our reasons for any belief are good, inasmuch as we would not be able to determine whether the reasons we have are the ones we ought to have. But there would be none that we ought to have if the causal genesis of a belief were not logically distinct from its rational warrant.

. . . The argument purports to show only that, if determinism is true, we can have no discernibly good reason to believe it. But, after all, determinism may be true, one's reasons for believing it may really be his reasons, and his reasons might actually be very good reasons. Yet this evades the argument's central and specific contention that we could then never be in a position to determine that they *are* good reasons, unless by "good reason" we choose to mean "what some one or more persons just happen to believe." Supposing that the latter disastrous (because itself self-defeating, as the *Theatetus* shows) alternative is not preferred, we must admit that, if determinism is true, what we consider good reasons for believing any proposition are, so far as we are concerned, simply the reasons we happen to have (thanks altogether to a more or less favorable "genetic endowment, together with certain environmental influences both when we were embryos and ever since").

Much of the apparent force of criticisms depends on references to *necessary* causal conditions when it is the issue of necessary *and sufficient* causal conditions that is at point. "The fact that there was a causal explanation for my advancing these views, that I should, for example, be thinking differently if my brain were differently constituted, would not prove that I do not genuinely hold them," etc. But no proponent of the argument that determinism is self-defeating need deny that one would have different thoughts, or no thoughts at all, if his brain were differently constituted. He may even acknowledge that one would have different thoughts in the delirium of a high fever or in a state of narcosis. There are necessary causal conditions of rational judgment. But the issue is not whether certain differences in cerebral and neural constitution would result in differences of thought, but instead, whether there can be any reason to believe that every thought is the result of conditions exhaustively describable in terms of one's brain and nervous system. That every thought is so conditioned one might entertain as a guiding principle of scientific inquiry or as a generalization from controlled experiments, and nothing in the argument that determinism is self-defeating could possibly show that he is ill-advised or wrong. The argument does not assume or imply that determinism is false. All the argument does is to raise, and answer in the negative, the question whether, if every thought were so conditioned, we could have recognizably good reasons to entertain anything, including the methodological principle or empirical generalization that every thought is so conditioned.

* * *

In deterministic treatments of moral responsibility, it is often said that, even though our brains and nervous systems are deterministic mechanisms analogous to computing machines, this would not prohibit our making the usual, or something enough like the usual, contrasts between free and unfree, responsible and nonresponsible behavior. Similarly, it may be said that the important distinction between reasoned judgment and baseless opinion can be interpreted or reinterpreted in conformity with the view that all the events in our lives have necessary and sufficient causal conditions. And one might think that if this is satisfactorily done, any argument against determinism would lose its force.

But it is important to see that the argument that determinism is self-defeating is quite compatible with, and so could not be affected by, the accomplishment of this. Since it does not even suggest that determinism is false, it cannot be viewed as showing that no one could do whatever would count as doing it. Perhaps someone will be so favored by his brain and nervous system that he gets it done. All that the argument establishes is that one would no more be able to justify his confidence that it had been done than a computer can assess its programs and circuitry.

Perhaps the readiest criticism of the argument . . . is that if *it* is sound, then *it* is self-defeating. Reasoned assessments of beliefs are surely temporal undertakings. Now temporal undertakings for which there are no necessary and sufficient causal conditions are random occurrences, mere chance events. But, however, we may decide that reasoned assessments ought to be positively characterized, obviously they are *not* random occurrences. Yet since this is what is really implied by the argument at hand, there could be no reason to believe that the argument is sound if it is.

A criticism of this type rests upon the assumption that every event is either random or the result of necessary and sufficient causal conditions, and the argument that determinism is self-defeating is perhaps the best way of showing that the exhaustiveness of this dichotomy cannot be maintained. Here it seems to be enough to note that, in employing the dichotomy as exhaustive, the criticism begs the question which is central to the argument. If one who advances the criticism is not to do so in a merely gratuitous manner, he must suppose that there is some reasonable basis for accepting the exhaustiveness of the dichotomy. But that the exhaustiveness of the dichotomy is rationally defensible, if it really is exhaustive, is exactly what the argument is at such pains to deny. The argument denies this, not by *assuming* that the dichotomy is false, but by *showing* that it must be false if anything is reasonably believable. The argument admits that the dichotomy may be exhaustive and claims only that, if it is, there is no rational assessment of arguments. The onus of showing that this is not the case is on the critic.

What the argument does premise is what presumably no one is ready to deny: there is a difference between simply happening to be right about the merits of a position and being able rationally to defend one's belief that he is right. And it holds that, if determinism is true, any effort in the latter direction could at best just happen to be worthwhile. For then it could only be declared of us, by some being more happily circumstanced, that "each of us . . . thinks what he does think, and that is all there is to be said on the matter; which of us thinks *truly* is a question which . . . is, and eternally must remain, without an answer."

Now for all its negativity, this result appears to imply something positive. If no one can with reason believe even that determinism is true unless determinism is false, it seems clear that one must hold it to be false in so far as he believes that he exercises a power of rational judgment. And if so, then a theoretical disproof of determinism, if not impossible, is superfluous. Since to work to disprove it, no less than to support it, is hopeless unless it is false, the only responsible alternative is to deny it at the outset. Since we can proceed in no other way but on the presumption of its falsity, we must presume that we are in so far forth possessed of "free will" and of such rights, privileges, and responsibililties as may thereunto appertain. But this, after all, was precisely Kant's conclusion, and if we have given it fresh support here, with it we may end: "I say every being that cannot act except under the idea of freedom is just for that reason in a practical point of view really free, that is to say, all laws which are inseparably connected with freedom have the same force for him as if his will had been shown to be free in itself by a proof theoretically conclusive."

Discussion Questions

1. How does Jordan define determinism? Would Fichte agree with this definition? Would Hume? Would Lucas?

2. How is Jordan's argument like or unlike the argument in the last section of Lucas's paper?

3. State Jordan's "narrower" and "wider" arguments in your own words. What objections can you see to these arguments?

4. What are the two major types of criticism which Jordan considers? Are Jordan's replies to them satisfactory? Why or why not?

5. How does Jordan use the distinction between necessary conditions and sufficient conditions in his reply to one criticism of his argument? Are you convinced by the point he makes? Why or why not?

6. What is Jordan's final conclusion? Give your reasons for agreeing or disagreeing with it.

Comment: Feodor Dostoevsky
"Notes from Underground"

Man has always and everywhere—whoever he may be—preferred to do as he chose, and not in the least as his reason or advantage dictated; and one may choose to do something even if it is against one's own advantage, and sometimes one *positively should* (that is my idea). One's own free and unfettered choice, one's own whims, however wild, one's own fancy, overwrought though it sometimes may be to the point of madness—that is that same most desirable good which we overlooked and which does not fit into any classification, and against which all theories and systems are continually wrecked. And why on earth do all those sages assume that man must needs strive after some normal, after some rationally desirable good? All man wants is an absolutely *free* choice, however dear that freedom may cost him and wherever it may lead him to. Well, of course, if it is a matter of choice, then the devil only knows . . .

"Ha-ha-ha! But there's really no such thing as choice, as a matter of fact, whatever you may say," you interrupt, me with a laugh. "Today science has succeeded in so far dissecting man that at least we now know that desire and the so-called free will are nothing but—"

One moment, gentlemen. I am coming to that myself, and I don't mind telling you that I was even feeling a little nervous. I was just about to say that choice depended on the devil only knows what and that that was all to the good, but I suddenly remember science and—and the words died on my lips. And you took advantage of it and began to speak. It is, of course, quite true that if one day they really discover some formula of all our desires and whims, that is to say, if they discover what they all depend on, by what laws they are governed, how they are disseminated, what they are aiming at in one case and another, and so on, that is, a real mathematical formula, man may perhaps at once stop feeling any desire and, I suppose, most certainly will. For who would want to desire according to a mathematical formula? And that is not all. He will at once be transformed from a man into an organ-stop, or something of the sort. For what is man without desires, without free will, and without the power of choice but a stop in an organ pipe? What do you think? Let us calculate the probabilities: is it or is it not likely to happen?

"Well," you decide, "in the majority of cases our desires are mistaken from a mistaken idea of what is to our advantage. Sometimes we desire absolute nonsense because in our stupidity we see in this nonsense the easiest way of attaining some conjectural good."

Very well, and when all that is explained and worked out on paper (which is quite possible, for it would be absurd and unreasonable to assume that man will never discover other laws of nature), the so-called desires will of course no longer exist. For when one day desire comes completely to terms with reason we shall of course reason and not desire, for it is obviously quite impossible to *desire* nonsense while retaining our reason and in that way knowingly go against our reason and wish to harm ourselves. And when all desires and reasons can be actually calculated (for one day the laws of our so-called free will are bound to be discovered) something in the nature of a mathematical table may in good earnest be compiled so that all our desires will in effect arise in accordance with this table. For if it is one day calculated and proved to me, for instance, that if I thumb my nose at a certain person it is because I cannot help thumbing my nose at him, and that I have to thumb my nose at him with that particular thumb, what *freedom* will there be left to me, especially if I happen to be a scholar and have taken my degree at a university? In that case, of course, I should be able to calculate my life for thirty years ahead. In short, if this were really to take place, there would be nothing left for us to do: we should have to understand everything whether we wanted to or not. And, generally speaking, we must go on repeating to ourselves incessantly that at a certain moment and in certain circumstances nature on no account asks us for our permission to do anything; that we have got to take her as she is, and not as we imagine her to be; and that if we are really tending towards mathematical tables and rules of thumb and—well—even towards test tubes, then what else is there left for us to do but to accept everything, test tube and all. Or else the test tube will come by itself and will be accepted whether you like it or not. . . .

I repeat for the hundredth time that here is one case, one case only, when man can deliberately and consciously desire something that is injurious, stupid, even outrageously stupid, just because he wants *to have the right* to desire for himself even what is very stupid and not to be bound by an obligation to desire only what is sensible. For this outrageously stupid thing, gentlemen, this whim of ours, may really be more accounted by us than anything else on earth, especially in certain cases. And in particular it may be more valuable than any good even when it is quite obviously bad for us and contradicts the soundest conclusions of our reason about what is to our advantage, for at all events it preserves what is most precious and most important to us, namely, our personality and our individuality. Indeed some people maintain that this is more precious than anything else to man. Desire, of course, can, if it chooses, come to terms with reason, especially if people do not abuse it and make use of it in moderation; this is useful and sometimes even praiseworthy. But very often and indeed mostly desire is utterly and obstinately at loggerheads wiht reason and—and, do you know, that, too, is useful and occasionally even praiseworthy. Let us suppose, gentlemen, that man is not stupid. (As a matter of fact, it cannot possibly be said that man is stupid, if only from the one consideration that if he is, then who is wise?) But if he is not stupid, he is monstrously ungrateful Phenomenally ungrateful. I'm even inclined to believe that the best definition of man is—a creature who walks on two legs and is ungrateful.

. . . Now let me ask you this question: what can you expect of man seeing that he is a being endowed with such strange qualities? Why, shower all the earthly blessings upon him, drown him in happiness, head over ears, so that only bubbles should be visible on its surface, as on the surface of water; bestow such economic prosperity upon him as would leave him with nothing else to do but sleep, eat cakes, and only worry about keeping world history going—and even then he will, man will, out of sheer ingratitude, out of sheer desire to injure you personally, play a dirty trick on you. He would even risk his cakes and ale and deliberately set his heart on the most deadly trash, the most uneconomic absurdity, and do it, if you please, for the sole purpose of infusing into this positive good sense his deadly fantastic element. It is just his fantastic dreams, his most patent absurdities, that he will desire above all else for the sole purpose of proving to himself (as though that were so necessary) that men are still men and not keys of a piano on which the laws of nature are indeed playing any tune they like, but are in danger of going on playing until no one is able to desire anything except a mathematical table. And that is not all: even if he really were nothing but a piano-key, even if this were proved to him by natural science and mathematically, even then he would refuse to come to his senses, but would on purpose, just in spite of everything, do something out of sheer ingratitude; actually, to carry his point. And if he has no other remedy, he will plan destruction and chaos, he will devise all sorts of sufferings, and in the end he will carry his point! He will send a curse over the world, and as only man can curse (this is his privilege which distinguishes him from other animals), he may by his curse alone attain his object, that is, really convince himself that he is a man and not a piano-key! If you say that this, too, can be calculated by the mathematical table—chaos, and darkness, and curses—so that the mere possibility of calculating it all beforehand would stop it all and reason would triumph in the end—well, if that were to happen man would go purposely mad in order to rid himself of reason and carry his point! I believe this is so, I give you my word for it; for it seems to me that the whole meaning of human life can be summed up in the one statement that man only exists for the purpose of proving to himself every minute that he is a man and not an organ-stop! Even if it means physical suffering, even if it means turning his back on civilisation, he will prove it. And how is one after that to resist the temptation to rejoice that all this has not happened yet and that so far desire depends on the devil alone knows what.

You shout at me (if, that is, you will deign to favour me with raising voices) that no one wants to deprive me of my free will, that all they are concerned with is to arrange things in such a way that my will should of itself, of its own will, coincide with my normal interests, with the laws of nature and arithmetic.

But, good Lord, gentlemen, what sort of a free will can it be once it is all a matter of mathematical tables and arithmetic, when the only thing to be taken into account will be that twice-two-makes-four? Twice-two will make four even without my will. Surely, free will does not mean that!

Gentlemen, I am joking of course, and I'm afraid my jokes are rather poor, but you can't after all take everything as a joke. How do you know I'm not joking with a heavy heart? Gentlemen, I'm worried by all sorts of questions; please, answer them for me. For instance, you want to cure man of his old habits and reform his will in accordance with the demands of science and common sense. But how do you know that man not only could but *should* be remade like that? And what leads you to conclude that human desires must *necessarily* be reformed? In short, how do you know that such a reformation will be a gain to man? And, if one is to put all one's cards on the table, why are you so *utterly* convinced that not to go counter to the real normal gains guaranteed by the conclusions of reason and arithmetic is always so certainly right for man and is a universal law so far as mankind is concerned? For at present it is only a supposition on your part. Let us assume it is a law of logic, but how do you know that it is also a human law?

CHAPTER FIVE
WHAT MAKES AN ACT RIGHT? THE PROBLEM OF MORALITY

Moral judgments have to do with the free actions of human beings in matters of right and wrong. Human beings are continually making moral judgments on their own conduct and that of others. The acts approved of are called right or good. Those condemned are labeled wrong or evil. The term *moral* comes from the Latin *mores* meaning "way of life." The related word *ethics* derives from the Greek word *ethos* meaning "custom." Today we apply the term morals more to conduct, and ethics more to the study of moral conduct.

In his little book *Christian Behavior,* C.S. Lewis stresses that morality is concerned with three things: 1) the inner workings within each individual; 2) the harmony and fair play between individuals; and 3) the general purpose of life taken as a whole. In discussing these three aspects of morality, Lewis uses the illustration of a fleet or convoy of ships sailing in formation. The voyage is deemed successful only if three conditions are fulfilled. First, each individual ship is seaworthy and has her engines in good running order. Second, the ships do not get in each other's way and collide. And third, the ships reach their proper destination.

Thus, ethics or moral philosophy is that part of philosophy that treats norms or values, ideas about good and bad, right and wrong, what should and should not be done. It also sometimes includes political and legal philosophy. In many European countries the academic discipline which touches all these subjects is called "philosophy of law," with the term translated as law (German *Recht,* French *droit*) including the moral principles undergirding it.

What is the standard of morals? What is that which makes an action right? One foundational answer to the question "What is good?" is given by *utilitarianism.* According to the utilitarians, an action is right if it is useful in promoting happiness. Pleasure is good, pain is bad, and happiness is a sum of pleasures.

John Stuart Mill (1806–1873) accepts the general position of Jeremy Bentham (1748–1832), who used the phrase "the greatest happiness of the greatest number." Bentham stressed that nature places humankind under the guidance of two masters, pain and pleasure, who alone determine how we shall and should act out our lives. The most important change Mill made in utilitarianism was to add a qualitative standard. Human beings with refined faculties are dissatisfied with pleasures of the body. They seek the higher pleasures of the mind.

Many followers of Bentham and Mill are *subjectivists,* who assert that all values are relative to each individual or group of individuals. According to one kind of subjectivism, to claim that something is good or right is simply to say "I like it." For this kind of subjectivist, justification for making value judgments is how a person feels. It would seem to be futile for them to argue about values, for no matter how much one reasons or how thoroughly one examines the consequences, in the end one must conclude with "I like it" or "I approve of it."

Another of the great systems of ethics was set forth by Immanuel Kant (1724–1804). Kant's moral philosophy is sometimes called formalism because he was looking for moral principles which are inherently right or wrong apart from all particular circumstances. Kant saw moral philosophy as concerned with oughtness, not isness. Kant's principle—"act so as to use humanity, whether in your own person or in the person of another, always as an end, never as merely a means" has received more widespread approval than any other part of his moral philosophy.

Followers of Kant (and Plato before him), often labeled objectivists (or absolutists), maintain that values are grounded in reality separate from man. According to objectivists, what is good is independent of what any particular person thinks or likes. Moreover, it is independent of what any particular society affirms or sanctions. The objectivist stresses that there are moral laws which are eternally true and universally binding, no matter what individuals or societies of a particular period happen to think.

Excerpts from Joseph Fletcher's *Situation Ethics* are included here both because Fletcher writes cogently and clearly about key ethical issues and because we have found that students are immensely interested in the topics he raises. According to Fletcher, there are in the end only three basic approaches we can take in making moral decisions: 1) Kantian legalism; 2) decision-making based upon no principles (antinomianism); and 3) situational ethics. Fletcher's Christian situation ethics affirms only one norm or principle that is always good and right, regardless of the circumstances: love or *agapē*. Everything else, without exception, is only valid if it serves love in a given situation.

Friedrich Nietzsche (1844–1901) disagreed with Bentham, Mill, Kant, and Fletcher on several key points, the most basic of which involves his affirmation of human inequality. Even though some scholars point to a series of phases in his work, the general thrust of Nietzsche would seem to be the following: his hostility to Christianity, his emphasis on "God is dead," his concept of the *Übermensch* (superman), and the "transvaluation of values." Nietzsche's new morality was a reversal of traditional ethical values. His reference to the doctrine of eternal recurrence was his power to say "yes" to life instead of the Schopenhauerian "no." By affirming this doctrine of eternal recurrence Nietzsche seems to be saying that he could embrace the idea that his whole life, every agony and humiliation, would be repeated numerous times throughout eternity. Nietzsche's moral theory is more social than personal. Those theories are said to be right which are biologically useful to a given species or for a certain type of man.

In the end, do we characterize ethics as a theoretical or a practical study? Well, it is obviously not practical in the sense that it tells us exactly what we must do in any given situation. We must decide for ourselves. On the other hand, moral philosophy is not purely a theoretical activity. Most of us do not study it simply for the fun of it. The inquiry arises from the problems of real life. And to ask, when confronted with conflicting standards of conduct, whether there is good reason to affirm one and reject the others, is really to ask which, if any, is right. Perhaps Plato is not at all out of date when he describes moral philosophy as the inquiry into "how we ought to live." (*Republic*, 352, D.)

We are born total egoists, with the potential of maturing into or becoming beings who give as well as take. While philosophers are not involved in the practical process of making us into social beings, they are concerned with understanding what the relationship between the individual and society should be. What rights or benefits should we expect to receive from society and what duties or obligations do we owe to others? Perhaps each time we make a choice involving a value decision we are operating in terms of a fundamental ethical/moral dichotomy: Shall we strive primarily for our own benefit, or shall we give greater weight to the benefit of other people? The options for decisions would seem to lie between egoism and altruism (some would say between heaven and hell). The egoist in essence claims that the proper concern in life is to maximize one's own welfare no matter what happens to other people. The altruist's chief concern is to work for the good of others. In this final analysis, each of us must decide where we choose to stand between egoism and altruism, hell and heaven. Our choices should not be made lightly.

A. THE UTILITARIAN VIEW

Jeremy Bentham: *An Introduction to the Principles of Morals and Legislation*

John Stuart Mill: *Utilitarianism*

Jeremy Bentham (1748–1832) was born in London and was graduated from Queen's College, Oxford, in 1763. Bentham founded the philosophy known as Utilitarianism. He thought that men should judge ideas, institutions, and actions on the basis of their utility (usefulness). Bentham's criticisms brought about many needed reforms.

John Stuart Mlll (1806–1873) became the leader of the utilitarian movement. Mill was born in London and was educated completely by his father. He entered the East India Company as a clerk at 17, became director of the company, retired after 33 years of service and was elected to Parliament in 1865. Mill's efforts to formulate the principles of scientific method are merely of historical interest, but his views in ethics and politics are stll relevant to contemporary concerns.

CHAPTER I OF THE PRINCIPLE OF UTILITY (Bentham)

I

Nature has placed mankind under the governance of two sovereign masters, *pain* and *pleasure*. It is for them alone to point out what we ought to do, as well as to determine what we shall do. On the one hand, the standard of right and wrong, on the other, the chain of causes and effects, are fastened to their throne. They govern us in all we do, in all we say, in all we think: every effort we can make to throw off our subjection, will serve but to demonstrate and confirm it. In words, a man may pretend to abjure their empire: but, in reality, he will remain subject to it all the while. The *principle of utility* recognizes this subjection, and assumes it for the foundation of that system, the object of which is to tear the fabric of felicity by the hands of reason and of law. Systems which attempt to question it, deal in sounds instead of sense, in caprice instead of reason, in darkness instead of light.

But enough of metaphor and declamation: it is not by such means that moral science is to be improved.

II

The principle of utility is the foundation of the present work: it will be proper, therefore, at the outset to give an explicit and determinate account of what is meant by it. By the principle of utility is meant that principle which approves or disapproves of every action whatsoever, according to the tendency which it appears to have to augment or diminish the happiness of the party whose interest is in question: or, what is the same thing in other words, to promote or to oppose that happiness. I say of every action whatsoever; and, therefore, not only of every action of a private individual, but of every measure of government.

III

By utility is meant that property in any object, whereby it tends to produce benefit, advantage, pleasure, good, or happiness (all this in the present case comes to the same thing), or (what comes again to the same thing) to prevent the happening of mischief, pain, evil, or unhappiness to the part whose interest is considered: if that party be the community in general, then the happiness of the community: if a particular individual, then the happiness of that individual.

IV

The interest of the community is one of the most general expressions that can occur in the phraseology of morals: no wonder that the meaning of it is often lost. When it has a meaning, it is this. The community is a fictitious *body*, composed of the individual persons who are considered as constituting, as it were, its *members*. The interest of the community then is, what?—the sum of the interests of the several members who compose it.

V

It is in vain to talk of the interest of the community, without understanding what is the interest of the individual. A thing is said to promote the interest, or to be *for* the interest, of an individual, when it tends to add to the sum total of his pleasures: or, what comes to the same thing, to diminish the sum total of his pains.

VI

An action, then, may be said to be conformable to the principle of utility, or, for shortness' sake, to utility (meaning with respect to the community at large), when the tendency it has to augment the happiness of the community is greater than any which it has to diminish it.

VII

A measure of government (which is but a particular kind of action, performed by a particular person or persons) may be said to be conformable to or dictated by the principle of utility, when in like manner the tendency which it has to augment the happiness of the community is greater than any which it has to diminish it.

* * *

X

Of an action that is conformable to the principle of utility, one may always say either that it is one that ought to be done, or at least that it is not one that ought not to be done. One may say also, that it is right it should be done; at least that it is not wrong it should be done: that it is a right action; at least that it is not a wrong action. When thus interpreted, the words *ought*, and *right* and *wrong*, and others of that stamp, have a meaning: when otherwise, they have none.

XI

Has the rectidude of this principle been ever formally contested? It should seem that it had, by those who have not known what they have been meaning. Is it susceptible of any direct proof? It should seem not: for that which is used to prove everything else, cannot itself be proved: a chain of proofs must have their commencement somewhere. To give such proof is as impossible as it is needless.

XII

Not that there is or ever has been that human creature breathing, however stupid or perverse, who has not on many, perhaps on most occasions of his life, deferred to it. By the natural constitution of the human frame, on most occasions of their lives men in general embrace this principle, without thinking of it: if not for the ordering of their own actions, yet for the trying of their own actions, as well as of those of other men. There have been, at the same time, not many, perhaps, even of the most intelligent, who have been disposed to embrace it purely and without reserve. There are even few who have not taken some occasion or other to quarrel with it, either on account of their not understanding always how to apply it, or on account of some prejudice or other which they were afraid to examine into, or could not bear to part with. For such is the stuff that man is made of: in principle and in practice, in a right track and in a wrong one, the rarest of all human qualities is consistency.

XIII

When a man attempts to combat the principle of utility, it is with reasons drawn, without his being aware of it, from that very principle itself. His arguments, if they prove anything, prove not that the principle is *wrong*, but that, according to the applications he supposes to be made of it, it is *misapplied*. Is it possible for a man to move the earth? Yes, but he must first find out another earth to stand upon.

XIV

To disprove the propriety of it by arguments is impossible; but, from the causes that have been mentioned, or from some confused or partial view of it, a man may happen to be disposed not to relish it. Where this is the case, if he thinks the settling of his opinions on such a subject worth the trouble, let him take the following steps, and at length, perhaps, he may come to reconcile himself it it.

1. Let him settle with himself, whether he would wish to discard this principle altogether; if so, let him consider what it is that all his reasonings (in matters of politics especially) can amount to?

2. If he would, let him settle with himself, whether he would judge and act without any principle, or whether there is any other he would judge and act by?

3. If there be, let him examine and satisfy himself whether the principle he thinks he has found is really any separate intelligible principle; or wheher it be not a mere principle in words, a kind of phrase, which at bottom expresses neither more nor less than the mere averment of his own unfounded sentiments; that is, what in another person he might be apt to call caprice?

4. If he is inclined to think that his own approbation or disapprobation, annexed to the idea of an act, without any regard to its consequences, is a sufficient foundation for him to judge and act upon, let him ask himself whether his sentiment is to be a standard of right and wrong, with respect to every other man, or whether every man's sentiment has the same privilege of being a standard to itself?

5. In the first case, let him ask himself whether his principle is not despotical, and hostile to all the rest of the human race?

6. In the second case, whether it is not anarchical, and whether at this rate there are not as many different standards of right and wrong as there are men? and whether even to the same man, the same thing, which is right today, may not (without the least change in its nature) be wrong tomorrow? and whether the same thing is not right and wrong in the same place at the same time? and in either case, whether all argument is not at an end? and whether, when two men have said, "I like this," and "I don't like it," they can (upon such a principle) have anything more to say?

7. If he should have said to himself, No: for that the sentiment which he proposes as a standard must be grounded on reflection, let him say on what particulars the reflection is to turn? If on particulars having relation to the utility of the act, then let him say whether this is not deserting his own principle, and borrowing assistance from that very one in opposition to which he sets it up: or if not on those particulars, on what other particulars?

8. If he should be for compounding the matter, and adopting his own principle in part, and the principle of utility in part, let him say how far he will adopt it?

9. When he has settled with himself where he will stop, then let him ask himself how he justifies to himself the adopting it so far? and why he will not adopt it any farther?

10. Admitting any other principle than the principle of utility to be a right principle, a principle that it is right for a man to pursue; admitting (what is not true) that the word *right* can have a meaning without reference to utility, let him say whether there is any such thing as a *motive* that a man

can have to pursue the dictates of it: if there is, let him say what the motive is, and how it is to be distinguished from those which enforce the dictates of utility: if not, then lastly let him say what it is this other principle can be good for?

CHAPTER III OF THE FOUR SANCTIONS
OR SOURCES OF PAIN AND PLEASURE

I

It has been shown that the happiness of the individuals, of whom a community is composed, that is, their pleasures and their security, is the end and the sole end which the legislator ought to have in view: the sole standard in conformity to which each individual ought, as far as depends upon the legislator, to be *made* to fashion his behavior. But whether it be this or anything else that is to be *done*, there is nothing by which a man can ultimately be *made* to do it, but either pain or pleasure. Having taken a general view of these two grand objects (*viz.*, pleasure, and what comes to the same thing—immunity from pain) in the character of *final* causes; it will be necessary to take a view of pleasure and pain itself, in the character of *efficient* causes or means.

II

There are four distinguishable sources from which pleasure and pain are in use to flow: considered separately, they may be termed the *physical*, the *poltical*, the *moral*, and the *religious*; and inasmuch as the pleasures and pains belonging to each of them are capable of giving a binding force to any law or rule of conduct, they may all of them be termed *sanctions*.

III

If it be in the present life, and from the ordinary course of nature, not purposely modified by the interposition of the will of any human being, nor by any extraordinary interposition of any superior invisible being, that the pleasure or the pain takes place or is expected, it may be said to issue from, or to belong to, the *physical sanction*.

IV

If at the hands of a *particular* person or set of persons in the community, who under names correspondent to that of *judge*, are chosen for the particular purpose of dispensing it, according to the will of the sovereign or supreme ruling power in the state, it may be said to issue from the *political sanction*.

V

If at the hands of such *chance* persons in the community, as the party in question may happen in the course of his life to have concerns with, according to each man's spontaneous disposition, and not according to any settled or concerted rule, it may be said to issue from the *moral* or *popular sanction*.

VI

If from the immediate hand of a superior invisible being, either in the present life, or in a future, it may be said to issue from the *religious sanction*.

VII

Pleasures or pains which may be expected to issue from the *physical, political, or moral* sanctions, must all of them be expected to be experienced, if ever, in the *present* life: those which may be expected to issue from the *religious* sanction, may be expected to be experienced either in the *present* life or in a *future*.

* * *

IX

A man's goods, or his person, are consumed by fire. If this happened to him by what is called an accident, it was a calamity: if by reason of his own imprudence (for instance, from his neglecting to put his candle out), it may be styled a punishment of the physical sanction: if it happened to him by the sentence of the political magistrate, a punishment belonging to the political sanction—that is, what is commonly called a punishment: if for want of any assistance which his *neighbor* withheld from h im out of some dislike to his *moral* character, a punishment of the *moral* sanction: if by an immediate act of *God's* displeasure, manifested on account of some *sin* committed by him, or through any distraction of mind, occasioned by the dread of such displeasure, a punishment of the *religious* sanction.

X

As to such of the pleasures and pains belonging to the religious sanction, as regard a future life, of what kind these may be, we cannot know. These lie not open to our observation. During the present life they are matter only of expectation: and, whether that expectation be derived from natural or revealed religion, the particular kind of pleasure or pain, if it be different from all those which lie open to our observation, is what we can have no idea of. The best ideas we can obtain of such pains and pleasures are altogether unliquidated in point of quality. In what other respects our ideas of them *may* be liquidated, will be considered in another place.

XI

Of these four sanctions, the physical is altogether, we may observe, the groundwork of the political and the moral: so is it also of the religious, in as far as the latter bears relation to the present life. It is included in each of those other three. This may operate in any case (that is, any of the pains or pleasures belonging to it may operate) independently of *them:* none of *them* can operate but by means of this. In a word, the powers of nature may operate of themselves; but neither the magistrate, nor men at large, *can* operate, n or is God in the case in question *supposed* to operate, but through the powers of nature.

* * *

CHAPTER IV   VALUE OF A LOT OF PLEASURE OR PAIN, HOW TO BE MEASURED.

I

Pleasures, then, and the avoidance of pains are the *ends* which the legislator has in view: it behooves him therefore to understand their *value.* Pleasures and pains are the *instruments* he has to work with: it behooves him therefore to understand their force, which is again, in another point of view, their value.

II

To a person considered *by himself*, the value of a pleasure or pain considered *by itself*, will be greater or less, according to the four following circumstances:

1. Its *intensity.*
2. Its *duration.*
3. Its *certainty* or *uncertainty.*
4. Its *propinquity* or *remoteness.*

III

These are the circumstances which are to be considered in estimating a pleasure or a pain considered each of them by itself. But when the value of any pleasure or pain is considered for the purpose of estimating the tendency of any *act* by which it is produced, there are two other circumstances to be taken into the account; these are:

5. Its *fecundity,* or the chance it has of being followed by sensations of the *same* kind: that is, pains, if it be a pleasure: pains, if it be a pain.

6. Its *purity,* or the chance it has of *not* being followed by sensations of the *opposite* kind: that is, pains if it be a pleasure: pleasures, if it be a pain.

These two last, however, are in strictness scarcely to be deemed properties of the pleasures or the pain itself; they are not, therefore, in strictness to be taken into the account of the value of that pleasure or that pain. They are in strictness to be deemed properties only of the act, or other event, by which such pleasure or pain has been produced; and accordingly are only to be taken into the account of the tendency of such act or such event.

IV

To a *number* of persons, with reference to each of whom the value of a pleasure or a pain is considered, it will be greater or less, according to seven circumstances: to wit, the six preceding ones; *viz.,*

1. Its *intensity.*
2. Its *duration.*
3. Its *certainty* or *uncertainty.*
4. Its *propinquity* or *remoteness.*
5. Its *fecundity.*
6. Its *purity.*

And one other: to wit:

7. Its *extent;* that is, the number of persons to whom it *extends;* or (in other words) who are affected by it.

V

To take an exact account, then, of the general tendency of any act, by which the interests of a community are affected, proceed as follows. Begin with any one person of those whose interests seem most immediately to be affected by it; and take an account:

1. Of the value of each distinguishable *pleasure* which appears to be produced by it in the *first* instance.

2. Of the value of each *pain* which appears to be produced by it in the *first* instance.

3. Of the value of each pleasure which appears to be produced by it *after* the first. This constitutes the *fecundity* of the first *pleasure* and the *impurity* of the first *pain.*

4. Of the value of each *pain* which appears to be produced by it after the first. This constitutes the *fecundity* of the first *pain*, and the *impurity* of the first pleasure.

5. Sum up all the values of all the *pleasures* on the one side, and those of all the pains on the other. The balance, if it be on the side of pleasure, will give the *good* tendency of the act upon the whole, with respect to the interests of that *individual* person; if on the side of pain, the *bad* tendency of it upon the whole.

6. Take an account of the *number* of persons whose interests appear to be concerned; and repeat the above process with respect to each. *Sum up* the numbers expressive of the degrees of *good* tendency, which the act has, with

respect to each individual, in regard to whom the tendency of it is *good* upon the whole: do this again with respect to each individual, in regard to whom the tendency of it is *bad* upon the whole. Take the *balance;* which, if on the side of *pleasure,* will give the general *good tendency* of the act, with respect to the total number or community of individuals concerned; if on the side of pain, the general *evil tendency,* with respect to the same community.

VI

It is not to be expected that the process should be strictly pursued previously to every moral judgment, or to every legislative or judicial operation. It may, however, be always kept in view: and as near as the process actually pursued on these occasions approaches to it, so near will such process approach to the charcter of an exact one.

UTILITARIANISM (Mill)

It is quite compatible with the principle of utility to recognise the fact, that some *kinds* of pleasure are more desirable and more valuable than others. It would be absurd that while, in estimating all other things, quality is considered as well as quantity, the estimation of pleasures should be supposed to depend on quantity alone.

If I am asked, what I mean by difference of quality in pleasures, or what makes one pleasure more valuable than another, merely as a pleasure, except its being greater in amount, there is but one possible answer. Of two pleasures, if there be one to which all or almost all who have experience of both give a decided preference, irrespective of any feeling of moral obligation to prefer it, that is the more desirable pleasure. If one of the two is, by those who are competently acquainted with both, placed so far above the other that they prefer it, even though knowing it to be attended with a greater amount of discontent, and would not resign it for any quantity of the other pleasure which their nature is capable of, we are justified in ascribing to the preferred enjoyment a superiority in quality, so far outweighing quantity as to render it, in comparison, of small account.

Now it is an unquestionable fact that those who are equally acquainted with, and equally capable of appreciating and enjoying, both, do give a most marked preference to the manner of existence which employs their higher faculties. Few human creatures would consent to be changed into any of the lower animals, for a promise of the fullest allowance of a beast's pleasures; no intelligent human being would consent to be a fool, no instructed person would be an ignoramus, no person of feeling and conscience would be selfish and base, even though they should be persuaded that the fool, the dunce, or the rascal is better satisfied with his lot than they are with theirs. They would not resign what they possess more than he for the most complete satisfaction of all the desires which they have in common with him. If they ever fancy they would, it is only in cases of unhappiness so extreme, that to escape from it they would exchange their lot for almost any other, however undesirable in their own eyes. A being of higher faculties requires more to make him happy, is capable probably of more acute suffering, and certainly accessible to it at more points, than one of an inferior type; but in spite of these liabilities, he can never really wish to sink into what he feels to be a lower grade of existence.

* * *

. . . It is indisputable that the being whose capacities of enjoyment are low, has the greatest chance of having them fully satisifed; and a highly endowed being will always feel that any happiness which he can look for, as the world is constituted, is imperfect. But he can learn to bear its imperfections, if they are at all bearable; and they will not make him envy the being who is indeed unconscious of the imperfections, but only because he feels not at all the good which those imperfections qualify. It is better to be a human being dissatisfied than a pig satisfied; better to be Socrates dissatisfied than a fool satisfied. And if the fool, or the pig, are of a different opinion, it is because they only know their own side of the question. The other party to the comparison knows both sides.

Discussion Questions

1. According to Bentham, what are the "two sovereign masters" that point out what we should and shall do? Do you agree? Why or why not?

2. Restate, in your own words, the principle of utility. How important is this principle to Bentham's ethics?

3. Does Bentham distinguish clearly between pleasure and goodness?

4. Is it Bentham's opinion that people do, in fact, live by the principle of utility? Can the validity of this principle be proven, according to Bentham?

5. Bentham's "hedonic calculus," or measurement of pleasures and pains, is proposed as our criterion in deciding how we should act. Do you think it is adequate? Why or why not?

6. In what way does Mill modify Bentham's principle of utility? Can he do that and remain a consistent utilitarian?

B. AGAINST CONVENTIONAL MORALITY

Friedrich Nietzsche: *Beyond Good and Evil*

Friedrich Wilhelm Nietzsche (1844–1900) was one of the most controversial philosophers of modern times. Born in Prussia, the son of a Lutheran minister, he became at 24 years of age professor of classics at the University of Basel in Switzerland. There he became a close friend of the composer Richard Wagner, although this friendship ended in hostility. Nietzsche taught at the university for only 10 years and then retired because of poor health. He then devoted his time and energy to his writing. In 1889 Nietzsche suffered a mental breakdown from which he never recovered.

Nietzsche is considered one of the greatest German stylists, along with Luther and Goethe. He was also an admirer of classical Greek civilization. His first book, *The Birth of Tragedy* (1872), proclaimed a revolutionary theory about the nature of Greek tragedy.

Nietzsche was critical of religion. In *Thus Spake Zarathustra* (1883-1885) he claimed "God is dead." He meant that religion had lost its meaningfulness and power over people, and could no longer serve as the foundation for moral values.

PART NINE

Every enhancement of the type "man" has so far been the work of an aristocratic society—and it will be so again and again—a society that believes in the long ladder of an order of rank and differences in value between man and man, and that needs slavery in some sense or other. Without that *pathos of distance* which grows out of the ingrained difference between strata—when the ruling caste constantly looks afar and looks down upon subjects and instruments and just as constantly practices obedience and command, keeping down and keeping at a distance—that other, more mysterious pathos could not have grown up either—the craving for an ever new widening of distances within the soul itself, the development of ever higher, rarer, more remote, further-stretching, more comprehensive states—in brief, simply the enhancement of the type "man," the continual "self-overcoming of man," to use a moral formula in a supra-moral sense.

To be sure, one should not yield to humanitarian illusions about the origins of an aristocractic society (and thus of the presupposition of this enhancement of the type "man"): truth is hard. Let us admit to ourselves, without trying to be considerate, how every higher culture on earth so far has *begun*. Human beings whose nature was still natural, barbarians in every terrible sense of the word, men of prey who were still in possession of unbroken strength of will and lust for power, hurled themselves upon weaker, more civilized, more peaceful races, . . .

Corruption as the expression of a threatening anarchy among the instincts and of the fact that the foundation of the affects, which is called "life," has been shaken: corruption is something totally different depending on the organism in which it appears. When, for example, an aristocracy, like that of France at the beginning of the Revolution, throws away its privileges with a sublime disgust and sacrifices itself to an extravagance of its own moral feelings, that is corruption; it was really only the last act of that centuries-old corruption which had led them to surrender, step by step, their governmental prerogatives, demoting themselves to a mere *function* of the monarchy (finally even to a mere ornament and showpiece). The essential characteristic of a good and healthy aristocracy, however, is that it experiences itself *not* as a function (whether of the monarchy or the commonwealth) but as their *meaning* and highest justification—that it therefore accepts with a good conscience the sacrifice of untold human beings who, *for its sake,* must be reduced and lowered to incomplete human beings, to slaves, to instruments. Their fundamental faith simply has to be that society must *not* exist for society's sake but only as the foundation and scaffolding on which a choice type of being is able to raise itself to its higher task and to a higher state of *being* . . .

Refraining mutually from injury, violence, and exploitation and placing one's will on a par with that of someone else—this may become, in a certain rough sense, good manners among individuals if the appropriate conditions are present (namely, if these men are actually similar in strength and value standards and belong together in *one* body). But as soon as this principle is extended, and possibly even accepted as the *fundamental principle of society,* it immediately proves to be what it really is—a will to the *denial* of life, a principle of disintegration and decay.

Here we must beware of superficiality and get to the bottom of the matter, resisting all sentimental weakness: life itself is *essentially* appropriation, injury, overpowering of what is alien and weaker; suppression, hardness, imposition of one's own forms, incorporation and at least, at its mildest, exploitation—but why should one always use those words in which a slanderous intent has been imprinted for ages?

Even the body within which individuals treat each other as equals, as suggested before—and this happens in every healthy aristocracy—if it is a living and not a dying body, has to do to other bodies what the individuals within it refrain from doing to each other: it will have to be an incarnate will to power, it will strive to grow, spread, seize, become predominant—not from any morality or immorality but because it is *living* and because life simply *is* will to power. But there is no point on which the ordinary consciousness of Europeans resists instruction as on this: everywhere people are now raving, even under scientific disguises, about coming conditions of society in which "the exploitative aspect" will be removed—which sounds to me as if they promised to invent a way of life that would dispense with all organic functions. "Exploitation" does not belong to a corrupt or imperfect and primitive society: it belongs to the *essence* of what lives, as a basic organic function; it is a consequence of the will to power, which is after all the will of life.

If this should be an innovation as a theory—as a reality it is the *primordial fact* of all history; people ought to be honest with themselves at least that far.

Wandering through the many subtler and coarser moralities which have so far been prevalent on earth, or still are prevalent, I found that certain features recurred regularly together and were closely associated—until I finally discovered two basic types and one basic difference.

There are *master morality* and *slave morality*—I add immediately that in all the higher and more mixed cultures there also appear attempts at mediation between these two moralities, and yet more often the interpenetration and mutual misunderstanding of both, and at times they occur directly alongside each other—even in the same human being, within a *single* soul. The moral discrimination of values has originated either among a ruling group whose consciousness of its difference from the ruled group was accompanied by delight—or among the ruled, the slaves and dependents of every degree.

In the first case, when the ruling group determines what is "good," the exalted, proud states of the soul are experienced as conferring distinction and determining the order of rank. The noble human being separates from himself those in whom the opposite of such exalted, proud states finds expression: he despises them. It should be noted immediately that in this first type of morality the opposition of "good" and "*bad*" means approximately the same as "noble" and "contemptible." (The opposition of "good" and "*evil*" has a different origin.) One feels contempt for the cowardly, the anxious, the petty, those intent on narrow utility; also for the suspicious with their unfree glances, those who humble themselves, the doglike people who allow themselves to be maltreated, the begging flatterers, above all the liars: it is part of the fundamental faith of all aristocrats that the common people lie. "We truthful ones"—thus the nobility of ancient Greece referred to itself.

It is obvious that moral designations were everywhere first applied to *human beings* and only later, derivatively, to actions. Therefore it is a gross mistake when historians of morality start from such questions as: why was the compassionate act praised? The noble type of man experiences *itself* as determining values; it does not need approval; it judges, "what is harmful to me is harmful in itself"; it knows itself to be that which first accords honor to things; it is *value-creating*. Everything it knows as part of itself it honors: such a morality is self-glorification. In the foreground there is the feeling of fullness, of power that seeks to overflow, the happiness of high tension, the consciousness of wealth that would give and bestow: the noble human being, too, helps the unfortunate, but not, or almost not, from pity, but prompted more by an urge begotten by excess of power. The noble human being honors himself as one who is powerful, also as one who has power over himself, who knows how to speak and be silent, who delights in being severe and hard with himself and respects all severity and hardness.

* * *

A morality of the ruling group, however, is most alien and embarrassing to the present taste in the severity of its principle that one has duties only to one's peers; that against beings of a lower rank, against everything alien, one may behave as one pleases or "as the heart desires," and in any case "beyond good and evil"—here pity and like feelings may find their place. The capacity for, and the duty of, long gratitude and long revenge—both only among one's peers—refinement in repaying, the sophisticated concept of friendship, a certain necessity for having enemies (as it were, as drainage ditches for the affects of envy, quarrelsomeness, exuberance—at bottom, in order to be capable of being good *friends*): all these are typical characteristics of noble morality which, as suggested, is not the morality of "modern ideas" and therefore is hard to empathize with today, also hard to dig up and uncover.

It is different with the second type of morality, *slave morality*. Suppose the violated, oppressed, suffering, unfree, who are uncertain of themselves and weary, moralize: what will their moral valuations have in common? Probably, a pessimistic suspicion about the whole condition of man will find expression, perhaps a condemnation of man along with his condition. The slave's eye is not favorable to the virtues of the powerful: he is skeptical and suspicious, *subtly* suspicious, of all the "good" that is honored there—he would like to persuade himself that even their happiness is not genuine. Conversely, those qualities are brought out and flooded with light which serve to ease existence for those who suffer: here pity, the complaisant and obliging hand, the warm heart, patience, industry, humility, and friendliness are honored—for here these are the most useful qualities and almost the only means for enduring the pressure of existence. Slave morality is essentially a morality of utility.

Here is the place for the origin of that famous opposition of "good" and "evil": into evil one's feelings project power and dangerousness, a certain terribleness, subtlety, and strength that does not permit contempt to develop. According to slave morality, those who are "evil" thus inspire fear; according to master morality it is precisely those who are "good" that inspire, and wish to inspire, fear, while the "bad" are felt to be contemptible.

The opposition reaches its climax when, as a logical consequence of slave morality, a touch of disdain is associated also with the "good" of this morality—this may be slight and benevolent—because the good human being has to be *undangerous* in the slaves' way of thinking: he is good-natured, easy to deceive, a little stupid perhaps, *un bonhomme*. Wherever slave morality becomes preponderant, language tends to bring the words "good" and "stupid" closer together.

One last fundamental difference: the longing for *freedom*, the instinct for happiness and the subtleties of the feeling of freedom belong just as necessarily to slave morality and morals as artful and enthusiastic reverence and devotion are the regular symptom of an aristocratic way of thinking and evaluating.

* * *

Discussion Questions

1. What kind of society has promoted every "enhancement of the type 'man'"? How does Nietzche characterize this society?

2. In Nietzsche's aristocratic ideal, it is appropriate to use other human beings as a means to an end. When?

3. How does Nietzsche define life? Do you agree? Why or why not?

4. What does Nietzsche appear to mean by the term "will to power"?

5. What are Nietzsche's two basic types of morality? What are the chief differences between the two?

6. Can you think of any governmental systems in the twentieth century which might have been influenced by Nietzschean thought?

7. Are you persuaded by Nietzsche's ideas? Why or why not?

C. A PRINCIPLED VIEW

Immanuel Kant:
Fundamental Principles of the Metaphysics of Morals

Immanuel Kant (1724–1804), the German philosopher, was another great builder of a systematic philosophy. In Kant's view, knowledge is confined to objects of possible experience, and the role of philosophy is to examine the limits of possible experience and judgment. The knowledge of these limits, however, provides us with a system of categories and principles with which we can either solve the problems raised by philosophers or show them to be impossible to solve. Kant's views in metaphysics are of mainly historical interest, but his ethical views are still important in current discussion.

FIRST SECTION
TRANSITION FROM THE COMMON RATIONAL KNOWLEDGE
OF MORALITY TO THE PHILOSOPHICAL

Nothing can possibly be conceived in the world, or even out of it, which can be called good, without qualification, except a good will. Intelligence, wit, judgement, and the other *talents* of the mind, however they may be named, or courage, resolution, perseverance, as qualities of temperament, are undoubtedly good and desirable in many respects; but these gifts of nature may also become extremely bad and mischievous if the will which is to make use of them, and which, therefore, constitutes what is called *character*, is not good.

* * *

There are even some qualities which are of service to this good will itself and may facilitate its action, yet which have no intrinsic unconditional value, but always presuppose a good will, and this qualifies the esteem that we justly have for them and does not permit us to regard them as absolutely good. Moderation in the affections and passions, self-control, and calm deliberation are not only good in many respects, but even seem to constitute part of the intrinsic worth of the person; but they are far from deserving to be called good without qualification, although they have been so unconditionally praised by the ancients. For without the principles of a good will, they may become extremely bad, and the coolness of a villain not only makes him far more dangerous, but also directly makes him more abominable in our eyes than he would have been without it.

A good will is good not because of what it performs or effects, not by its aptness for the attainment of some proposed end, but simply by virtue of the volition; that is, it is good in itself, and considered by itself is to be esteemed much higher than all that can be brought about by it in favour of any inclination, nay even of the sum total of all inclinations. Even if it should happen that, owing to special disfavour of fortune, or the niggardly provision of a step-motherly nature, this will should wholly lack power to accomplish its purpose, if with its greatest efforts it should yet achieve nothing; and there should remain only the good will (not, to be sure, a mere wish, but the summoning of all means in our power), then, like a jewel, it would still shine by its own light, as a thing which has its whole value in itself. Its usefulness or fruitfulness can neither add nor take away anything from this value.

* * *

In the physical constitution of an organized being, that is, a being adapted suitably to the purposes of life, we assume it as a fundamental principle that no organ for any purpose will be found but what is also the fittest and best adapted for that purpose. Now in a being which has reason and a will, if the proper object of nature were its *conservation,* its *welfare,* in a word, its *happiness,* then nature would have hit upon a very bad arrangement in selecting the reason of the creature to carry out this purpose. For all the actions which the creature has to perform with a view to this purpose, and the whole rule of its conduct, would be far more surely prescribed to it by instinct, and that end would have been attained thereby much more certainly than it ever can be by reason.

* * *

. . . but there lies at the root of these judgements the idea that our existence has a different and far nobler end, for which, and not for happiness, reason is properly intended, and which must, therefore, be regarded as the supreme condition to which the private ends of man must, for the most part, be postponed.

For as reason is not competent to guide the will with certainty in regard to its objects and the satisfaction of all our wants (which it to some extent even multiplies), this being an end to which an implanted instinct would have led with much greater certainty; and since, nevertheless, reason is imparted to us as a practical faculty, i.e., as one which is to have influence on the *will,* therefore, admitting that nature generally in the distrubution of her capacities has adapted the means to the end, its true destination must be to produce a *will,* not merely good as a *means* to something else, but *good in itself,* for which reason was absolutely necessary. This will then, though not indeed the sole and complete good, must be the supreme good and the condition of every other, even of the desire of happiness. Under these circumstances, there is nothing inconsistent with the wisdom of nature in the fact that the cultivation of the reason, which is requisite for the first and unconditional purpose, does in many ways interfere, at least in this life, with the attainment of the second, which is always conditonal, namely, happiness. Nay, it may even reduce it to nothing, without nature thereby failing of her purpose. For reason recognizes the establishment of a good will as its highest practical destination. . . .

I omit here all actions which are already recognized as inconsistent with duty, although they may be useful for this or that purpose, for with these the question whether they are done *from duty* cannot arise at all, since they even conflict with it. I also set aside those actions which really conform to duty, but to which men have *no* direct *inclination,* performing them because they are impelled thereto by some other inclination. For in this case we can readily distinguish whether the action which agrees with duty is done *from duty,* or from a selfish view. It is much harder to make this distinction when the action accords with duty and the subject has besides a *direct* inclination to it. For example, it is always a matter of duty that a dealer should not overcharge an inexperienced purchaser; and wherever there is much commerce the prudent tradesman does not overcharge, but keeps a fixed price for everyone, so that a child buys of him as well as any other. Men are thus *honestly* served; but this is not enough to make us believe that the tradesman has so acted from duty and from principles of honesty: his own advantage required it; it is out of the question in this case to suppose that he might besides have a direct inclination in favour of the buyers, so that, as it were, from love he should give no advantage to one over another. Accordingly the action was done neither from duty nor from direct inclination, but merely with a selfish view.

On the other hand, it is a duty to maintain one's life; and, in addition, everyone has also a direct inclination to do so. But on this account the often anxious care which most men take for it has no intrinsic worth, and their maxim has no moral import. They preserve their life as *duty requires,* no doubt, but not *because duty requires.* On the other hand, if adversity and hopeless sorrow have completely taken away the relish for life; if the unfortunate one, strong in mind, indignant at his fate rather than desponding or dejected, wishes for death, and yet preserves his life without loving it—not from inclination or fear, but from duty—then his maxim has a moral worth.

To be beneficent when we can is a duty; and besides this, there are many minds so sympathetically constituted that, without any other motive of vanity or self-interest, they find a pleasure in spreading joy around them and can take delight in the satisfaction of others so far as it is their own work. But I maintain that in such a case an action of this kind, however proper, however amiable it may be, has nevertheless no true moral worth, but is on a level with other inclinations, e.g., the inclination to honour, which, if it is happily directed to that which is in fact of public utility and accordant with duty and consequently honourable, deserves praise and encouragement, but not esteem. For the maxim lacks the moral import, namely, that such actions be done *from duty,* not from inclination. Put the case that the mind of that philanthropist were clouded by sorrow of his own, extinguishing all sympathy with the lot of others, and that, while he still has the power to benefit others in distress, he is not touched by their trouble because he is absorbed with his own; and now suppose that he tears himself out of this dead insensibility, and performs the action without any inclination to it, but simply from duty, then first has his action its genuine moral worth. Further still; if nature has put little sympathy in the heart of this or that man; if he, supposed to be an upright man, is by temperament cold and indifferent to the sufferings of others, perhaps because in respect of his own he is provided with the special gift of patience and fortitude and supposes, or even requires, that others should have the same—and such a man would certainly not be the meanest product of nature—but if nature had not specially framed him for a philanthropist, would he not still find in himself a source from whence to give himself a far higher worth than that of a good-natured temperament could be? Unquestionably. It is just in this that the moral worth of the character is brought out which is incomparably the highest of all, namely, that he is beneficent, not from inclination, but from duty.

To secure one's own happiness is a duty, at least indirectly; for discontent with one's condition, under a pressure of many anxieties and amidst unsatisfied wants, might easily become a great *temptation to transgression of duty.* But here again, without looking to duty, all men have already the strongest and most intimate inclination to happiness, because it is just in this idea that all inclinations are combined in one total.

* * *

The second proposition is: That an action done from duty derives its moral worth, *not from the purpose* which is to be attained by it, but from the maxim by which it is determined, and therefore does not depend on the realization of the object of the action, but merely on the *principle of volition* by which the action has taken place, without regard to any object of desire. It is clear from what precedes that the purposes which we may have in view in our actions, or their effects regarded as ends and springs of the will, cannot give to actions any unconditional or moral worth. In what, then, can their worth lie, if it is not to consist in the will and in reference to its expected effect? It cannot lie anywhere but in the *principle of the will* without regard to the ends which can be attained by the action. For the will stands between its a *priori* principle, which is formal, and its a *posteriori* spring, which is material, as between two roads, and as it must be determined by something, it follows that it must be determined by the formal principle of volition when an action is done from duty, in which case every material principle has been withdrawn from it.

The third proposition, which is a consequence of the two preceding, I would express thus: *Duty is the necessity of acting from respect for the law.* I may have *inclination* for an object as the effect of my proposed action, but I cannot have *respect* for it, just for this reason, that it is an effect and not an energy of will. . . .

. . . Now an action done from duty must wholly exclude the influence of inclination and with it every object of the will, so that nothing remains which can determine the will except objectively the *law*, and subjectively *pure respect* for this practical law, and consequently the maxim that I should follow this law even to the thwarting of all my inclinations.

Thus the moral worth of an action does not lie in the effect expected from it, nor in any principle of action which requires to borrow its motive from this expected effect. For all these effects—agreeableness of one's condition and even the promotion of the happiness of others—could have been also brought about by other causes, so that for this there would have been no need of the will of a rational being; whereas it is in this alone that the supreme and unconditional good can be found. The pre-eminent good which we call moral can therefore consist in nothing else than *the conception of law* in itself, *which certainly is only possible in a rational being*, in so far as this conception, and not the expected effect, determines the will. This is a good which is already present in the person who acts accordingly, and we have not to wait for it to appear first in the result.

But what sort of law can that be, the conception of which must determine the will, even without paying any regard to the effect expected from it, in order that this will may be called good absolutely and without qualification? As I have deprived the will of every impulse which could arise to it from obedience to any law, there remains nothing but the universal conformity of its actions to law in general, which alone is to serve the will as a principle, i.e., I am never to act otherwise than *so that I could also will that my maxim should become a universal law.* Here, now, it is the simple conformity to law in general, without assuming any particular law applicable to certain actions, . . .

I do not, therefore, need any far-reaching penetration to discern what I have to do in order that my will may be morally good. Inexperienced in the course of the world, incapable of being prepared for all its contingencies, I only ask myself: Canst thou also will that thy maxim should be a universal law?

SECOND SECTION
TRANSITION FROM POPULAR MORAL PHILOSOPHY
TO THE METAPHYSIC OF MORALS

* * *

From what has been said, it is clear that all moral conceptions have their seat and origina completely *a priori* in the reason, and that, moreover, in the commonest reason just as truly as in that which is in the highest degree speculative; that they cannot be obtained by abstraction from any empirical, and therefore merely contingent, knowledge; that it is just this purity of their origin that makes them worthy to serve as our supreme practical principle, and that just in proportion as we add anything empirical, we detract from their genuine influence and from the absolute value of actions; that it is not only of the greatest necessity, in a purely speculative point of view, but is also of the greatest practical importance to derive these notions and laws from pure reason, to present them pure and unmixed, and even to determine the compass of this practical or pure rational knowledge, i.e., to determine the whole faculty of pure practical reason; and, in doing so, we must not make its principles dependent on the particular nature of human reason, though in speculative philosophy this may be permitted, or may even at times be necessary; but since moral laws ought to hold good for every rational creature, we must derive them from the general concept of a rational being.

Everything in nature works according to laws. Rational beings alone have the faculty of acting according *to the conception* of laws, that is according to principles, i.e., have a *will*. Since the deduction of actions from principles requires *reason*, the will is nothing but practical reason.

* * *

All imperatives are expressed by the word *ought* [or *shall*], and thereby indicate the relation of an objective law of reason to a will, which from its subjective constitution is not necessarily determined by it (an obligation). They say that something would be good to do or to forbear, but they say it to a will which does not always do a thing because it is conceived to be good to do it. That is practically *good*, however, wh ich determines the will by means of the conceptions of reason, and consequently not from subjective causes, but objectively, that is on principles which are valid for every rational being as such. It is distinguished from the *pleasant*, as that which influences the will only by means of sensation from merely subjective causes, valid only for the sense of this or that one, and not as a principle of reason, which holds for every one.

A perfectly good will would therefore be equally subject to objective laws (viz., laws of good), but could not be conceived as *obliged* thereby to act lawfully, because of itself from its subjective constitution it can only be determined by the conception of good. Therefore no imperatives hold for the Divine will, or in general for a *holy* will; *ought* is here out of place, because the volition is already of itself necessarily in unison with the law. Therefore imperatives are only formulae to express the relation of objective laws of all volition to the subjective imperfection of the will of this or that rational being, e.g., the human will.

Now all *imperatives* command either *hypothetically* or *categorically*. The former represent the practical necessity of a possible action as means to something else that is willed (or at least which one might possibly will). The categorical imperative would be that which represented an action as necessary of itself without reference to another end, i.e., as objectively necessary.

Since every practical law represents a possible action as good and, on this account, for a subject who is practically determinable by reason, necessary, all imperatives are formulae determining an action which is necessary according to the principle of a will good in some respects. If now the action is good only as a means *to something else*, then the imperative is *hypothetical;* if it is conceived as good *in itself* and consequently as being necessarily the principle of a will which of itself conforms to reason, then it is *categorical*.

* * *

The categorical imperative which declares an action to be objectively necessary in itself without reference to any purpose, i.e., without any other end, is valid as an *apodeictic* (practical) principle.

* * *

There is *one* end, however, which may be assumed to be actually such to all rational beings (so far as imperatives apply to them, viz., as dependent beings), and, therefore, one purpose which they not merely *may* have, but which we may with certainty assume that they all actually *have* by a natural necessity, and this is *happiness*. The hypothetical imperative which expresses the practical necessity of an action as means to the advancement of happiness is *assertorial*. We are not to present it as necessary for an uncertain and merely possible purpose, but for a purpose which we may presuppose with certainty and *a priori* in every man, because it belongs to his being. Now skill in the choice of means to his own greatest well-being may be called *prudence*, in the narrowest sense. And thus the imperative which refers to the choice of means to one's own happiness, i.e., the precept of prudence, is still always *hypothetical*; the action is not commanded absolutely, but only as means to another purpose.

Finally, there is an imperative which commands a certain conduct immediately, without having as its condition any other purpose to be attained by it. This imperative is *categorical*. It concerns not the matter of the action, or its intended result, but its form and the principle of which it is itself a result; and what is essentially good in it consists in the mental disposition, let the consequence be what it may. This imperative may be called that of *morality*.

* * *

There is therefore but one categorical imperative, namely, this: *Act only on that maxim whereby thou canst at the same time will that it should become a universal law.*

Now if all imperatives of duty can be deduced from this one imperative as from their principle, then, although it should remain undecided what is called *duty* is not merely a vain notion, yet at least we shall be able to show what we understand by it and what this notion means.

Since the universality of the law according to which effects are produced constitutes what is properly called *nature* in the most general sense (as to form), that is the existence of things so far as it is determined by general laws, the imperative of duty may be expressed thus: *Act as if the maxim of thy action were to become by thy will a universal law of nature.*

Now I say: man and generally any rational being *exists* as an end in himself, *not merely as a means* to be arbitrarily used by this or that will, but in all his actions, whether they concern himself or other rational beings, must be always regarded at the same time as an end. All objects of the inclinations have only a conditional worth, for if the inclinations and the wants founded on them did not exist, then their object would be without value. But the inclinations, themselves being sources of want, are so far from having an absolute worth for which they should be desired that on the contrary it must be the universal wish of every rational being to be wholly free from them. Thus the worth of any object which is *to be acquired* by our action is always conditional. Beings whose existence depends not on our will but on nature's, have nevertheless, if they are irrational beings, only a relative value as means, and are therefore called *things;* rational beings, on the contrary, are called *persons,* because their very nature points them out as ends in themselves, that is as something which must not be used merely as means, and so far therefore restricts freedom of action (and is an object of respect). These, therefore, are not merely subjective ends whose existence has a worth *for us* as an effect of our action, but *objective ends,* that is, things whose existence is an end in itself; an end moreover for which no other can be substituted, which they should subserve *merely* as means, for otherwise nothing whatever would possess *absolute worth;* but if all worth were conditioned and therefore contingent, then there would be no supreme practical principle of reason whatever.

* * *

This principle that humanity and generally every rational nature is *an end in itself* (which is the supreme limiting condition of every man's freedom of action), is not borrowed from experience, *first*, because it is universal, applying as it does to all rational beings whatever, and experience is not capable of determining anything about them; *secondly*, because it does not present humanity as an end to men (subjectively), that is, an object which men do of themselves actually adopt as an end; but as an objective end which must as a law constitute the supreme limiting condition of all our subjective ends, let them be what we will; it must therefore spring from pure reason.

* * *

What then is it which justifies virtue or the morally good disposition, in making such lofty claims? It is nothing less than the privilege it secures to the rational being of participating in the giving of universal laws, by which it qualifies him to be a member of a possible kingdom of ends, a privilege to which he was already destined by his own nature as being an end in himself and, on that account, legislating in the kingdom of ends; free as regards all laws of physical nature, and obeying those only which he himself gives, and by which his maxims can belong to a system of universal law, to which at that same time he submits himself.

* * *

Discussion Questions

1. Kant emphasizes that a "good will" is the only thing good without further qualification. Is he persuasive? Why or why not?

2. What is reason's noble end, according to Kant?

3. Why does Kant maintain that only actions done "from duty" have moral worth? Do you agree with him? Why or why not?

4. Do you ever seem to have a conflict between what you believe you ought to do (duty) and what you want to do (inclination)? If yes, give some examples.

5. Kant argues that morality should not be based upon experience. Why does he argue in this way?

6. Kant states, "Everything in nature works according to laws. Rational beings alone have the faculty of acting according to the conception of laws—that is, according to principles, that is, have a will." Restate in your own words what Kant means. Do you agree with him?

7. How does Kant distinguish between a hypothetical and a categorical imperative? Give examples of each.

8. How does Kant distinguish between "persons" and "things"? Do you agree with him? Why or why not?

9. What are the essential differences between Kant's views and those of Bentham and Mill?

D. A SITUATIONAL VIEW

Joseph Fletcher: *Situation Ethics*

Joseph Fletcher (b. 1905) is an ordained minister of the Protestant Episcopal Church. He was professor of pastoral theology and Christian ethics of the Episcopal Theological School from 1944 to 1970 and visiting professor of medical ethics at the University of Virginia in 1970. Professor Fletcher is also well known as a lecturer and author.

Situation Ethics proclaims that moral systems are too shallow to provide continuous and ongoing answers. Fletcher's methodology presupposes individual responsibility, declaring that every person must decide for himself or herself what is good and right.

THREE APPROACHES

There are at bottom only three alternative routes or approaches to follow in making moral decisions. They are: (1) the legalistic; (2) the antinomian, the opposite extreme—i.e., a lawless or unprincipled approach; and (3) the situational. . . .

* * *

Approaches to Decision-Making

1. Legalism

With this approach one enters into every decision-making situation encumbered with a whole apparatus of prefabricated rules and regulations. Not just the spirit but the letter of the law reigns. Its principles, codified in rules, are not merely guidelines or maxims to illuminate the situation; they are *directives* to be followed. Solutions are preset, and you can "look them up" in a book—a Bible or a confessor's manual.

* * *

Legalism in the Christian tradition has taken two forms. In the Catholic line it has been a matter of legalistic *reason,* based on nature or natural law. These moralists have tended to adumbrate their ethical rules by applying human reason to the facts of nature, both human and subhuman, and to the lessons of historical experience. By this procedure they claim to have adduced universally agreed and therefore valid "natural" moral laws. Protestant moralists have followed the same adductive and deductive tactics.

They have taken Scripture and done with it what the Catholics do with nature. Their Scriptural moral law is, they argue, based on the words and sayings of the Law and the Prophets, the evangelists and apostles of the bible. It is a matter of legalistic *revelation*. One is rationalistic, the other biblicistic; one natural, the other Scriptural. But both are legalistic.

2. *Antinomianism*

Over against legalism, as a sort of polar opposite, we can put antinomianism. This is the approach with which one enters into the decision-making situation armed with no principles or maxims whatsoever, to say nothing of *rules*. In every "existential moment" or "unique" situation, it declares, one must rely upon the situation of itself, *there and then*, to provide its ethical solution.

* * *

While legalists are preoccupied with law and its stipulations, the Gnostics are so flatly opposed to law—even in principle—that their moral decisions are random, unpredictable, erratic, quite anomalous. Making moral decisions is a matter of spontaneity; it is literally unprincipled, purely *ad hoc* and casual. They follow no forecastable course from one situation to another. They are, exactly, anarchic—i.e., without a rule. They are not only "unbound by the chains of law" but actually sheer extemporizers, impromptu and intellectually irresponsible. They not only cast the old Torah aside; they even cease to think seriously and *care-fully* about the demands of love as it has been shown in Christ, the love norm itself. The baby goes out with the bath water!

* * *

3. *Situationism*

A third approach, in between legalism and antinomian unprincipledness, is situation ethics. (To jump from one polarity to the other would be only to go from the frying pan to the fire.) The situationist enters into every decision-making situation fully armed with the ethical maxims of his community and its heritage, and he treats them with respect as illuminators of his problems. Just the same he is prepared in any situation to compromise them or set them aside *in the situation* if love seems better served by doing so.

Situation ethics goes part of the way with natural law, by accepting reason as the instrument of moral judgment, while rejecting the notion that the good is "given" in the nature of things, objectively. It goes part of the way with Scriptural law by accepting revelation as the source of the norm while rejecting all "revealed" norms or laws but the one command—to love God in the neighbor. The situationist follows a moral law or violates it according to love's need. For example, "Almsgiving is a good thing *if* . . ." The situationist never says, "Almsgiving is a good thing. Period!" His decisions are hypothetical, not categorical. Only the commandement to love is categorically good.

William Temple put it this way: "Universal obligation attaches not to particular judgments of conscience but to conscientiousness. What acts are right may depend on circumstances . . . but there is an absolute obligation to will whatever may on each occasion be right." Our obligation is relative *to* the situation, but obligation *in* the situation is absolute. We are only "obliged" to tell the truth, for example, if the situation calls for it; if a murderer asks us his victim's whereabouts, our duty might be to lie. . . . We have to find out what is "fitting" to be truly ethical, to use H.R. Niebuhr's word for it in his *The Responsible Self*. Situation ethics aims at a contextual appropriateness—not the "good" or the "right" but the *fitting*.

* * *

One competent situationist, speaking to students, explained the position this way. Rules are "like 'Punt on fourth down,' or 'Take a pitch when the count is three balls.' These rules are part of the wise player's know-how, and distinguish him from the novice. But they are not unbreakable. The best players are those who know when to ignore them. In the game of bridge, for example, there is a useful rule which says 'Second hand low.' But have you ever played with anyone who followed the rule slavishly? You say to him (in exasperation), 'Partner, why didn't you play your ace? We could have set the hand.' And he replies, unperturbed, 'Second hand low!' What is wrong? The same thing that was wrong when Kant gave information to the murderer. He forgot the purpose of the game. . . . He no longer thought of winning the hand, but of being able to justify himself by invoking the rule."

* * *

The situational factors are so primary that we may even say "circumstances alter rules and principles." It is said that when Gertrude Stein lay dying she declared, "It is better to ask questions than to give answers, even good answers." This is the temper of situation ethics. It is empirical, fact-minded, data conscious, inquiring. . . .

* * *

As we shall see, *Christian* situation ethics has only one norm or principle or law (call it what you will) that is binding and unexceptionable, always good and right regardless of the circumstances. That is "love"—the *agapē* of the summary commandment to love God and the neighbor. Everything else without exception, all laws and rules and principles and ideals and norms, are only *contingent*, only valid *if they happen* to serve love in any situation. . . .

* * *

... Love is for people, not for principles; i.e., it is personal—and therefore when the impersonal universal conflicts with the personal particular, the latter prevails in situation ethics. . . .

* * *

SOME PRESUPPOSITIONS

* * *

Four Working Principles

1. *Pragmatism*

In the first place, this book is consciously inspired by American *pragmatism*. Forty years ago when the author became a theological student, he was a professed advocate of the Pierce-James-Dewey analysis of human knowledge. . . .

* * *

We must realize, however, that pragmatism, as such is no self-contained world view. It is a method, precisely. It is not a substantive faith, and properly represented it never pretends to be. Pragmatism of itself yields none of the norms we need to measure or verify the very success that pragmatism calls for! To be correct or right a thing—a thought or an action—must *work*. Yes. But work to what end, for what purpose, to satisfy what standard or ideal or norm? Like any other method, pragmatism as such is utterly without any way of answering this question. Yet this is the decisive question.

The very first question in all ethics is, *What* do I want? Only after this is settled (pleasure in hedonism, adjustment in naturalism, self-realization in eudaemonism, etc.) can we ask about the *why* and the *how* and the *who* and the *when* and the *where* and the *which!* The primary issue is the "value" problem, our choice of our *summum bonum*.

* * *

Christianly speaking, as we shall see, the norm or measure by which any thought or action is to be judged a success of failure, i.e., right or wrong, is *love*. . . .

* * *

2. *Relativism*

In our attempt to be situational, to be contemporary in our understanding of conscience, we can pin another label on our method. It is *relativistic*. . . . The situationist avoids words like "never" and "perfect" and "always" and "complete" as he avoids the plague, as he avoids "absolutely."

* * *

To be relative, of course, means to be relative *to* something. To be "absolutely relative" (an uneasy combination of terms) is to be inchoate, random, unpredictable, unjudgeable, meaningless, amoral—rather in the antinomian mode. There must be an absolute or norm of some kind if there is to be any true relativity. This is the central fact in the normative relativism of a situation ethic. It is not anarchic (i.e., without an *archē*, an ordering principle). In *Christian* situationism the ultimate criterion is, as we shall be seeing, "agapeic love." It relativizes the absolute, it does not absolutize the relative!

3. *Positivism*

The other approach is theological *positivism* (or "positive theology"), in which faith propositions are "posited" or affirmed voluntaristically rather than rationalistically. It is a-rational but not ir-rational, outside reason but not against it. Its starting point is like anselm's *Credo ut intelligam* in the *Proslogion* (first chapter); thinking supported by faith rather than faith supported by thinking. Although it does not exclude reason, reason goes to work because of the commitment and in its service. Thus Christian ethics "posits" faith in God and *reasons* out what obedience to his commandment to love requires in any situation. . . .

* * *

. . . Any moral or value judgment in ethics, like a theologian's faith proposition, is a *decision*—not a conclusion. It is a choice, not a result reached by force of logic, Q.E.D. The hedonist cannot "prove" that pleasure is the highest good, any more than the Christian can "prove" his faith that *love* is! . . .

* * *

4. *Personalism*

Ethics deals with human relations. Situation ethics puts people at the center of concern, not things. Obligation is to persons, not to things; to subjects, not objects. The legalist is a *what* asker (What does the law say?); the situationist is a *who* asker (Who is to be helped?). that is, situationists are *personalistic*. . . .

* * *

. . . Martin Buber's "dialogic" thesis about *I-Thou*—i.e., that true existence lies in personal relationships, not in *I-it* (relation to mere things)—has greatly influenced man theory in such theological work as Maritain's, Berdyaev's, and Tillich's. . . .

Kant's second maxim holds: Treat persons as ends, never as means. . . .

* * *

Speaking more timidly than a situationist would, but solidly on the point, Temple says: "It is doubtful if any act is right 'in itself.' Every act is a link in a chain of causes and effects. It cannot be said that it is wrong to take away a man's possessions against his will, for that would condemn all taxation—or the removal of a revolver from a homicidal maniac; neither of these is stealing—which is always wrong; though high authority has held that a starving man may steal a loaf rather than die of hunger, because life is of more value than property and should be chosen first for preservation if both cannot be preserved together. The rightness of an act, then, nearly always and perhaps always, depends on the way in which the act is related to circumstances; this is what is meant by calling it relatively right; . . ."

* * *

Bishop Pike tries to be a consistent situationist. He sets "existential" ethics over against "ontological" ethics in a very promising way. But it never really comes off! He says stoutly, "As St. Thomas Aquinas reminded us, a negative particular destroys an affirmative universal." He says this in pointing out that even in the Apocrypha, Judith is praised for lying to Holofernes and using her sex (though she remained a *technical* virgin, according to the canonical story) whoringly in order to murder him. Yet for all this sturdy ethical evaluation of Judith's situational action "to save Israel;" Pike ends with the opinion that a justifiable violation of a sound principle (e.g., homicide is wrong) is never *good*, however "right" situationally!

He cannot disentangle himself from the intrinsicalists' net. He *thinks* of right and wrong as real things, "ontologically," after all. He says, "What we have is not an exception to the rules which makes [the action] *good* or even neutral in character, but a balance of goods and evils and a resulting choice of the greater of two goods, the lesser of two evils (though . . . the choice may be, in the situation, *the right thing*)" (his italics). This is the talk of ontological or intrinsic ethics, not of existential or extrinsic ethics!

A common objection to situation ethics is that it calls for more critical intelligence, more factual information, and more self-starting commitment to righteousness than most people can bring to bear. We all know the army veteran who "wishes the war was back" because he could tell the good guys from the bad buys by the uniforms they wore. There are those who say situationism ignores the reality of human sin or egocentricity, and fails to appreciate the finitude of human reason.

* * *

This contextual, situational, clinical case method (or neocasuistry), this way of dealing with decision, is too full of variables to please some people. They like better to latch on to a few well-anchored constants, sanctioned in law, and ignore all the variables. That is law's way. But it is not love's way. . . .

* * *

Said Paul to the saints at Philippi: "And this I pray, that your love may abound yet more and more in knowledge and in all judgment." Here, in a few words, are the four pillars of the method of Christian ethics, in the order of the apostle's words: (1) a prayerful reliance upon God's grace; (2) the law of love as the norm; (3) knowledge of the facts, of the empirical situation in all its variety and relativity and particularity; and (4) judgment—i.e., decision—which is a matter of responsibility in humility.

This reference to humility, we might add, is no mere pretty moralism; it is the voice of grim realism. . . .

Discussion Questions

1. Do you agree with Fletcher's statement that there are at bottom only three alternative approaches to follow in making moral decisions? Why or why not?

2. Is Fletcher fair in his definitions of legalism? Why or why not?

3. What is Fletcher's understanding of how the major Western religions fit into his definitions? Do you agree?

4. What does Fletcher mean by the statement "only the commandment to love is categorically good"?

5. In what sense does Fletcher see himself as a pragmatist? In what sense is he not a pragmatist?

6. Do you agree with Fletcher that situation ethics puts people at the center of concern, not things? Why or why not?

7. Does Fletcher affirm that an act is right in itself? How does this question relate to the distinction between ontological or intrinsic ethics and existential or extrinsic ethics?

8. Are you persuaded by Fletcher's overall thesis of situation ethics? Why or why not?

E. A RELIGIOUS VIEW

C.S. Lewis: *Mere Christianity*

C.S. Lewis (1898–1963) was a British religious writer. He was Professor of Renaissance and Medieval Literature at Cambridge University from 1955 to 1963, and Fellow of Magdalen College, Oxford, from 1925 to 1954.

Originally trained as a philosopher at Oxford, Lewis combined literary scholarship and the writing of fiction with clear and persuasive argumentation for traditional Christianity. Lewis's religious works continue to be best sellers, and much of his writing is directly or indirectly of philosophical interest.

THE LAW OF HUMAN NATURE

Every one has heard people quarrelling. Sometimes it sounds funny and sometimes it sounds merely unpleasant; but however it sounds, I believe we can learn something very important from listening to the kinds of things they say. They say things like this: "How'd you like it if anyone did the same to you?"—"That's my seat, I was there first"—"Leave him alone, he isn't dong you any harm"—"Why should you shove in first?"—"Give me a bit of your orange, I gave you a bit of mine"—"Come on, you promised." People say things like that every day, educated people as well as uneducated, and children as well as grown-ups.

Now what interests me about all these remarks is that the man who makes them is not merely saying that the other man's behaviour does not happen to please him. He is appealing to some kind of standard of behaviour which he expects the other man to know about. And the other man very seldom replies: "To hell with your standard." Nearly always he tries to make out that what he has been doing does not really go against the standard, or that if it does there is some special excuse. . . .

* * *

Now this Law or Rule about Right and Wrong used to be called the Law of Nature. Nowadays, when we talk of the "laws of nature" we usually mean things like gravitation, or heredity, or the laws of chemistry. But when the older thinkers called the Law of Right and Wrong "the Law of Nature," they really meant the Law of *Human* Nature. The idea was that, just as all bodies are governed by the law of gravitation and organisms by biological laws, so the creature called man also had *his* law—with this great difference, that a body could not choose whether it obeyed the law of gravitation or not, but a man could choose either to obey the Law of Nature or to disobey it.

We may put this in another way. Each man is at every moment subjected to several sets of law but there is only one of these which he is free to disobey. As a body, he is subjected to gravitation and cannot disobey it; if you leave him unsupported in mid-air, he has no more choice about falling than a stone has. . . .

* * *

This law was called the Law of Nature because people thought that every one knew it by nature and did not need to be taught it. They did not mean, of course, that you might not find an odd individual here and there who did not know it, just as you find a few people who are colour-blind, or have no ear for a tune. But taking the race as a whole, they thought that the human idea of decent behaviour was obvious to every one. And I believe they were right. . . .

* * *

I know that some people say the idea of a Law of Nature or decent behaviour known to all men is unsound, because different civilisations and different ages have had quite different moralities.

But this is not true. There have been differences between their moralities, but these have never amounted to anything like a total difference. If anyone will take the trouble to compare the moral teaching of, say, the ancient Egyptians, Babylonians, Hindus, Chinese, Greeks and Romans, what will really strike him will be how very like they are to each other and to our own. Some of the evidence for this I have put together in the appendix of another book called *The Abolition of Man;* but for our present purpose I need only ask the reader to think what a totally different morality would mean. Think of a country where people were admired for running away in battle, or where a man felt proud of doublecrossing all the people who had been kindest to him. You might just as well try to imagine a country where two and two made five. Men have differed as regards what people you ought to be unselfish to—whether it was only your own family, or your fellow countrymen, or everyone. But they have always agreed that you ought not to put yourself first. Selfishness has never been admired. Men have differed as to whether you should have one wife or four. But they have always agreed that you must not simply have any woman you liked.

* * *

It seems, then, we are forced to believe in a real Right and Wrong. People may be sometimes mistaken about them, just as people sometimes get their sums wrong; but they are not a matter of mere taste and opinion any more than the mutliplication table. Now if we are agreed about that, I go on to my next point, which is this. None of us are really keeping the Law of Nature. If there are any exceptions among you, I apologize to them. . . .

* * *

If you take a thing like a stone or a tree, it is what it is and there seems no sense in saying it ought to have been otherwise. Of course you may say a stone is "the wrong shape" if you want to use it for a rockery, or that a tree is a bad tree because it does not give you as much shade as you expected. But all you mean is that the stone or tree does not happen to be convenient for some purpose of your own. You are not, except as a joke, blaming them for that. You really know, that, given the weather and the soil, the tree could not have been any different. What we, from our point of view, call a "bad" tree is obeying the laws of its nature just as much as a "good" one.

Now have you noticed what follows? It follows that what we usually call the laws of nature—the way weather works on a tree for example—may not really be *laws* in the strict sense, but only in a manner of speaking.

When you say that falling stones always obey the law of gravitation, is not this much the same as saying that the law only means "what stones always do"? You do not really think that when a stone is let go, it suddenly remembers that it is under orders to fall to the ground. You only mean that, in fact, it does fall. In other words, you cannot be sure that there is anything over and above the facts themselves, any law about what ought to happen, as distinct from what does happen.

* * *

But if you turn to the Law of Human Nature, the Law of Decent Behavior, it is a different matter. That law certainly does not mean "what human beings, in fact, do"; for as I said before, many of them do not obey this law at all, and none of them obey it completely. The law of gravity tells you what stones do if you drop them; but the Law of Human Nature tells you what human beings ought to do and do not. In other words, when you are dealing with humans, something else comes in above and beyond the actual facts. You have the facts (how men do behave) and you also have something else (how they ought to behave). In the rest of the universe there need not be anything but the facts.

* * *

. . . A man occupying the corner seat in the train because he got there first, and a man who slipped into it while my back was turned and removed my bag, are both equally inconvenient. But I blame the second man and do not blame the first. I am not angry—except perhaps for a moment before I come to my senses—with a man who trips me up by accident; I am angry with a man who tries to trip me up even if he does not succeed. Yet the first has hurt me and the second has not. . . .

* * *

. . . this Rule of Right and Wrong, or Law of Human Nature, or whatever you call it, must somehow or other be a real thing—a thing that is really there, not made up by ourselves. And yet it is not a fact in the ordinary sense, in the same way as our actual behaviour is a fact. It begins to look as if we shall have to admit that there is more than one kind of reality; that, in this particular case, there is something above and beyond the ordinary facts of men's behaviour, and yet quite definitely real—a real law, which none of us made, but which we find pressing on us.

* * *

THE THREE PARTS OF MORALITY

There is a story about a schoolboy who was asked what he thought God was like. He replied that, as far as he could make out, God was "The sort of person who is always snooping round to see if anyone is enjoying himself and then trying to stop it." And I am afraid that is the sort of idea that the word Morality raises in a good many people's minds: something that interferes, something that stops you having a good time. In reality, moral rules are directions for running the human machine.

* * *

. . . There are two ways in which the human machine goes wrong. One is when human individuals drift apart from one another, or else collide with one another and do one another damage, by cheating or bullying. The other is when things go wrong inside the individual—when the different parts of him (his different faculties and desires and so on) either drift apart or interfere with one another. You can get the idea plain if you think of us as a fleet of ships sailing in formation. The voyage will be a success only, in the first place, if the ships do not collide and get in one another's way; and, secondly, if each ship is seaworthy and has her engines in good order. As a matter of fact, you cannot have either of these two things without the other. If the ships keep on having collisions they will not remain seaworthy very long. On the other hand, if their steering gears are out of order they will not be able to avoid collisions. Or, if you like, think of humanity as a band playing a tune. To get a good result, you need two things. Each player's individual instrument must be in tune and also each must come in at the right moment so as to combine with all the others.

But there is one thing we have not yet taken into account. We have not asked where the fleet is trying to get to, or what piece of music the band is trying to play. The instruments might be all in tune and might all come in at the right moment, but even so the performance would not be a success if they had been engaged to provide dance music and actually played nothing but Dead Marches. And however well the fleet sailed, its voyage would be a failure if it were meant to reach New York and actually arrived at Calcutta.

Morality, then, seems to be concerned with three things. Firstly, with fair play and harmony between individuals. Secondly, with what might be called tidying up or harmonising the things inside each individual. Thirdly, with the general purpose of human life as a whole: what man was made for: what course the whole fleet ought to be on: what tune the conductor of the band wants it to play.

Discussion Questions

1. What method does Lewis use to begin his argument for the recognition of the Moral Law?

2. What does Lewis mean by the Moral Law? What other synonyms does he use for the same thing?

3. Do you think Lewis's view that there is a Moral Law is true or false? Why?

4. What does Lewis conclude about the difference between people and things as they relate to the Moral Law?

5. Lewis concludes that morality is concerned with three things. What are they? How persuasive is Lewis's analogy about sailing the sea of life?

COMMENT: Hermann Hesse
"Preface" from *Steppenwolf*

This book contains the records left us by a man whom, according to the expression he often used himself, we called the Steppenwolf. . . .

* * *

Some years ago the Steppenwolf, who was then approaching fifty, called on my aunt to inquire for a furnished room. He took the attic room on the top floor and the bedroom next to it, returned a day or two later with two trunks and a big case of books and stayed nine or ten months with us. He lived by himself very quietly, and but for the fact that our bedrooms were next door to each other—which occasioned a good many chance encounters on the stairs and in the passage—we should have remained practically unacquainted. For he was not a sociable man. Indeed, he was unsociable to a degree I had never before experienced in anybody. He was, in fact, as he called himself, a real wolf of the Steppes, a strange, wild, shy—very shy—being from another world than mine. How deep the loneliness into which his life had drifted on account of his disposition and destiny and how consciously he accepted this loneliness as his destiny, I certainly did not know until I read the records he left behind him. . . .

* * *

By chance I was there at the very moment when the Steppenwolf entered our house for the first time and became my aunt's lodger. He came at noon. The table had not been cleared and I still had half an hour before going back to the office. I have never forgotten the odd and very conflict-ing impressions he made on me at this first encounter. He came through the glazed door, having just rung the bell, and my aunt asked him in the dim light of the hall what he wanted. The Steppenwolf, however, first threw up his sharp, closely cropped head and sniffed around nervously before he either made any answer or announced his name.

"Oh, it smells good here," he said, and at that he smiled and my aunt smiled too. For my part, I found this matter of introducing himself ridiculous and was not favorably impressed.

"However," said he, "I've come about the room you have to let."

I did not get a good look at him until we were all three on our way up to the top floor. Though not very big, he had the bearing of a big man. He wore a fashionable and comfortable winter overcoat and he was well, though carelessly, dressed, clean-shaven, and his cropped head showed here and there a streak of grey. He carried himself in a way I did not at all like at first. There was something weary and undecided about it that did not go with his keen and striking profile nor with the tone of his voice. Later, I found out that his health was poor and that walking tired him. With a peculiar smile—at that time equally unpleasant to me—he contemplated the stairs, the walls, and windows, and the tall old cupboards on the staircase. All this seemed to please and at the same time to amuse him. Altogether he gave the impression of having come out of an alien world, from another continent perhaps. He found it all very charming and a little odd. I cannot deny that he was polite, even friendly. He agreed at once and without objection to the terms for lodging and breakfast and so forth, and yet about the whole man there was a foreign and, as I chose to think, disagreeable or hostile atmosphere. He took the room and the bedroom too, listened attentively and amiably to all he was told about the heating, the water, the service and the rules of the household, agreed to everything, offered at once to pay a sum in advance—and yet he seemed at the same time to be outside it all, to find it comic to be doing as he did and not to take it seriously. It was as though it were a very odd and new experience for him, occupied as he was with quite other concerns, to be renting a room and talking to people in German. . . .

* * *

I have already given some account of the Steppenwolf's outward appearance. He gave at the very first glance the impression of a significant, an uncommon, and unusually gifted man. His face was intellectual, and the abnormally delicate and mobile play of his features reflected a soul of extremely emotional and unusually delicate sensibility. When one spoke to him and he, as was not always the case, dropped conventionalities and said personal and individual things that came out of his own alien world, then a man like myself came under his spell on the spot. He had thought more than other men, and in matters of the intellect he had that calm objectivity, that certainty of thought and knowledge, such as only really intellectual men have, who have no axe to grind, who never wish to shine, or to talk others down, or to appear always in the right.

I remember an instance of this in the last days he was here, if I can call a mere fleeting glance he gave me an example of what I mean. It was when a celebrated historian, philosopher, and critic, a man of European fame, had announced a lecture in the school auditorium. I had succeeded in persuading the Steppenwolf to attend it, though at first he had little desire to do so. We went together and sat next to each other in the lecture hall. When the lecturer ascended the platform and began his address, many of his hearers, who had expected a sort of prophet, were disappointed by his rather dapper appearance and conceited air. And when he proceeded, by way of introduction, to say a few flattering things to the audience, thanking them for their attendance in such numbers, the Steppenwolf threw me a quick look, a look which criticized both the words and the speaker of them—an unforgettable and frightful look which spoke volumes! It was a look that did not simply criticize the lecturer, annihilating the famous man with its delicate but crushing irony. That was the least of it. It was more sad than ironical; it was indeed utterly and hopelessly sad; it conveyed a quiet despair, born partly of conviction, partly of a mode of thought which had become habitual with him. This despair of his not only unmasked the conceited lecturer and dismissed with its irony the matter at hand, the expectant attitude of the public, the somewhat presumptuous title under which the lecture was announced—no, the Steppenwolf's look pierced our whole epoch, its whole overwrought activity, the whole surge and strife, the whole vanity, the whole superficial play of a shallow, opinionated intellectuality. And alas! the look went still deeper, went far below the faults, defects and hopelessness of our time, our intellect, our culture alone. It went right to the heart of all humanity, it bespoke eloquently in a single second the whole despair of a thinker, of one who knew the full worth and meaning of man's life. . . .

* * *

It was soon obvious that his days were spent with his thoughts and his books, and that he pursued no practical calling. He lay always very late in bed. Often he was not up much before noon. . . .

* * *

He took me into his room, which smelt strongly of tobacco, and took out a book from one of the heaps, turned the leaves and looked for the passage.

"This is good too, very good," he said, "listen to this: 'A man should be proud of suffering. All suffering is a reminder of our high estate.' Fine! Eighty years before Nietzsche. But that is not the sentence I meant. Wait a moment, here I have it. This: 'Most men will not swim before they are able to.' Is not that witty? Naturally, they won't swim! They are born for the solid earth, not for the water. And naturally they won't think. They are made for life, not for thought. Yes, and he who thinks, what's more, he who makes thought his business, he may go far in it, but he has bartered the solid earth for the water all the same, and one day he will drown."

He had got hold of me now. I was interested; and I stayed on a short while with him; and after that we often talked when we met on the stairs or in the street. On such occasions I always had at first the feeling that he was being ironical with me. But it was not so. He had a real respect for me, . . . He was so convinced and conscious of his isolation, his swimming in the water, his uprootedness, that a glimpse now and then of the orderly daily round—the punctuality, for example, that kept me to my office hours, or an expression let fall by a servant or tramway conductor—acted on him literally as a stimulus without in the least arousing his scorn. At first all this seemed to me a ridiculous exaggeration, the affectation of a gentleman of leisure, a playful sentimentality. But I came to see more and more that from the empty spaces of his lone wolfishness he actually really admired and loved our little bourgeois world as something solid and secure, as the home and peace which must ever remain far and unattainable, with no road leading from him to them. He took off his hat to our charwoman, a worthy person, every time he met her, with geniune respect; . . .

* * *

. . . A wolf of the Steppes that had lost its way and strayed into the towns and the life of the herd, a more striking image could not be found for his shy loneliness, his savagery, his restlessness, his homesickness, his homelessness.

And now that we come to these records of Haller's, these partly diseased, partly beautiful, and thoughtful fantasies, I must confess that if they had fallen into my hands by chance and if I had not known their author, I should most certainly have thrown them away in disgust. But owing to my acquaintance with Haller I have been able, to some extent, to understand them, and even to appreciate them. I should hesitate to share them with others if I saw in them nothing but the pathological fancies of a single and isolated case of a diseased temperament. But I see something more in them. I see them as a document of the times, for Haller's sickness of the soul, as I now know, is not the eccentricity of a single individual, but the sickness of the times themselves, the neurosis of that generation to which Haller belongs, a sickness, it seems, that by no means attacks the weak and worthless only but, rather, precisely those who are strongest in spirit and richest in gifts.

These records, however much or however little of real life may lie at the back of them, are not an attempt to disguise or to palliate this wide-spread sickness of our times. They are an attempt to present the sickness itself in its actual manifestation. They mean, literally, a journey through hell, a sometimes fearful, sometimes courageous journey through the chaos of a world whose souls dwell in darkness, a journey undertaken with the determination to go through hell from one end to the other, to give battle to chaos, and to suffer torture to the full.

A remark of Haller's gave me the key to this interpretation. He said to me once when we were talking of the so-called horrors of the Middle Ages: "These horrors were really nonexistent. A man of the Middle Ages would detest the whole mode of our present-day life as something far more than horrible, far more than barbarous. Every age, every culture, every custom and tradition has its own character, its own weakness and its own strength, its beauties and ugliness; accepts certain sufferings as matters of course, puts up patiently with certain evils. Human life is reduced to real suffering, to hell, only when two ages, two cultures and religions overlap. A man of the Classical Age who had to live in medieval times would suffocate miserably just as a savage does in the midst of our civilisation. Now there are times when a whole generation is caught in this way between two ages, two modes of life, with the consequence that it loses all power to understand itself and has no standard, no security, no simple acquiescence. Naturally, every one does not feel this equally strongly. A nature such as Nietzsche's had to suffer our present ills more than a generation in advance. What he had to go through alone and misunderstood, thousands suffer today."

I often had to think of these words while reading the records. Haller belongs to those who have been caught between two ages, who are outside of all security and simple acquiescence. He belongs to those whose fate it is to live the whole riddle of human destiny heightened to the pitch of a personal torture, a personal hell.

Therein, it seems to me, lies the meaning these records can have for us, and because of this I decided to publish them. For the rest, I neither approve nor condemn them. Let every reader do as his conscience bids him.

CHAPTER SIX
HOW SHOULD WE LIVE? THE PROBLEM OF THE GOOD LIFE

In one sense the question "How should we live?" is quite unanswerable: different individuals should live in different ways in different situations. But in another sense we can seek some common good, or value, for everyone, simply because there is a common human nature and a common human life. Whether we are old, young, male, female, black, white, wise, foolish, teacher, nurse, mother, or mechanic, we are all human beings; we all experience birth, death, growth, pain, love, humor, curiosity, and a thousand other things that make up our common humanity. Of *this* we ask: What is it *for*? What should we aim at? How should we live? Not *qua* child or *qua* nurse or *qua* male but *qua* human, how should we live?

C. S. Lewis uses the image of a fleet of sailing ships to explain that morality has three parts. The sailing orders tell the ships first how to avoid bumping into each other, second how each ship is to stay shipshape, and third where the whole fleet is going, why the ships are at sea in the first place. We are like ships; we need to know not only how to avoid harming each other, but also how to be shipshape ourselves, and above all why we are afloat, why we are alive at all. Most modern discussions of ethics or values omit this third question and discuss only the first two. Yet this third question is the most important one of all.

Another way to state this question is: What is the goal, or end, or supreme value of human life? What is the end for which everything else is a means? And if there are more than one, which is the greatest good, the *summum bonum*? We seek some things as means toward other things (e.g., lemonade to quench our thirst, hammers to nail wood together, cars to travel in); but there seem to be a few things we seek as ends, for their own sake (e.g., beauty, pleasure, or knowledge). What is the supreme end? What is the end of life as a whole? What justifies everything else in life as a means? Why do we get out of bed in the morning? ("To go to work," we may reply. But then why do we go to work? "To make money." But why make money? "To buy food." Why buy food? "To live." But why live? You see, repeating the child's profound question "Why?" brings us squarely up against the philosophical concept of the *summum bonum* or supreme end.)

You may be thinking, "But 'the end does not justify the means.'" We mean by that saying that a morally good end does not justify a morally evil means; e.g., we should not kill the rich to feed the poor. But in a more general sense the end certainly *does* justify the means. Nothing else can. A "means" *means* a means *to an end.* Take away the end (e.g., the value of nailing the wood together) and the means (the hammer) becomes meaningless. The question then is: What is the end that justifies, or gives value to, all the desirable things we seek?

In other questions in philosophy there seems to have been some progress over the past 2500 years or so; but on this question, the basic, perennial answers keep recurring in the philosophy and literature of each age in essentially the same way. Most of these possible candidates for the *summum bonum* are reviewed in the selection from St. Thomas: wealth, honor, fame, power, health, pleasure, virtue, and God. By logically eliminating all the other candidates, Thomas tries to prove the conclusion that "no created good (nothing other than God) constitutes man's happiness," or final end. ('Happiness' is used by many pre-modern writers to mean not just subjective satisfaction but objective fulfillment, attaining the really highest good.)

This last point brings out the fact that values do seem to have an objective aspect to them, that they are not merely a matter of taste or private opinion. For we *argue* about them. We say things like: "How *could* you sacrifice your family for your career?" or "How foolish of you to compromise your virtue for money!" or "How good of you to work so hard for this worthy cause." Whichever side of such arguments is right, the point is that we do argue about values, and we do not argue about mere taste (e.g., I like olives and not yogurt; you like yogurt and not olives).

People differ about values, They choose different values as their *summum bonum.* The sociologist or psychologist asks the question: What values *do* people choose? The philosopher asks the question: What values *should* they choose? What is a *wise* choice? (e.g., Is wisdom really more valuable than money? Is a clean soul really more valuable than a clean body?)

Kierkegaard has usefully classified the possible answers to the question of the *summum bonum* into three categories. He calls them the three "stages of life's way," implying that life is a learning process in which we should move from lower to higher values. The three states are "the aesthetic" (meaning not "fine arts" but *pleasure*, being pleased, getting what I desire for myself), "the ethical" (meaning not merely socially acceptable behavior but obedience to moral laws universally known to us by conscience) and "the religious" (meaning not merely adherence to a visible creed, code, and cult of worship but an individual's lived relationship with God).

These three "stages" could be seen as corresponding to three aspects of the self: body, soul, and spirit. The aesthetic, or "hedonistic," or pleasure-seeking answer says that the objective good is pleasure and that the human subject is essentially the body with its desires. The ethical answer says that the objective good is virtue, or duty, or justice, and that the human subject is essentially a conscious, choosing soul, mind, will, or ego. The "religious" answer says that the objective good is God, or our union with God, and that the essence of the human subject is the spirit, or heart: something deeper than the rational ego, something which is related to God by "faith," "hope," and "charity".

"Spirit" does not mean just "mind" here, and "heart" does not mean just "feelings." The kind of love ("charity") emphasized by religious believers is neither rational love (love of what reason tells you ought to be loved— that is *justice*) nor physical love (desire, pleasure). Pascal distinguishes it from the other two levels in a famous passage in his *Pensees*:

> The infinite distance between body and mind symbolizes the infinitely more infinite distance between mind and charity, for charity is supernatural. . . . Out of all bodies together we could not succeed in creating one little thought. It is impossible, and of a different order. Out of all bodies and minds we could not extract one impulse of true charity. It is impossible, and of a different, supernatural, order. . . . All bodies, the firmament, the stars, the earth and its kingdoms are not worth the least of minds, for it knows them all and itself too, while bodies know nothing. All bodies together and all minds together and all their products are not worth the least impulse of charity. This is of an infinitely superior order.

The first three selections in this unit represent these three options. The first, one of the most brilliant expositions of the hedonistic (pleasure-seeking) way of life, comes not from a hedonist but from an antihedonist, Kierkegaard, who sets up an attractive hedonism in the first half of *Either/Or* precisely in order to refute it in the second half, which represents the ethical answer. (Kierkegaard's final answer is the religious.)

The selection is quite short; yet the essence of hedonism is quite simple—indeed, that is one of its attractions. To be pleased, interested, "turned on"—this is its good: pleasure, not in the object, but in having my own way.

Like most philosophical hedonists, Kierkegaard prefers a witty "high-brow" hedonism to the simple, popular "wine, women and song"; but both in practice result in emptiness and despair (a theme of much comtemporary cinema: cf. *Shampoo, Alfie, Carnal Knowledge, Blow-Up*).

The critique of hedonism that Kierkegaard offers in the "Or" half of *Either/Or* does not moralize but psychologizes, daring the self-forgetful aesthete to "know thyself" and to choose. The "either-or" between aesthetic and ethical is not between *im*moral and moral but between *a*moral and moral. Just as indifference is farther from love than hate is, so amorality, or indifference to good and evil, is farther from morality than positive evil and rebellion, which at least has the courage to choose a side, even if the wrong side. The aesthete does not choose, does not will. The hedonist is a passive enjoyer, not an active willer.

The major options within the aesthetic are also dealt with in the first six articles of the excerpt from Thomas Aquinas. (The seventh is essentially the ethical and the eighth the religious.)

For the ethical answer, we have included the beginning and the ending of the overall argument in Plato's *Republic*, the most famous and influential book in the entire history of philosophy. Its fundamental conclusion is that justice is the supreme good, or value, or "profit," both for the individual and the State; that it is more "profitable" in itself, even if not rewarded in any way, than injustice, even if the injustice is rewarded in every way.

Plato means by "justice" more than legal behavior or fair dealings between people; he means health of soul in an individual and in a state. The *Republic* distinguishes three parts of the soul or psyche (mind, "spirited part" or will, and desires) and three classes in the state (rulers, soldiers, and producers). The content of justice is described as (1) wisdom (in the mind and in the rulers) (2) courage (in the will and in the soldiers) and (3) self-control, or moderation (in the desires and in the producers). With (4) justice, they constitute the "four cardinal virtues."

After the Aquinas section, which contrasts the religious answer with seven others, the excerpt from St. Anselm's *Proslogium* describes the *summum bonum* of union with God not as an alternative to but as the fulfillment of everything desirable, every value contained in all the other candidates. It is not, like Aquinas', a rigorous logical analysis, but a poetic word-picture designed to move the whole person.

The concluding "comment" is an outlined reorganization of the only strictly philosophical book in the Bible, *Ecclesiastes*. The author appeals to no faith or divine revelation, and asks the question of the *summum bonum* in the light of his experience "under the sun" only. His answer is essentially that of many modern "existentialists" over 2000 years later: life is "vanity of vanities," purposeless "striving after wind"; there *is* no *summum bonum*. We have included this selection as a challenge to the reader: can any of the answers considered survive Eccelsiastes' critique?

The selection concludes with the assertion that while everything in the world is "beautiful in its time," we find a desire for something more than time in our heart. Here is a puzzle worthy of some thought: what do you value most deeply, from your heart? If it is something in time, how can it survive Ecclesiastes' critique, especially the fact that its end is death? If it is something in eternity rather than time, how can you love or value something you have never experienced? In the spirit of Socrates, we conclude with a question which remains open.

A. A HEDONISTIC ANSWER

Soren Kierkegaard: *Either/Or*

Soren Kierkegaard (1813–1855) was a melancholy, introspective, hunchbacked, witty Danish bachelor whose maverick psychological and spiritual probings, expressed in an incredible wealth of styles and pseudonyms, alienated the provincial Danish literary and ecclesiastical establishments of his time, and became well known to the rest of the world only after World War I. His new, antirationalistic, introspective way of philosophizing without a "system" laid the foundations for "depth psychology," for "neo-orthodox theology," and for twentieth-century Existentialism.

---

(1) Starting from a principle is affirmed by people of experience to be a very reasonable procedure; I am willing to humor them, and so begin with the principle that all men are bores. Surely no one will prove himself so great a bore as to contradict me in this. . . .

(2) Boredom is the root of all evil. Strange that boredom, in itself so staid and stolid, should have such power to set in motion. The influence it exists is altogether magical, except that it is not the influence of attraction, but of repulsion.

(3) In the case of children, the ruinous character of boredom is universally acknowledged. Children are always well-behaved as long as they are enjoying themselves. . . .

(4) All men are bores. The word itself suggests the possibility of a subdivision. It may just as well indicate a man who bores others as one who bores himself. Those who bore others are the mob, the crowd, the infinite multitude of men in general. Those who bore themselves are the elect, the aristocracy; and it is a curious fact that those who do not bore themselves usually bore others, while those who bore themselves entertain others. Those who do not bore themselves are generally people who, in one way or

another, keep themselves extremely busy; these people are precisely on this account the most tiresome, the most utterly unendurable.

(5) . . . some people believe that the end and aim of life is work . . . I assume that it is the end and aim of every man to enjoy himself . . .

(6) Everyone who feels bored cries out for change. With this demand I am in complete sympathy . . . (to) insure against sticking fast in some relationship of life, and make possible the realization of a complete freedom.

(7) One must guard against friendship . . . it is impossible for one human being to be anything to another human being except to be in his way. . . .

(8) The essential thing is never to stick fast. . . . One must never enter into the relation of marriage. Husband and wife promise to love one another for eternity. This is all very fine, but it does not mean very much; for if their love comes to an end in time, it will surely be ended in eternity. If, instead of promising forever, the parties would say until Easter, or until May-day comes, there might be some meaning in what they say; for then they would have said something definite, and also something that they might be able to keep. . . .

* * *

(9) Let others complain that the age is wicked; my complaint is that it is wretched, for it lacks passion. Men's thoughts are thin and flimsy like lace, they are themselves pitiable like the lacemakers. The thoughts of their hearts are too paltry to be sinful. For a worm it might be regarded as a sin to harbor such thoughts, but not for a being made in the image of God. Their lusts are dull and sluggish, their passions sleepy. They do their duty, these shopkeeping souls, but they clip the coin a trifle . . . they think that even if the Lord keeps ever so careful a set of books, they may still cheat Him a little. Out upon them! This is the reason my soul always turns back to the Old Testament and to Shakespeare. I feel that those who speak there are at least human beings: they hate, they love, they murder their enemies, and curse their descendants throughout all generations, they sin.

* * *

(10) The essence of pleasure does not lie in the thing enjoyed, but in the accompanying consciousness. If I had a humble spirit in my service, who, when I asked for a glass of water, brought me the world's costliest wines blended in a chalice, I should dismiss him, in order to teach him that pleasure consists not in what I enjoy, but in having my own way.

* * *

(11) Something wonderful has happened to me. I was carried up into the seventh heaven. There all the gods sat assembled. By special grace I was granted the favor of a wish. "Will you," said Mercury, "have youth, or beauty, or power, or a long life, or the most beautiful maiden, or any of the

other glories we have in the chest? Choose, but only one thing." For a moment I was at a loss. Then I addressed myself to the gods as follows: "Most honorable comtemporaries, I choose this one thing, that I may always have the laugh on my side." Not one of the gods said a word, on the contrary, they all began to laugh. Hence I concluded that my request was granted, and found that the gods knew how to express themselves with taste; for it would hardly have been suitable for them to have answered gravely: "It is granted thee."

* * *

(12) My grief is my castle, which like an eagle's nest is built high up on the mountain peaks among the clouds; nothing can storm it. From it I fly down into reality to seize my prey; but I do not remain down there, I bring it home with me, and this prey is a picture I weave into the tapestries of my palace. There I live as one dead. . . . I sit like an old man, grey-haired and thoughtful, and explain the pictures in a voice as soft as a whisper; and at my side a child sits and listens, although he remembers everything before I tell it.

* * *

(13) My life is absolutely meaningless. When I consider the different periods into which it falls, it seems like the word *Schnur* in the dictionary, which means in the first place a string, in the second, a daughter-in-law. The only thing lacking is that the word *Schnur* should mean in the third place a camel, in the fourth, a dust-brush.

* * *

VOLUME II: THE CRITIQUE OF THE 'AESTHETIC'

(14 You are outside yourself . . . you believe that only a restless spirit is alive, whereas all men of experience think that only a quiet spirit is truly alive; for you, an agitated sea is the image of life, for me it is still, deep waters.

(15) . . . one is not tempted to pity you but rather to wish that some day the circumstances of your life may tighten upon you the screws in its rack and compel you to come out with what really dwells in you; that they may begin the sharper inquisition of the rack which cannot be beguiled by nonsense and witticisms. Life is a masquerade, you explain, and for you this is inexhaustible material for amusement; and so far, no one has succeeded in knowing you; for every revelation you make is always an illusion, it is only in this way that you are able to breathe and prevent people from pressing importunely upon you and obstructing your respiration. Your occupation consists in preserving your hiding-place, and that you succeed in doing, for your mask is the most enigmatical of all. In fact you are nothing; you are merely a relation to others, and what you are you are by virtue of this relation. . . .

(16) Do you not know that there comes a midnight hour when every one has to throw off his mask? Do you believe that life will always let itself be mocked? Do you think you can slip away a little before midnight in order to avoid this? Or are you not terrified by it? I have seen men in real life who so long deceived others that at last their true nature could not reveal itself. . . . Or can you think of anything more frightful than that it might end with your nature being resolved into a multiplicity, that you really might become many, become, like those unhappy demoniacs, a legion, and you thus would have lost the inmost and holiest thing of all in a man, the unifying power of personality? Truly, you should not jest with that which is not only serious but dreadful. . . . if you have, or rather if you will to have the requisite energy, you can win what is the chief thing in life—win yourself, acquire your own self.

(17) What is it, then, that I distinguish in my either/or? Is it good and evil? No, I would only bring you up to the point where the choice between the evil and the good acquires significance for you. Everything hinges upon this. As soon as one can get a man to stand at the crossroads in such a position that there is no recourse but to choose, he will choose the right. . . .

(18) My either/or does not in the first instance denote the choice between good and evil, it denotes the choice whereby one chooses good *and* evil, or excludes them. Here the question is under what determinants one would contemplate the whole of existence and would himself live. That the man who chooses good and evil chooses the good is indeed true, but this becomes evident only afterwards; for the aesthetical is not the evil but neutrality, and that is the reason why I affirmed that it is the ethical which constitutes the choice. It is, therefore, not so much a question of choosing between willing the good *or* the evil, as of choosing to *will*; but by this in turn the good and the evil are posited.

Discussion Questions

1. Is the "principle" Kierkegaard begins with serious or not? Does it function as a premise to an argument or not?

2. Why do you think Kierkegaard calls the "aesthetic" alternatives the boring and the interesting rather than the painful and the pleasant?

3. What is the significance of the fact that the aesthete does not enjoy the world but only himself? Does paragraph 10 mean that power is a greater good than pleasure?

4. Why are friendship and especially marriage threatening to the aesthete?

5. Must one agree with the aesthetic way of life to make the criticism of modern life in paragraph 9? Why or why not?

6. How do you interpret the suggestive and puzzling paragraph 12?

7. *Why*, for Kierkegaard, does hedonism culminate in emptiness?

8. What is the basic psychological critique of the aesthete in Volume II? Compare Pascal on page 369.

9. What, for Kierkegaard, was the function of suffering (paragraph 15)? Can you illustrate this with a real experience?

10. Interpret the story of Cinderella in terms of paragraph 16.

11. *Why* is the choice between amorality and morality more important than the choice between immorality and morality?

12. Have you ever spent any time alone, perhaps in a dark room free from distractions, asking yourself who you are and what the meaning of your life is? If not, why not? If so, what did you find?

B. AN ETHICAL ANSWER

Plato: *The Republic*

Plato (428–348 B.C.) was the first systematic philosopher. No one knows how much in his thirty dialogues came from his master, Socrates, who wrote nothing, and how much from Plato, who used Socrates as his literary mouthpiece; but in these dialogues nearly every major question in the next 2400 years of Western philosophy is raised. Thus Ralph Waldo Emerson said that "Plato is philosophy and philosophy is Plato," and Alfred North Whitehead called the whole history of Western philosophy "a series of footnotes to Plato."

BOOK 2

I thought that was the end of our talk, but it seems it was only the prelude. Glaucon, who is always bold in everything, wouldn't accept Thrasymachus's surrender. "Socrates," he said, "do you want to *seem* like you've persuaded us that it's in every way better to be just than unjust, or do you really want to persuade us?"

"Really," I said, "—if it's up to me."

"Well, you aren't succeeding," he said, "Look, does there seem to you to be a kind of good that we choose to have for its own sake and not for its consequences—joy, for instance, and harmless pleasures that bring nothing beyond their immediate enjoyment?"

"Yes, Glaucon, it seems so to me."

"And a kind we cherish both for itself and for its consequences—like thinking, seeing, and health?"

"Yes," I said.

"Do you see a third form of good that includes exercise, being cured, and earning a living? We call these things arduous but beneficial, and we choose to have them not for themselves but only for their consequences—for the profit and other benefits they bring."

"Yes," I said, "but what is this all leading up to?"

"In which class do you place justice?"

"In the most beautiful one, I think—among the things a man must cherish both for themselves and for their consequences if he's going to be truly happy."

"That's not what most people think; they put it with the arduous things that ought to be shunned for themselves but pursued for profit and a reputation based on appearance."

"I know. Thrasymachus has been disparaging justice as being like that for some time now. Glaucon, while extolling injustice. But I seem to be a slow learner."

"Listen," he said, "it seems to me that Thrasymachus was tamed too easily. It was like charming a snake. But the presentation wasn't up to my expectations on either side: I want to hear what justice and injustice each *are* and what power each of them has by itself when in the soul. Leave profits and consequences out of it. So if it seems all right to you, here's what I'll do: I'll revive Thrasymachus's argument and first present the popular view of the nature and origin of justice. Then I'll maintain that all who practice it do so unwillingly, not as a good but as a necessity. Finally, I'll argue that this attitude is reasonable, because people actually believe the unjust life is the better. That's not how it seems to me, Socrates; it's an opinion that Thrasymachus and hordes of others have drummed into me until I'm thoroughly baffled. But I've never heard the argument for the superiority of justice presented as I'd like—I mean justice extolled for its own sake—and I think I can hear it from you. So I'll praise the unjust life as forcefully as I can and in the process show you how I want you to do the opposite. Do you approve of my plan?"

"Oh yes, Glaucon. That's a topic an intelligent man can enjoy discussing again and again."

"Fine," he said, "I'll begin with my first subject then: the nature and origin of justice.

"People say that injustice is by nature good to inflict but evil to suffer. Men taste both of its sides and learn that the evil of suffering it exceeds the good of inflicting it. Those unable to flee the one and take the other therefore decide it pays to make a pact neither to commit nor to suffer injustice. It was here that men began to make laws and covenants, and to call whatever the laws decreed 'legal' and 'just.' This, they say, is both the origin and the essence of justice, a thing midway between the best condition—committing injustice without being punished—and the worst—suffering injustice without getting revenge. Justice is therefore a compromise; it isn't cherished as a good, but honored out of inability to do wrong. A real 'man,' capable of injustice, would never make a pact with anyone. He'd be insane if he did. That, Socrates, is the popular view of the nature of justice and of the conditions under which it develops.[1]

"That men practice justice unwillingly out of inability to do wrong may be seen by considering a hypothetical situation: Give two men, one just and the other unjust, the opportunity to do anything they want and then observe where their desires take them. We'll catch the just man ending up in the same place as the unjust. This is because human nature always wants more, and pursues that as a natural good. But nature has been diverted by convention and forced to honor equality.

"Our two men would have the opportunity I mentioned if we gave them the power once given to the ancestor of Gyges, the famous king of Lydia. They say he was once a shepherd serving the man who was then king. One day a great earthquake opened a chasm in the place where he was pasturing sheep. Astonished, he climbed down into the fissure and saw, among other fabulous things, a hollow bronze horse with windows in it. He peeped inside and saw the body of a man, seemingly larger than life and wearing only a golden ring. He took the ring and left. Later he wore it to the monthly meeting of shepherds, at which they made their reports to the king. As he was sitting there with the others he happened to turn the setting of the ring toward him. Suddenly he became invisible, and the others began to speak of him as though he were gone. Amazed, he turned the setting away from him again and reappeared. After further experiments had convinced him that the ring indeed had the power to make him visible and invisible at will, he contrived to become a messenger to the king. He seduced the queen, with her help murdered the king, and usurped the throne of Lydia.

"Now if there were two such rings and we gave one to our just man and one to the unjust, no one, they say, would have the iron will to restrain himself when he could with impunity take what he liked from the market, slip into houses and sleep with anyone he wanted or kill whomever he wished, free people from jail, and like a god among mortals, do whatever he pleased. In that situation there'd be no difference between our two men; both would act alike. So a person may use this as evidence that no one is willingly just, since whenever a man thinks he can get away with injustice he does it. Justice is practiced only under compulsion, as someone else's good—not our own. Everyone really believes that injustice pays better than justice; rightly, according to this argument. Because if a man had the power to do wrong and yet refused to touch other people's property, discerning men would consider him a comtemptible dolt, though they'd openly praise him and deceive one another for fear of being harmed.

"We'll be able to make a proper judgment on these two ways of life

---

[1]The first presentation in literature of the "social contract" theory of justice.

only if we contrast the perfectly just man with the perfectly unjust. Make each a perfect specimen of his kind. The unjust man should act like a skilled craftsman. An accomplished doctor or navigator distinguishes between what's possible and impossible in his field and attempts the one but ignores the other. And if he botches something he knows how to straighten it out. So with our accomplished criminal: he should discriminate nicely and get away with his crimes. If caught he's a bungler. And injustice's highest perfection is to *seem* just without *being* so. Deprive our perfectly unjust man of nothing, therefore, but lend him utter perfection: Let him contrive the greatest reputation for justice while committing the most heinous crimes, and if he should bungle something, grant him the ability to straighten it out; give him the persuasion to sway juries when informers denounce him, and the wealth, influence, courage, and vigor to use force when force must be used.

"Alongside this paragon of perfidy let us place our perfectly just man—a man noble and simple, desiring, in Aeschylus's words, 'not to *seem*, but to *be* good.' All right, let's take away seeming. A reputation for justice will bring him honor and rewards and make it uncertain whether he practices justice for its own sake or for the rewards. So strip him of everything but justice and make him the exact opposite of our other specimen. Let him win the worst reputation for injustice while leading the justest of lives, to test him and see if his justice holds up against ill repute and its evil effects. And let him persevere until death, seeming unjust while being just, so we may examine the extremes of justice and injustice and decide which makes the happier life."

"Uncanny, Glaucon!" I cried. "You've scoured these two types of our judgment as though they were bronzes."

"I do my best, Socrates. Now with these two men before us it shouldn't be hard to tell what sort of life awaits each. And if it sounds uncouth, Socrates, don't blame me, but the champions of injustice. They say our just man will be whipped, racked, chained, and after having his eyes burnt out and suffering every torment, be run up on a stake and impaled, and so learn that one ought 'not to *be*, but to *seem* just.' . . .

Glaucon and the others urged me by all means to take up the defense and track down the truth about what justice and injustice are and the benefits of each. So I told them my plan: "I don't think this will be an easy investigation—it'll take sharp eyes. Now since we're not very bright, here's how I suggest we go about it: if you told a man with poor eyes to read something small at a distance and he noticed that the same thing was written elsewhere in large letters on a larger background, he'd probably jump for joy because he could read the big writing first and then examine the small to see if both were really the same."

"True," said Adeimantus, "but where do you see something like that in our search?"

"I think I've got an idea," I said. "Isn't justice found in a state as well as in an individual?"

"Certainly," he said.

"And a state is larger than an individual?"

"Of course."

"Then maybe justice is also larger in a state and easier to observe. So let's first inquire what justice is like in states. Then we can examine it in the individual and see if the smaller resembles the larger."

"Good idea, Socrates."

"If we watch a city coming into being in words, we may also see its justice and injustice come into being, and when it's finished we should have a better chance of seeing what we're after. Shall we try it that way? Consider this carefully—I think it'll be a lot of work."

"We have," said Adeimantus. "Let's try it."

BOOK 9

"Now that we've gotten this far," I said, "let's go back to that statement made at the beginning, which brought us here: that it pays for a man to be perfectly unjust if he appears to be just. Isn't that what someone said?"

"Yes."

"Then since we've agreed what power justice and injustice each have, let's have a discussion with him."

"How?"

"By molding in words an image of the soul, so that the one who said that will realize what he was saying."

"What kind of image?"

"Oh, something like those natures the myths tell us were born in ancient times—the Chimaera, Scylla, Cerberus, and others in which many different shapes were supposed to have grown into one."

"So they tell us," he said.

"Then mold one figure of a colorful, many-headed beast with heads of wild and tame animals growing in a circle all around it; one that can change and grow all of them out of itself."

"That's a job for a skilled artist. Still, words mold easier than wax or clay, so consider it done."

"And another of a lion, and one of a man. Make the first by far the biggest, the second second largest."

"That's easier, and already done."

"Now join the three together so that they somehow grow."

"All right."

"Next mold the image of one, the man. around them all, so that to someone who can't see what's inside but looks only at the container it appears to be a single animal, man."

"I have."

"Then shall we inform the gentleman that when he says it pays for this man to be unjust, he's saying that it profits him to feast his multifarious beast and his lion and make them grow strong, but to starve and enfeeble the man in him so that he gets dragged wherever the animals lead him, and instead of making them friends and used to each other, to let them bite and fight and eat each other?"

"That's just what he's saying by praising injustice."

"The one who says justice pays, however, would be saying that he should practice and say whatever will give the most mastery to his inner man, who should care for the many-headed beast like a farmer, raising and domesticating its tame heads and preventing the wild ones from growing, making the lion's nature his partner and ally, and so raise them both to be friends to each other and to him."

"That's exactly what he means by praising justice."

"So in every way the commender of justice is telling the truth, the other a lie. Whether we examine pleasure, reputation, or profit, we find that the man who praises justice speaks truly, the one who disparages it disparages sickly and knows nothing of what he disparages."

"I don't think he does at all."

"Then let's gently persuade him—his error wasn't intended—by asking him a question: 'Shouldn't we say that the traditions of the beautiful and the ugly have come about like this: Beautiful things are those that make our bestial parts subservient to the human—or rather, perhaps, to the divine—part of our nature, while ugly ones are those that enslave the tame to the wild?' Won't he agree?"

"If he takes my advice."

"'On this argument then, can it pay for a man to take money unjustly if that means making his best part a slave to the worst? If it wouldn't profit a man to sell his son or his daughter into slavery—to wild and evil men at that—even if he got a fortune for it, then if he has no pity on himself and enslaves the most godlike thing in him to the most godless and polluted, isn't he a wretch who gets bribed for gold into a destruction more horrible than Euriphyle's, who sold her husband's life for a necklace?'"

"Much more horrible," said Glaucon.

". . . everyone is better off being ruled by the godlike and intelligent; preferably if he has it inside, but if not, it should be imposed on him from without so that we may all be friends and as nearly alike as possible, all steered by the same thing."

"Yes, and we're right." he said.

"Law, the ally of everyone in the city, clearly intends the same thing, as does the rule of children, which forbids us to let them be free until we've instituted a regime in them as in a city. We serve their best part with a similar part in us, install a like guardian and ruler in them, and only then set them free."

"Clearly."

"Then how, by what argument, Glaucon, can we say that it pays for a man to be unjust or self-indulgent or to do something shameful to get more money or power if by doing so he makes himself worse?"

"We can't," he said.

"And how can it pay to commit injustice without getting caught and being punished? Doesn't getting away with it make a man even worse? Whereas if a man gets caught and punished, his beastlike part is taken in and tamed, his tame part is set free, and his whole soul acquires justice and temperance and knowledge. Therefore his soul recovers its best nature and attains a state more honorable than the state the body attains when it acquires health and strength and beauty, by as much as the soul is more honorable than the body."

"Absolutely."

"Then won't a sensible man spend his life directing all his efforts to this end?"

Discussion Questions

1. Book I of the *Republic* is basically a dialog between Socrates and Thrasymachus on the two questions (a) whether justice is more profitable than injustice and (b) what justice is. Which question must be answered first? Why? Which is more pratically important to us? Why? Which of the two is the question of the passage you read here?

2. Explain in your own words the threefold subdivision of goods on the first page. How does this help to define the difference between the viewpoints of Socrates and popular opinion?

3. Prove from the text that by "justice" Plato means not just external deeds, but an internal state of soul. What significance do you see in the fact that the term "justice" has changed its meaning in this way between Plato's time and our own?

4. What is the educational value of taking the "Devil's advocate" position as Glaucon does?

5. Explain the "social contract theory" (the footnoted paragraph) in your own words. What would be an opposing theory? Formulate the question to which these two theories are contrary answers.

6. What is the connection between the question of justice's *origin* and the question of justice's *nature*? Can you find the same connection between the origin and nature of each of the following? (a) humanity (b) conscience (c) religion (d) sexuality (e) artistic inspiration?

7. What is the *point* of the story of the Ring of Gyges? Compare it with the ring in Tolkien's *Lord of the Rings* if you know it, or with the Ring of the Nibelungs (in the mythical *Niebelungenlied* or in Wagner's opera).

8. Why must Plato contrast the *perfectly* just and unjust lives? Isn't this unrealistic, since no one is perfectly just or unjust?

9. How does the Book of Job make the same experiment to test the hero's motives for being good as Plato's experiment in the *Republic*?

10. Why does Plato turn from individual justice to political justice at the end of the passage from Book 2?

11. Explain the point of the image of the many-headed beast at the beginning of Book 9. How is this Plato's basic answer to his question in Book 2?

12. Does the conclusion about punishment in the last long paragraph logically follow? If so, from what premises?

13. How would Plato rate the following lives in terms of "profit" or happiness (rank them #1, 2, 3, 4)? (A) doing evil and suffering evil, (B) doing no evil and suffering no evil, (C) doing evil and suffering no evil, (D) doing no evil and suffering evil.

14. Does the conclusion in the very last sentence necessarily follow? Why or why not?

C. A RELIGIOUS ANSWER

Thomas Aquinas: *Summa Theologiae*

St. Thomas Aquinas (1225–1274), greatest of medieval philosophers and perhaps the greatest theologian of all time, exemplified the medieval ideal of a rational synthesis of Christian theology and Greek philosophy (especially Aristotle) in voluminous works of tightly and carefully defined arguments, notably his enormous *Summa Theologiae* (summary of theology). About 6000 ordinary-length pages written "for beginners," it remained unfinished because shortly before his death an experience of God's immediate presence left him unwilling to write another word: "Compared with what I have seen, all I have written seems to be straw." This "straw" is only the most ambitious and complete philosophical and theological system ever constructed.

QUESTION 2
OF THOSE THINGS IN WHICH MAN'S HAPPINESS CONSISTS *(IN EIGHT ARTICLES)*

First Article
Whether Man's Happiness Consists in Wealth?

We proceed thus to the First Article:—

Objection 1. It would seem that man's happiness consists in wealth. For since happiness is man's last end, it must consist in that which has the greatest hold on man's affections. Now this is wealth: for it is written

(Eccles. x. 19): *All things obey money.* Therefore man's happiness consists in wealth.

Obj. 2. Further, according to Böethius (*De Consol.* iii), happiness is *a state of life made perfect by the aggregate of all good things.* Now money seems to be the means of possessing all things: for, as the Philosopher says (*Ethic.* v. 5), money was invented, that it might be a sort of guarantee for the acquisition of whatever man desires. Therefore happiness consists in wealth.

Obj. 3. Further, since the desire for the sovereign good never fails, it seems to be infinite. But this is the case with riches more than anything else; since *a covetous man shall not be satisfied with riches* (Eccles. v. 9). Therefore happiness consists in wealth.

On the contrary, Man's good consists in retaining happiness rather than in spreading it. But as Böethius says (*De Consol.* ii), *wealth shines in giving rather than in hoarding: for the miser is hateful, whereas the generous man is applauded.* Therefore man's happiness does not consist in wealth.

I answer that, It is impossible for man's happiness to consist in wealth. For wealth is twofold, as the Philosopher says (*Polit.* i. 3), viz., natural and artificial. Natural wealth is that which serves man as a remedy for his natural wants: such as food, drink, clothing, cars, dwellings, and such like, while artificial wealth is that which is not a direct help to nature, as money, but is invented by the art of man, for the convenience of exchange, and as a measure of things saleable.

Now it is evident that man's happiness cannot consist in natural wealth. For wealth of this kind is sought for the sake of something else, viz., as a support of human nature: consequently it cannot be man's last end, rather is it ordained to man as to its end. Wherefore in the order of nature, all such things are below man, and made for him, according to Ps. viii. 8: *Thou hast subjected all things under his feet.*

And as to artificial wealth, it is not sought save for the sake of natural wealth; since man would not seek it except because, by its means, he procures for himself the necessaries of life. Consequently much less can it be considered in the light of the last end. Therefore it is impossible for happiness, which is the last end of man, to consist in wealth.

Reply Obj. 1. All material things obey money, so far as the multitude of fools is concerned, who know no other than material goods, which can be obtained for money. But we should take our estimation of human goods not from the foolish but from the wise: just as it is for a person, whose sense of taste is in good order, to judge whether a thing is palatable.

Reply Obj. 2. All things saleable can be had for money: not so spiritual things, which cannot be sold. Hence it is written (Prov. xvii. 16): *What doth it avail a fool to have riches, seeing he cannot buy wisdom.*

Reply Obj. 3. The desire for natural riches is not infinite: because they suffice for nature in a certain measure. But the desire for artificial wealth is infinite, for it is the servant of disordered concupiscence, which is not curbed, as the Philosopher makes clear (*Polit.* i. 3). Yet this desire for wealth is infinite otherwise than the desire for the sovereign good. For the more perfectly the sovereign good is possessed, the more it is loved, and other things despised: because the more we possess it, the more we know it. Hence it is written, (Ecclus. xxiv. 29): *They that eat me shall yet hunger.* Whereas in the desire for wealth and for whatsoever temporal goods, the contrary is the case: for when we already possess them, we despise them, and seek others: which is the sense of Our Lord's words (Jo. iv. 13): *Whosoever drinketh of this water,* by which temporal goods are signified, *shall thirst again.* The reason of this is that we realize more their insufficiency when we possess them: and this very fact shows that they are imperfect, and that the sovereign good does not consist therein.

Second Article
Whether Man's Happiness Consists in Honors?

We proceed thus to the Second Article:—

Objection 1. It would seem that man's happiness consists in honors. For happiness or bliss is *the reward of virtue,* as the Philosopher says (*Ethic.* i. 9). But honor more than anything else seems to be that by which virtue is rewarded, as the Philosopher says (*Ethic.* iv. 3). Therefore happiness consists especially in honor.

Obj. 2. Further, that which belongs to God and to persons of great excellence seems especially to be happiness, which is the perfect good. But that is honor, as the Philosopher says (*Ethic.* iv. 3). Moreover, the Apostle says (1 Tim. i. 17): *To . . . the only God be honor and glory.* Therefore happiness consists in honor.

Obj. 3. Further, that which man desires above all is happiness. But nothing seems more desirable to man than honor: since man suffers loss in all other things, lest he should suffer loss of honor. Therefore happiness consists in honor.

On the contrary, Happiness is in the happy. But honor is not in the honored, but rather in him who honors, and who offers deference to the person honored, as the Philosopher says (*Ethic.* i. 5). Therefore happiness does not consist in honor.

I answer that, It is impossible for happiness to consist in honor. For honor is given to a man on account of some excellence in him; and consequently it is a sign and attestation of the excellence that is in the person honored. Now a man's excellence is in proportion, especially, to his happiness, which is man's perfect good; and to its parts, *i.e.,* those goods by which he has a certain share of happiness. And therefore honor can result from happiness, but happiness cannot principally consist therein.

Reply Obj. 1. As the Philosopher says (*ibid.*), honor is not that reward of virtue, for which the virtuous work: but they receive honor from men by way of reward, *as from those who have nothing greater to offer.* But virtue's true reward is happiness itself, for which the virtuous work: whereas if they worked for honor, it would no longer be a virtue, but ambition.

Reply Obj. 2. Honor is due to God and to persons of great excellence as a sign of attestation of excellence already existing: not that honor makes them excellent.

Reply Obj. 3. That man desires honor above all else, arises from his natural desire for happiness, from which honor results, as stated above. Wherefore man seeks to be honored especially by the wise, on whose judgment he believes himself to be excellent or happy.

Third Article
Whether Man's Happiness Consists in Fame or Glory?

We proceed thus to the Third Article:—

Objection 1. It would seem that man's happiness consists in glory. For happiness seems to consist in that which is paid to the saints for the trials they have undergone in the world. But this is glory: for the Apostle says (Rom. viii. 18) *The sufferings of this time are not worthy to be compared with the glory to come, that shall be revealed in us.* Therefore happiness consists in glory.

Obj. 2. Further, good is diffusive of itself, as stated by Dionysius (*Div. Nom.* iv.). But man's good is spread abroad in the knowledge of others by glory more than by anything else: since, according to Ambrose, glory consists *in being well known and praised.* Therefore man's happiness consists in glory.

Obj. 3. Further, happiness is the most enduring good. Now this seems to be fame or glory; because by this men attain to eternity after a fashion. Hence Böethius says (*De Consol.* ii): *You seem to beget unto yourselves eternity, when you think of your fame in future time.* Therefore man's happiness consists in fame or glory.

On the contrary, Happiness is man's true good. But it happens that fame or glory is false: for as Böethius says (*De Consol.* iii), *many owe their renown to the lying reports spread among the people. Can anything be more shameful? For those who receive false fame, must needs blush at their own praise.* Therefore man's happiness does not consist in fame or glory.

I answer that, Man's happiness cannot consist in human fame or glory. For glory consists *in being well known and praised,* as Ambrose says. Now the thing known is related to human knowledge otherwise than to God's knowledge: for human knowledge is caused by the things known, whereas God's knowledge is the cause of the things known. Wherefore the perfection of human good, which is called happiness, cannot be caused by human knowledge: but rather human knowledge of another's happiness proceeds from, and, in a fashion, is caused by, human happiness itself, inchoate or perfect. Consequently man's happiness cannot consist in fame or glory. On the other hand, man's good depends on God's knowledge as its cause. And therefore man's beautitude depends, as on its cause, on the glory which man has with God; according to Ps. xc. 15, 16: *I will deliver him, and I will glorify him; I will fill him with length of days, and I will show him my salvation.*

Furthermore, we must observe that human knowledge often fails, especially in contingent singulars, such as are human acts. For this reason human glory is frequently deceptive. But since God cannot be deceived, His glory is always true; hence it is written (2 Cor. x. 18): *He . . . is approved . . . whom God commendeth.*

Reply Obj. 1. The Apostle speaks then, not of the glory which is with men, but of the glory which is from God, with His Angels. Hence it is written (Mark viii. 38): *The Son of Man shall confess him in the glory of His Father, before His angels.*

Reply Obj. 2. A man's good which, through fame or glory, is in the knowledge of many, if this knowledge be true, must needs be derived from good existing in the man himself: and hence it presupposes perfect or inchoate happiness. But if the knowledge be false, it does not harmonize with the thing: and thus good does not exist in him who is looked upon as famous. Hence it follows that fame can nowise make man happy.

Reply Obj. 3. Fame has no stability; in fact, it is exactly ruined by false report. And if sometimes it endures, this is by accident. But happiness endures of itself, and for ever.

Fourth Article
Whether Man's Happiness Consists in Power?

We proceed thus to the Fourth Article:—

Objection 1. It would seem that happiness consists in power. For all things desire to become like to God, as to their last end and first beginning. But men who are in power, seem, on account of the similarity of power, to be most like to God: hence also in Scripture they are called *gods* (Exod. xxii. 28),—*Thou shalt not speak ill of the gods.* Therefore happiness consists in power.

Obj. 2. Further, happiness is the perfect good. But the highest perfection for man is to be able to rule others; which belongs to those who are in power. Therefore happiness consists in power.

Obj. 3. Further, since happiness is supremely desirable, it is contrary to that which is before all to be shunned. But, more than aught else, men shun servitude, which is contrary to power. Therefore happiness consists in power.

On the contrary, Happiness is the perfect good. But power is most imperfect. For as Böethius says (*De Consol.* iii), *the power of man cannot relieve the gnawings of care, nor can it avoid the thorny path of anxiety:* and further on: *Think you a man is powerful who is surrounded by attendants, whom he inspires with fear indeed, but whom he fears still more?* Therefore happiness does not consist in power.

I answer that, It is impossible for happiness to consist in power; and this for two reasons. First because power has the nature of principle, as is stated in *Metaph.* v. 12, whereas happiness has the nature of last end.— Secondly, because power has relation to good and evil: whereas happiness is man's proper and perfect good. Wherefore some happiness might consist in the good use of power, which is by virtue, rather than in power itself.

Now four general reasons may be given to prove that happiness consists in none of the foregoing external goods. First, because, since happiness is man's supreme good, it is incompatible with any evil. Now all the foregoing can be found both in good and in evil men.—Secondly, because, since it is the nature of happiness to *satisfy of itself,* as stated in *Ethic.* i. 7, having gained happiness, man cannot lack any needful good. But after acquiring any one of the foregoing, man may still lack many goods that are necessary to him; for instance, wisdom, bodily health, and such like.— Thirdly, because, since happiness is the perfect good, no evil can accrue to anyone therefrom. This cannot be said of the foregoing: for it is written (Eccles. v. 12) that *riches* are sometimes *kept to the hurt of the owner;* and the same may be said of the other three.—Fourthly, because man is ordained to happiness through principles that are in him; since he is ordained thereto naturally. Now the four goods mentioned above are due rather to external causes, and in most cases to fortune; for which reason they are called goods of fortune. Therefore it is evident that happiness nowise consists in the foregoing.

Reply Obj. 1. God's power is His goodness: hence He cannot use His power otherwise than well. But it is not so with men. Consequently it is not enough for man's happiness, that he become like God in power, unless he become like Him in goodness also.

Reply Obj. 2. Just as it is a very good thing for a man to make good use of power in ruling many, so is it a very bad thing if he makes a bad use of it. And so it is that power is towards good and evil.

Reply Obj. 3. Servitude is a hindrance to the good use of power: therefore is it that men naturally shun it; not because man's supreme good consists of power.

Fifth Article
Whether Man's Happiness Consists in Any Bodily Good?

We proceed thus to the Fifth Article:—

Objection 1. It would seem that man's happiness consists in bodily goods. For it is written (Ecclus. xxx. 16): *There is no riches above the riches of the health of the body.* But happiness consists in that which is best. Therefore it consists in the health of the body.

Obj. 2. Further, Dionysius says (*Div. Nom.* v), that *to be* is better than *to live,* and *to live* is better than all that follows. But for man's being and living, the health of the body is necessary. Since, therefore, happiness is man's supreme good, it seems that health of the body belongs more than anything else to happiness.

Obj. 3. Further, the more universal a thing is, the higher the principle from which it depends; because the higher a cause is, the greater the scope of its power. Now just as the causality of the efficent cause consists in its flowing into something, so the causality of the end consists in its drawing the appetite. Therefore, just as the First Cause is that which flows into all things, so the last end is that which attracts the desire of all. But being itself is that which is most desired by all. Therefore man's happiness consists most of all in things pertaining to his being, such as the health of the body.

On the contrary, Man surpasses all other animals in regard to happiness. But in bodily goods he is surpassed by many animals; for instance, by the elephant in longevity, by the lion in strength, by the stag in fleetness. Therefore man's happiness does not consist in goods of the body.

I answer that, It is impossible for man's happiness to consist in the goods of the body; and this for two reasons. First, because, if a thing be ordained to another as to its end, its last end cannot consist in the preservation of its being. Hence a captain does not intend as a last end, the preservation of the ship entrusted to him, since a ship is ordained to something else as its end, viz., to navigation. Now just as the ship is entrusted to the captain that he may steer its course, so man is given over to his will and reason; according to Ecclus. xv. 14; *God made man from the beginning and left him in the hand of his own counsel.* Now it is evident that man is ordained to something as his end: since man is not the supreme good. Therefore the last end of man's reason and will cannot be the preservation of man's being.

Secondly, because, granted that the end of man's will and reason be the preservation of man's being, it could not be said that the end of man is some good of the body. For man's being consists in soul and body; and though the being of the body depends on the soul, yet the being of the human soul depends not on the body, as shown above (I, Q. 75, A. 2); and the very body is for the soul, as matter for its form, and the instruments for the man that puts them into motion, that by their means he may do his work. Wherefore all goods of the body are ordained to the goods of the soul, as to their end. Consequently happiness, which is man's last end, cannot consist in goods of the body.

Reply Obj. 1. Just as the body is ordained to the soul, as its end, so are external goods ordained to the body itself. And therefore it is with reason that the good of the body is preferred to external goods, which are signified by *riches,* just as the good of the soul is preferred to all bodily goods.

Reply Obj. 2. Being taken simply, as including all perfection of being, surpasses life and all that follows it; for thus being itself includes all these. And in this sense Dionysius speaks. But if we consider being itself as participated in this or that thing, which does not possess the whole perfection of being, but has imperfect being, such as the being of any creature; then it is evident that being itself together with an additional perfection is more excellent. Hence in the same passage Dionysius says that things that live are better than things that exist, and intelligent better than living things.

Reply Obj. 3. Since the end corresponds to the beginning; this argument proves that the last end is the first beginning of being, in Whom every perfection of being is: Whose likeness, according to their proportion, some desire as to being only, some as to living being, some as to being which is living, intelligent and happy. And this belongs to few.

Sixth Article
Whether Man's Happiness Consists in Pleasure?

We proceed thus to the Sixth Article:—

Objection 1. It would seem that man's happiness consists in pleasure. For since happiness is the last end, it is not desired for something else, but other things for it. But this answers to pleasure more than to anything else: *for it is absurd to ask anyone what is his motive in wishing to be pleased* (*Ethic.* x. 2). Therefore happiness consists principally in pleasure and delight.

Obj. 2. Further, *the first cause goes more deeply into the effect than the second cause* (*De Causis* 1). Now the causality of the end consists in its attracting the appetite. Therefore, seemingly that which moves most the appetite, answers to the notion of the last end. Now this is pleasure: and a sign of this is that delight so far absorbs man's will and reason, that it causes him to despise other goods. Therefore it seems that man's last end, which is happiness, consists principally in pleasure.

Obj. 3. Further, since desire is for good, it seems that what all desire is best. But all desire delight; both wise and foolish, and even irrational creatures. Therefore delight is the best of all. Therefore happiness, which is the supreme good, consists in pleasure.

On the contrary, Böethius says (*De Consol.* iii): *Any one that chooses to look back on his past excesses, will perceive that pleasures have a sad ending: and if they can render a man happy, there is no reason why we should not say that the very beasts are happy too.*

I answer that, Because bodily delights are more generally known, *the name of pleasure has been appropriated to them* (*Ethic.* vii. 13), although other delights excel them: and yet happiness does not consist in them. Because in every thing, that which pertains to its essence is distinct from its proper accident: thus in man it is one thing that he is a mortal rational animal, and another that he is a risible animal. We must therefore consider that every delight is a proper accident resulting from happiness, or from some part of happiness; since the reason that a man is delighted is that he has some fitting good, either in reality, or in hope, or at least in memory. Now a fitting good, if indeed it be the perfect good, is precisely man's happiness:

and if it is imperfect, it is a share of happiness, either proximate, or remote, or at least apparent. Therefore it is evident that neither is delight, which results from the perfect good, the very essence of happiness, but something resulting therefrom as its proper accident.

But bodily pleasure cannot result from the perfect good even in that way. For it results from a good apprehended by sense, which is a power of the soul, which power makes use of the body. Now good pertaining to the body, and apprehended by sense, cannot be man's perfect good. For since the rational soul excels the capacity of corporeal matter, that part of the soul which is independent of a corporeal organ, has a certain infinity in regard to the body and those parts of the soul which are tied down to the body: just as immaterial things are in a way infinite as compared to material things, since a form is, after a fashion, contracted and bounded by matter, so that a form which is independent of matter is, in a way, infinite. Therefore sense, which is a power of the body, knows the singular, which is determinate through matter: whereas the intellect, which is a power independent of matter, knows the universal, which is abstracted from matter, and contains an infinite number of singulars. Consequently it is evident that good which is fitting to the body, and which causes bodily delight through being apprehended by sense, is not man's perfect good, but is quite a trifle as compared with the good of the soul. Hence it is written (Wisd. vii.9) that *all gold in comparison of her, is as a little sand.* And therefore bodily pleasure is neither happiness itself, nor a proper accident of happiness.

Reply Obj. 1. It comes to the same whether we desire good, or desire delight, which is nothing else than the appetite's rest in good: thus it is owing to the same natural force that a weighty body is borne downwards and that it rests there. Consequently just as good is desired for itself, so delight is desired for itself and not for anything else, if the preposition *for* denote the final cause. But if it denote the formal or rather the motive cause, thus delight is desirable for something else, *i.e.,* for the good, which is the object of that delight, and consequently is its principle, and gives it its form: for the reason that delight is desired is that it is rest in the thing desired.

Reply Obj. 2. The vehemence of desire for sensible delight arises from the fact that operations of the senses, through being the principles of our knowledge, are more perceptible. And so it is that sensible pleasures are desired by the majority.

Reply Obj. 3. All desire delight in the same way as they desire good: and yet they desire delight by reason of the good and not conversely, as stated above (*ad* 1). Consequently it does not follow that delight is the supreme and essential good, but that every delight results from some good, and that some delight results from that which is the essential and supreme good.

Seventh Article
Whether Some Good of the Soul Constitutes Man's Happiness?

We proceed thus to the Seventh Article:—

Objection 1. It would seem that some good of the soul constitutes man's happiness. For happiness is man's good. Now this is three-fold, external goods, goods of the body, and goods of the soul. But happiness does not consist in external goods, nor in goods of the body, as shown above (AA. 4, 5). Therefore it consists in goods of the soul.

Obj. 2. Further, we love that for which we desire good, more than the good that we desire for it: thus we love a friend for whom we desire money, more than we love money. But whatever good a man desires, he desires it for himself. Therefore he loves himself more than all other goods. Now happiness is what is loved above all: which is evident from the fact that for its sake all else is loved and desired. Therefore happiness consists in some good of man himself: not, however, in goods of the body; therefore, in goods of the soul.

Obj. 3. Further, perfection is something belonging to that which is perfected. But happiness is a perfection of man. Therefore happiness is something belonging to man. But it is not something belonging to the body, as shown above (A. 5). Therefore it is something belonging to the soul; and thus it consists in goods of the soul.

On the contrary, As Augustine says (*De Doctr. Christ:* i. 22), *that which constitutes the life of happiness is to be loved for its own sake.* But man is not to be loved for his own sake, but whatever is in man is to be loved for God's sake. Therefore happiness consists in no good of the soul.

I answer that, As stated above (Q. 1, A. 8), the end is twofold: namely, the thing itself, which we desire to attain, and the use, namely, the attainment or possession of that thing. If, then, we speak of man's last end, as to the thing itself which we desire as last end, it is impossible for man's last end to be the soul itself or something belonging to it. Because the soul, considered in itself, is as something existing in potentiality: for it becomes knowing actually, from being potentially knowing; and actually virtuous, from being potentially virtuous. Now since potentiality is for the sake of act as for its fulfilment, that which in itself is in potentiality cannot be the last end. Therefore the soul itself cannot be its own last end.

In like manner neither can anything belonging to it, whether power, habit, or act. For that good which is the last end, is the perfect good fulfilling the desire. Now man's appetite, otherwise the will, is for the universal good. And any good inherent to the soul is a participated good, and consequently a portioned good. Therefore none of them can be man's last end.

But if we speak of man's last end, as to the attainment or possession thereof, or as to any use whatever of the thing itself desired as an end, thus does something of man, in respect of his soul, belong to his last end: since man attains happiness through his soul. Therefore the thing itself which is desired as end, is that which constitutes happiness, and makes man happy; but the attainment of this thing is called happiness. Consequently we must say that happiness is something belonging to the soul; but that which constitutes happiness is something outside the soul.

Reply Obj. 1. Inasmuch as this division includes all goods that man can desire, thus the good of the soul is not only power, habit, or act, but also the object of these, which is something outside. And in this way nothing hinders us from saying that what constitutes happiness is a good of the soul.

Reply Obj. 2. As far as the proposed objection is concerned, happiness is loved above all, as the good desired; whereas a friend is loved as that for which good is desired; and thus, too, man loves himself. Consequently it is not the same kind of love in both cases. As to whether man loves anything more than himself with the love of friendship, there will be occasion to inquire when we treat of Charity.

Reply Obj. 3. Happiness itself, since it is a perfection of the soul, is an inherent good of the soul; but that which constitutes happiness, viz., which makes man happy, is something outside his soul, as stated above.

Eighth Article
Whether Any Created Good
Constitutes Man's Happiness?

We proceed thus to the Eighth Article:—

Objection 1. It would seem that some created good constitutes man's happiness. For Dionysius says (*Div. Nom.* vii) that Divine wisdom *unites the ends of first things to the beginnings of second things,* from which we may gather that the summit of a lower nature touches the base of the higher nature. But man's highest good is happiness. Since then the angel is above man in the order of nature, as stated in the First Part (Q. 111, A. 1), it seems that man's happiness consists in man somehow reaching the angel.

Obj. 2. Further, the last end of each thing is that which, in relation to it, is perfect: hence the part is for the whole, as for its end. But the universe of creatures which is called the macrocosm, is compared to man who is called the microcosm (*Phys.* viii.2), as perfect to imperfect. Therefore man's happiness consists in the whole universe of creatures.

Obj. 3. Further, man is made happy by that which lulls his natural desire. But man's natural desire does not reach out to a good surpassing his capacity. Since then man's capacity does not include that good which surpasses the limits of all creation, it seems that man can be made happy by some created good. Consequently some created good constitutes man's happiness.

On the contrary, Augustine says (*De Civ. Dei* xix. 26): *As the soul is the life of the body, so God is man's life of happiness: of Whom it is written: "Happy is that people whose God is the Lord"* (Ps. cxliii. 15).

I answer that, It is impossible for any created good to constitute man's happiness. For happiness is the perfect good, which lulls the appetite altogether; else it would not be the last end, if something yet remained to be desired. Now the object of the will, *i.e.,* of man's appetite, is the universal good; just as the object of the intellect is the universal true. Hence it is evident that naught can lull man's will, save the universal good. This is to be found, not in any creature, but in God alone; because every creature has goodness by participation. Wherefore God alone can satisfy the will of man, according to the words of Ps. cii. 5: *Who satisfieth thy desire with good things.* Therefore God alone constitutes man's happiness.

Reply Obj. 1. The summit of man does indeed touch the base of the angelic nature, by a kind of likeness; but man does not rest there as in his last end, but reaches out to the universal fount itself of good, which is the common object of happiness of all the blessed, as being the infinite and perfect good.

Reply Obj. 2. If a whole be not the last end, but ordained to a further end, then the last end of a part thereof is not the whole itself, but something else. Now the universe of creatures, to which man is compared as part to whole, is not the last end, but is ordained to God, as to its last end. Therefore the last end of man is not the good of the universe, but God himself.

Reply Obj. 3. Created good is not less than that good of which man is capable, as of something intrinsic and inherent to him: but it is less than the good of which he is capable, as of an object, and which is infinite. And the participated good which is in an angel, and in the whole universe, is a finite and restricted good.

Discussion Questions

1.   Identify the following structural elements of a *Summa* "article":
(a) the question; (b) the answer given by Aquinas' opponent;
(c) the reasons for that answer; (d) the answer given by Aquinas;
(e) the reasons for that answer. What other structural element is added in each article? Why is this important?

2.   Does Aquinas's highly compressed, logical style "turn you off" or "turn you on"? Why? What does your reaction tell you about yourself? Why do you suppose it turns off many contemporary students but did not turn off medieval students?

3.   Which of the candidates for happiness seems strongest to you? Why?

4.   Why does Aquinas identify "happiness" with "the final end"? Does

anyone ever seek happiness as a means? Does anyone ever seek anything other than happiness for some other end than happiness?

5. Does Aquinas mean by "happiness" something subjective? Would he say, "If you feel happy, you're happy"? If so, how could he argue about it? If not, why do many people today feel that way?

6. Did Aquinas forget any major candidates for happiness?

7. Compare Aquinas's list of candidates with that of Ecclesiastes on pages 264–269: does either one include the other? Compare the candidates for happiness presented in a novel of search like Sartre's *Nausea*, Hesse's *Siddhartha*, or Dostoyevski's *The Brothers Karamazov*.

8. Think of people you know—friends, famous people, or characters in literature—who exemplify each of the eight candidates Aquinas considers. What do their lives and characters and destinies add to his logical analysis? Do they confirm it in each case?

9. Because of its condensed style, many students find this passage difficult. Because of its subject matter, its importance, and its connection with our experience, many students find it quite intelligible. Which was your primary reaction? You can test whether you understand any given passage very simply: can you put it in your own words? If not, only words, not ideas, have passed from the author's mind into yours.

10. Identify and put in your own words what you think is the strongest argument for each candidate (i.e., the strongest objection to Aquinas's answer). Is Aquinas's reply adequate each time? If not, why not?

D. ANOTHER RELIGIOUS ANSWER

St. Anselm: *Proslogion*

St. Anselm (1033–1109), born in Lombardy, abbot at Bec in Normandy, then Archbishop of Canterbury in England, was a leading figure in the twelfth century renaissance and the rise of Scholasticism. Nearly all of the works of Plato and Aristotle had been lost for centuries, and until the rediscovery of Aristotle in the thirteenth century, philosophy was largely confined to logical and theological questions. But the spirit of Greek philosophy, especially that of Plato, was kept alive especially through the continued influence of St. Augustine (345–430 A.D.), Anselm's philosophical master.

. . . 'one thing is necessary.' This is that one thing necessary, which contains every good, or rather which is wholly, uniquely, entirely, and solely good. (Ch. 23)

    Now arouse yourself, my soul, attend with all your mind, and think as much as you can about the nature and extent of so great a good. For if each good thing is delightful, think carefully how delightful must be that good which holds within it the joy of every good and not such a good as we experience in created things, but as different as Creator is from creature. For if life that is created is good, how good must life of the Creator be? (Ch. 24)

He who would enjoy this good, what will be his and what will not be his? He will have whatever he wants, and what he does not want he will not have. There will be those goods of body and soul such as 'the eye has not seen, nor the ear heard, nor has the heart of man understood.' So why do you wander about so, little man, seeking goods for your body and soul? Love that one good in which are all goods, and it suffices. Desire that one good that is every good, and that is enough. What does my flesh love, what does my soul desire? Whatever you love, whatever you desire, it is there, it is there indeed.

If beauty delights you, 'the just shall shine as the sun.' If you enjoy that speed, strength, and freedom of the body that nothing can withstand, 'they will be like the angels of God.' for 'that which was sown in a natural body, shall rise as a spiritual body,' by a power beyond nature. If it is a long and healthy life you desire, there is there a healthy eternity and an eternity of health, since 'the just will live for ever,' and 'the salvation of the just is from the Lord.' If you want abundance, they shall be satisfied 'when the glory of God shall appear.' If it is drink you desire, 'they will drink of the fullness of the house of God.' If it is melody, there the choirs of angels sing together unceasingly before God. If you delight in any pleasure that is not impure but pure, 'they shall drink from the torrent of the pleasures' of God. If it is wisdom you crave, the wisdom of God himself will show itself to them. If it is friendship that delights you, they will love God more than themselves, and each other as themselves; God will love them more than they love themselves, because it is through him that they have love for him and themselves and one another; and it is through his own self that God loves both himself and them. If your joy is in unity, there will be one will for them all, for they will have nothing except the one will of God. If it is power you want, their wills will be all powerful just like God's will. For as God can do what he wills in his own power, so through him they will be able to do what they will; for they will want nothing but his will, and therefore he will want whatever they want; and what God wills must be. If it is honour and riches that you aim at, God will set his good and faithful servants over many things; even more, they will be called and will be 'gods' and 'sons of God,' and where his Son is they will be also, 'heirs of God and co-heirs with Christ.' If it is true security that you long for, that security, or rather that good, will never in any way fail them for they certainly will not lose it of their own free will, and the God who loves them will not take it away against their will from those who love him; and there is nothing more powerful than God, which could separate him and them against their will.

Where there is such and so great a good, how rich and how great must be the joy! If man abounded in all these things, how great would be the joy of his heart, that needy heart, well-versed in, indeed overwhelmed by, suffering. Question within yourself, could you hold the joy of so great a bliss? But surely if another whom you loved in every way as yourself, had that same bliss, your joy would be double, for you would rejoice no less for him than for yourself. And if two or three or many more had this same blessedness, you would rejoice for each of them as much as you do for yourself, if you loved each one as yourself. So in that perfection of charity of countless blessed angels and men, where no one loves another any less than he loves himself, they will all rejoice for each other as they do for themselves. If the heart of man can scarcely hold the joy that comes to him from so great a good, how will it hold so many and such great joys? In so far as each one loves another, so he will rejoice in the other's good; and as in that perfection of happiness each one will love God imcomparably more than he loves himself or others, so he will rejoice more and beyond reckoning in the happiness of God than in that of himself and of everyone else. But if they love God with their whole heart, mind and soul, while as yet their whole heart, mind and soul is not equal to the dignity of that love, truly they will so rejoice with their whole heart and mind and soul that their whole heart and mind and soul will not suffice for the fullness of their joy. (Ch. 25)

. . . It is a joy that fills the whole heart, mind and soul, indeed it fills the whole of a man, and yet joy beyond measure remains. The whole of that joy cannot enter into those who rejoice, but those who rejoice can enter wholly into that joy.

But, of course, that joy in which Your chosen ones will rejoice, 'neither has eye seen, nor ear heard, nor has it entered into the heart of man.' So as yet, Lord, I have not spoken about or understood how greatly your blessed ones rejoice. They will rejoice as much as they love, and they will love as much as they know. How much will they know you, Lord, how much will they love you? Truly in this life 'neither has eye seen, nor ear heard, nor has it entered into the heart of man' how much they will know and love you in that life.

My God, I pray that I may so know you and love you that I may rejoice in you. And if I may not do so fully in this life, let me go steadily on to the day when I come to that fullness. Let the knowledge of you increase in me here, and there let it come to its fullness. Let your love grow in me here, and there let it be fullfilled, so that here my joy may be in a great hope, and there in full reality. . . . Meanwhile, let my mind meditate on it, let my tongue speak of it, let my heart love it, let my mouth preach it, let my soul hunger for it, my flesh thirst for it, and my whole being desire it, until I enter into the joy of my Lord. (Ch. 26)

Discussion Questions

1. Do you think one must believe what Anselm belives in order to be moved by his writing? Why or why not?

2. Some students dislike both the rationalistic style of Aquinas *and* the emotional style of Anselm. How can this be?

3. What is Anselm's overall argument, the "bare bones" beneath the rhetorical polish? What are its premises and what is its conclusion? Evaluate it.

4. The passage can be treated not only as an *argument* but also as a *description* of the *summum bonum*. What is the central, unifying feature in all the elements of this description?

5. How is joy multiplied, according to Anselm? Is this true in this life, after death, or both?

6. Distinguish joy from satisfaction or contentment. Have you ever experienced a joy that is not just satisfaction? When? How would Anselm interpret that experience?

7. How would a hedonist interpret Anselm? How would Anselm interpret the hedonist? How could this dispute be settled, do you think? How can you tell whether love of God is only a substitution for love of earthly pleasure or vice versa?

COMMENT: The Bible
Ecclesiastes

Title and Author: "The words of the Preacher, the son of David, king of Jerusalem." (1:1)

Conclusion: "Vanity of vanities, says the Preacher, vanity of vanities! All is vanity." (1:2)

Argument: "What does man gain by the toil at which he toils under the sun?" (1:3)

The Attempt to Find Value in Wisdom: "I the Preacher have been king over Israel in Jerusalem. And I applied my mind to see and to search out by wisdom all that is done under heaven; it is an unhappy business that God has given to the sons of men to be busy with. I have seen everything that is done under the sun; and behold, all is vanity and a striving after wind. . . . I said to myself, 'I have acquired great wisdom, surpassing all who were over Jerusalem before me; and my mind has had great experience in wisdom and knowledge.' And I applied my mind to know wisdom and to know madness and folly. I perceived that this also is but a striving after wind. For in much wisdom is much vexation, and he who increases knowledge increases sorrow." (1:12–14, 15–18)

The Valuelessness of Wisdom: Nothing Makes Any Ultimate Difference: "So I turned to consider wisdom and madness and folly. . . . Then I saw that wisdom excels folly as light excels darkness. The wise man has his eyes in his head, but the fool walks in darkness; and yet I perceived that one fate comes to all of them. Then I said to myself, 'What befalls the fool will befall me also; why then have I been so very wise? And I said to myself that this also is vanity. For of the wise man as of the fool there is no enduring remembrance, seeing that in the days to come all will have been long forgotten. How the wise man dies just like the fool! So I hated life, because what is done under the sun was grievous to me; for all is vanity and a striving after wind. I hated all my toil in which I had toiled under the sun, seeing that I must leave it to the man who will come after me; and who knows whether he will be a wise man or a fool? Yet he will be master of all for which I toiled and used my wisdom under the sun. This also is vanity. So I turned about and gave my heart up to despair over the toil of my labors under the sun." (2:12–20)

"Everything before them is vanity, since one fate comes to all, to the righteous and the wicked, to the good and the evil, to the clean and the unclean, to him who sacrifices and him who does not sacrifice. As is the good man, so is the sinner; and he who swears is as he who shuns an oath. This is an evil in all that is done under the sun, that one fate comes to all." (9:1–3)

"Again I saw that under the sun the race is not to the swift, nor the battle to the strong, nor bread to the wise, nor riches to the intelligent, nor favor to men of skill; but time and chance happen to them all. . . . I have also seen this example of wisdom under the sun, and it seemed great to me. There was a little city with few men in it; and a great king came against it and besieged it, building great siegeworks against it. But there was found in it a poor wise man, and he by his wisdom delivered the city. Yet no one remembered that poor man." (9:11, 13–15)

The Attempt to Find Value in Pleasure: "I said to myself, 'Come now, I will make a test of pleasure; enjoy yourself.' But behold, this also was vanity. I said of laughter, 'It is mad,' and of pleasure, 'What use is it?' I searched with my mind how to cheer my body with wine—my mind still guiding me with wisdom—and how to lay hold on folly, till I might see what was good for the sons of men to do under heaven during the few days of their life. I made great works; I built houses and planted vineyards for myself; I made myself gardens and parks, and planted in them all kinds of fruit trees. I made myself pools from which to water the forest of growing trees. I bought male and female slaves, and had slaves who were born in my house; I had also great possessions of herds and flocks, more than any who had been before me in Jerusalem. I also gathered for myself silver and gold and the treasure of kings and provinces; I got singers, both men and women, and many concubines, man's delight. So I became great and surpassed all who were before me in Jerusalem; also my wisdom remained with me. And whatever my eyes desired I did not keep from them; I kept my heart from no pleasure, for my heart found pleasure in all my toil, and this was my reward for all my toil. Then I considered all that my hands had done and the toil I had spent in doing it, and behold, all was vanity and a striving after wind, and there was nothing to be gained under the sun." (2:1–11)

The Valuelessness of Pleasure: Death Removes All: "For the fate of the sons of men and the fate of beasts is the same: as one dies, so dies the other. They all have the same breath, and man has no advantage over the beasts; for all is vanity. All go to one place; all are from the dust, and all turn to dust again. Who knows whether the spirit of man goes upward and the spirit of the beast goes down to the earth?" (3:19–21)

"But he who is joined with all the living has hope, for a living dog is better than a dead lion. For the living know that they will die, but the dead know nothing, and they have no more reward; but the memory of them is lost. Their love and their hate and their envy have already perished, and they have no more for ever any share in all that is done under the sun." (9:4–6)

"Remember also your Creator in the days of your youth, before the evil days come, and the years draw nigh, when you will say, 'I have no pleasure in them'; before the sun and the light and the moon and the stars are darkened and the clouds return after the rain; in the day when the keepers of the house tremble, and the strong men are bent, and the grinders cease because they are few, and those that look through the windows are dimmed, and the doors on the street are shut; when the sound of the grinding is low, and one rises up at the voice of a bird, and all the daughters of song are brought low; they are afraid also of what is high, and terrors are in the way; the almond tree blossoms, and the grasshopper drags itself along and desire fails; because man goes to his eternal home and the mourners go about the streets; before the silver cord is snapped, or the golden bowl is broken, or the pitcher is broken at the fountain, or the wheel broken at the cistern, and the dust returns to the earth as it was, and the spirit returns to God who gave it. Vanity of vanities, says the Preacher; all is vanity." (12:1–8)

The Attempt to Find Value in Morality: "Two are better than one, because they have a good reward for their toil. For if they fall, one will lift up his fellow; but woe to him who is alone when he falls and has not another to lift him up. Again, if two lie together, they are warm; but how can one be warm alone? And though a man might prevail against one who is alone, two will withstand him. A threefold cord is not quickly broken." (4:9–12)

"Cast your bread upon the waters, for you will find it after many days. Give a portion to seven, or even to eight, for you know not what evil may happen on earth." (11:1)

The Valuelessness of Morality: The Problem of Evil: "I saw that in the place of justice, even there was wickedness, and in the place of righteousness, even there was wickedness." (3:16)

"Again I saw all the oppressions that are practiced under the sun. And behold, the tears of the oppressed, and they had no one to comfort them! On the side of their oppressors there was power, and there was no one to comfort them. And I thought the dead who are already dead more fortunate than the living who are still alive; but better than both is he who has not yet been, and has not seen the evil deeds that are done under the sun." (4:1–3)

"In my vain life I have seen everything; there is a righteous man who perishes in his righteousness, and there is a wicked man who prolongs his life in his evil-doing. Be not righteous overmuch, and do not make yourself overwise; why should you destroy yourself?" (7:15–16)

"There is a vanity which takes place on earth, that there are righteous men to whom it happens according to the deeds of the wicked, and there are wicked men to whom it happens according to the deeds of the righteous. I said that this also is vanity." (8:14)

"Dead flies make the perfumer's ointment give off an evil odor; so a little folly outweighs wisdom and honor." (10:1)

The Attempt to Find Value in Conventional Piety: "Because sentence against an evil deed is not executed speedily, the heart of the sons of men is fully set to do evil. Though a sinner does evil a hundred times and prolongs his life, yet I know that it will be well with those who fear God, because they fear before him; but it will not be well with the wicked, neither will he prolong his days like a shadow, because he does not fear before God." (8:11–13)

"The end of the matter; all has been heard. Fear God, and keep his commandments; for this is the whole duty of man. For God will bring every deed into judgment, with every secret thing, whether good or evil." (12:13–14)

The Valuelessness of Conventional Piety: The Unknowableness of God: "There is an evil which I have seen under the sun, and it lies heavy upon men: a man to whom God gives wealth, possessions, and honor, so that he lacks nothing of all that he desires, yet God does not give him power to enjoy them, but a stranger enjoys them; this is vanity, it is a sore affliction." (6:1–2)

"Consider the work of God; who can make straight what he has made crooked? In the day of prosperity be joyful, and in the day of adversity consider; God has made the one as well as the other, so that man may not find out anything that will be after him." (7:13–14)

"Then I saw all the work of God, that man cannot find out the work that is done under the sun. However much man may toil in seeking he will not find it out; even though a wise man claims to know, he cannot find it out." (8:17)

"As you do not know how the spirit comes to the bones in the womb of a woman with child, so you do not know the work of God who makes everything." (11:5)

The Valuelessness of Human Life: Time as Cyclic

A generation goes, and a generation comes,
    but the earth remains for ever.

The sun rises and the sun goes down.
    and hastens to the place where it rises.

The wind blows to the south,
    and goes round to the north;
round and round goes the wind,
    and on its circuits the wind returns.

All streams run to the sea,
    but the sea is not full;
to the place where the streams flow,
    there they flow again.

All things are full of weariness;
    a man cannot utter it;
the eye is not satisfied with seeing,
    nor the ear filled with hearing.

What has been is what will be,
    and what has been done is what will be done;
    and there is nothing new under the sun.

Is there a thing of which it is said,
   'See, this in new'?

It has been already,
   in the ages before us.

There is no remembrance of former things,
   nor will there be any remembrance
of later things yet to happen
   among those who come after. (1:4–11)

For everything there is a season, and a time for every matter under
heaven:

a time to be born, and a time to die;
a time to plant, and a time to pluck up what is planted;
a time to kill, and a time to heal;
a time to break down, and a time to build up;
a time to weep, and a time to laugh;
a time to mourn, and a time to dance;
a time to cast away stones, and a time to gather stones together;
a time to embrace, and a time to refrain from embracing;
a time to seek, and a time to lose;
a time to keep, and a time to cast away;
a time to rend, and a time to sew;
a time to keep silence, and a time to speak;
a time to love, and a time to hate;
a time for war, and a time for peace.

What gain has the worker from his toil? (3:1–10)

I have seen the business that God has given to the sons of men to be busy
with. He has made everything beautiful in its time; also (however) he has
put eternity into man's mind [heart, desire] . . . ." (3:11)

PART THREE
WHAT MAY WE HOPE?

CHAPTER SEVEN
IS THERE A GOD?
THE PROBLEM
OF GOD'S EXISTENCE

To some people the whole idea of giving *arguments* for or against the existence of God seems strange. These people assume that belief in God is a matter of faith and that faith is opposed to or excludes reason. This assumption is made by many nonreligious people and is reinforced by religious believers who see faith as a "leap in the dark," a wholly nonrational commitment. However, there is a long tradition in such major religions as Christianity, Judaism, and Islam, which says that "reasons to believe" can be given. Those whom we might call "rational believers" often hold that philosophical arguments can be given for the existence of God, and that historical evidence can be given for the reality of miraculous events in the history of their religion, such as the parting of the Red Sea or the resurrection of Christ. Such rational believers usually hold that faith includes commitment and is *more* than mere intellectual assent, but they argue that faith builds on reason rather than being opposed to it. The selection from Thomas Aquinas on pages 276-80 is a good representation of this point of view.

Before we discuss the arguments themselves it is necessary to make clear what is meant by "God." Although some religions have believed in a god or gods limited in power and having human or even animal form, when we speak of God today we are generally thinking of the God found in the Jewish, Christian, and Islamic traditions. This God has the following characteristics:

1. *God is real*, not just an idea in human minds or an abstraction.
2. *God is not material*—does not have a size or shape or weight or a spatial location.
3. *God is a person*, not merely a force or tendency.
   By saying that someone is a person we mean that this person has knowledge, including both self-awareness and awareness of other things, and will or choice. God's knowledge and will are conceivd of as without limitation.
4. *God is all-knowing or omniscient*—knows everything that it is possible to know.
5. *God is all-powerful or omnipotent*—can bring about anything that is not either self-contradictory or contradictory to the idea of being brought about by God.
   A manifestation of God's power that is important to Jewish, Christian, and Islamic belief is God's creation of the universe and continuing control of it.
6. *God is the creator and ruler of the universe.*
   Finally, God is seen as supremely good and the source of moral goodness.
7. *God is perfectly good and the source of all goodness.*

Many of these characteristics can be the starting points of arguments for the existence of God. For instance, philosophers have argued from the existence of morality to God as the source of moral goodness, from the existence of the physical universe to God as the first cause of the universe, and so on. The general pattern of these arguments is to take some basic aspect of our experience, such as our moral experience or our experience of the physical universe and argue that the basic part of our experience cannot be explained without the existence of God. For instance the universe seems to be orderly and understandable: Could this be the case if it was not the result of design by a mind and power much greater than our own?

Arguments *against* the existence of God often take one of two forms. In the first, an attempt is made to show that all of our experience can be explained and understood without reference to God. The second form of argument against the existence of God takes some element of our experience, such as evil and suffering, and argues that this part of our experience is incompatible with the existence of God.

It is true that there are arguments for and against the existence of God which proceed not from experience but from the definition or idea of God. These are often of considerable philosophical interest, and can show us a good deal about the nature and limitations of our idea of God. However, it seems to most philosophers that we cannot move from the realm of ideas to the realm of reality merely by argument; merely analyzing ideas will not show that God does or does not exist.

In this section we have not tried to examine every argument for and against the existence of God, only some of those which have been most important and influential in the history of philosophy. We have tried to choose arguments which can be understood without too much background in the history of philosophy. In addition to arguments for and against the existence of God we have included criticisms of those arguments.

We begin with the statement of the arguments by a major theologian and philosopher, Thomas Aquinas (1225–1274). Aquinas raises the question of whether we *can* prove God's existence and concludes that we can. He then gives his summary of "five ways" of proving God's existence. However, the medieval philosophers were in the habit of arguing questions both rigorously and vigorously, giving both sides of the question. So Aquinas gives arguments against his conclusions as well as for them. "Can we prove God's existence? It would seem not . . ." "Does God exist? It would seem not . . ." In fact Aquinas *begins* with the objections, then later gives counterarguments; this was one typical pattern of medieval "disputation." The two objections Aquinas gives to the existence of God were mentioned earlier in this introduction: The first is the existence of evil, which is a major obstacle to belief in God for many people; The second is based on the idea that we can explain and understand the universe without God. "We have have no need of that hypothesis," as one scientist is reported to have said.

The most discussed of Aquinas's arguments for God's existence are the first three, which taken as a group are often called the Cosmological Argument, and the last, which is a version of the Argument from Design. Because Aquinas's statement of these arguments is very compressed and based on philosophical ideas which are hard for students today to understand, we have included a reflection on Aquinas's argument by a contemporary follower of Aquinas, Edward Sillem.

We next turn to the major objections to the arguments for existence of God, and to the problem of evil. We give one classical statement of these objections by the eighteenth-century philosopher David Hume. We then give a restatement and assessment of the Cosmological Argument by Bruce Reichenbach, another contemporary philosopher. The debate about these arguments still goes on and is still a lively one. A reply to the objection from evil is taken from a popular textbook written several years ago by one of the editors of the present book. It seemed better to use this selection, which summarizes a number of philosophical and religious answers to the problem of evil, rather than try to give brief quotations out of context from a number of philosophers and theologians who have written on this subject.

The Comment for this section is taken from a book by Robert Farrar Capon, an Episcopal priest who has written a number of lively and interesting books on theological themes. Father Capon uses humor and metaphor to point out the limitations of even our best attempts to think about realities far beyond our limited selves.

A. GOD DOES EXIST

St. Thomas Aquinas: *Summa Theologica*

St. Thomas Aquinas (1225–1274), Italian theologian and philosopher, was a member of the Dominican Order. Aquinas taught at the University of Paris and elsewhere. Perhaps the greatest of the medieval philosophers and one of the great philosophical system builders, Aquinas attempted to investigate every theological question by applying reason to the Christian revelation. The results of his investigations appear in his two great systematic expositions of theology, the *Summa Theologica* and the *Summa Contra Gentiles*, both of which contain much of philosophical interest.

SECOND ARTICLE. WHETHER IT CAN BE DEMONSTRATED THAT GOD EXISTS?

We proceed thus to the Second Article:—

Objection 1. It seems that the existence of God cannot be demonstrated. For it is an article of faith that God exists. But what is of faith cannot be demonstrated, because a demonstration produces scientific knowledge, whereas faith is of the unseen, as is clear from the Apostle (Heb. xi. 1). Therefore it cannot be demonstrated that God exists.

Obj. 2. Further, essence is the middle term of demonstration. But we cannot know in what God's essence consists, but solely in what it does not consist, as Damascene says. Therefore we cannot demonstrate that God exists.

Obj. 3. Further, if the existence of God were demonstrated, this could only be from His effects. But His effects are not proportioned to Him, since He is infinite and His effects are finite, and between the finite and infinite there is no proportion. Therefore, since a cause cannot be demonstrated by an effect not proportioned to it, is seems that the existence of God cannot be demonstrated.

On the contrary, The Apostle says: *The invisible things of Him are clearly seen, being understood by the things that are made* (Rom. i. 20). But this would not be unless the existence of God could be demonstrated through the things that are made; for the first thing we must know of anything is, whether it exists.

I answer that, Demonstration can be made in two ways: One is through the cause, and is called *propter quid,* and this is to argue from what is prior absolutely. The other is through the effect, and is called a demonstration *quia*; this is to argue from what is prior relatively only to us. When an effect is better known to us than its cause, from the effect we proceed to the knowledge of the cause. And from every effect the existence of its proper cause can be demonstrated, so long as its effects are better known to us; because, since every effect depends upon its cause, if the effect exists, the cause must pre-exist. Hence the existence of God, in so far as it is not self-evident to us, can be demonstrated from those of His effects which are known to us.

Reply Obj. 1. The existence of God and other like truths about God, which can be known by natural reason, are not articles of faith, but are preambles to the articles; for faith presupposes natural knowledge, even as grace presupposes nature and perfection the perfectible. Nevertheless, there is nothing to prevent a man, who cannot grasp a proof, from accepting, as a matter of faith, something which in itself is capable of being scientifically known and demonstrated.

Reply Obj. 2. When the existence of a cause is demonstrated from an effect, this effect takes the place of the definition of the cause in proving the cause's existence. This is especially the case in regard to God, because, in order to prove the existence of anything, it is necessary to accept as a middle term the meaning of the name, and not its essence, for the question of its essence follows on the question of its existence. Now the names given to God are derived from His effects, as will be later shown. Consequently, in demonstrating the existence of God from His effects, we may take for the middle term the meaning of the name *God.*

Reply Obj. 3. From effects not proportioned to the cause no perfect knowledge of that cause can be obtained. Yet from every effect the existence of the cause can be clearly demonstrated, and so we can demonstrate the existence of God from His effects; though from them we cannot know God perfectly as He is in His essence.

THIRD ARTICLE. WHETHER GOD EXISTS?

We proceed thus to the Third Article:—

Objection 1. It seems that God does not exist; because if one of two contraries be infinite, the other would be altogether destroyed. But the name *God* means that He is infinite goodness. If, therefore, God existed, there would be no evil discoverable; but there is evil in the world. Therefore God does not exist.

Obj. 2. Further, it is superfluous to suppose that what can be accounted for by a few principles has been produced by many. But it seems that everything we see in the world can be accounted for by other principles, supposing God did not exist. For all natural things can be reduced to one principle, which is nature; and all voluntary things can be reduced to one principle, which is human reason, or will. Therefore there is no need to suppose God's existence.

On the contrary, It is said in the person of God: *I am Who am* (Exod. iii. 14).

I answer that, The existence of God can be proved in five ways.

The first and more manifest way is the argument from motion. It is certain, and evident to our senses, that in the world some things are in motion. Now whatever is moved is moved by another, for nothing can be moved except it is in potentiality to that towards which it is moved; whereas a thing moves inasmuch as it is in act. For motion is nothing else than the reduction of something from potentiality to actuality. But nothing can be reduced from potentiality to actuality, except by something in a state of actuality. Thus that which is actually hot, as fire, makes wood, which is potentially hot, to be actually hot, and thereby moves and changes it. Now it is not possible that the same thing should be at once in actuality and potentiality in the same respect, but only in different respects. For what is actually hot cannot simultaneously be potentially hot; but it is simultaneously potentially cold. It is therefore impossible that in the same respect and in the same way a thing should be both mover and moved, *i.e.,* that it should move itself. Therefore, whatever is moved must be moved by another. If that by which it is moved be itself moved, then this also must needs be moved by another, and that by another again. But this cannot go on to infinity, because then there would be no first mover, and, consequently, no other mover, seeing that subsequent movers move only inasmuch as they are moved by the first mover; as the staff moves only because it is moved by the hand. Therefore it is necessary to arrive at a first mover, moved by no other; and this everyone understands to be God.

The second way is from the nature of efficient cause. In the world of sensible things we find there is an order of efficient causes. There is no case known (neither is it, indeed, possible) in which a thing is found to be the efficient cause of itself; for so it would be prior to itself, which is impossible. Now in efficient causes it is not possible to go on to infinity, because in all efficient causes following in order, the first is the cause of the intermediate cause, and the intermediate is the cause of the ultimate cause, whether the intermediate cause be several, or one only. Now to take away the cause is to take away the effect. Therefore, if there be no first cause among efficient causes, there will be no ultimate, nor any intermediate, cause. But if in efficient causes it is possible to go on to infinity, there will be no first efficient cause, neither will there be an ultimate effect, nor any intermediate efficient causes; all of which is plainly false. Therefore it is necessary to admit a first efficient cause, to which everyone gives the name of God.

The third way is taken from possibility and necessity, and runs thus. We find in nature things that are possible to be and not to be, since they are found to be generated, and to be corrupted, and consequently, it is possible for them to be and not to be. But it is impossible for these always to exist, for that which can not-be at some time is not. Therefore, if everything can not-be, then at one time there was nothing in existence. Now if this were true, even now there would be nothing in existence, because that which does not exist begins to exist only through something already existing. Therefore, if at one time nothing was in existence, it would have been impossible for anything to have begun to exist; and thus even now nothing would be in existence—which is absurd. Therefore, not all beings are merely possible, but there must exist something the existence of which is necessary. But every necessary thing either has its necessity caused by another, or not. Now it is impossible to go on to infinity in necessary things which have their necessity caused by another, as has been already proved in regard to efficient causes. Therefore we cannot but admit the existence of some being having of itself its own necessity, and not receiving it from another, but rather causing in others their necessity. This all men speak of as God.

The fourth way is taken from the gradation to be found in things. Among beings there are some more and some less good, true, noble, and the like. But *more* and *less* are predicated of different things according as they resemble in their different ways something which is the maximum, as a thing is said to be hotter according as it more nearly resembles that which is hottest; so that there is something which is truest, something best, something noblest, and, consequently, something which is most in being, for those things that are greatest in truth are greatest in being, as it is written in *Metaph.* ii. Now the maximum in any genus is the cause of all in that genus, as fire, which is the maximum of heat, is the cause of all hot things, as is said in the same book. Therefore there must also be something which is to all beings the cause of their being, goodness, and every other perfection; and this we call God.

The fifth way is taken from the governance of the world. We see that things which lack knowledge, such as natural bodies, act for an end, and this is evident from their acting always, or nearly always, in the same way, so as to obtain the best result. Hence it is plain that they achieve their end, not fortuitously, but designedly. Now whatever lacks knowledge cannot move towards an end, unless it be directed by some being endowed with knowledge and intelligence; as the arrow is directed by the archer. Therefore some intelligent being exists by whom all natural things are directed to their end; and this being we call God.

Reply Obj. 1. Augustine says: *Since God is the highest good, He would not allow any evil to exist in His works, unless His omnipotence and goodness were such as to bring good even out of evil.* This is part of the infinite goodness of God, that He should allow evil to exist, and out of it produce good.

Reply Obj. 2. Since nature works for a determinate end under the direction of a higher agent, whatever is done by nature must be traced back to God as to its first cause. So likewise whatever is done voluntarily must be traced back to some higher cause other than human reason and will, since these can change and fail; for all things that are changeable and capable of defect must be traced back to an immovable and self-necessary first principle, as has been shown.

Discussion Questions

1.   State in your own words an objection to the idea that God's existence can be proved. Is your objection similar to any of those given by Aquinas? How might Aquinas reply to your objection?

2.   In what kind of cases do we argue from an effect to a cause? How are these cases similar or dissimilar to arguing to the existence of God from the existence of the universe?

3.   What might Aquinas mean by saying that the existence of God is not an article of faith, because it can be known by reason? Do you agree or disagree with what you understand him to mean?

4.   Do you think that Aquinas's two objections to the existence of God can be answered along the lines indicated in his Replies? If not, why not? If you think they can, how could Aquinas's brief replies be expanded and developed?

5.   All of the first three arguments given by Aquinas are similar in structure. What are the common elements in these arguments? In what important ways are they different?

6.   Take one of Aquinas's arguments and state it in your own words. Which premises seem most open to question? Develop an objection to a premise used by Aquinas or answer a possible objection.

7.   Aquinas uses quotations from Scripture in several places. What part do these quotations play in his argument? Does Aquinas's use of these quotations mean that he is appealing to faith rather than reason?

8.   Give your own version of one of Aquinas's arguments and either develop an objection to it or defend it against a possible objection.

9.   Are you convinced by Aquinas's arguments? Why or why not?

10.   What is the major objection to God's existence? Can it be answered?

B. COMMENT ON AQUINAS

Edward Sillem: *Ways of Thinking About God*

Edward Sillem (b. 1916) is an English philosopher and theologian and a Lecturer in Philosophy at St. John's Seminary, Guilford, England. He has written several books on problems connected with the arguments for the existence of God, including *George Berkeley and the Proofs for the Existence of God* (1957) and one of the best contemporary discussions of Aquinas's arguments, *Ways of Thinking About God* (1961), from which this selection is taken. For dramatic purposes, Professor Sillem has written this discussion as if Aquinas himself were discussing his arguments with contemporary philosophers.

I should like to mention, in a very summary fashion, a number of points which I must leave those of you who write about my arguments for the existence of God to discuss in detail amongst yourselves. Needless to say, I intend the following remarks for the special consideration of those who claim to be exponents of my proofs for the existence of God. Though they may not agree with some of the points I am going to make, I venture to suggest that they should consider each of them in their discussions of the Five Ways. If this had been done some years ago, I am sure that many disputes over the interpretation of my arguments might have been avoided altogether, and Thomist philosophers might have something to offer that would strike the attention of all serious thinkers, of your own or of any other time.

1. I suggest that there is really only one complete argument for the existence of God in my *Summa Theologica* and *Contra Gentes*, and that this argument comprises the two distinct stages of which I have spoken. The first stage argues from contingent to necessary being, and the second shows that necessary being must be self-subsistent Being, and thence perfect, infinite, eternal, and one in Being.

2. The first stage of the argument is as metaphysical in character as the second. But whereas the first stage is purely philosophical in that it reasons from the date of experience, the second stage is theological, that is to say, it is a metaphysical intepretation of the biblical and revealed teaching about God offered by a theologian to show how God has revealed Himself to us, and how we can think the truths about Himself He has revealed to us. Following my idea of theology as a dialogue between faith and reason I wrote Quaestiones 3-11 of the *Summa* to show how by His revelation God answers the questions the philosopher comes to ask about uncaused, necessary and non-limited being.

3. I compressed the first stage of the argument within the narrow confines of article 3 giving the Five Ways. Here, as in chapter 13 of the *Contra Gentes*, I only intended to establish that the universe is an effect dependent on a being (or beings) which is (or are) uncaused, nonlimited, necessary and intelligent. They are not, therefore, so much five complete or independent arguments for God's existence as five complementary ways into one complete argument. An example may make my point clearer. Let us imagine a number of men on a mountain-climbing expedition splitting into five

different parties to commence the difficult first phase of their climb, and let us suppose that they all agree to meet, if possible, at five points not far distant from each other about one-third the way up; we would say that they planned to begin their one expedition of climbing the mountain by commencing in five different ways along five different routes. We would not say that there were five independent expeditions of climbing the mountain, because, after completing the first third of their climb, the parties arranged to meet and complete their climb together. So it is with the Five Ways: they begin to converge together in Quaestio 3, but it is not till Quaestio 11 that they all finally arrive together at the top, or at the conclusion of the whole operation.

I took the Five Ways of set purpose mainly from the works of Aristotle, because I knew that they would appeal to the Aristotelian ways of thinking which I was doing my best to foster in the mediaeval schools, and because I wanted to make Aristotle better known to my brother theologians at the time. I cast the arguments into the succinct form in which you know them now, becuase I was writing the *Summa Theologica* for the benefit of students beginning their theology, and I only required them to have summaries of the full arguments which professional philosophers would need. I still regard the main intention of the Five Ways as sound, that is to say, I still hold that we can argue validly from changing to unchangeable being, from beings which happen to exist to being which must exist, from limited to nonlimited being, from an intelligible universe to a mind responsible for its formation, though I would revise my judgement about the merits of the arguments as they are stated in the Five Ways, had I realized when committing the Five Ways to writing that they were to become the focal point for discussion amongst philsophers for centuries to come, and that they were going to be paraded by many as the 'traditional' arguments for God's existence, I would never have presented them just as they are. I would never have imagined that I could let Aristotle plead the full case for Christian theism before the philsophers of the world, as I could allow him to plead the case I set him to plead on behalf of reason before the theologians of the thirteenth century. If, then, you wish to present the full reasoning of the first stage of the argument for the existence of God before philosophers today, I cannot see that any good is to be gained by adhering literally and exclusively to the text of the Five Ways. The Five Ways need to be rethought and re-argued in detail with contemporary thinkers, and they ought to be revised so as to make room for the study of the basic problems of modern philosophy which need to be studied with great care. The Five Ways do not need to be scrapped, but improved and enriched by being kept in contact with modern developments in philosophy. The whole way of thinking this stage of the argument needs to be freed from the rigid Aristotelian mould in which I considered it advisable to cast the Five Ways. There is no justification whatsoever for saying that anyone who criticizes the use at the present day of the Five Ways in their mediaeval format must be prejudiced against my whole treatment of the argument for God's existence, for the Five Ways as they stand were never intended to meet the requirements of serious philosophical discussion of the problems of theism in the present century.

4. In my view it is necessary to take all the Five Ways together as five parts of one whole argument designed to show that the universe is an effect. The example of the mountain-climbing expedition should make this point clear. We establish that the universe is an effect by showing that it is contingent, i.e. dependent or suspended in its being: there must therefore be a cause on which it depends. The Five Ways convert the question 'does God exist?' into the question 'who is the cause of the contingent universe?' In the context of the argument for the existence of God contingent being is to be understood to mean, not just that which happens to exist whereas it might as well never have existed or, as I have expressed the idea in this talk, that which is not self-necessitated in its existence, but also that which changes and is changed in its being, is limited and intelligible in its being, though it is clearly not the source of its own intelligibility. We have to show that the universe is contingent not merely in the weaker sense associated exclusively with the third Way, but in the radical and fuller sense which results from climbing the Five Ways together. I suggest that the whole strength of the first stage of the argument comes from understanding contingeny in this full sense.

For those who take them separately, I must point out how little I actually claimed to have established at the end of each of the Five Ways. Considering the caution and restraint with which I worded the conclusion of each Way, I deplore the unaccountable persistency with which many Thomist writers regard the Five Ways as providing five independent and complete arguments for God's existence. I chose the little expression 'quod omnes dicunt Deum esse' with which each Way finishes because I expected everyone to understand that I used the word 'God' each time to refer, not to the God of the Christian faith whose existence I was trying to establish, nor to God as He has revealed Himself to us, but to God as we had to define Him nominally at the beginning of the argument. The *Deus* mentioned at the end of each Way is just the being whom all entering upon the first stage of the argument agree at the beginning to call God, and whom they agree must exist as cause if we can show that the universe is an effect. Having, then, established in the Five Ways that the universe is an effect, we end by concluding that a being we all agreed to call God exists. I admit that it is not clear from the Five Ways alone that there is only one cause of the world. I included the Five Ways under Quaestio 2, not because I regarded the whole argument as ending where article 3 finished so that I could pass on to some other topic in Quaestio 3, but because in Quaestio 2 I was concerned to show that reason on its own can know God, not by actually proving that I can myself, but by producing evidence to show that non-Christian philosophers had come to some knowledge of Him. I certainly did not intend anyone to think that, because I did not add a fourth article to Quaestio 2, reason unaided by faith could not in principle come to know more about God than is contained in the Five Ways. In brief, I never intended article 3 to decide or finish anything about God's existence once and for all: I intended it to present the challenge to reason with which it concludes and with which the theologian confronts reason, that, in the full sense of the term, the universe is contingent and depends on necessary being.

Discussion Questions

1. Sillem uses the device of writing his discussion of Aquinas as if Aquinas himself were speaking to a present-day audience. Do you think Aquinas himself would agree with all that Sillem has him say? Why or why not?

2. Did Sillem's discussion help you understand Aquinas's arguments better? If so, in what way? If not, why not?

3. Aquinas as represented by Sillem says that all five ways are part of one argument. Give in your own words the reasons given for saying this. Do you agree or disagree that the five ways make up one argument? Give your reasons.

4. Sillem has Aquinas says that if he were alive today he would revise his arguments. How might he do this? Why might he want to do it?

5. What is the "challenge to reason" which Sillem has Aquinas state is the main purpose of the five ways? How should reason meet this challenge in your view?

C. GOD DOES NOT EXIST

David Hume:
Dialogues on Natural Religion

David Hume (1711–1776), a Scottish philosopher, is a major figure in modern philosophy. Hume began with an empiricist position that all knowledge is confined to what we can learn from our senses and arrived at a position of complete scepticism in every department of human thought. While some philosophers accept Hume's sceptical conclusions in one or more areas (e.g., his religious scepticism) a great part of Hume's importance for modern philosophy is the formidable challenge he offers, a challenge which must be taken up by any nonsceptical philosophical theory. Some of Hume's most important works are the *Treatise of Human Nature*, the *Enquiry Concerning Human Understanding*, and *Dialogues on Natural Religion*, from which this selection is taken.

In the dialogue, Demea represents a metaphysical approach to religion somewhat like that of Aquinas, Cleanthes a more empirical approach, and Philo a sceptical approach. It is usually thought that Philo represents Hume's own point of view, but some philosophers believe that Cleanthes also sometimes represents Hume's view.

Not to lose any time in circumlocutions, said Cleanthes, addressing himself to Demea, much less in replying to the pious declamations of Philo, I shall briefly explain how I conceive this matter. Look round the world: Contemplate the whole and every part of it: You will find it to be nothing but one great machine, subdivided into an infinite number of lesser machines, which again admit of subdivisions to a degree beyond what human senses and faculties can trace and explain. All these various machines, and even their most minute parts, are adjusted to each other with an accuracy which ravishes into admiration all men who have ever contemplated them. The curious adapting of means to ends, throughout all nature, resembles exactly, though it much exceeds, the productions of human contrivance— of human design, thought, wisdom, and intelligence. Since therefore the effects resemble each other, we are led to infer, by all the rules of analogy, that the causes also resemble, and that the Author of Nature is somewhat similar to the mind of man, though possessed of much larger faculties, proportioned to the grandeur of the work which he has executed. By this argument *a posteriori*, and by this argument alone, do we prove at once the existence of a Deity and his similarity to human mind and intelligence.

I shall be so free, Cleanthes, said Demea, as to tell you that from the beginning I could not approve of your conclusion concerning the similarity of the Deity to men, still less can I approve of the mediums by which you endeavor to establish it. What! No demonstration of the Being of God! No abstract arguments! No proofs *a priori!* Are these which have hitherto been so much insisted on by philosophers all fallacy, all sophism? Can we reach no farther in this subject than experience and probability? I will say not that this is betraying the cause of a Deity; but surely, by this affected candor, you give advantages to atheists which they never could obtain by the mere dint of argument and reasoning.

What I chiefly scruple in this subject, said Philo, is not so much that all religious arguments are by Cleanthes reduced to experience, as that they appear not to be even the most certain and irrefragable of that inferior kind. That a stone will fall, that fire will burn, that the earth has solidity, we have observed a thousand and a thousand times; and when any new instance of this nature is presented, we draw without hesitation the accustomed inference. The exact similarity of the cases gives us a perfect assurance of a similar event, and a stronger evidence is never desired nor sought after. But wherever you depart, in the least, from the similarity of the cases, you diminish proportionably the evidence; and may at last bring it to a very weak *analogy*, which is confessedly liable to error and uncertainty. After having experienced the circulation of the blood in human creatures, we make no doubt that it takes place in Titius and Maevius; but from its circulation in frogs and fishes it is only a presumption, though a strong one, from analogy that it takes place in men and other animals. The analogical reasoning is much weaker when we infer the circulation of the sap in vegetables from our experience that the blood circulates in animals; and those who hastily followed that imperfect analogy are found, by more accurate experiments, to have been mistaken.

If we see a house, Cleanthes, we conclude, with the greatest certainty, that it had an architect or builder because this is precisely that species of effect which we have experienced to proceed from that species of cause. But surely you will not affirm that the universe bears such a resemblance to a house that we can with the same certainty infer a similar cause, or that the analogy is here entire and perfect. The dissimilitude is so striking that the utmost you can here pretend to is a guess, a conjecture, a presumption concerning a similar cause; and how that pretension will be received in the world, I leave you to consider.

It would surely be very ill received, replied Cleanthes; and I should be deservedly blamed and detested did I allow that the proofs of a Deity amounted to no more than a guess or conjecture. But is the whole adjustment of means to ends in a house and in the universe so slight a resemblance? the economy of final causes? the order, proportion, and arrangement of every part? Steps of a stair are plainly contrived that human legs may use them in mounting; and this inference is certain and infallible. Human legs are also contrived for walking and mounting; and this inference, I allow, is not altogether so certain because of the dissimilarity which you remark; but does it, therefore, deserve the name only of presumption or conjecture?

Good God! cried Demea, interrupting him, where are we? Zealous defenders of religion allow that the proofs of a Deity fall short of perfect evidence! And you, Philo, on whose assistance I depended in proving the adorable mysteriousness of the Divine Nature, do you assent to all these extravagant opinions of Cleanthes? For what other name can I give them? or, why spare my censure when such principles are advanced, supported by such an authority, before so young a man as Pamphilus?

You seem not to apprehend, replied Philo, that I argue with Cleanthes in his own way, and, by showing him the dangerous consequences of his tenets, hope at last to reduce him to our opinion. But what sticks most with you, I observe, is the representation which Cleanthes has made of the argument *a posteriori*; and, finding that the argument is likely to escape your hold and vanish into air, you think it so disguised that you can scarcely believe it to be set in its true light. Now, however much I may dissent, in other respects, from the dangerous principle of Cleanthes, I must allow that he has fairly represented that argument, and I shall endeavor so to state the matter to you that you will entertain no further scruples with regard to it.

Were a man to abstract from everything which he knows or has seen, he would be altogether incapable, merely from his own ideas, to determine what kind of scene the universe must be, or to give the preference to one state or situation of things above another. For as nothing which he clearly conceives could be esteemed impossible or implying a contradiction, every chimera of his fancy would be upon an equal footing; nor could he assign any just reason why he adheres to one idea or system, and rejects the others which are equally possible.

Again, after he opens his eyes and contemplates the world as it really is, it would be impossible for him at first to assign the cause of any one event, much less of the whole of things, or of the universe. He might set his fancy a rambling, and she might bring him in an infinite variety of reports and representations. These would all be possible; but, being all equally possible, he would never of himself give a satisfactory account for his preferring one of them to the rest. Experience alone can point out to him the true cause of any phenomenon.

Now, according to this method of reasoning, Demea, it follows (and is, indeed, tacitly allowed by Cleanthes himself) that order, arrangement, or the adjustment of final causes, is not of itself any proof of design, but only so far as it has been experienced to proceed from that principle. For aught we can know *a priori*, matter may contain the source of spring of order originally within itself, as well as mind does; and there is no more difficulty in conceiving that the several elements, from an internal unknown cause, may fall into the most exquisite arrangement, than to conceive that their ideas, in the great universal mind, from a like internal unknown cause, fall into that arrangement. The equal possibility of both these suppositions is allowed. But, by experience, we find (according to Cleanthes) that there is a difference between them. Throw several pieces of steel together, without shape or form, they will never arrange themselves so as to compose a watch. Stone and mortar and wood, without an architect, never erect a house. But the ideas in a human mind, we see, by an unknown, inexplicable economy, arrange themselves so as to form the plan of a watch or house. Experience, therefore, proves that there is an original principle of order in mind, not in matter. From similar effects we infer similar causes. The adjustment of means to ends is alike in the universe, as in a machine of human contrivance. The causes, therefore, must be resembling.

I was from the beginning scandalized, I must own, with this resemblance which is asserted between the Deity and human creatures, and must conceive it to imply such a degradation of the Supreme Being as no sound theist could endure. With your assistance, therefore, Demea, I shall endeavor to defend what you justly call the adorable mysteriousness of the Divine Nature, and shall refute this reasoning of Cleanthes, provided he allows that I have made a fair representation of it.

When Cleanthes had assented, Philo, after a short pause, proceeded in the following manner.

That all inferences, Cleanthes, concerning fact are founded on experience, and that all experimental reasonings are founded on the supposition that similar causes prove similar effects, and similar effects similar causes, I shall not at present much dispute with you. But observe, I entreat you, with what extreme caution all just reasoners proceed in the transferring of experiments to similar cases. Unless the cases be exactly similar, they repose no perfect confidence in applying their past observation to any particular phenomenon. Every alteration of circumstances occasions a doubt concerning the event; and it requires new experiments to prove certainly that the new circumstances are of no moment or importance. A change in bulk, situation, arrangement, age, disposition of the air, or surrounding bodies—any of these particulars may be attended with the most unexpected consequences. And unless the objects be quite familiar to us, it is the highest temerity to expect with assurance, after any of these changes, an event similar to that which before fell under our observation. The slow and deliberate steps of philosophers here, if anywhere, are distinguished from the precipitate march of the vulgar, who, hurried on by the smallest similitude, are incapable of all discernment or consideration.

But can you think, Cleanthes, that your usual phlegm and philosophy have been preserved in so wide a step as you have taken when you compared to the universe houses, ships, furniture, machines; and, from their similarity in some circumstances, inferred a similarity in their causes? Thought, design, intelligence, such as we discover in men and other animals, is no more than one of the springs and principles of the universe, as well as heat or cold, attraction or repulsion, and is a hundred others which fall under daily observation. It is an active cause by which some particular parts of nature, we find, produce alterations on other parts. But can a conclusion, with any propriety, be transferred from parts to the whole? Does not the great disproportion bar all comparison and inference? From observing the growth of a hair, can we learn anything concerning the generation of a man? Would the manner of a leaf's blowing, even though perfectly known, afford us any instruction concerning the vegetation of a tree?

But allowing that we were to take the *operations* of one part of nature upon another for the foundation of our judgment concerning the *origin* of the whole (which never can be admitted), yet why select so minute, so weak, so bounded a principle as the reason and design of animals is found to be upon this planet? What peculiar privilege has this little agitation of the brain which we call *thought*, that we must thus make in the model of the whole universe? Our partiality in our own favor does indeed present it on all occasions, but sound philoosphy ought carefully to guard against so natural an illusion.

So far from admitting, continued Philo, that the operations of a part can afford us any just conclusion concerning the origin of the whole, I will not allow any one part to form a rule for another part if the latter be very remote from the former. Is there any reasonable ground to conclude that the inhabitants of other planets possess thought, intelligence, reason, or anything similar to these faculties in men? When nature has so extremely diversified her manner of operation in this small globe, can we imagine that she incessantly copies herself throughout so immense a universe? And if thought, as we may well suppose, be confined merely to this narrow corner and has even there so limited a sphere of action, with what propriety can we assign it for the original cause of all things? The narrow views of a peasant who makes his domestic economy the rule for the government of kingdoms is in comparison a pardonable sophism.

But were we ever so much assured that a thought and reason resembling the human were to be found throughtout the whole universe, and were its activity elsewhere vastly greater and more commanding than it appears in this globe; yet I cannot see why the operations of a world constituted, arranged, adjusted, can with any propriety be extended to a world which is in its embryo-state, and is advancing towards that constitution and arrangement. By observation we know somewhat of the economy, action, and nourishment of a finished animal; but we must transfer with great caution that observation to the growth of a foetus in the womb, and still more to the formation of an animalcule in the loins of its male parent. Nature, we find, even from our limited experience, possesses an infinite number of springs and principles which incessantly discover themselves on every change of her position and situation. And what new and unknown principles would actuate her in so new and unknown a situation as that of the formation of a universe, we cannot, without the utmost temerity, pretend to determine.

A very small part of this great system, during a very short time, is very imperfectly discovered to us; and do we thence pronounce decisively concerning the origin of the whole?

Admirable conclusion! Stone, wood, brick, iron, brass, have not, at this time, in this minute globe of earth, an order or arrangement without human art and contrivance; therefore, the universe could not originally attain its order and arrangement without something similar to human art. But is a part of nature a rule for another part very wide of the former? Is it a rule for the whole? Is a very small part a rule for the universe? Is nature in one situation a certain rule for nature in another situation vastly different from the former?

And can you blame me, Cleanthes, if I here imitate the prudent reserve of Simonides, who, according to the noted story, being asked by Hiero, *What God was*? desired a day to think of it, and then two days more; and after that manner continually prolonged the term, without ever bringing in his definition or description? Could you even blame me if I had answered, at first, *that I did not know*, and was sensible that this subject lay vastly beyond the reach of my faculties? You might cry out sceptic and railer, as much as you pleased; but, having found in so many other subjects much more familiar the imperfections and even contradictions of human reason, I never should expect any success from its feeble conjectures in a subject so sublime and so remote from the sphrere of our observation. When two *species* of objects have always been observed to be conjoined together, I can *infer*, by custom, the existence of one wherever I *see* the existence of the other; and this I call an argument form experience. But how this argument can have place where the objects, as in the present case, are single, individual, without parallel or specific resemblance, may be difficult to explain. And will any man tell me with a serious countenance that an orderly universe must arise from some thought and art like the human because we have experience of it? To ascertain this reasoning it were requisite that we had experience of the origin of worlds; and it is not sufficient, surely, that we have seen ships and cities arise from human art and contrivance . . .

Now, Cleanthes, said Philo, with an air of alacrity and triumph, mark the consequences. *First*, by this method of reasoning you renounce all claim to infinity in any of the attributes of the Deity. For, as the cause ought only to be proportioned to the effect, and the effect, so far as it falls under our cognizance, is not infinite, what pretensions have we, upon your suppositions, to ascribe that attribute to the divine Being? You will still insist that, by removing him so much from all similarity to human creatures, we give in to the most arbitrary hypothesis, and at the same time weaken all proofs of his existence.

Secondly, you have no reason, on your theory, for ascribing perfection to the Deity, even in his finite capacity; or for supposing him free from every error, mistake, or incoherence, in his undertakings. There are many inexplicable difficulties in the works of nature which, if we allow a perfect author to be proved *a priori*, are easily solved, and become only seeming difficulties from the narrow capacity of man, who cannot trace infinite relations. But according to your method of reasoning, these difficulties become all real; and, perhaps, will be insited on as new instances of likeness to human art and contrivance. At least, you must acknowledge that it is impossible for us to tell, from our limited views, whether this system contains any great faults or deserves any considerable praise if compared to other possible and even real systems. Could a peasant, if the *Aeneid* were read to him, pronounce that poem to be absolutely faultless, or even assign to it its proper rank among the productions of human wit, he who had never seen any other production?

But were this world ever so perfect a production, it must still remain uncertain whether all the excellences of the work can justly be ascribed to the workman. If we survey a ship, what an exalted idea must we form of the ingenuity of the carpenter who framed so complicated, useful, and beautiful a machine? And what surprise must we feel when we find him a stupid mechanic who imitated others, and copied an art which, through a long succession of ages, after multiplied trials, mistakes, corrections, deliberations, and controversies, had been gradually improving? Many worlds might have been botched and bungled, throughout an eternity, ere this system was struck out; much labor lost; many fruitless trials made; and a slow but continued improvement carried on during infinite ages in the art of world-making. In such subjects, who can determine where the truth, nay, who can conjecture where the probability lies, amidst a great number of hypotheses which may be proposed, and a still greater which may be imagined?

And what shadow of an argument, continued Philo, can you produce from your hypothesis to prove the unity of the Deity? A great number of men join in building a house or ship, in rearing a city, in framing a commonwealth; why may not several deities combine in contriving and framing a world? This is only so much greater similarity to human affairs. By sharing the work among several, we may so much further limit the attributes of each, and get rid of that extensive power and knowledge which must be supposed in one deity, and which, according to you, can only serve to weaken the proof of his existence. And if such foolish, such vicious creatures as man can yet often unite in framing and executing one plan, how much more those deities or demons, whom we may suppose several degrees more perfect?

To multiply causes without necessity is indeed contrary to true philosophy, but this principle applies not to the present case. Were one deity antecedently proved by your theory who were possessed of every attribute requisite to the production of the universe, it would be needless, I own (though not absurd), to suppose any other deity existent. But while it is still a question whether all these attributes are united in one subject or dispersed among several independent beings; by what phenomena in nature can we pretend to decide the controversy? Where we see a body raised in a scale, we are sure that there is in the opposite scale, however concealed from sight, some counterposing weight equal to it; but it is still allowed to doubt whether that weight be an aggregate of several distinct bodies or one uniform united mass. And if the weight requisite very much exceeds anything which we have ever seen conjoined in any single body, the former supposition becomes still more probable and natural. An intelligent being of such vast power and capacity as is necessary to produce the universe—or, to speak in the language of ancient philosophy, so prodigious an animal—exceeds all analogy and even comprehension.

But further, Cleanthes, men are mortal, and renew their species by generation; and this is common to all living creatures. The two great sexes of male and female, says Milton, animate the world. Why must this circumstance, so universal, so essential, be executed from those numerous and limited deities? Behold, then, the theogeny of ancient times brought back upon us.

And why not become a perfect anthropomorphite? Why not assert the deity or deities to be corporeal, and to have eyes, a nose, mouth, ears, etc.? Epicurus maintained that no man had ever seen reason but in a human figure; therefore, the gods must have a human figure. And this argument, which is deservedly so much ridiculed by Cicero, becomes, according to you, solid and philosophical.

In a word, Cleanthes, a man who follows your hypothesis is able, perhaps, to assert or conjecture that the universe sometime arose from something like design; but beyond that position he cannot ascertain one single circumstance, and is left afterwards to fix every point of his theology by the utmost license of fancy and hypothesis. This world, for aught he knows, is very faulty and imperfect, compared to a superior standard; and was only the first rude essay of some infant deity who afterwards abandoned it, ashamed of his lame performance; it is the work only of some dependent, inferior deity, and is the object of derision to his superiors; it is the production of old age and dotage in some superannuated deity; and ever since his death has run on at adventures, from the first impulse and active force which it received from him. You justly give signs of horror, Demea, at these strange suppositions; but these, and a thousand more of the same kind, are Cleanthes' suppositions, not mine. From the moment the attributes of the Deity are supposed finite, all these have place. And I cannot, for my part, think that so wild and unsettled a system of theology is, in any respect, preferable to none at all. . . .

What you ascribe to the fertility of my invention, replied Philo, is entirely owing to the nature of the subject. In subjects adapted to the narrow compass of human reason there is commonly but one determination which carries probability or conviction with it; and to a man of sound judgment all other suppositions but that one appear entirely absurd and chimerical. But in such questions as the present, a hundred contradictory views may preserve a kind of imperfect analogy, and invention has here full scope to exert itself. Without any great effort of thought, I believe that I could, in an instant, propose other systems of cosmogony which would have some faint appearance of truth; though it is a thousand, a million to one if either yours or any one of mine be the true system.

For instance, what if I should revive the old Epicurean hypothesis? This is commonly, and I believe justly, esteemed the most absurd system that has yet been proposed; yet I know not whether, with a few alterations, it might not be brought to bear a faint appearance of probability. Instead of supposing matter infinite, as Epicurus did, let us suppose it finite. A finite number of particles is only susceptible of finite transpositions; and it must happen, in an eternal duration, that every possible order or position must be tried an infinite number of times. This world, therefore, with all its events, even the most minute, has before been produced and destroyed, and will again be produced and destroyed, without any bounds and limitations. No one who has a conception of the powers of infinite, in comparison of finite, will ever scruple this determination.

But this supposes, said Demea, that matter can acquire motion without any voluntary agent or first mover.

And where is the difficulty, replied Philo, of that supposition? Every event, before experience, is equally difficult and incomprehensible; and every event, after experience, is equally easy and intelligible. Motion, in many instances, from gravity, from elasticity, from electricity, begins in matter, without any known voluntary agent; and to suppose always, in these cases, an unknown voluntary agent is mere hypothesis—and hypothesis attended with no advantages. The beginning of motion in matter itself is as conceivable *a priori* as its communication from mind and intelligence.

Besides, why may not motion have been propagated by impulse through all eternity, and the same stock of it, or nearly the same, be still upheld in the universe? As much as is lost by the composition of motion, as much is gained by its resolution. And whatever the causes are, the fact is certain that matter is and always has been in continual agitation, as far as human experience or tradition reaches. There is not probably, at present, in the whole universe, one particle of matter at absolute rest.

And this very consideration, too, continued Philo, which we have stumbled on in the course of the argument suggests a new hypothesis of cosmogony that is not absolutely absurd and improbable. Is there a system, an order, an economy of things, by which matter can preserve that perpetual agitation which seems essential to it, and yet maintain a constancy in the forms which it produces? There certainly is such an economy, for this is actually the case with the present world. The continual motion of matter, therefore, in less than infinite transpositions, must produce this economy or order; and, by its very nature, that order, when once established, supports itself for many ages if not to eternity. But wherever matter is so poised, arranged, and adjusted, as to continue in perpetual motion, and yet preserve a constancy in the forms, its situation must, of necessity, have all the same appearance of art and contrivance which we observe at present. All the parts of each form must have a relation to each other and to the whole; and the whole itself must have a relation to the other parts of the universe, to the element in which the form subsists, to the materials with which it repairs its waste and decay, and to every other form which is hostile or friendly. A defect in any of these particulars destroys the form; and the matter of which it is composed is again set loose, and is thrown into irregular motions and fermentations till it unite itself to some other regular form. If no such form be prepared to receive it, and if there be a great quantity of this corrupted matter in the universe, the universe itself is entirely disordered, whether it be the feeble embryo of a world in its first beginnings that is thus destroyed or the rotten carcass of one languishing in old age and infirmity. In either case, a chaos ensues till infinite though innumerable revolutions produce, at last, some forms whose parts and organs are so adjusted as to support the forms amidst a continued succession of matter.

Suppose (for we shall endeavor to vary the expression) that matter were thrown into any position by a blind, unguided force; it is evident that this first position must, in all probability, be the most confused and most disorderly imaginable, without any resemblance to those works of human contrivance which, along with a symmetry of parts, discover an adjustment of means to ends and a tendency to self-preservation. If the actuating force cease after this operation, matter must remain forever in disorder, and continue an immense chaos, without any proportion or activity. But suppose that the actuating force, whatever it be, still continues in matter, this first position will immediately give place to a second which will likewise, in all probability, be as disorderly as the first, and so on through many successions of changes and revolutions. No particular order or position ever continues a moment unaltered. The original force, still remaining in activity, gives a perpetual restlessness to matter. Every possible situation is produced, and instantly destroyed. If a glimpse or dawn of order appears for a moment, it is instantly hurried away and confounded by that never-ceasing force which actuates every part of matter.

Thus the universe goes on for many ages in a continued succession of chaos and disorder. But is it not possible that it may settle at last, so as not to lose its motion and active force (for that we have supposed inherent in it), yet so as to preserve a uniformity of appearance, amidst the continual motion and fluctuation of its parts? This we find to be the case with the universe at present. Every individual is perpetually changing, and every part of every individual; and yet the whole remains, in appearance, the same. May we not hope for such a position or rather be assured of it from the eternal revolutions of unguided matter; and may not this account for all the appearing wisdom and contrivance which is in the universe? Let us contemplate the subject a little, and we shall find that this adjustment if attained by matter of a seeming stability in the forms, with a real and perpetual revolution or motion of parts, affords a plausible, if not a true, solution of the difficulty.

It is in vain, therefore, to insist upon the uses of the parts in animals or vegetables, and their curoius adjustment to each other. I would fain know how an animal could subsist unless its parts were so adjusted? Do we not find that it immediately perishes whenever this adjustment ceases, and that its matter, corrupting, tries some new form? It happens indeed that the parts of the world are so well adjusted that some regular form immediately lays claim to this corrupted matter; and if it were not so, could the world subsist? Must it not dissolve, as well as the animal, and pass through new positions and situations till in great but finite succession it fall, at last, into the present or some such order?

It is well, replied Cleanthes, you told us that this hypothesis was suggested on a sudden, in the course of the argument. Had you had leisure to examine it, you would soon have perceived the insuperable objections to which it is exposed. No form, you say, can subsist unless it possess those powers and organs requisite for its subsistence; some new order or economy must be tried, and so on, without intermission, till at last some order which can support and maintain itself is fallen upon. But according to this hypothesis, whence arise the many conveniences and advantages which men and all animals possess? Two eyes, two ears are not absolutely necessary for the subsistence of the species. Human race might have been propagated and preserved without horses, dogs, cows, sheep, and those innumerable fruits and products which serve to our satisfaction and enjoyment. If no camels had been created for the use of man in the sandy deserts of Africa and Arabia, would the world have been dissolved? If no loadstone had been framed to give that wonderful and useful direction to the needle, would human society and the human kind have been immediately extinguished? Though the maxims of nature be in general very frugal, yet instances of this kind are far from being rare; and any one of them is a sufficient proof of design—and of a benevolent design—which gave rise to the order and arrangement of the universe.

At least, you may safely infer, said Philo, that the foregoing hypothesis is so far incomplete and imperfect, which I shall not scruple to allow. But can we ever reasonably expect greater success in any attempts of this nature? Or can we ever hope to erect a system of cosmogony that will be liable to no exceptions, and will contain no circumstance repugnant to our limited and imperfect experience of the analogy of nature? Your theory itself cannot surely pretend to any such advantage; even though you have run into *anthropomorphism*, the better to preserve a conformity to common experience. Let us once more put it to trial. In all instances which we have ever seen, ideas are copied from real objects, and are ectypal, not archetypal, to express myself in learned terms. You reverse this order and give thought the precedence. In all instances which we have ever seen, thought has no influence upon matter except where that matter is so conjoined with it as to have an equal reciprocal influence upon it. No animal can move immediately anything but the members of its own body; and, indeed, the equality of action and reaction seems to be an universal law of nature; but your theory implies a contradiction to this experience. These instances, with many more which it were easy to collect (particularly the supposition of a mind or system of thought that is eternal or, in other words, an animal ingenerable and immortal)—these instances, I say, may teach all of us sobriety in condemning each other, and let us see that as no system of this kind ought ever to be received from a slight analogy, so neither ought any to be rejected on account of a small incongruity. For that is an inconvenience from which we can justly pronounce no one to be exempted.

All religious systems, it is confessed, are subject to great and insuperable difficulties. Each disputant triumphs in his turn, while he carries on an offensive war, and exposes the absurdities, barbarities, and pernicious tenets of his antagonist. But all of them, on the whole, prepare a complete triumph for the *sceptic*, who tells them that no system ought ever to be embraced with regard to such subjects; for this plain reason, that no absurdity ought ever to be assented to with regard to any subject. A total suspense of judgment is here our only reasonable resource. And if every attack, as is commonly observed, and no defence among theologians is successful, how complete must be *his* victory who remains always, with all mankind, on the offensive, and has himself no fixed station or abiding city which he is ever, on any occasion, obliged to defend?

* * *

But if so many difficulties attend the argument *a posteriori*, said Demea, had we not better adhere to that simple and sublime argument *a priori* which, by offering to us infallible demonstration, cuts off at once all doubt and difficulty? By this argument, too, we may prove the *infinity* of the Divine attributes, which, I am afraid, can never be ascertained with certainty from any other topic. For how can an effect which either is finite or, for aught we know, may be so—how can such an effect, I say, prove an infinite cause? The unity, too, of the Divine Nature it is very difficult, if not absolutely impossible, to deduce merely from contemplating the works of nature; nor will the uniformity alone of the plan, even were it allowed, give us any assurance of that attribute. Whereas the argument *a priori* . . .

You seem to reason, Demea, interposed Cleanthes, as if those advantages and conveniences in the abstract argument were full proofs of its solidity. But it is first proper, in my opinion, to determine what argument of this nature you choose to insist on; and we shall afterwards, from itself, better than from its *useful* consequences, endeavor to determine what value we ought to put upon it.

The argument, replied Demea, which I would insist on is the common one. Whatever exists must have a cause or reason of its existence, it being absolutely impossible for anything to produce itself or be the cause of its own existence. In mounting up, therefore, from effects to causes, we must either go on in tracing an infinite succession, without any ultimate cause at all, or must at last have recourse to some ultimate cause that is *necessarily* existent. Now, that the first supposition is absurd may be thus proved. In the infinite chain or succession of causes and effects, each single effect is determined to exist by the power and efficacy of that cause which immediately preceded; but the whole eternal chain or succession, taken together, is not determined or caused by anything; and yet it is evident that it requires a cause or reason, as much as any particular object which begins to exist in time. The question is still reasonable why this particular succession of causes existed from eternity, and not any other succession or no succession at all. If there be no necessarily existent being, any supposition which can be formed is equally possible; nor is there any more absurdity in nothing's having existed from eternity than there is in that succession of causes which constitutes the universe. What was it, then, which determined something to exist rather than nothing, and bestowed being on a particular possibility, exclusive of the rest? *External causes*, there are supposed to be none. *Chance* is a word without a meaning. Was it *nothing*? But that can never produce anything. We must, therefore, have recourse to a necessarily existent Being who carries the *reason* of his existence in himself; and who cannot be supposed not to exist, without an express contradiction. There is, consequently, such a Being—that is, there is a Deity.

I shall not leave it to Philo, said Cleanthes (though I know that the starting objections is his chief delight), to point out the weakness of this metaphysical reasoning. It seems to me so obviously ill-grounded, and at the same time of so little consequence to the cause of true piety and religion, that I shall myself venture to show the fallacy of it.

I shall begin with observing that there is an evident absurdity in pretending to demonstrate a matter of fact, or to prove it by any arguments *a priori*. Nothing is demonstrable unless the contrary implies a contradiction. Nothing that is distinctly conceivable implies a contradiction. Whatever we conceive as existent, we can also conceive as non-existent. There is no being, therefore, whose non-existence implies a contradiction. Consequently thre is no being whose existence is demonstrable. I propose this argument as entirely decisive, and am willing to rest the whole controversy upon it.

It is pretended that the Deity is a necessarily existent being; and this necessity of his existence is attempted to be explained by asserting that, if we knew his whole essence or nature, we should perceive it to be as impossible for him not to exist, as for twice two not to be four. But it is evident that this can never happen, while our faculties remain the same as at present. It will still be possible for us, at any time, to conceive the non-existence of what we formerly conceived to exist; nor can the mind ever lie under a necessity of supposing any object to remain always in being; in the same manner as we lie under a necessity of always conceiving twice two to be four. The words, therefore, *necessary existence* have no meaning; or, which is the same thing, none that is consistent.

But further, why may not the material universe be the necessarily existent Being, according to this pretended explication of necessity? We dare not affirm that we know all the qualities of matter; and, for aught we can determine, it may contain some qualities which, were they known, would make its nonexistence appear as great a contradiction as that twice two is five. I find only one argument employed to prove that the material world is not the necessarily existent Being; and this argument is derived from the contingency both of the matter and the form of the world. "Any particle of matter", it is said, "may be *conceived* to be annihilated, and any form may be *conceived* to be altered. Such an annihilation or alteration, therefore, is not impossible." But it seems a great partiality not to perceive that the same argument extends equally to the Deity, so far as we have any conception of Him; and that the mind can at least imagine him to be non-existent, or his attributes to be altered. It must be some unknown, inconceivable qualities which can make his non-existence appear impossible or his attributes unalterable: And no reason can be assigned why these qualities may not belong to matter. As they are altogether unknown and inconceivable, they can never be proved incompatible with it.

Add to this that in tracing an eternal succession of objects it seems absurd to inquire for a general cause or first author. How can anything that exists from eternity have a cause, since that relation implies a priority in time and a beginning of existence?

In such a chain, too, or succession of objects, each part is caused by that which preceded it, and causes that which succeeds it. Where then is the difficulty? But the *whole*, you say, wants a cause. I answer that the uniting of these parts into a whole, like the uniting of several distinct countries into one kingdom, or several distinct members into one body, is performed merely by an arbitrary act of the mind, and has no influence on the nature of things. Did I show you the particular causes of each individual in a collection of twenty particles of matter, I should think it very unreasonable should you afterwards ask me what was the cause of the whole twenty. This is sufficiently explained in explaining the cause of the parts.

Though the reasonings which you have urged, Cleanthes, may well excuse me, said Philo, from starting any further difficulties; yet I cannot forbear insisting still upon another topic. It is observed by arithmeticians that the products of 9 compose always either 9 or some lesser product of 9 if you add together all the characters of which any of the former products is composed. Thus, of 18, 27, 36, which are products of 9, you make 9 by adding 1 to 8, 2 to 7, 3 to 6. Thus 369 is a product also of 9; and if you add 3, 6, and 9, you make 18, a lesser product of 9. To a superficial observer so wonderful a regularity may be admired as the effect either of chance or design; but a skillful algebraist immediately concludes it to be the work of necessity, and demonstrates that it must forever result from the nature of these numbers. Is it not probable, I ask, that the whole economy of the universe is conducted by a like necessity, though no human algebra can furnish a key which solves the difficulty? And instead of admiring the order of natural beings, may it not happen that, could we penetrate into the intimate nature of bodies, we should clearly see why it was absolutely impossible they could ever admit of any other disposition? So dangerous is it to introduce this idea of necessity into the present question! and so naturally does it afford an inference directly opposite to the religious hypothesis!

But dropping all these abstractions, continued Philo, and confining ourselves to more familiar topics, I shall venture to add an observation that the argument *a priori* has seldom been found very convincing, except to people of a metaphysical head who have accustomed themselves to abstract reasoning, and who, finding from mathematics that the understanding frequently leads to truth through obscurity, and contrary to first appearances, have transferred the same habit of thinking to subjects where it ought not to have place. Other people, even of good sense and the best inclined to religion, feel always some deficiency in such arguments, though they are not perhaps able to explain distinctly where it lies—a certain proof that men ever did and ever will derive their religion from other sources than from this species of reasoning.

I am indeed persuaded, said Philo, that the best and indeed the only method of bringing everyone to a due sense of religion is by just representations of the misery and wickedness of men. And for that purpose a talent of eloquence and strong imagery is more requisite than that of reasoning and argument. For is it necessary to prove what everyone feels within himself? It is only necessary to make us feel it, if possible, more intimately and sensibly.

The people, indeed, replied Demea, are sufficiently convinced of this great and melancholy truth. the miseries of life, the unhappiness of man, the general corruptions of our nature, the unsatisfactory enjoyment of pleasures, riches, honors—these phrases have become almost proverbial in all languages. And who can doubt of what all men declare from their own immediate feeling and experience?

In this point, said Philo, the learned are perfectly agreed with the vulgar; and in all letters, *sacred* and *profane*, the topic of human misery has been insisted on with the most pathetic eloquence that sorrow and melancholy could inspire. The poets, who speak from sentiment, without a system, and whose testimony has therefore the more authority, abound in images of this nature. From Homer down to Dr. Young, the whole inspired tribe have ever been sensible that no other representation of things would suit the feeling and observation of each individual.

As to authorities, replied Demea, you need not seek them. Look round this library of Cleanthes. I shall venture to affirm that, except authors of particular sciences, such as chemistry or botany, who have no occasion to treat of human life, there is scarce one of those innumerable writers from whom the sense of human misery has not, in some passage or other, extorted a complaint and confession of it. At least, the chance is entirely on that side; and no one author has ever, so far as I can recollect, been so extravagant as to deny it.

There you must excuse me, said Philo: Leibniz has denied it, and is perhaps the first who ventured upon so bold and paradoxical an opinion; at least, the first who made it essential to his philosophical system.

And by being the first, replied Demea, might he not have been sensible of his error? For is this a subject in which philosophers can propose to make discoveries especially in so late an age? And can any man hope by a simple denial (for the subject scarcely admits of reasoning) to bear down the united testimony of mankind, founded on sense and consciousness?

And why should man, added he, pretend to an exemption from the lot of all other animals? The whole earth, believe me, Philo, is cursed and polluted. A perpetual war is kindled amongst all living creatures. Necessity, hunger, want stimulate the strong and courageous; fear, anxiety, terror agitate the weak and infirm. The first entrance into life gives anguish to the new-born infant and to its wretched parent; weakness, impotence, distress attend each stage of that life, and it is, at last, finished in agony and horror.

Observe, too, says Philo, the curious artifices of nature in order to embitter the life of every living being. The stronger prey upon the weaker and keep them in perpetual terror and anxiety. The weaker, too, in their turn, often prey upon the stronger, and vex and molest them without relaxation. Consider that innumerable race of insects, which either are bred on the body of each animal or, flying about, infix their stings in him. These insects have others still less than themselves which torment them. And thus on each hand, before and behind, above and below, every animal is surrounded with enemies which incessantly seek his misery and destruction.

Man alone, said Demea, seems to be, in part, an exception to this rule. For by combination in society he can easily master lions, tigers, and bears, whose greater strength and agility naturally enable them to prey upon him.

On the contrary, it is here chiefly, cried Philo, that the uniform and equal maxims of nature are most apparent. Man, it is true, can, by combination, surmount all his *real* enemies and become master of the whole animal creation; but does he not immediately raise up to himself *imaginary* enemies, the demons of his fancy, who haunt him with superstitious terrors and blast every enjoyment of life? His pleasure, as he imagines, becomes in their eyes a crime; his food and repose give them umbrage and offence; his very sleep and dreams furnish new materials to anxious fear; and even death, his refuge from every other ill, presents only the dread of endless and innumerable woes. Nor does the wolf molest more the timid flock than superstition does the anxious beast of wretched mortals.

Besides, consider, Demea: This very society by which we surmount those wild beasts, our natural enemies, what new enemies does it not raise to us? What woe and misery does it not occasion? Man is the greatest enemy of man. Oppression, injustice, contempt, contumely, violence, sedition, war, calumny, treachery, fraud—by these they mutually torment each other, and they would soon dissolve that society which they had formed were it not for the dread of still greater ills which must attend their separation.

But though these external insults, said Demea, from animals, from men, from all the elements, which assault us from a frightful catalogue of woes, they are nothing in comparison of those which arise within ourselves, from the distempered condition of our mind and body. How many lie under the lingering torment of disease? Hear the pathetic enumeration of the great poet.

> Intestine stone and ulcer, colic-pangs,
> Demoniac frenzy, moping melancholy,
> And moon-struck madness, pining atrophy,
> Marasmus, and wide-wasting pestilence.
> Dire was the tossing, deep the groans: *Despair*
> Tended the sick, busiest from couch to couch.
> And over them triumphant *Death* his dart
> Shook: but delay'd to strike, though oft invok'd
> With vows, as their chief good and final hope.

The disorders of the mind, continued Demea, though more secret, are not perhaps less dismal and vexatious. Remorse, shame, anguish, rage, disappointment, anxiety, fear, dejection, despair—who has ever passed through life without cruel inroads from these tormentors? How many have scarcely ever felt any better sensations? Labor and poverty, so abhorred by everyone, are the certain lot of the far greater number; and those few privileged persons who enjoy ease and opulence never reach contentment or true felicity. All the goods of life united would not make a very happy man, but all the ills united would make a wretch indeed; and any one of them almost (and who can be free from every one), nay, often the absence of one good (and who can possess all) is sufficient to render life ineligible.

Were a stranger to drop on a sudden into this world, I would show him, as a specimen of its ills, a hospital full of diseases, a prison crowded with malefactors and debtors, a field of battle strewed with carcases, a fleet foundering in the ocean, a nation languishing under tyranny, famine, or pestilence. To turn the gay side of life to him and give him a notion of its pleasures—whither should I conduct him? To a ball, to an opera, to court? He might justly think that I was only showing him a diversity of distress and sorrow.

There is no evading such striking instances, said Philo, but by apologies which still further aggravate the charge. Why have all men, I ask, in all ages, complained incessantly of the miseries of life? . . . They have no just reason, says one: These complaints proceed only from their discontented, repining, anxious disposition. . . . And can there possibly, I reply, be a more certain foundation of misery than such a wretched temper?

But if they were really as unhappy as they pretend, says my antagonist, why do they remain in life? . . .

Not satisfied with life, afraid of death.

This is the secret chain, say I, that holds us. We are terrified, not bribed to the continuance of our existence.

It is only a false delicacy, he may insist, which a few refined spirits indulge, and which has spread these complaints among the whole race of mankind. . . . And what is the delicacy, I ask, which you blame? Is it anything but a greater sensibility to all the pleasures and pains of life? And if the man of a delicate, refined temper, by being so much more alive than the rest of the world, is only so much more unhappy, what judgment must we form in general of human life?

Let men remain at rest, says our adversary, and they will be easy. They are willing artificers of their own misery. . . . No! reply I: An anxious languor follows their repose; disappointment, vexation, trouble, their activity and ambition.

I can observe something like what you mention in some others, replied Cleanthes; but I confess I feel little or nothing of it in myself, and hope that it is not so common as you represent it.

If you feel not human misery yourself, cried Demea, I congratulate you on so happy a singularity. Others, seemingly the most prosperous, have not been ashamed to vent their complaints in the most melancholy strains. Let us attend to the great, the fortunate emperor, Charles V, when, tired with human grandeur, he resigned all his extensive dominions into the hands of his son. In the last harangue which he made on that memorable occasion, he publicly avowed *that the greatest prosperities which he had ever enjoyed had been mixed with so many adversities that he might truly say he had never enjoyed any satisfaction or contentment.* But did the retired life in which he sought for shelter afford him any greater happiness? If we may credit his son's account, his repentance commenced the very day of his resignation.

Cicero's fortune, from small beginnings, rose to the greatest luster and renown; yet what pathetic complaints of the ills of life do his familiar letters, as well as philosophical discourses, contain? And suitably to his own experience, he introduces Cato, the great, the fortunate Cato protesting in his old age that had he a new life in his offer he would reject the present.

Ask yourself, ask any of your acquaintance, whether they would live over again the last ten or twenty years of their life. No! but the next twenty, they say, will be better:

> And from the dregs of life, hope to receive
> What the first sprightly running could not give.

Thus, at last, they find (such is the greatness of human misery, it reconciles even contradictions) that they complain at once of the shortness of life and of its vanity and sorrow.

And is it possible, Cleanthes, said Philo, that after all these reflections, and infinitely more which might be suggested, you can still persevere in your anthropomorphism, and assert the moral attributes of the Deity, his justice, benevolence, mercy, and rectitude, to be of the same nature with these virtues in human creatures? His power, we allow, is infinite; whatever he wills is executed; but neither man nor any other animal is happy; therefore, he does not will their happiness. His wisdom is infinite; he is never mistaken in choosing the means to any end; but the course of nature tends not to human or animal felicity; therefore, it is not established for that purpose. Through the whole compass of human knowledge there are no inferences more certain and infallible than these. In what respect, then, do his benevolence and mercy resemble the benevolence and mercy of men?

Epicurus' old questions are yet unanswered.

Is he willing to prevent evil, but not able? then is he impotent. Is he able, but not willing? then is he malevolent. Is he both able and willing? whence then is evil?

You ascribe, Cleanthes (and I believe justly), a purpose and intention to nature. But what, I beseech you, is the object of that curious artifice and machinery which she has displayed in all animals—the preservation alone of individuals, and propagation of the species? It seems enough for her purpose, if such a rank be barely upheld in the universe, without any care or concern for the happiness of the members that compose it. No resource for this purpose: no machinery in order merely to give pleasure or ease: no fund of pure joy and contentment: no indulgence without some want or necessity accompanying it. At least, the few phenomena of this nature are overbalanced by opposite phenomena of still greater importance.

Our sense of music, harmony, and indeed beauty of all kinds, gives satisfaction, without being absolutely necessary to the preservation and propagation of the species. But what racking pains, on the other hand, arise from gouts, gravels, megrims, toothaches, rheumatisms, where the injury to the animal machinery is either small or incurable? Mirth, laughter, play, frolic seem gratuitous satisfactions which have no further tendency; spleen, melancholy, discontent, superstition are pains of the same nature. How then does the divine benevolence display itself, in the sense of you anthropomorphites? None but we mystics, as you were pleased to call us, can account for this strange mixture of phenomena, by deriving it from attributes infinitely perfect but incomprehensible.

And have you, at last, said Cleanthes smiling, betrayed your intentions, Philo? Your long agreement with Demea did indeed a little suprise me, but I find you were all the while erecting a concealed battery against me. And I must confess that you have now fallen upon a subject worthy of your noble spirit of opposition and controversy. If you can make out the present point, and prove mankind to be unhappy or corrupted, there is an end at once of all religion. For to what purpose establish the natural attributes of the Deity, while the moral are still doubtful and uncertain?

You take umbrage very easily, replied Demea, at opinions the most innocent and the most generally received, even amongst the religious and devout themselves; and nothing can be more surprising than to find a topic like this—concerning the wickedness and misery of man—charged with no less than atheism and profaneness. Have not all pious divines and preachers who have indulged their rhetoric on so fertile a subject; have they not easily, I say, given a solution of any difficulties which may attend it? This world is but a point in comparison of the universe; this life but a moment in comparison of eternity. The present evil phenomena, therefore, are rectified in other regions, and in some future period of existence. And the eyes of men, being then opened to large views of things, see the whole connection of general laws, and trace, with adoration, the benevolence and rectitude of the Deity through all the mazes and intricacies of his providence.

No! replied Cleanthes, no! These arbitrary suppositions can never be admitted, contrary to matter of fact, visible and uncontroverted. Whence can any cause be known but from its known effects? Whence can any hypothesis be proved but from the apparent phenomena? To establish one hypothesis upon another is building entirely in the air; and the utmost we ever attain by these conjectures and fictions is to ascertain the bare possibility of our opinion, but never can we, upon such terms, establish its reality.

The only method of supporting divine benevolence—and it is what I willingly embrace—is to deny absolutely the misery and wickedness of man. Your representations are exaggerated; your melancholy views mostly fictitious; your inferences contrary to fact and experience. Health is more common than sickness; pleasure than pain; happiness than misery. And for one vexation which we meet with, we attain, upon computation, a hundred enjoyments.

Admitting your position, replied Philo, which yet is extremely doubtful, you must at the same time allow that, if pain be less frequent than pleasure, it is infinitely more violent and durable. One hour of it is often able to outweigh a day, a week, a month of our common insipid enjoyments; and how many days, weeks, and months are passed by several in the most acute torments? Pleasure, scarcely in one instance, is ever able to reach ecstasy and rapture; and in no one instance can it continue for any time at its highest pitch and altitude. The spirits evaporate, the nerves relax, the fabric is disordered, and the enjoyment quickly degenerates into fatigue and uneasiness. But pain often, good god, how often! rises to torture and agony; and the longer it continues, it becomes still more genuine agony and torture. Patience is exhausted, courage languishes, melancholy seizes us, and nothing terminates our misery but the removal of its cause or another event which is the sole cure of all evil, but which, from our natural folly, we regard with still greater horror and consternation.

But not to insist upon these topics, continued Philo, though most obvious, certain, and important, I must use the freedom to admonish you, Cleanthes, that you have put the controversy upon a most dangerous issue, and are unawares introducing a total scepticism into the most essential articles of natural and revealed theology. What! no method of fixing a just foundation for religion unless we allow the happiness of human life, and maintain a continued existence even in this world, with all our present pains, infirmities, vexations, and follies, to be eligible and desirable! But this is contrary to everyone's feeling and experience; it is contrary to an authority so established as nothing can subvert. No decisive proofs can ever be produced against this authority; nor is it possible for you to compute, estimate, and compare all the pains and all the pleasures in the lives of all men and of all animals; and thus, by your resting the whole system of religion on a point which, from its very nature, must forever be uncertain, you tacitly confess that that system is equally uncertain.

But allowing you what never will be believed, at least, what you never possibly can prove, that animal or, at least, human happiness in this life exceeds its misery, you have yet done nothing; for this is not, by any means, what we expect from infinite power, infinite wisdom, and infinite goodness. Why is there any misery at all in the world? Not by chance, surely. From some cause then. Is it from the intention of the Deity? But he is perfectly benevolent. Is it contrary to his intention? But he is almighty. Nothing can shake the solidity of this reasoning, so short, so clear, so decisive, except we assert that these subjects exceed all human capacity, and that our common measures of truth and falsehood are not applicable to them—a topic which I have all along insisted on, but which you have, from the beginning, rejected with scorn and indignation.

But I will be contented to retire still from this intrenchment, for I deny that you can ever force me in it. I will allow that pain or misery in man is *compatible* with infinite power and goodness in the Deity, even in your sense of these attributes: what are you advanced by all these concessions? A mere possible compatibility is not sufficient. You must *prove* these pure, unmixed and uncontrollable attributes from the present mixed and confused phenomena, and from these alone. A hopeful undertaking! Were the phenomena ever so pure and unmixed, yet, being finite, they would be insufficient for that purpose. How much more, where they are also so jarring and discordant!

Here, Cleanthes, I find myself at ease in my argument. Here I triumph. Formerly, when we argued concerning the natural attributes of intelligence and design, I needed all my sceptical and metaphysical subtilty to elude your grasp. In many views of the universe and of its parts, particularly the latter, the beauty and fitness of final causes strike us with such irresistible force that all objections appear (what I believe they really are) mere cavils and sophisms; nor can we then imagine how it was ever possible for us to repose any weight on them. But there is no view of human life or of the condition of mankind from which, without the greatest violence, we can infer the moral attributes or learn that infinite benevolence, conjoined with infinite power and infinite wisdom, which we must discover by the eyes of faith alone. It is your turn now to tug the laboring oar, and to support your philosophical subtilties against the dictates of plain reason and experience.

Discussion Questions

1. How is Cleanthes' version of the Argument from Design like or unlike Aquinas's fifth way? Do Philo's criticisms of Cleanthes always apply to Aquinas's version? Why or why not?

2. State in your own words one of Philo's objections to Cleanthes' argument and give a reply to it on behalf of Aquinas or Cleanthes.

3. State one of Cleanthes' objections to Demea's argument and give a reply to it.

4. State one of Philo's objections to Demea's argument and give a reply to it.

5. How is Demea's argument like or unlike Aquinas's first three ways? Do the criticisms in the dialogue apply to Aquinas's version?

6. In Hume's dialogue Philo represents himself as a defender of religion. Does he in fact seem to be defending or attacking religious belief? Why?

7. Does Philo paint too gloomy a picture of human existence? Why or why not?

8. Philo claims that if you say that God's goodness is in any way similar to human goodness, you are guilty of anthropomorphism (thinking of God as human). Is this a reasonable accusation? Why or why not?

9. Would it be satisfactory from a religious point of view to accept a view like Philo's? Why or why not?

10. Is Demea's reply to Philo satisfactory? Why or why not? How would you reply to Philo?

D. A MODERN DEFENSE
OF THE COSMOLOGICAL ARGUMENT

Bruce Reichenbach: *The Cosmological Argument*

Bruce Reichenbach (b. 1943) is an American philosopher. He is Professor of Philosophy at Augsburg College, Minnesota, the author of numerous articles in philosophy and of two books, *Is Man the Phoenix*? a study of immortality (1978), and *The Cosmological Argument*: *A Reassessment*, from which this selection is taken.

We may summarize the detailed argument as follows:

(S_1) A contingent being exists.
    a. This contingent being is caused either (1) by itself, or (2) by another.
    b. If it were caused by itself, it would have to precede itself in existence, which is impossible.
(S_2) Therefore, this contingent being (2) is caused by another, i.e. depends on something else for its existence.
(S_3) That which causes (provides the sufficient reason for) the existence of any contingent being must be either (3) another contingent being, or (4) a non-contingent (necessary) being.
    c. If 3, then this contingent cause must itself be caused by another, and so on to infinity.
(S_4) Therefore, that which causes (provides the sufficient reason for) the existence of any contingent being must be either (5) an infinite series of contingent beings, or (4) a necessary being.
(S_5) An infinite series of contingent beings (5) is incapable of yielding a sufficient reason for the existence of any being.
(S_6) Therefore, a necessary being (4) exists.

We have here what appears, at least initially, to be a true and valid cosmological argument. From what appear to be true premises we have argued to a valid conclusion. Our task must be to defend the premises and steps of this argument against their various critics, both historical and contemporary, so that we may see whether our initial judgment as to the truth of this argument can be sustained.

THE MATERIAL UNIVERSE AND THE NECESSARY BEING

It has been the contention of some philosophers that one need not make the move from the necessary being to God at all. The identity of this being can be determined without having to invoke the existence of a being (such as a personal deity) which exists transcendent to sense experience. Rather, the necessary being is the universe itself. Wallace Matson writes:

> The world itself might be the necessary being after all: infinite in power and maximal in goodness, but neither containing nor presupposing any personal intelligence. . . . The world might be conceived of as having (nontemporally) actualized itself—more simply, as having just always been here, so to speak, automatically. It is hard to see why the argument should not lead to this conclusion just as well as to the orthodox one.

The same point was made several centuries ago by David Hume: "Why may not the material universe be the necessarily existing being, according to this pretended explication of necessity?"

Those who argue in this fashion are making two points. First, they are claiming that as the cosmological argument stands it cannot *validly* conclude that this necessary being is God. In order to make such a move legitimately, the argument must be further supplemented. . . . for example, . . . the cosmological argument should be supplemented by the argument from design. With this general contention I agree; in light of the premises of the argument, to move from the necessary being to a personal deity requires additional argumentation. We shall say more on this later.

Secondly, and more importantly, they are contending that one need not conclude that the necessary being in S_6 is divine at all. Indeed, it is quite conceivable (or even evident) that this necessary being can be identified with the world or material universe. We need not conclude to a personal divinity, introduced from a religious sphere external to the argument; the world itself could be the necessary being, as that which "nontemporally actualized itself."

But is the world or material universe a proper candidate for the position of necessary being? I think not. The totality or world or universe is nothing over and above the sum total of its constituents. But all its constituents are contingent beings; what exists in the universe could conceivably not exist. Now if the components, as contingent, could conceivably not exist, then the totality or world which they compose could likewise conceivably not exist, for if all the constituents ceased to exist at the same time (which is possible), the totality of which they constitute the parts would likewise cease to exist. And if the whole which now exists can conceivably not be, it is contingent. Thus, the world cannot be the necessary being for which we argue, for if it were, it would possess contradictory properties: it would be necessary because it is the necessary being to which the cosmological proof argues, and it would be contingent because it is the totality of contingent beings.

Matson responds to this by noting that it is meaningless to apply the notion of "cause" to the totality of contingent beings. That which is contingent is caused; but causation can only meaningfully take place within the context of a totality. "The universe is the framework within which causal explanations operate. . . . It is quite beyond their scope to link the universe to anything [beyond itself]. To ask for the cause of the universe is to ask a question similar to 'When is time?' or 'Where is space?'" Consequently, to inquire about the cause of this totality is to move outside the framework within which the question of causation can be meaningfully asked. As such, the contention that the totality is contingent and caused is meaningless.

. . . Though it be granted that causation can take place only within a totality, there is no reason to restrict the notion of "totality" simply to the totality of contingent beings. There are many kinds of totalities, some of which are relevant to the problem before us. There can be, for example, a totality of all existent beings or a totality of all things which are causes. That is, the notion of "totality" can be satisfied in the inclusion of all contingent and necessary beings in the whole, and it is within this resulting totality of existents that we can meaningfully inquire concerning the contingency or causation of the totality of contingent beings. Thus, far from being meaningless, the question of the contingency or causation of the totality of contingent beings can be asked within a meaningful framework. Just as we can ask for the cause of the totality of tulips within the totality of the world, we can ask for the cause of the totality of contingent beings within the totality of existents or totality of causes.

Thus, it seems that we cannot identify the world or material universe with the necessary being, for the world itself is contingent and requires an explanation or cause for its existence.

IDENTIFICATION IS EXTRINSIC TO THE ARGUMENT

What about the move from the necessary being to God? Is not such a move likewise unjustified from the premises in the argument? And does not such a move cast doubt upon the validity of the whole argument? To answer this, we must determine whether the move from a necessary being to God is essential at all to the validity of the cosmological argument. Is such a move essential, such that the questioning of such an identification throws in doubt the validity of the entire argument?

That such a move was part of the traditional formulation by St. Thomas Aquinas has already been pointed out above. But though he did identify this being as God, he recognized that the argument to prove the existence of a necessary being must be kept distinct from the analysis of its essence. He writes, "When the existence of a thing has been ascertained, there remains the further question of the manner of its existence, in order that we may know its essence." The distinct purpose of his cosmological arguments in Question Two was to show that this being exists. The determination of who this necessary being is and what it is like was the concern of the questions which followed after St. Thomas' arguments to show that this being exists. Thus, though he did perhaps commit himself too early in his Five Ways to an identification of this being with God, St. Thomas himself seemed to recognize a distinction between the argument which endeavors to prove the existence of some being, and the arguments which seek to determine who this being is through a determination of the essence or further properties of this being.

Likewise, nowhere in the argument we developed did we make such an identification nor did we need to do so. The argument is perfectly valid and quite complete without it. Just as it is one thing to prove something's existence and quite another to determine its properties, so it is one thing to prove a necessary being exists and another to identify this being with the being called God, or to further research what other names, derived from other spheres of experience like the religious sphere, are appropriate to it. Such research commences subsequent to the argument for existence. Thus, since the cosmological argument, as I see it, does not need to further determine who this being is which we have proven to exist, further identification (beyond the fact that it is a necessary being) is extrinsic to the validity of the argument. Consequently, though the traditional move from the necessary being to God is without justification from the argument itself, such should not be construed as a criticism of the argument per se, for identification is not really part of it.

SOME PROGRAMMATIC SUGGESTIONS

Granted that the identification of this being is extrinsic to the cosmological argument per se, stil the question remains, Is this necessary being God? Can this being be identified with a personal deity? What is this being like which we have shown to necessarily exist? Who is this necessary being?

Though such a question, as we have shown, is not an intrinsic part of the cosmological argument, some programmatic suggestions toward the identification of such a being might still be in order. Three steps are necessary in order to discover whether the necessary being is to be identified with God. First of all, the characteristics of this necessary being must be determined. From what we have already said in other chapters about this being, some of these characteristics can be noted. The being which exists is a necessary being, a being which is such that if it exists is a necessary being, a being which is such that if it exists, it cannot not exist. That is, it can neither be brought into existence nor pass out of existence. It is eternal. Moreover, as a non-contingent being it partakes of those essential qualities which are the opposite of those of a contingent being. That is, it is uncaused and independent of all else (*a se*). And since it is not dependent on anything else, it cannot be limited by another being. Hence, it must be a non-finite being. Finally, from the cosmological argument itself we can see that it must be the sufficient reason not only for the existence of all contingent beings, but also for its own existence. As such, it must be self-sufficient and self-sustaining. Accordingly, by means of reason alone, we can discover some of the characteristics of this necessary being: it is independent of all beings, not finite, self-sufficient, self-sustaining, the uncaused cause of all contingent beings, and eternal. Perhaps other characteristics can be determined in this manner.

The second step of the programme will involve the determination of what God is like. As with the necessary being, it must be determined what properties and characteristics can be meaningfully predicated of God. Some attributes have been accorded prominence in traditional theology. According to the Nicene Creed, God is one God, the "Maker of heaven and earth." He is both the creator and sustainer of the universe; by the Word of God all things came to be and continue to exist, for in Him we "live and move and have our being." This act of creation was a free act on His part;

there was no necessity that He create the world. Thus, the world is dependent on Him, but He is independent of it. He is self-sufficient, needing no other being in order to act, and self-sustaining, needing no other being in order to exist. Likewise He is non-finite in His being, for He cannot be limited by any other being.

Another important attribute is His eternality. God was before the foundation of the worlds; He is the great "I am," the eternally present now. God never came into existence, nor will He ever pass out of existence. Finally, He is personal and good; He is the personal Deity which is the very source and standard for goodness in the world. Thus, God may be partially characterized as independent of all things, self-sufficient and self-sustaining, non-finite, the uncaused cause and sustainer of the universe, personal and good. These attributes are by no means exhaustive, but they do embody some of the more important concepts predicated of God. Further analysis of the attributes of God will constitute the task of the second stage.

The third and final phase involves the method of correlation. If the characteristics of the necessary being correlate with those of the Deity, and if none of the Deity's characteristics conflict with those of the necessary being, then the probability that they are one and same being has been established. From the above it is obvious that many of the characteristics do indeed correlate. Further analysis is necessary to discover other correlations, and to see whether there are any conflicts. This analysis or correlation constitutes the third-phase of the programme.

That the identification between the necessary being and God is possible can be seen from the correlation of the attributes for these two beings. Indeed, that there is such an identification has been the conclusion of most philosophers who have engaged in philosophical theology. Witness the general heading under which the arguments fall: proofs for the existence of God. However, we must remind ourselves that such a programme, such an identification, extends beyond the boundaries of the cosmological argument proper. This method of correlation is a programme which commences after we have shown that a necessary being necessarily exists if we are to adequately account for the existence of a contingent being.

ARGUMENT AND BELIEF

One final question remains: What is the relationship of the cosmological argument to religious belief? Must one who sees the logic of the argument become a committed theist? The answer I believe is twofold. First, if the cosmological argument, as presented above, is a true and valid argument, and if the above programmatic suggestions can be successfully carried out such that the necessary being can be identified with God, then certainly an important religious dogma has been rationally established. That is, it has then been shown that there are good reasons for believing in the existence of a divine being, that such a belief is most rational and reasonable. To believe in God is not to commit intellectual suicide.

Secondly, however, it is quite possible that someone could see the validity of the argument and see the validity of identification of this being with God, and yet not believe in or commit himself to this Deity. It is not to be expected that an argument to prove the existence of a being should at the same time produce in the hearer a desire to trust himself to this being.

This is, of course, a statement about the relationship between reason and faith, between argument and commitment. For most individuals it is one thing to rationally acknowledge the truth of an argument or the truth of a statement, but it is quite another to incorporate this rational conclusion as an integral part of their life style. This is not to say that such would not be the ideal; most certainly it would. From an ideal standpoint, the establishment of the rational probability or improbability of something should result in an act of commitment or rejection on the part of those who agree with the rational conclusion. Likewise, beliefs should be based upon reason and fact, such that beliefs could be evaluated as rational or irrational. It is to say, however, something about the psychology of belief, i.e., that individuals by and large are not converted by rational argument, but out of deep, existential realization of their plight.

To Kierkegaard and his twentieth century followers, this must appear most paradoxical. On one hand, I am affirming the Kierkegaardian position that faith is not an act of reason but an act of commitment and that despair—the wanting to die and inability to do so—leads or can lead to this faith. The leap of faith, the act of personal commitment, the ultimate risk, follows upon the recognition of the state of despair. To speak of plights— dread, anxiety, despair, melancholy—and the resulting movement from this into the religious stage is welcome to their ears. But to likewise affirm that this faith ideally should be reasonable is the clashing of Hegelian cymbals, the treading again of the muddy, wellworn path to "the system." They assert that the truth on the human level is to be found in the inwardness and passion with which a doctrine is held. As passionate believing and passionate grasping, the inwardness of the ultimate choice and decision thrives not on rational synthesis, but on absolute paradox; the greater the paradox, the greater the inwardness called for. Faith is not believing the rational; it is appropriating the irrational, the contradictory. Faith as rational is impossible.

Beyond the suggestion that "rational faith" might provide a more ultimate paradox for the Kierkegaardian to grasp hold of, I want to affirm that faith and reason are not such strange bedfellows as one might be led to believe. Indeed, they are related as cultivator and harvester. Reason plows the furrows, cutting the ground, separating what is to be separated, planting seeds of ideas, putting back together what belongs as such. It prepares the bed by breaking the clods of rational doubt. But its work is in vain if the grain does not grow and is not reaped, if it is not cut and bound and used. Without fruit, without action, it is simply a mental charade; it is to plant the field without concern for harvest. Reason should prepare the way for faith; faith as commitment should either grow out of reason or be based upon rational conclusions such that faith can be conceived to be either rational or irrational.

Kierkegaard was correct when he saw that faith was a matter of the heart, an act of commitment and inwardness rather than an act of reason (of the rational faculty). But he failed to see that faith, insofar as it is or is not *based* upon reason, can be either a rational act or an irrational act. Commitment to the improbable, absurd, or irrational is faith, it is true, but irrational faith. It is as if the explorer would cast aside the compass and chart with the assertion, "It is the movement, not the direction, that counts." Faith becomes a meaningful act when good reasons can be given for the action, when exploration is guided by compass.

Kierkegaard was, of course, describing human existence, seeing man as he acted and made decisions. Here Kierkegaard is on solid ground. It must be granted that most humans make decisions of commitment on grounds other than rational. The politician sways the crowd not by reason, but by emotion. The "sawdust trail" evangelist stirs his audience by passion or fear, not by rational debate. The communications media rarely give arguments in their advertisements or commercials; music, humor, and beautiful, sexy women convey the message. But again, to say that this is the way we normally do make decisions is not to say that this is the way decisions ought to be made. Nor is it to say that, ultimately, good reasons should not be given for the decision or action. Reason might not psychologically precipitate the action, but it should provide a basis for an analysis of that commitment.

But is not this admission concerning the common human decision-making process fatal to our argument? If Kierkegaard was correct in his analysis of the usual decision-making process, is then our argument without value, despite all our talk about "the ideal way" to make decisions? I think not. Granted that it is highly unlikely that the above argument will convert the atheist to theism or convince the agnostic to adopt religious belief in God; yet perhaps it will answer or cast light on some of the pressing questions of reason which surround the debate about the reasonableness of a belief in God. With questions of reason aside, the ground has been prepared for the planting of reasoned belief.

Discussion Questions

1. How is Reichenbach's argument similar to those of Aquinas? How is it different? Which argument seems better? Why?

2. Does Reichenbach's discussion answer some of Hume's objections? How?

3. In what ways would Reichenbach agree or disagree with Sillem's view of the nature and purpose of arguments for the existence of God?

4. What does Reichenbach mean by "contingent" and "necessary" being? How might Hume criticize his ideas?

5. How does Reichenbach argue that the "necessary being" or the Cosmological Argument is the same as the God of traditional theism? Are you convinced by his argument? Why or why not?

F. SOME ANSWERS TO THE PROBLEM OF EVIL

Richard L. Purtill: *Thinking About Religion*

Richard L. Purtill (b. 1931) an American philosopher, is one of the editors of this book and Professor of Philosophy at Western Washington University, in the state of Washington. He is the author of about thirty articles in philosophical journals and of fifteen books, including five novels, three textbooks in logic, and three introductory textbooks: *Philosophically Speaking* (1975), *Thinking About Ethics* (1976), and *Thinking About Religion* (1978), from which this selection is taken.

Most of us lead fairly sheltered lives with respect to both suffering and moral evil. We are not likely to know a major criminal or see a major crime, and if a friend or relative has a severe accident or illness, he or she is likely to be hidden away in a hospital, where his or her suffering is out of our sight if not out of our minds. Thus our first experience of real moral evil or severe suffering is sometimes shattering. But such experiences seem to push people toward religious belief as often as they push them away from it, and religious believers as a group certainly are as familiar with sin and suffering as are nonbelievers.

Most people would agree that the existence of suffering and evil in the world is a challenge to religious belief. But what sort of challenge, and how strong a challenge? To get this clear, let us consider three possible claims that might be made about the way in which the existence of evil and suffering should affect our belief in God:

Claim I. If a good, all-powerful God existed, He would not permit any suffering or moral evil at all. Since suffering and moral evil obviously do exist, such a God does not exist.

This claim breaks down into two parts: that a good God would not permit suffering, and that a good God would not permit moral evil. Since most religious believers think of Heaven as a place without moral evil and without suffering, we might put this more picturesquely by saying that Claim I is the claim that a good God would create only a Heaven, and would not create a world such as the one we see around us.

The first answer a religious believer might give to this claim would begin with a distinction. If God had created a world of creatures without freedom of choice, with no free will, moral evil would of course have been impossible. And a world without the possibility of moral evil might well be a world without suffering, since suffering would seem to serve no purpose in such a world. But, the religious believer might claim, if you have a world containing persons with genuine freedom of choice, then suffering is a necessary element of such a world, for only by suffering can persons develop character.

This seems to be true in a very basic way. For if we never had unpleasant experiences—if everything occurred just as we wanted it, or if we liked everything that occurred—then it would be hard to see how we could even realize ourselves as persons distinct from other persons and from our environment. If a baby received everything it wanted as soon as it formed the wish, then it would think of persons and things outside itself as mere extensions of its own personality, like its fingers and toes. But if we do not get what we want or do not like what we get, we suffer—that, basically, is what suffering is.

So if other persons did precisely what we wanted or if we were always pleased with what they did, we would not recognize them as distinct persons. But beyond this, it is when we first begin to realize that other persons can be hurt just as we can, that we really see them as persons. A toy or doll or machine cannot be hurt, and we need not consider its feelings. But persons are not toys or dolls or machines, and it is when we begin to realize this that we begin to develop morally. Some of the most horrifying crimes have been committed by "moral solipsists"—people who do not seem to realize that there are other persons besides themselves, who treat other persons as things. Without the realization of pain in ourselves and in other persons, we would all be solipsists. Moral growth begins when we realize "This action hurts that other person. *I* wouldn't like to be hurt; he doesn't either."

There are several replies that could be made at this stage of the argument. The supporters of Claim I might try to argue that we do not have free choice and therefore, even if pain and suffering were a means of moral development in free persons, this does not justify *our* pain and suffering. The issue of free will is a complex one, and for the moment we will merely say that religious believers who use the kind of reply to Claim I discussed above are taking it for granted that we do have free choice and that most other people also take this for granted. They may be wrong, but arguments would be needed to show this.

A second objection which could be raised to the religious believers' reply to Claim I is the fact of animal suffering. Animals do not seem to have moral choice, and therefore cannot commit moral evil. But they do suffer physical pain, and this cannot be explained as necessary for their moral development since they do not have moral characters. This is a difficult objection to answer, if only because we have no inside knowledge of what animals feel. It is clear, however, that pain serves a biological purpose in enabling animals to survive, and that an animal that felt no pain would not avoid damage or death very long. The religious believer may agree that if God had created the world only for the sake of animals, it might have been a world without death and damage and perhaps therefore without pain. But if one of the reasons for the creation of this world was the moral development of persons, then it must be a world with danger and suffering. How animal suffering fits into the whole picture we may not completely understand, but if we can find a satisfactory solution to the problem of human suffering, we may have confidence that there is also a solution to the problem of suffering in animals.

We have seen at least a plausible answer to the question as to why a good God would allow some suffering: because without it the development of character is impossible. While of course more could be said about the questions raised so far, let us now consider a second claim, which could be put forward even by those who might grant what we have said up to this point.

Claim II. Even granted that there is a reason for permitting some moral evil and some suffering, if a good God existed, He would not allow the *amount* of moral evil and suffering which does in fact exist. Therefore a good God does not exist.

This is a much more difficult claim to deal with because it involves matters of amount and proportion. If it is granted that a good God could allow *some* evil and suffering, then where can a line be drawn? How much evil and suffering is too much for a good God to allow? And how much would not be too much? Half as much as actually exists? A tenth? A hundredth?

An important point to consider is the relation between permitting moral evil and permitting pain and suffering. If God allows human beings to make choices which are genuinely free, and some of those choices are morally wrong choices, what will be the result? Given that there are possibilities of causing pain and suffering to others and that some people by wrong moral choices exploit those possibilities for their own ends, then what could God do without taking away human freedom? If God steps in to nullify the bad results of the use of human freedom, how will people learn not to make wrong moral choices?

The difficulty, of course, is that wrong moral choices often hurt the innocent rather than the guilty. Most of us would have far fewer difficulties about the amount of pain and suffering in the world if suffering were always proportionate to wrongdoing: if no innocent person ever suffered and if each evildoer suffered in exact proportion to his sins. But innocent people do suffer and people seem to suffer out of all proportion for relatively minor failings. A few minutes of careless driving can lead to untold anguish for the driver and for innocent people he may involve in an accident.

At least a partial answer can be given to this difficulty by seeing that we often realize the wrongness of our moral choices only when these choices do cause suffering to innocent people. Someone who is relatively powerless to harm others—a child, for example—may have selfish or destructive attitudes which, because of his powerlessness, do no harm, but which are destroying the person's capacity for love and appreciation of things outside himself. It can happen that if people do manage to do some harm to others, and see the effect of their selfishness and hatred, this brings them at last to a realization of what they have become.

All very well, it might be replied, for the person who realizes and perhaps repents and reforms. But the innocent people are still injured, through no fault of their own. This objection brings us to our third and final claim, which might be put in this way:

Claim III.   Setting aside the total amount of suffering, a good God will not cause or allow innocent persons to suffer for the sins of others. Since innocent people do suffer for the sins of others, a good, all-powerful God does not exist.

This claim is an attempt to detour around the question of how *much* suffering might be justified and to claim that certain *kinds* of suffering, which do seem to occur, are incompatible with the existence of a God in the traditional sense—both all good and all-powerful. Certainly some human beings—at least very young children—seem to be without any personal guilt of any kind. And some of these innocent human beings do seem to suffer more than could possibly be needed for the formation of their own character.

Different religious traditions have different answers to this problem. In this chapter I will discuss some answers to this problem which are part of the Christian religious tradition, since this is the one which is most likely to have affected, either positively or negatively, most people who will be reading this.

The two answers to the problem of suffering to be discussed are first, the doctrine of *original sin*, and second, the doctrine of *vicarious atonement*. Since these are theological doctrines, which are supposed to be known by revelation from God and not by argument, philosophy cannot directly decide the question of their truth or falsity. But we can consider the philosophical question as to whether these doctrines make sense and whether, *if* true, they would solve the problem of the suffering of innocent persons.

Insofar as religious believers are merely defending their views against attack or answering a challenge, it is enough for them to show that their views are understandable and that they do meet the challenge. Of course repelling an attack is merely avoiding defeat; if the religious believer wants to convince anyone that his answers are true and should be accepted, different kinds of argument will be needed. But for the moment we are merely concerned to answer the nonbeliever's objections.

The notion of *original sin* in Christian theology is based, at least in part, on the story in the book of Genesis which is part of the Jewish Torah as well as of the Christian Old Testament. But most Jews would reject this doctrine, at least in the form which Christian theology has given it, so we will talk only of the Christian version of the doctrine. Within Christianity there is a wide variety of interpretations of the idea of original sin, and it will be helpful to separate the historical question from the ethical question involved. The historical question is that of how literally we are to take the Adam and Eve story in Genesis, while the ethical question is the justi-fiability of letting someone here and now suffer for something done at an earlier time by other persons, even if those persons were the ancestors of those who now suffer.

In our introductory story I pictured the priest as making two points about the historical question—first, that there is no scientific impossibility in the origin of the human race from a single couple, and secondly, that the essentials of the doctrine of original sin are that the human race as a whole has in some way from the beginning refused obedience to God, thereby creating a separation from God which is the source of such things as war, disease, etc. that cause suffering to innocent persons.

This is a very general and cautious statement of the doctrine, but Christians in a good many denominations and traditions would agree that the doctrine means *at least* this. At any rate, this statement is enough to enable us to raise the ethical question, which is the question of collective guilt, or collective responsibility. Are we to regard human beings as prop-erly responsible only for their own actions and mistakes, or is there a sense in which, *as* human beings, they can share a collective responsibility and even a collective guilt?

When we discuss this question in the context of such present-day problems as white guilt for past injustices to black persons, similar ques-tions come up. Because I am a descendant of racial groups who have exploited and enslaved other groups, do I have some responsibility for reparation to those groups? In cases like this it helps to see that I have inherited many advantages from my ancestors so that it is only fair that I should inherit their liabilities, just as someone who inherits a family busi-ness must expect to inherit its debts as well as the stock and the good will.

Can we apply this analogy to the human race as a whole? Can we say that in inheriting life itself as well as the many advantages of centuries of human civilization, we must also accept some responsibility for the sins and errors of our ancestors? Perhaps so. But the difficulty seems to be that some of us seem to get mainly the advantages and some of us mainly the disadvantages. If suffering were evenly distributed over all people who were personally innocent, we might be willing to grant that they were bearing their part in the responsibilities inherited from past generations. But suffering is not equally distributed: of two innocent persons, one seems to suffer out of all proportion, the other hardly at all. The moral equation still does not seem to balance, even if we accept some responsibility of later generations for the morally wrong choices of earlier ones.

And, of course, at least some people would dig in their heels at this point, refusing to admit there is any justice in "inherited" responsibilities. The question really is how we should regard the human race: as a number of unconnected units not owing anything to one another, or as a sort of organic unity in which both benefits and responsibilities are shared.

To give the full answer of traditional Christianity to the problem of the apparently unjust distribution of suffering, we must go on to discuss the second doctrine, that of *vicarious atonement*. According to this doctrine the suffering of one person can benefit others; specifically, one person's suffering can make up for the wrong moral choices of another. For the Christian, the suffering and death of Christ was "for our sins," and his suffering and death somehow earned a new chance for the human race, so that through Christ's actions we can again be united to God. Some Christians would go on to say that by their sufferings, those who are personally innocent of moral evil can somehow unite themselves with the sufferings of Christ and that by their suffering they do what is within their power to make up for the sins of others and to help reunite the human race to God.

Two major objections are made to this doctrine by nonbelievers. The first is that the doctrine is nonsensical, and the second is that even if it makes sense it is immoral. The objection that the doctrine doesn't make sense can be put in the following way: "My morally wrong choices are my own responsibility. Perhaps if *I* am punished for my wrong moral choices I will be sorry for what I have done, but at any rate I have brought the punishment on myself. But how can there ever be any connection between my wrongdoing and the sufferings of Christ or the suffering of some other innocent person who may be completely unknown to me? To say that the suffering of that person makes up for my wrongdoing makes no sense."

There are three different levels on which a religious believer might attempt to answer this objection. On the first level, he can point out that if a punishment is merely nullified, with no one paying for wrongdoing, we are inclined to treat the offense lightly and do the same thing again. If we are punished ourselves, resentment and anger may get in the way of repentance. But if someone else generously takes on the consequences of our wrongdoing, then our realization of and appreciation of the other person's self-sacrifice can provide a very powerful motive for repentance, if the least spark of love or gratitude remains in us.

On an even deeper level, it can be pointed out that what some have called the *law of exchange* is fundamental to human experience. Human beings can help one another physically, literally bearing one another's burdens. They can help one another mentally by teaching or counseling one another. In these cases the help is most effective when we literally or in an extended sense take the place of the other person. If I lift the bundle from your shoulders, then you are no longer carrying it. The best teacher is the one who can put himself in the student's place and appreciate the problem from the student's point of view; the best counselor is the one who can appreciate the feelings and desires of the person he is trying to help.

There is a long Christian tradition which says that we can also help others by putting ourselves in their place in another sense and bearing the suffering that is the consequence of their actions. Sydney Carton, in *A Tale of Two Cities*, takes the place of another man in the condemned cell; many friends, or husbands or wives or parents or children have given up their lives for their loved ones or taken on their sufferings. Christians remember the words of Christ about taking up their cross and following Him, and the saying that "greater love has no man than that he lay down his life for his friend."

At this stage the moral objection may be raised: It is not *fair*, it may be said, to let one person suffer for another. Each person should take the consequences of his own wrongdoing: No one should be asked or allowed to bear the sufferings deserved by another. There are two cases to consider here: one, the case of a volunteer, the other, the case of someone who has not consciously chosen to suffer for others. To forbid, on moral grounds, that one person should voluntarily take on the burdens of another seems very strange. To most human beings self-sacrificing love has seemed the best and noblest thing in human experience: Not to allow us to suffer for those we love would be to rob love of what seems to many to be its highest expression.

But what about those who have not deliberately chosen to suffer for others? Accepting a voluntary sacrifice is one thing; demanding an involuntary sacrifice is surely another. Here again we must distinguish two possibilities. Some people who suffer for others without deliberately choosing to are glad when they realize what they have accomplished for the other person. If they had been asked and if they had fully realized what was involved, they would gladly have volunteered. Some people, however, even if they had been asked to make a sacrifice for others and even if they had realized the good they could have done for them, might still have refused. And since suffering for others to whom we have no obligation is above and beyond the call of duty, we cannot say that the refusal is morally wrong.

However, in the Christian view, what God has in mind for all of us human beings is that we should love one another as Christ loved us—that is, love one another enough to suffer and die for one another. In this view the purpose of human beings is to form a community of love, what St. Paul called the mystical body of Christ. Each member of this community of love will be either explicitly or implicitly volunteers, glad either in advance or in retrospect to sacrifice themselves for others. Thus the suffering of the innocent is not wasted and is not an imposition of them. In the long run persons of good will who have suffered will be glad that they have suffered—glad for their own sake, or glad for the sake of others.

What about the suffering of those who are not persons of good will, who hate and reject others? Some of it, in the Christian view, will be deserved, will be simply what they have brought on themselves. Some of it, Christians will hope, may be part of a process that will lead to repentance and reform. But does any person suffer for the sake of others who has not deserved that suffering and who will not in the long run be glad of that suffering? The answer most Christians would give is no. Suffering for others is a privilege, a share in Christ's work. Those who have no share in Christ have no share in His work.

If these Christian doctrines are true, then they may offer a solution to the problem of apparently undeserved suffering in this world. But some Christians at least still hold that it is possible, by misuse of our free will, to separate ourselves from God forever—to condemn ourselves to eternal separation from all that is good and so to eternal suffering. The moral question raised by unbelievers, which also troubles many Christians, is "How could a good God permit anyone to suffer eternally?" Surely no puny action of ours could *deserve* such punishment, and no benefit to others could arise from such punishment.

Christians have been divided on this issue. Some great representatives of the Christian tradition have dared to hope that since St. Paul tells us that God "desires all men to be saved and to come to the knowledge of God," His will will not in the long run be frustrated by our rebellions. They have hoped that after a process, perhaps very long and very painful, even the worst of human beings will choose to accept the offer of love in God.

However, here the issue of freedom is crucial. If freedom is really genuine, then it must include the possibility of choosing evil and rejecting good. Our own unhappy experience shows us that we sometimes reject joy and peace simply because we stubbornly insist on our own way. God wants all men to freely choose Him, but if we are genuinely free, then may some men not choose to reject God? And if they freely so choose and persist in this refusal, then what can be the result but eternal separation from the good?

An intermediate position between Universalism—the belief that all persons will someday be united with God—and the traditional belief that at least some persons are eternally punished, is the view that separation from God will eventually lead to nonexistence: that in rejecting God we reject all goods including the good of existence, which also comes from God, and that the person who rejects God eventually passes out of existence. Some Christians would support this idea on Biblical grounds; fire, which is used as the symbol of Hell's sufferings not only hurts but eventually destroys. Some may never accept God, but if so they will not always exist to reject God.

Many Christians, however, cannot reconcile this interpretation with God's revelation as they understand it, and conclude that some who reject God will be allowed to exist and maintain their rejection eternally. What the state of those persons will be is perhaps unimaginable to us; the important thing is that we could be like them. They have rejected God of their own free will and God has merely followed through His gift of free will by not forcing them to accept Him. We too have free will, and we too could so abuse it as to reject everything outside ourselves and be left to ourselves eternally. Thus some Christians see the idea of eternal punishment as the inescapable corollary of free will.

The nonbeliever's final objection might center on this point. Granted that the price of free will is this high; why should God have created creatures with free will? Many religious believers, Christian and non-Christian, would reply that anything good brings with it corresponding dangers. A plant cannot suffer but equally cannot feel enjoyment. An animal cannot worry about the future but equally cannot hope for or anticipate the future. Beings without free will could not reject God but equally could not accept God of their own choice. These religious believers hold that likeness to God consists in being able to know *and* to choose. Our knowledge is incomplete but is nevertheless real knowledge, and our choices, however imperfect, are genuine choices. God allows us to make our choices; He does not make them for us or force us to make them.

To the determinist the whole idea of individual choice seems mistaken. In a determinist view every event has *determining* causes; for every event B there is a previous event A such that when A occurred B was bound to occur. This is quite distinct from the more modest view that every event has *enabling* causes: that for any event B, there must be some previous event A which *enabled* B to happen, if A *had not* occurred, *B could not have* occurred. Even this view may be too broad, since it seems to lead to an infinite regress of causes. But at any rate, all of the events we experience certainly have enabling causes, including our own choices. If I had not been born, had not learned English, etc., I could not have chosen to write these words.

The most important single thing to notice about the arguments for determinism is that almost all such arguments from science or experience confuse enabling causes and determining causes. From the obvious fact that all events in our experience have enabling causes it is concluded, illegitimately, that all events have determining causes. There are also purely logical arguments for determinism, but when carefully examined, all such arguments turn out to assume what they are attempting to prove.

There are also theological arguments for determinism. But for the moment the situation can be summed up as follows: There are no conclusive arguments against the idea that human beings have free will, which is to say that some human choices have no determining causes. If God has given us free will we can see that *some* moral evil must be possible, and that at least some pain and suffering will be necessary to form our moral character. If moral evil causes suffering and if God cannot remove the suffering without frustrating its operation in forming moral character, then the amount of suffering in the world does not seem a conclusive argument against the existence of a good God. The suffering of innocent persons seems the hardest problem to solve, but granted the Christian idea that God wants to form us into a community of self-sacrificing love, we can see the part that suffering might play. The notion of eternal suffering poses a final problem, but perhaps the possibility of final rejection of God is an inescapable consequence of free will.

If these arguments are successful, then the religious believer has shown that the existence of moral evil and suffering does not provide an argument against religious belief. In the following chapters we will consider whether there are any successful arguments for religious belief. If there are not, the situation is a standoff, and neither the believer nor the unbeliever can claim victory. But if there are good arguments for religious belief, then the failure of objections based on moral evil and suffering would be a step in showing that religious belief is *more* rational than nonbelief.

Surprisingly enough, the argument from evil is the only major argument which has been advanced against the existence of God, in the sense of being an attempt to *disprove* His existence. There have been a number of attempts to explain away belief in God on psychological or sociological grounds, but we can see, by briefly considering several points, that such explanations do not *disprove* God's existence.

The first point is that merely offering an alternative explanation does not disprove any theory or idea. First an alternative theory must be shown to be coherent and to fit the known facts. Once this has been done we are faced with two *possible* explanations. We can reasonably reject the established theory in favor of a new theory only if the new theory can be shown to be *superior* on some grounds to the established theory.

The second point is that in general the question of the origin of our beliefs is logically irrelevant to the truth or falsity of those beliefs. The appeal to the alleged origins of our beliefs as a substitute for arguments pro or con about the beliefs themselves is called by logicians the *genetic fallacy*, and is condemned in most elementary logic books.

The final point is that plausible explanations of ideas in terms of their psychological origins can almost always be given on both sides of an argument, and tend to cancel each other out.

The force of these last two points is that even if psychology or sociology were able to give a completely plausible explanation of the origin of our religious beliefs in psychological terms, this would not settle the question of the truth or falsity of those beliefs. Unless we begin with a prejudgment that a belief is false and a predisposition to accept any other possible explanation, psychological or sociological explanations of our beliefs carry little weight.

Discussion Questions

1. Give an argument for Claim I. What assumptions do you have to make to support Claim I? Can these assumptions be defended?

2. Give an argument in support of Claim II. How much suffering does your argument assume that a good God would allow? Could an argument be given that a good God would not allow more than this amount?

3. Give an argument in support of Claim III. What moral principles are presupposed by your argument? How could these be defended?

4. What answers can you find for the problem of evil? Are these answers satisfactory?

5. Whether or not you accept the doctrines of original sin and vicarious atonement, do you think that someone who does accept them would be able to use them to give a satisfactory solution to the problem of evil? Why or why not?

COMMENT: Robert Farrer Capon
"Hunting the Divine Fox"

Fable

Once upon a time, in the mud at the bottom of a tidal pool, there lived an oyster. By oyster's standards, he had a good life: The sea water was clean and full of plankton, and the green warmth of the light at low tide made him grow and prosper.

Next to him lived a stone with whom he sometimes talked. It was very much the same size, shape and color as he, and was good, if undemanding, company. As a matter of fact, their conversations gave the oyster a definite feeling of superiority. He loved to dwell at length on the differences that underlay their apparent similarity. Rocks, he would say, are merely mineral. Oysters may be mineral on the outside; but inside, they are bona fide members of the animal kingdom.

One day, however, the stone surprised him by coming up with a rejoinder. It pointed out that there were nevertheless some advantages to being further down the evolutionary scale. Rocks had fewer enemies than oysters. Starfish and oyster drills, it observed, were no threat to stones; to the oyster they were a matter of life or death. Furthermore, the stone told him, it was getting just a little tired of being put down by an oyster with airs. He might get a lesson in humility if he would listen to some of the things starfish say about oysters—things which the oyster never heard because he was too busy being mortally afraid, but which the stone heard regularly, and with amusement.

Starfish, it seems, have a very low opinion of oysters. They eat them, but they always refer to them as "nothing more than a rock with a stomach." In fact, what passes for humor among starfish is rather like Polish jokes, except that the punch line invariably has to do with how stupid it is to be an animal and not be able to move about. The worst thing one starfish can call another is "sessile creature."

The oyster terminated the discussion huffily and went into a state of profound depression. To have everything he had been so proud of become the butt of underwater ethnic wisecracks made life not worth living. Existence, he concluded, was nothing but a cruel joke. All the faith he once had in the grand design of the evolutionary scheme forsook him. Better to believe in nothing than dignify this farce of a world with pretensions of order. He became an anti-evolutionist, and stopped saying his prayers.

For a while, righteous indignation made the losing of his religion rather fun, as it always does; but as summer wore on into fall and the water began its slow progress to winter's cold, he became merely sour—angry at the universe, but even more angry with himself for having let it turn him into a grouch. Finally, in desperation, he decided he would pray once again; but this time with a difference. No more mumbling of set pieties. He saw himself as a Job among oysters; he would open his shell and curse his day.

And the oyster spoke and said, "Let the day perish wherein I was spawned, and the night in which it was said, A seed oyster has appeared. Why is light given to him that is in misery, and life to the bitter in soul? Why do I live my days in doubt and darkness? O, that one would hear me, and tell me openly of the glories above. Behold, my desire is, that the Almighty would answer me."

And, to his utter astonishment, a voice said, "All right, all right. But I have to make it short. It's Friday afternoon.

"It's all true. There are things you never even dreamed of. All kinds of stuff. And with moves you couldn't imagine if you tried. As a matter of fact, that's your problem. There you sit with a rock on one side and a starfish on the other. My apologies. It's a limited field of vision, I admit, but in the evolutionary-scale business, you've got to put a lot of things near the bottom. Spoils the effect if you don't.

"Anyway, the moves. I'll tell you a few. Basketball. College basketball, especially. The best ones are so flashy, they make you laugh for not being able to believe the guy actually made the shot. And squirrels going through trees. One of my best effects. You know the last time a squirrel missed his footing? I keep track of these things. It was May 3rd, 1438. Definitely a record.

"And it's not all slapdash, either. I've got creatures so graceful, they almost break your heart. When it comes to exquisite moves, my favorite maybe is girls' knees. Lovely. Some people think that's a funny thing to get excited about, but in this line of work, there's no substitute for enthusiasm.

"Seriously. If you take the knee thing and really go all the way with it, you get my absolute favorite for loveliness, a prima ballerina. Talk about moves. It's like Ernie DiGregorio, Marcel Marceau and Squirrel Nutkin all rolled together—but as a girl, which makes it that much better. Terrific.

"Listen, though. It's almost sundown, and I have to set a good example. As I said, your basic problem is your point of view. There really are all these great moves, but you unfortunately don't know from motion. If you're going into business as the world's first philosophical oyster, it's O.K. by me. But just so you shouldn't get it all wrong, I'll give you one piece of advice: Think very carefully. Remember that all this stuff really is, but it can't possibly *be* the way you *think*. Or, to turn it around: The way you *think* about things will never be exactly the same as the way they *are*. But enough, I really have to run. *Mazel tov.*"

And with that, the voice ceased and the oyster was left alone with his thoughts. He felt both humbler and more elated than ever before. He resolved to philosphize no matter what the difficulties, and, in order to make the best use of the voice's advice, he decided to put himself in a methodical frame of mind. What follows is a transcript of his train of thought.

1. There is motion. I, as an oyster, can distinguish two sorts. The first is *being moved* (e.g., both the stone and myself can be moved by oystermen). The second is *moving* on one's own. The stone cannot do this at all. I can move the part of myself within my shell but I cannot move my whole self from place to place. The starfish can move from place to place.

2. The voice was quite clear on the existence of more mobile creatures than the starfish. Let me see what I can say about the prima ballerina:

> Starfish move; ballerinas move.
> Starfish attack oysters.
> Can starfish attack ballerinas?

This is problematical. Perhaps a tentative solution would be that since the ballerina's motion is apparently far more eminent than the starfish's, a ballerina would invariably move in such a way as to avoid starfish. There are unresolved difficulties however:

a. I do not know whether starfish and ballerinas occupy the same medium.
b. I do not know whether starfish have any interest in attacking ballerinas.

3. Let me begin again:

Starfish move; ballerinas move.
Starfish are deadly to oysters.
Are ballerinas deadly to oysters?

One line of approach would seem to be that, since the voice says that ballerinas are his absolute favorite for loveliness, and since loveliness and deadliness do not seem to be compatible, the ballerina cannot be deadly to the oyster. (This depends, of course, on what is meant by loveliness and deadliness. It also might depend on whether a ballerina's possible deadliness to the oyster proceeds out of her nature, as the starfish's does, or out of some accidental or acquired taste, as it were. If the latter were true, then it might be that not every ballerina is deadly to oysters.) In any case, there is not enough evidence to resolve the question.

4. Even though the voice's enthusiasm for the world of higher motion seems to have suspended my own doubts, it is disturbing to think how easily a skeptical oyster could argue from all this that ballerinas do not exist, but rather are nothing more than a distracting hypothesis invented by oysters who cannot face the grimness of existence without flinching.

5. Tentatively, I shall list the following as the chief properties of the prima ballerina:
a. Mobility (like the starfish's, but better).
b. Invulnerability to starfish (likely).
c. Loveliness (on faith).
d. Deadliness (possible, but not certain).
There is a good deal unresolved here. Perhaps it would be useful to consider next what ballerinas are for. This is fascinating but tiring. At least, though, the sea water seems refreshing again.

Chinese Proverb

He who hammers at things over his head
easily hits nail right on thumb

—And he who hammers higher does it easier still.

Unless our philosophical oyster gets a firm grip on the truth that discourse about realities other than himself is always couched in analogies, parables, images and paradoxes, he could very well conclude his definitive treatise *On The Prima Ballerina* by proving that ballerinas have five feet and glide along the ocean bottom at four miles per hour. And unless we, who are unfathomably further from our major subject than the oyster, are a hundred times more careful, we will say even stranger things about God—and be just as unaware as the oyster that we have almost completely missed the mark.

CHAPTER EIGHT
WHAT IS THE MEANING OF LIFE? THE PROBLEM OF MEANING

Each of us holds a view of himself or herself and the world in which we live. Each of us feels, thinks, and hopes in such a way that, in effect, says: "This is what it means to be human."

Both philosophy and science are interested in the explanation and meaning of things. In science, the emphasis is more upon a description of the laws of phenomena and upon causal relationships. Philosophy is interested in the "why" as well as the "how." Philosophy is concerned with questions of purpose, and in the relation between particular facts and the larger scheme of things.

Meaning is found in a variety of ways. Many say meaning is obtained by devotion to that which has a lasting significance and is beyond the self. For them, relationships with others are prescribed by universal principles, not by what is pleasant and convenient. An overall purpose and meaning is stressed. Others stress that one should submit everything to the control of reason. Still others point to the pleasure-full life as the happy life.

Some Oriental minds point to Nirvana, the cessation of desire and thus of pain, as the ultimate meaning of life. Our excerpt from Buddha's earliest sermons show an Oriental way to absolute oneness and egolessness through the cessation of what we in the West usually think of as the two most distinctively human activities of the psyche: the desire of the will (first sermon) and the speculations of the intellect (second sermon).

In this section we have presented excerpts from Viktor Frankl, C. S. Lewis, Albert Camus, and the *Humanist Manifesto*.

Frankl's "logotherapy" stresses that man's search for meaning is the primary motivational force in life. This meaning is concrete and specific; it must be fulfilled by each individual person. Frankl turns for support to a survey of around 8,000 students from 48 colleges, conducted by John Hopkins University. In this survey, 78 percent of the students noted that their first goal was finding a purpose and meaning to life.

From his concentration camp experiences Frankl learned that there is a kind of value which has little to do with material things and one's possessions, or with the way one is treated. Under very adverse circumstances of terrible psychic and physical stress one can find meaning and preserve a spiritual freedom and independence of mind. Even in the worst of circumstances one can still choose one's attitude to the situation. Is one worthy of his or her suffering? This is the key question for Frankl.

Humanism is a philosophical view that accepts human beings as the ultimate source of values and meaning. It strives to preserve and enhance all things human and to allow the potentiality of each individual to be realized. Its basic assumption is that man is educable because man has basic good will toward his fellow man.

There are several different meanings that the term "humanism" brings to mind. The material we have included emphasizes the following:

1. The universe is self-existing and not created; man has emerged as the result of a continuous process.

2. Religion has value only as a *means* for achieving higher ends in the here and now.

3. An economic order should be established such that the equitable distribution of the means of life be possible. If our future choice is between despair and hope, humanists affirm faith and hope. Reason and compassion must be tied to science and democracy in order for humanity to survive and build constructive social and moral values.

Albert Camus claims that there is only one serious philosophical problem: suicide. He means that the fundamental question of philosophy is judging whether life is or is not worth living. Camus' universe is divested of all illusions and lights; man is a stranger. For Camus, the sphere of the "ought" is inoperative. All value judgments are discarded in favor of factual judgments. For Camus' "absurd man," the universe is not something we explain or solve, it is something we can only experience and describe. Like Sisyphus, we push our stones up the slope and then watch the stone rush down the other side. Perhaps the classic statement in summary of this position is found in Shakespeare's *Macbeth*:

Out, out brief candle!
Life's but a walking shadow, a poor player
That struts and frets his hour upon the stage
And then is heard no more. It is a tale
Told by an idiot, full of sound and fury,
Signifying nothing.

A final point of view, represented by C. S. Lewis, is that there exists in the universe a power greater than man that is ultimately responsible for truth, beauty, goodness, and the meaning of persons. Human beings are not alone in a hostile universe. Meaning, purpose, and values are present, and can be discovered by all of us.

We hear and read today much about the loss of a sense of meaning in life and the resulting deterioration of modern society. Some claim that modern people have become the victims of the very instruments they value most. Indeed, our gains in power, our mastery of natural forces, and our addition to scientific knowledge may prove to be extremely dangerous because they have not been accompanied by similar progress in self-understanding.

We are no longer living under the illusion that more and bigger is better. Happiness and the good and meaningful life will not be ushered in that way. Our nuclear century has made it very clear that the quality of civilization cannot be equated with a material standard of living. In fact, human civilization may stand or fall by whether or not we foster the spiritual and moral values that distinquish human beings and grant them their only dignity.

We in the modern age are unclear about the intent, purpose, or explanation of the universe. It is this question of meaning which may frustrate us most. William Barrett notes in *Irrational Man* (pp. 64–65):

> Our time . . . is the first in which man has become thoroughly and completely problematic to himself. . . .
> An observer from another planet might well be struck by the disparity between the enormous power which our age has concentrated in its external life and the inner poverty which our art seeks to expose to view. . . . What man cannot do! He has greater power now than Prometheus or Icarus or any of those daring mythical heroes who were later to succumb to the disaster of pride. But if an observer from Mars were to turn his attention from these external appurtenances of power to the shape of man as revealed in our novels, plays, painting and sculpture, he would find there a creature full of holes and gaps, faceless, riddled with doubts and negations, starkly finite.

We trust the following excerpts will provide an opportunity to explore some of the alternative perspectives as they relate to the question: What is the meaning of life?

A. LIFE HAS NO MEANING

Albert Camus: *The Myth of Sisyphus*

Albert Camus (1913–1960) was born in Algeria and spent the early years of his life in North Africa until journalism took him to France. In 1942 he joined the French resistance against the Nazis and edited its underground newspaper, *Combat*. He won the 1957 Nobel prize for literature.

Camus is associated with the existentialist movement, a contemporary philosophy which stresses that there is no essential human nature. Instead, each individual creates his or her own essence, or character, by a free, responsible choice of interests and actions. Thus, "existence precedes essence," since essence is not completed until life, with its endless series of choices, is curtailed by death.

Camus' chief concern was with the freedom and responsibility of the individual, the alienation of the individual from society, and the difficulty of facing life without the comfort of believing in God or in absolute moral standards. In *The Myth of Sisyphus* (1942), from which our excerpt is taken, Camus stresses that the only serious philosophical problem is that of suicide. He concludes that man hangs on to life even though life has no meaning or purpose to justify it and is therefore "absurd." Camus' most widely read novels are *The Stranger* (1942), *The Plague* (1947), and *The Fall* (1957).

AN ABSURD REASONING

There is but one truly serious philosophical problem, and that is suicide. Judging whether life is or is not worth living amounts to answering the fundamental question of philosophy. All the rest—whether or not the world has three dimensions, whether the mind has nine or twelve categories—comes afterwards. These are games; one must first answer. And if it is true, as Nietzsche claims, that a philosopher, to deserve our respect, must preach by example, you can appreciate the importance of that reply, for it will precede the definitive act. These are facts the heart can feel; yet they call for careful study before they become clear to the intellect.

If I ask myself how to judge that this question is more urgent than that, I reply that one judges by the actions it entails. I have never seen anyone die for the ontological argument. Galileo, who held a scientific truth of great importance, abjured it with the greatest ease as soon as it endangered his life. In a certain sense, he did right. That truth was not worth the stake. Whether the earth or the sun revolves around the other is a matter of profound indifference. To tell the truth, it is a futile question. On the other hand, I see many people die because they judge that life is not worth living. I see others paradoxically getting killed for the ideas or illusions that give them a reason for living (what is called a reason for living is also an excellent reason for dying). I therefore conclude that the meaning of life is the most urgent of questions. . . .

* * *

Suicide has never been dealt with except as a social phenomenon. On the contrary, we are concerned here, at the outset, with the relationship between individual thought and suicide. An act like this is prepared within the silence of the heart, as is a great work of art. The man himself is ignorant of it. One evening he pulls the trigger or jumps. Of an apartment-building manager who had killed himself I was told that he had lost his daughter five years before, that he had changed greatly since, and that that experience had "undermined" him. A more exact word cannot be imagined. Beginning to think is beginning to be undermined. Society has but little connection with such beginnings. The worm is in man's heart. That is where it must be sought. One must follow and understand this fatal game that leads from lucidity in the face of existence to flight from light.

* * *

. . . Does the Absurd dictate death? This problem must be given priority over others, outside all methods of thought and all exercises of the disinterested mind. Shades of meaning, contraditions, the psychology that an "objective" mind can always introduce into all problems have no place in this pursuit and this passion. It calls simply for an unjust—in other words, logical—thought. That is not easy. It is always easy to be logical. It is almost impossible to be logical to the bitter end. Men who die by their own hand consequently follow to its conclusion their emotional inclination. Reflecting on suicide gives me an opportunity to raise the only problem to interest me: is there a logic to the point of death. I cannot know unless I pursue, without reckless passion, in the sole light of evidence, the reasoning of which I am here suggesting the source. This is what I call an absurd reasoning. Many have begun it. I do not yet know whether or not they kept to it.

It happens that the stage sets collapse. Rising, streetcar, four hours in the office or the factory, meal, sleep, and Monday Tuesday Wednesday Thursday Friday and Saturday according to the same rhythm—this path is easily followed most of the time. But one day the "why" arises and everything begins in that weariness tinged with amazement . . . .

* * *

Likewise and during every day of an unillustrious life, time carries us. But a moment always comes when we have to carry it. We live on the future: "tomorrow," "later on," "when you have made your way," "you will understand when you are old enough." Such irrelevancies are wonderful, for, after all, it's a matter of dying. Yet a day comes when a man notices or says that he is thirty. Thus he asserts his youth. But simultaneously he situates himself in relation to time. He takes his place in it. He admits that he stands at a certain point on a curve that he acknowledges having to travel to its end. He belongs to time, and by the horror that seizes him, he recognizes his worst enemy. Tomorrow, he was longing for tomorrow, whereas everything in him ought to reject it. . . .

* * *

. . . At certain moments of lucidity, the mechanical aspect of their gestures, their meaningless pantomime makes silly everything that surrounds them. A man is talking on the telephone behind a glass partition; you cannot hear him, but you see his imcomprehensible dumb show: you wonder why he is alive. . . .

* * *

. . . A man who has become conscious of the absurd is forever bound to it. A man devoid of hope and conscious of being so has ceased to belong to the future. That is natural. But it is just as natural that he should strive to escape the universe of which he is the creator. All the foregoing has significance only on account of this paradox. Certain men, starting from a critique of rationalism, have admitted to the absurd climate. Nothing is more instructive in this regard than to scrutinize the way in which they have elaborated their consequences.

* * *

It must be repeated that the reasoning developed in this essay leaves out altogether the most widespread spiritual attitude of our enlightened age: the one, based on the principle that all is reason, which aims to explain the world. It is natural to give a clear view of the world after accepting the idea that it must be clear. That is even legitimate, but does not concern the reasoning we are following out here. In fact, our aim is to shed light upon the step taken by the mind when, starting from a philosophy of the world's lack of meaning, it ends up by finding a meaning and depth in it. . . .

* * *

. . . I don't know whether this world has a meaning that transcends it. But I know that I do not know that meaning and that it is impossible for me just now to know it. What can a meaning outside my condition mean to me? I can understand only in human terms. What I touch, what resists me—that is what I understand. And these two certainties—my appetite for the absolute and for unity and the impossibility of reducing this world to a rational and reasonable principle—I also know that I cannot reconcile them. What other truth can I admit without lying, without bringing in a hope I lack and which means nothing within the limits of my condition?

If I were a tree among trees, a cat among animals, this life would have a meaning, or rather this problem would not arise, for I should belong to this world. I should *be* this world to which I am now opposed by my whole consciousness and my whole insistence upon familiarity. This ridiculous reason is what sets me in opposition to all creation. I cannot cross it out with a stroke of the pen. . . .

* * *

Now I can broach the notion of suicide. It has already been felt what solution might be given. At this point the problem is reversed. It was previously a question of finding out whether or not life had to have a meaning to be lived. It now becomes clear, on the contrary, that it will be lived all the better if it has no meaning. Living an experience, a particular fate, is accepting it fully. Now, no one will live this fate, knowing it to be absurd, unless he does everything to keep before him that absurd brought to light by consciousness. Negating one of the terms of the opposition on which he lives amounts to escaping it. To abolish conscious revolt is to elude the problem. The theme of permanent revolution is thus carried into individual experience. Living is keeping the absurd alive. Keeping it alive is, above all, contemplating it. . . . the absurd dies only when we turn away from it. One of the only coherent philosophical positions is thus revolt. It is a constant confrontation between man and his own obscurity. It is an insistence upon an impossible transparency. It challenges the world anew every second. Just as danger provided man the unique opportunity of seizing awareness, so metaphysical revolt extends awareness to the whole of experience. It is that constant presence of man in his own eyes. It is not aspiration, for it is devoid of hope. That revolt is the certainty of a crushing fate, without the resignation that ought to accompany it.

This is where it is seen to what a degree absurd experience is remote from suicide. It may be thought that suicide follows revolt—but wrongly. For it does not represent the logical outcome of revolt. It is just the contrary by the consent it presupposes. Suicide, like the leap, is acceptance at its extreme. Everything is over and man returns to his essential history. His future, his unique and dreadful future—he sees and rushes toward it. In its way, suicide settles the absurd. It engulfs the absurd in the same death. But I know that in order to keep alive, the absurd cannot be settled. It escapes suicide to the extent that it is simultaneously awareness and rejection of death. . . .

* * *

. . . It is essential to die unreconciled and not of one's own free will. Suicide is a repudiation. The absurd man can only drain everything to the bitter end, and deplete himself. The absurd is his extreme tension, which he maintains constantly by solitary effort, for he knows that in that consciousness and in that day-to-day revolt he gives proof of his only truth, which is defiance. . . .

* * *

. . . Being aware of one's life, one's revolt, one's freedom, and to the maximum, is living, and to the maximum . . .

* * *

THE ABSURD MAN

All systems of morality are based on the idea that an action has consequences that legitimize or cancel it. A mind imbued with the absurd merely judges that those consequences must be considered calmly. It is ready to pay up. In other words, there may be responsible persons, but there are no guilty ones, in its opinion. . . .

* * *

ABSURD CREATION

. . . For the absurd man it is not a matter of explaining and solving, but of experiencing and describing. Everything begins with lucid indifference.

Describing—that is the last ambition of an absurd thought. Science likewise, having reached the end of its paradoxes, ceases to propound and stops to contemplate and sketch the ever virgin landscape of phenomena. The heart learns thus that the emotion delighting us when we see the world's aspects comes to us not from its depth but from their diversity. Explanation is useless, but the sensation remains and, with it, the constant attractions of a universe inexhaustible in quantity. The place of the work of art can be understood at this point.

* * *

THE MYTH OF SISYPHUS

The gods had condemned Sisyphus to ceaselessly rolling a rock to the top of a mountain, whence the stone would fall back of its own weight. They had thought with some reason that there is no more dreadful punishment than futile and hopeless labor.

* * *

. . . Sisyphus is the absurd hero. He is, as much through his passions as through his torture. His scorn of the gods, his hatred of death, and his passion for life won him that unspeakable penalty in which the whole being is exerted toward accomplishing nothing. This is the price that must be paid for the passions of this earth. Nothing is told us about Sisyphus in the underworld. Myths are made for the imagination to breathe life into them. As for this myth, one sees merely the whole effort of a body straining to raise the huge stone, to roll it and push it up a slope a hundred times over; one sees the face screwed up, the cheek tight against the stone, the shoulder bracing the clay-covered mass, the foot wedging it, the fresh start with arms outstretched, the wholly human security of two earth-clotted hands. At the very end of his long effort measured by skyless space and time without depth, the purpose is achieved. Then Sisyphus watches the stone rush down in a few moments toward that lower world whence he will have to push it up again toward the summit. He goes back down to the plain.

It is during that return, that pause, that Sisyphus interests me. A face that toils so close to stones is already stone itself! I see that man going back down with a heavy yet measured step toward the torment of which he will never know the end. That hour like a breathing-space which returns as surely as his suffering, that is the hour of consciousness. At each of those moments when he leaves the heights and gradually sinks toward the lairs of the gods, he is superior to his fate. He is stronger than his rock.

If this myth is tragic, that is because its hero is conscious. Where would his torture be, indeed, if at every step the hope of succeeding upheld him? The workman of today works every day in his life at the same tasks, and his fate is no less absurd. But it is tragic only at the rare moments when it becomes conscious. Sisyphus, proletarian of the gods, powerless and rebellious, knows the whole extent of his wretched condition: it is what he thinks of during his descent. The lucidity that was to constitute his torture at the same time crowns his victory. There is no fate that cannot be surmounted by scorn.

* * *

If the descent is thus sometimes performed in sorrow, it can also take place in joy. This word is not too much. Again I fancy Sisyphus returning toward his rock, and the sorrow was in the beginning. When the images of earth cling too tightly to memory, when the call of happiness becomes too insistent, it happens that melancholy rises in man's heart: this is the rock's victory, this is the rock itself. The boundless grief is too heavy to bear. These are our nights of Gethsemane. But crushing truths perish from being acknowledged. Thus, Oedipus at the outset obeys fate without knowing it. But from the moment he knows, his tragedy begins. Yet at the same moment, blind and desperate, he realized that the only bond linking him to the world is the cool hand of a girl. Then a tremendous remark rings out: "Despite so many ordeals, my advanced age and the nobility of my soul make me conclude that all is well." Sophocles' Oedipus, like Dostoevsky's Kirilov, thus gives the recipe for the absurd victory. Ancient wisdom confirms modern heroism.

One does not discover the absurd without being tempted to write a manual of happiness. "What! by such narrow ways—?" There is but one world, however. Happiness and the absurd are two sons of the same earth. They are inseparable. It would be a mistake to say that happiness necessarily springs from the absurd discovery. It happens as well that the feeling of the absurd springs from happiness. "I conclude that all is well," says Oedipus, and that remark is sacred. It echoes in the wild and limited universe of man. It teaches that all is not, has not been, exhausted. It drives out of this world a god who had come into it with dissatisfaction and a preference for futile sufferings. It makes of fate a human matter, which must be settled among men.

All Sisyphus' silent joy is contained therein. His fate belongs to him.

His rock is his thing. Likewise, the absurd man, when he contemplates his torment, silences all the idols. In the universe suddenly restored to its silence, the myriad wondering little voices of the earth rise up. Unconscious, secret calls, invitations from all the faces, they are the necessary reverse and price of victory. There is no sun without shadow, and it is essential to know the night. The absurd man says yes and his effort will henceforth be unceasing. If there is a personal fate, there is no higher destiny, or at least there is but one which he concludes is inevitable and despicable. For the rest, he knows himself to be the master of his days. At that subtle moment when man glances backward over his life, Sisyphus returning toward his rock, in that slight pivoting he contemplates that series of unrelated actions which becomes his fate, created by him, combined under his memory's eye and soon sealed by his death. Thus, convinced of the wholly human origin of all that is human, a blind man eager to see who knows that the night has no end, he is still on the go. The rock is still rolling.

I leave Sisyphus at the foot of the mountain! One always finds one's burden again. But Sisyphus teaches the higher fidelity that negates the gods and raises rocks. He too concludes that all is well. This universe henceforth without a master seems to him neither sterile nor futile. Each atom of that stone, each mineral flake of that night-filled mountain, in itself forms a world. The struggle itself toward the heights is enough to fill a man's heart. One must imagine Sisyphus happy.

Discussion Questions

1. According to Camus, there is but one serious philosophical problem: suicide. Do you agree? Why or why not?

2. What does Camus mean by "the absurd?"

3. What do the "existential philosophies" conclude in the way of an escape from the absurd?

4. It is Camus' thesis that suicide should not follow logically from the notion of the absurd. Why not?

5. Knowing whether or not man is free doesn't interest Camus. Why not?

6. What is the myth of Sisyphus? Why is it an ideal example of Camus' central thesis?

7. Do you agree with Camus that life is absurd? Why or why not?

B. PEOPLE GIVE LIFE MEANING

The Humanist Manifesto

In 1933 a group of 34 liberal humanists in the United States drafted *Humanist Manifesto I*, defining therein the philosophical and religious principles that seemed fundamental to them. The commitment was to reason, science, and democracy. *Humanist Manifesto II* (1973) was first signed by 114 individuals of prominence and distinction. It has since been endorsed by many others from all walks of life as an important document for our time, committed to both human fulfillment and survival.

Humanism is defined in several key ways: any view in which the welfare and happiness of humankind in this life is primary; the Renaissance revolt against religious limitations on knowledge and a revival of classical learning; and a twentieth-century philosophy that rejects belief in all forms of the supernatural and considers the greater good of all humanity on earth as the supreme ethical goal.

HUMANIST MANIFESTO I

The time has come for widespread recognition of the radical changes in religious beliefs throughout the modern world. The time is past for mere revision of traditional attitudes. Science and economic change have disrupted the old beliefs. Religions the world over are under the necessity of coming to terms with new conditions created by a vastly increased knowledge and experience. In every field of human activity, the vital movement is now in the direction of a candid and explicit humanism. In order that religious humanism may be better understood we, the undersigned, desire to make certain affirmations which we believe the facts of our contemporary life demonstrate.

There is great danger of a final, and we believe fatal, identification of the word *religion* with doctrines and methods which have lost their significance and which are powerless to solve the problem of human living in the Twentieth Century. Religions have always been means for realizing the highest values of life. . . .

* * *

Today man's larger understanding of the universe, his scientific achievements, and his deeper appreciation of brotherhood have created a situation which requires a new statement of the means and purposes of religion. Such a vital, fearless, and frank religion capable of furnishing adequate social goals and personal satisfactions may appear to many people as a complete break with the past. While this age does owe a vast debt to traditional religions, it is none the less obvious that any religion that can hope to be a synthesizing and dynamic force for today must be shaped for the needs of this age. To establish such a religion is a major necessity of the present. It is a responsibility which rests upon this generation. We therefore affirm the following:

First: Religious humanists regard the universe as self-existing and not created.

Second: Humanism believes that man is a part of nature and that he has emerged as the result of a continuous process.

Third: Holding an organic view of life, humanists find that the traditional dualism of mind and body must be rejected.

* * *

Fifth: Humanism asserts that the nature of the universe depicted by modern science makes unacceptable any supernatural or cosmic guarantees of human values. Obviously humanism does not deny the possibility of realities as yet undiscovered, but it does insist that the way to determine the existence and value of any and all realities is by means of intelligent inquiry and by the assessment of their relation to human needs. Religion must formulate its hopes and plans in the light of the scientific spirit and method.

* * *

Eighth: Religious humanism considers the complete realization of human personality to be the end of man's life and seeks its development and fulfillment in the here and now. This is the explanation of the humanist's social passion.

* * *

Eleventh: Man will learn to face the crises of life in terms of his knowledge of their naturalness and probability. Reasonable and manly attitudes will be fostered by education and supported by custom. . . .

* * *

Fourteenth: The humanists are firmly convinced that existing acquisitive and profit-motivated society has shown itself to be inadequate and that a radical change in methods, controls, and motives must be instituted. A socialized and cooperative economic order must be established to the end that the equitable distribution of the means of life be possible. The goal of humanism is a free and universal society in which people voluntarily and intelligently cooperate for the common good. Humanists demand a shared life in a shared world.

* * *

HUMANIST MANIFESTO II

Preface

It is forty years since *Humanist Manifesto I* (1933) appeared. Events since then make that earlier statement seem far too optimistic. Nazism has shown the depths of brutality of which humanity is capable. Other totalitarian regimes have suppressed human rights without ending poverty. Science has sometimes brought evil as well as good. Recent decades have shown that inhuman wars can be made in the name of peace. The beginnings of police states, even in democratic societies, widespread government espionage, and other abuses of power by military, political, and industrial elites, and the continuance of unyielding racism, all present a different and difficult social outlook. In various societies, the demands of women and minority groups for equal rights effectively challenge our generation.

As we approach the twenty-first century, however, an affirmative and hopeful vision is needed. Faith, commensurate with advancing knowledge, is also necessary. In the choice between despair and hope, humanists respond in this *Humanist Manifest II* with a positive declaration for times of uncertainty. . . .

* * *

Humanity, to survive, requires bold and daring measures. We need to extend the uses of scientific method, not renounce them, to fuse reason with compassion in order to build constructive social and moral values. Confronted by many possible futures, we must decide which to pursue. The ultimate goal should be the fulfillment of the potential for growth in each human personality—not for the favored few, but for all of human-kind. Only a shared world and global measures will suffice.

A humanist outlook will tap the creativity of each human being and provide the vision and courage for us to work together. . . .

* * *

. . . views that merely reject theism are not equivalent to humanism. They lack commitment to the positive belief in the possibilities of human progress and to the values central to it. Many within religious groups, believing in the future of humanism, now claim humanist credentials. Humanism is an ethical process through which we all can move, above and beyond the divisive particulars, heroic personalities, dogmatic creeds, and ritual customs of past religions or their mere negation.

* * *

Religion

First: In the best sense, religion may inspire dedication to the highest eth-ical ideals. The cultivation of moral devotion and creative imagination is an expression of genuine "spiritual" experience and aspiration.

We believe, however, that traditional dogmatic or authoritarian religions that place revelation, God, ritual, or creed above human needs and experience do a disservice to the human species. Any account of nature should pass the tests of scientific evidence; in our judgment, the dogmas and myths of traditional religions do not do so. Even at this late date in human history, certain elementary facts based upon the critical use of scientific reason have to be restated. We find insufficient evidence for belief in the existence of a supernatural; it is either meaningless or irrelevant to the question of the survival and fulfillment of the human race. As non-theists, we begin with humans not God, nature not deity. . . .

* * *

. . . We need . . . radically new human purposes and goals. . . . Traditional religions often offer solace to humans, but, as often, they inhibit humans from helping themselves or experiencing their full potentialities. Such institutions, creeds, and rituals often impede the will to serve others. Too often traditional faiths encourage dependence rather than independence, obedience rather than affirmation, fear rather than courage. More recently they have generated concerned social action, with many signs of relevance appearing in the wake of the "God Is Dead" theologies. But we can discover no divine purpose or providence for the human species. While there is much that we do not know, humans are responsible for what we are or will become. No deity will save us; we must save ourselves.

Second: Promises of immortal salvation or fear of eternal damnation are both illusory and harmful. They distract humans from present concerns, from self-actualization, and from rectifying social injustices. Modern science discredits such historic concepts as the "ghost in the machine" and the "separable soul." Rather, science affirms that the human species is an emergence from natural evolutionary forces. As far as we know, the total personality is a function of the biological organism transacting in a social and cultural context. There is no credible evidence that life survives the death of the body. . . .

* * *

Ethics

Third: We affirm that moral values derive their source from human experience. Ethics is *autonomous* and *situational*, needing no theological or ideological sanction. Ethics stems from human need and interest. To deny this distorts the whole basis of life. Human life has meaning because we create and develop our futures. Happiness and the creative realization of human needs and desires, individually and in shared enjoyment, are continuous themes of humanism. We strive for the good life, here and now. The goal is to pursue life's enrichment despite debasing forces of vulgarization, commercialization, bureaucratization, and dehumanization.

Fourth: Reason and intelligence are the most effective instruments that humankind possesses. There is no substitute: neither faith nor passion suffices in itself. The controlled use of scientific methods, which have transformed the natural and social sciences since the Renaissance, must be extended further in the solution of human problems. But reason must be tempered by humility, since no group has a monopoly of wisdom or virtue. Nor is there any guarantee that all problems can be solved or all questions answered. Yet critical intelligence, infused by a sense of human caring, is the best method that humanity has for resolving problems. Reason should be balanced with compassion and empathy and the whole person fulfilled. Thus, we are not advocating the use of scientific intelligence independent of or in opposition to emotion, for we believe in the cultivation of feeling and love. As science pushes back the boundary of the known, one's sense of wonder is continually renewed, and art, poetry, and music find their places, along with religion and ethics.

The Individual

Fifth: The preciousness and dignity of the individual person is a central humanist value. Individuals should be encouraged to realize their own creative talents and desires. We reject all religious, ideological, or moral codes that denigrate the individual, suppress freedom, dull intellect, dehumanize personality. We believe in maximum individual autonomy consonant with social responsibility. Although science can account for the causes of behavior, the possibilities of individual *freedom of choice* exist in human life and should be increased.

Sixth: In the area of sexuality, we believe that intolerant attitudes, often cultivated by orthodox religions and puritanical cultures, unduly repress sexual conduct. The right to birth control, abortion, and divorce should be recognized. While we do not approve of exploitive, denigrating forms of sexual expression, neither do we wish to prohibit, by law or social sanction, sexual behavior between consenting adults. The many varieties of sexual exploration should not in themselves be considered "evil." Without countenancing mindless permissiveness or unbridled promiscuity, a civilized society should be a *tolerant* one. Short of harming others or compelling them to do likewise, individuals should be permitted to express their sexual proclivities and pursue their life-styles as they desire. We wish to cultivate the development of a responsible attitude toward sexuality, in which humans are not exploited as sexual objects, and in which intimacy, sensitivity, respect, and honesty in interpersonal relations are encouraged. Moral education for children and adults is an important way of developing awareness and sexual maturity.

Democratic Society

Seventh: To enhance freedom and dignity the individual must experience a full range of *civil liberties* in all societies. This includes freedom of speech and the press, political democracy, the legal right of opposition to governmental policies, fair judicial process, religious liberty, freedom of association, and artistic, scientific, and cultural freedom. It also includes a recognition of an individual's right to die with dignity, euthanasia, and the right to suicide. We oppose the increasing invasion of privacy, by whatever means, in both totalitarian and democratic societies. . . .

World Community

Twelfth: We deplore the division of humankind on nationalistic grounds. We have reached a turning point in human history where the best option is to *transcend the limits of national sovereignty* and to move toward the building of a world community in which all sectors of the human family can participate. Thus we look to the development of a system of world law and a world order based upon transnational federal government. This would appreciate cultural pluralism and diversity. It would not exclude pride in national origins and accomplishments nor the handling of regional problems on a regional basis. Human progress, however, can no longer be achieved by focusing on one section of the world, Western or Eastern, developed or underdeveloped. For the first time in human history, no part of humankind can be isolated from any other. Each person's future is in some way linked to all. We thus reaffirm a commitment to the building of world community, at the same time recognizing that this commits us to some hard choices.

Thirteenth: This world community must *renounce the resort to violence and force* as a method of solving international disputes. We believe in the peaceful adjudication of differences by international courts and by the developments of the arts of negotiation and compromise. War is obsolete. So is the use of nuclear, biological, and chemical weapons. It is a planetary imperative to reduce the level of military expenditures and turn these savings to peaceful and people-oriented uses.

Fourteenth: The world community must engage in *cooperative planning* concerning the use of rapidly depleting resources. The planet earth must be considered a single *ecosystem.* Ecological damage, resource depletion, and excessive population growth must be checked by international concord. . . .

* * *

Sixteenth: Technology is a vital key to human progress and development. We deplore any neo-romantic efforts to condemn indiscriminately all technology and science or to counsel retreat from its further extension and use for the good of humankind. We would resist any moves to censor basic scientific research on moral, political, or social grounds. Technology must, however, be carefully judged by the consequences of its use; harmful and destructive changes should be avoided. We are particularly disturbed when technology and bureaucracy control, manipulate, or modify human beings without their consent. Technological feasibility does not imply social or cultural desirability.

* * *

Humanity as a Whole

. . . We believe that humankind has the potential intelligence, good will, and cooperative skill to implement this commitment in the decades ahead.

Discussion Questions

1. Why, according to the writers of the *Humanist Manifesto I*, do we need a new statement of the means and purposes of religion?

2. Which events have occurred between *Manifesto I* and *II* which make the earlier statement seem too optimistic? Do you agree? Why or why not?

3. In the choice between despair and hope, *Humanist Manifesto II* responds with a positive statement. Is it persuasive? Why or why not?

4. What are the "bold and daring measures" which are needed for humanity to survive?

5. Why are views which simply reject theism not equivalent to humanism?

6. What do these humanists have to say about the individual?

7. In what ways do these humanists emphasize what they call a "world community"?

8. Should technology be a vital key to human progress and development? How?

9. What, if any, are the chief differences between *Humanist Manifesto I* and *II*?

C. LIFE MUST HAVE MEANING

Viktor Frankl: *Man's Search for Meaning*

Viktor E. Frankl (b. 1905), has been Professor of Psychiatry and Neurology at the University of Vienna Medical School and has been affiliated with the United States International University, Stanford University, and Harvard University in the United States. He is the leader and originator of the school of logotherapy (existential analysis) and the author of numerous books translated into at least fourteen languages, including Japanese and Chinese.

Dostoevski once said: "There is only one thing that I dread: not to be worthy of my sufferings." Viktor Frankl spent three years at Auschwitz and other Nazi prisons. Upon gaining his freedom he learned that almost his entire family had been killed. During—and undoubtedly partly because of—the suffering and degradation of those years, Dr. Frankl developed his theory of logotherapy, which some see as the most significant psychological movement of our day.

EXPERIENCES IN A CONCENTRATION CAMP

This book does not claim to be an account of facts and events but of personal experiences, experiences which millions of prisoners have suffered time and again. It is the inside story of a concentration camp, told by one of its survivors. This tale is not concerned with the great horrors, which have already been described often enough (though less often believed), but with the multitude of small torments. In other words, it will try to answer this question: How was everyday life in a concentration camp reflected in the mind of the average prisoner?

* * *

It is easy for the outsider to get the wrong conception of camp life, a conception mingled with sentiment and pity. Little does he know of the hard fight for existence which raged among the prisoners. This was an unrelenting struggle for daily bread and for life itself, for one's own sake or for that of a good friend.

* * *

In psychiatry there is a certain condition known as "delusion of reprieve." The condemned man, immediately before his execution, gets the illusion that he might be reprieved at the very last moment. . . .

* * *

Nearly everyone in our transport lived under the illusion that he would be reprieved, that everything would yet be well. . . .

* * *

We waited in a shed which seemed to be the anteroom to the disinfecting chamber. SS men appeared and spread out blankets into which we had to throw all our possessions, all our watches and jewelry. There were still naïve prisoners among us who asked, to the amusement of the more seasoned ones who were there as helpers, if they could not keep a wedding ring, a medal or a good-luck piece. No one could yet grasp the fact that everything would be taken away.

I tried to take one of the old prisoners into my confidence. Approaching him furtively, I pointed to the roll of paper in the inner pocket of my coat and said, "Look, this is the manuscript of a scientific book. I know what you will say; that I should be grateful to escape with my life, that that should be all I can expect of fate. But I cannot help myself. I must keep this manuscript at all costs; it contains my life's work. Do you understand that?"

Yes, he was beginning to understand. A grin spread slowly over his face, first piteous, then more amused, mocking, insulting, until he bellowed one word at me in answer to my question, a word that was ever present in the vocabulary of the camp inmates: "Shit!" At that moment I saw the plain truth and did what marked the culminating point of the first phase of my psychological reaction: I struck out my whole former life.

* * *

. . . we really had nothing now except our bare bodies—even minus hair; all we possessed, literally, was our naked existence. What else remained for us as a material link with our former lives? . . .

* * *

There were many . . . surprises in store for new arrivals. The medical men among us learned first of all: "Textbooks tell lies!" Somewhere it is said that man cannot exist without sleep for more than a stated number of hours. Quite wrong! I had been convinced that there were certain things I just could not do: I could not sleep without this or I could not live with that or the other. The first night in Auschwitz we slept in beds which were constructed in tiers. On each tier (measuring about six-and-a-half to eight feet) slept nine men, directly on the boards. Two blankets were shared by each nine men. We could, of course, lie only on our sides, crowded and huddled against each other . . .

* * *

The thought of suicide was entertained by nearly everyone, if only for a brief time. It was born of the hopelessness of the situation, the constant danger of death looming over us daily and hourly, and the closeness of the deaths suffered by many of the others. . . .

* * *

Apathy, the blunting of the emotions and the feeling that one could not care any more, were the symptoms arising during the second stage of the prisoner's psychological reactions, and which eventually made him insensitive to daily and hourly beatings . . .

* * *

What did the prisoner dream about most frequently? Of bread, cake, cigarettes, and nice warm baths. The lack of having these simple desires satisfied led him to seek wish-fulfillment in dreams. Whether these dreams did any good is another matter; the dreamer had to wake from them to the reality of camp life, and to the terrible contrast between that and his dream illusions.

I shall never forget how I was roused one night by the groans of a fellow prisoner, who threw himself about in his sleep, obviously having a horrible nightmare. Since I had always been especially sorry for people who suffered from fearful dreams or deliria, I wanted to wake the poor man. Suddenly I drew back the hand which was ready to shake him, frightened at the thing I was about to do. At that moment I became intensely conscious of the fact that no dream, no matter how horrible, could be as bad as the reality of the camp which surrounded us, and to which I was about to recall him.

* * *

When the last layers of subcutaneous fat had vanished, and we looked like skeletons disguised with skin and rags, we could watch our bodies beginning to devour themselves. The organism digested its own protein, and the muscles disappeared. Then the body had no powers or resistance left. One after another the members of the little community in our hut died. . . .

* * *

Undernourishment, besides being the cause of the general preoccupation with food, probably also explains the fact that the sexual urge was generally absent. Apart from the initial effects of shock, this appears to be the only explanation of a phenomenon which a psychologist was bound to observe in those all-male camps: that, as opposed to all other strictly male establishments—such as army barracks—there was little sexual perversion. . . .

* * *

The religious interest of the prisoners, as far and as soon as it developed, was the most sincere imaginable. The depth and vigor of religious belief often surprised and moved a new arrival. Most impressive in this connection were improvised prayers or services in the corner of a hut, or in the darkness of the locked cattle truck in which we were brought back from a distant work site, tired, hungry and frozen in our ragged clothing.

* * *

In spite of all the enforced physical and mental primitiveness of the life in a concentration camp, it was possible for spiritual life to deepen. Sensitive people who were used to a rich intellectual life may have suffered much pain (they were often of a delicate constitution), but the damage to their inner selves was less. They were able to retreat from their terrible surroundings to a life of inner riches and spiritual freedom. Only in this way can one explain the apparent paradox that some prisoners of a less hardy make-up often seemed to survive camp life better than did those of a robust nature . . .

* * *

. . . Humor was another of the soul's weapons in the fight for self-preservation. It is well known that humor, more than anything else in the human make-up, can afford an aloofness and an ability to rise above any situation, even if only for a few seconds . . .

The attempt to develop a sense of humor and to see things in a humorous light is some kind of a trick learned while mastering the art of living. . .

* * *

. . . everything that was not connected with the immediate task of keeping oneself and one's closest friends alive lost its value. . . .

* * *

It is very difficult for an outsider to grasp how very little value was placed on human life in camp. The camp inmate was hardened, but possibly became more conscious of this complete disregard of human existence when a convoy of sick men was arranged. The emaciated bodies of the sick were thrown on two-wheeled carts which were drawn by prisoners for many miles, often through snow-storms, to the next camp. If one of the sick men had died before the cart left, he was thrown on anyway—the list had to be correct! . . .

* * *

. . . The majority of prisoners suffered from a kind of inferiority complex. We all had once been or had fancied ourselves to be "somebody." Now we were treated like complete nonentities. (The consciousness of one's inner value is anchored in higher, more spiritual things, and cannot be shaken by camp life. But how many free men, let alone prisoners, possess it?) . . .

* * *

. . . The experiences of camp life show that man does have a choice of action. There were enough examples, often of a heroic nature, which proved that apathy could be overcome, irritability supressed. Man *can* preserve a vestige of spiritual freedom, of independence of mind, even in such terrible conditions of psychic and physical stress.

We who lived in concentration camps can remember the men who walked through the huts comforting others, giving away their last piece of bread. They may have been few in number, but they offer sufficient proof that everything can be taken from a man but one thing: the last of the human freedoms—to choose one's attitude in any given set of circumstances, to choose one's own way.

And there were always choices to make. Every day, every hour, offered the opportunity to make a decision, a decision which determined whether you would or would not submit to those powers which threatened to rob you of your very self, your inner freedom; which determined whether or not you would become the plaything of circumstance, renouncing freedom and dignity to become molded into the form of the typical inmate.

Seen from this point of view, the mental reactions of the inmates of a concentration camp must seem more to us than the mere expression of certain physical and sociological conditions. Even though conditions such as lack of sleep, insufficient food and various mental stresses may suggest that the inmates were bound to react in certain ways, in the final analysis it becomes clear that the sort of person the prisoner became was the result of an inner decision, and not the result of camp influences alone. Fundamentally, therefore, any man can, even under such circumstances, decide what shall become of him—mentally and spiritually. He may retain his human dignity even in a concentration camp. Dostoevski said once, "There is only one thing that I dread: not to be worthy of my sufferings."

* * *

An active life serves the purpose of giving man the opportunity to realize values in creative work, while a passive life of enjoyment affords him the opportunity to obtain fulfillment in experiencing beauty, art, or nature. But there is also purpose in that life which is almost barren of both creation and enjoyment and which admits of but one possibility of behavior: namely, in man's attitude to his existence, an existence restricted by external forces. A creative life and a life of enjoyment are banned to him. But not only creativeness and enjoyment are meaningful. If there is a meaning in life at all, then there must be a meaning in suffering. Suffering is an ineradicable part of life, even as fate and death. Without suffering and death human life cannot be complete.

The way in which a man accepts his fate and all the suffering it entails, the way in which he takes up his cross, gives him ample opportunity—even under the most difficult circumstances—to add a deeper meaning to his life. It may remain brave, dignified and unselfish. Or in the bitter fight for self-preservation he may forget his human dignity and become no more than an animal. Here lies the chance for a man either to make use of or to forego the opportunities of attaining the values that a difficult situation may afford him. And this decides whether he is worthy of his sufferings or not.

Do not think that these considerations are unworldly and too far removed from real life. It is true that only a few people are capable of reaching such high standards. Of the prisoners only a few kept their full inner liberty and obtained those values which their suffering afforded, but even one such example is sufficient proof that man's inner strength may raise him above his outward fate. Such men are not only in concentration camps. Everywhere man is confronted with fate, with the chance of achieving something through his own suffering.

* * *

[Some] people forgot that often it is just such an exceptionally difficult external situation which gives man the opportunity to grow spiritually beyond himself. Instead of taking the camp's difficulties as a test of their inner strength, they did not take their life seriously and despised it as something of no consequence. They preferred to close their eyes and to live in the past. Life for such people became meaningless.

Naturally only a few people were capable of reaching great spiritual heights. But a few were given the chance to attain human greatness even through their apparent worldly failure and death, an accomplishment which in ordinary circumstances they would never have achieved.

* * *

The prisoner who had lost faith in the future—his future—was doomed. With his loss of belief in the future, he also lost his spiritual hold; he let himself decline and became subject to mental and physical decay. Usually this happened quite suddenly, in the form of a crisis, the symptoms of which were familiar to the experienced camp inmate. We all feared this moment—not for ourselves, which would have been pointless, but for our friends. Usually it began with the prisoner refusing one morning to get dressed and wash or to go out on the parade grounds. No entreaties, no blows, no threats had any effect. He just lay there, hardly moving. If this crisis was brought about by an illness, he refused to be taken to the sick-bay or to do anything to help himself. He simply gave up. There he remained, lying in his own excreta, and nothing bothered him any more.

* * *

. . . any attempt to restore a man's inner strength in the camp had first to succeed in showing him some future goal. Nietzsche's words, "He who has a *why* to live for can bear with almost any *how*," could be the guiding motto for all psychotherapeutic and psychohygienic efforts regarding prisoners. Whenever there was an opportunity for it, one had to give them a *why*—an aim—for their lives, in order to strengthen them to bear the terrible *how* of their existence. Woe to him who saw no more sense in his life, no aim, no purpose, and therefore no point in carrying on. He was soon lost. . . .

* * *

. . . Questions about the meaning of life can never be answered by sweeping statements. "Life" does not mean something vague, but something very real and concrete, just as life's tasks are also very real and concrete. . . .

* * *

BASIC CONCEPTS OF LOGO-THERAPY

Logo-therapy or, as it has been called by some authors, "The Third Viennese School of Psychotherapy," focuses on the meaning of human existence as well as on man's search for such a meaning. According to logotherapy, the striving to find a meaning in one's life is the primary motivational force in man. That is why I speak of a *will to meaning* in contrast to the pleasure principle (or, as we could also term it, the *will to pleasure*) on which Freudian psychoanalysis is centered, as well as in contrast to the *will to power* stressed by Adlerian psychology.

The Will to Meaning

Man's search for meaning is a primary force in his life and not a "secondary rationalization" of instinctual drives. This meaning is unique and specific in that it must and can be fulfilled by him alone; only then does it achieve a significance that will satisfy his own will to meaning. There are some authors who contend that meanings and values are "nothing but defense mechanisms, reaction formations and sublimations." But as for myself, I would not be willing to live merely for the sake of my "defense mechanisms," nor would I be ready to die merely for the sake of my "reaction formations." Man, however, is able to live and even to die for the sake of his ideals and values!

A poll of public opinion was conducted a few years ago in France. The results showed that 89% of the people polled admitted that man needs "something" for the sake of which to live. Moreover, 61% conceded that there was something, or someone, in their own lives for whose sake they were even ready to die. I repeated this poll at my clinic in Vienna among both the patients and the personnel, and the outcome was practically the same as among the thousands of people screened in France; the difference was only 2%. In other words, the will to meaning is in most people *fact,* not *faith.*

* * *

I think the meaning of our existence is not invented by ourselves, but rather detected.

Psychodynamic research in the field of values is legitimate; the question is whether it is always appropriate. Above all, we must keep in mind that any exclusively psychodynamic investigation can, in principle, only reveal what is a driving force in man. Values, however, do not drive a man; they do not *push* him, but rather *pull* him. This is a difference, by the way, of which I am constantly reminded whenever I go through the doors of an American hotel. One of them has to be pulled while the other has to be pushed. Now, if I say man is *pulled* by values, what is implicitly referred to is the fact that there is always freedom involved: the freedom of man to make his choice between accepting or rejecting an offer, i.e., to fulfill a meaning potentiality or else to forfeit it.

However, it should be made quite clear that there cannot exist in man any such thing as a *moral drive*, or even a *religious drive*, in the same manner as we speak of man's being determined by basic instincts. Man is never driven to moral behavior; in each instance he decides to behave morally . . .

* * *

. . . Logotherapy deviates from psychoanalysis insofar as it considers man as a being whose main concern consists in fulfilling a meaning and in actualizing values, rather than in the mere gratification and satisfaction of drives and instincts, the mere reconciliation of the conflicting claims of id, ego and superego, or mere adaptation and adjustment to the society and environment.

* * *

The Meaning of Life

I doubt whether a doctor can answer this question in general terms. For the meaning of life differs from man to man, from day to day and from hour to hour. What matters, therefore, is not the meaning of life in general but rather the specific meaning of a person's life at a given moment. To put the question in general terms would be comparable to the question posed to a chess champion, "Tell me, Master, what is the best move in the world?" There simply is no such thing as the best or even a good move apart from a particular situation in a game and the particular personality of one's opponent. The same holds for human existence. One should not search for an abstract meaning of life. Everyone has his own specific vocation or mission in life; everyone must carry out a concrete assignment that demands fulfillment. Therein he cannot be replaced, nor can his life be repeated. Thus, everyone's task is as unique as is his specific opportunity to implement it.

As each situation in life represents a challenge to man and presents a problem for him to solve, the question of the meaning of life may actually be reversed. Ultimately, man should not ask what the meaning of his life is, but rather must recognize that it is *he* who is asked. In a word, each man is questioned by life; and he can only answer to life by *answering for* his own life; to life he can only respond by being responsible. Thus, logotherapy sees in responsibleness the very essence of human existence.

* * *

By declaring that man is a responsible creature and must actualize the potential meaning of his life, I wish to stress that the true meaning of life is to be found in the world rather than within man or his own *psyche*, as though it were a closed system. . . .

* * *

The Meaning of Suffering

. . . Suffering ceases to be suffering in some way at the moment it finds a meaning, such as the meaning of a sacrifice.

* * *

Freedom . . . is not the last word. Freedom is only part of the story and half of the truth. Freedom is but the negative aspect of the whole phenomenon whose positive aspect is responsibleness. In fact, freedom is in danger of degenerating into mere arbitrariness unless it is lived in terms of responsibleness. That is why *I recommend that the Statue of Liberty on the East Coast be supplemented by a Statue of Responsibility on the West Coast.*

* * *

A human being is not one thing among others; *things* determine each other, but *man* is ultimately self-determining. What he becomes—within the limits of endowment and environment—he has made out of himself. In the concentration camps, for example, in this living laboratory and on this testing ground, we watched and witnessed some of our comrades behave like swine while others behaved like saints. Man has both potentialities within himself; which one is actualized depends on decisions but not on conditions.

Our generation is realistic, for we have come to know man as he really is. After all, man is that being who has invented the gas chambers of Auschwitz; however, he is also that being who has entered those gas chambers upright, with the Lord's Prayer or the *Shema Yisrael* on his lips.

Discussion Questions

1. In what sense are these excerpts an account not of facts and events but of personal experiences? What exactly does Viktor Frankl describe?

2. What is apathy and what role did it play in the concentration camp?

3. Of what did prisoners dream most frequently? How is this different from the conclusions of Freud?

4. Did Frankl conclude that prisoners had any significant religious interest? Does this surprise you? Explain.

5. What role did Frankl discover that humor played? Does this surprise you? Why or why not?

6. What does Frankl mean when he concludes that "one's inner value is anchored in higher, more spiritual things"?

7. Frankl approvingly quotes Dostoevski: "There is only one thing that I dread: not to be worthy of my sufferings." What does this mean?

8. Why was it significant when a prisoner lost faith in the future?

9. For Frankl, is it more important that life have an abstract or a concrete meaning? Why?

10. What does Frankl say about the relationship between freedom and responsibility?

D. A WESTERN RELIGIOUS VIEW

C. S. Lewis: *Mere Christianity*

C. S. Lewis (1898–1963) was a British religious writer, a Professor of Renaissance and Medieval Literature at Cambridge University from 1955 to 1963, and Fellow of Magdalen College, Oxford, from 1925 to 1954. Originally trained as a philosopher at Oxford, Lewis combined literary scholarship and the writing of fiction with clear and persuasive argumentation for traditional Christianity. Over a decade after his death, Lewis's religious works continue to be best sellers, and much of his writing is directly or indirectly of philosophical interest. His book, *Miracles* (New York: Macmillan and Co., 1963), is a good introduction to his religious and philosophical positions.

* * *

Reality . . . is usually something you could not have guessed. That is one of the reasons I believe Christianity. It is a religion you could not have guessed. If it offered us just the kind of universe we have always expected, I should feel we were making it up. But, in fact, it is not the sort of thing anyone would have made up. It has just that queer twist about it that real things have. So let us leave behind all these boys' philosophies—these oversimple answers. The problem is not simple and the answer is not going to be simple either.

What is the problem? A universe that contains much that is obviously bad and apparently meaningless, but containing creatures like ourselves who know that it is bad and meaningless. There are only two views that face all the facts. One is the Christian view that this is a good world that has gone wrong, but still retains the memory of what it ought to have been. The other is the view called Dualism. Dualism means the belief that there are two equal and independent powers at the back of everything, one of them good and the other bad, and that this universe is the battlefield in which they fight out an endless war. I personally think that next to Christianity Dualism is the manliest and most sensible creed on the market. But it has a catch in it.

The two powers, or spirits, or gods—the good one and the bad one—

are supposed to be quite independent. They both existed from all eternity. Neither of them made the other, neither of them has any more right than the other to call itself God. Each presumably thinks it is good and thinks the other bad. One of them likes hatred and cruelty, the other likes love and mercy, and each backs its own view. Now what do we mean when we call one of them the Good Power and the other the Bad Power? Either we are merely saying that we happen to prefer the one to the other—like preferring beer to cider—or else we are saying that, whatever the two powers think about it, and whichever we humans, at the moment, happen to like, one of them is actually wrong, actually mistaken, in regarding itself as good. Now if we mean merely that we happen to prefer the first, then we must give up talking about good and evil at all. For good means what you ought to prefer quite regardless of what you happen to like at any given moment. If "being good" meant simply joining the side you happened to fancy, for no real reason, then good would not deserve to be called good. So we must mean that one of the two powers is actually wrong and the other actually right.

But the moment you say that, you are putting into the universe a third thing in addition to the two Powers: some law or standard or rule of good which one of the powers conforms to and the other fails to conform to. But since the two powers are judged by this standard, then this standard, or the Being who made this standard, is farther back and higher up than either of them, and He will be the real God. In fact, what we meant by calling them good and bad turns out to be that one of them is in a right relation to the real ultimate God and the other in a wrong relation to Him.

* * *

. . . how can anything happen contrary to the will of a being with absolute power?

But anyone who has been in authority knows how a thing can be in accordance with your will in one way and not in another. It may be quite sensible for a mother to say to the children, "I'm not going to go and make you tidy the schoolroom every night. You've got to learn to keep it tidy on your own." Then she goes up one night and finds the Teddy bear and the ink and the French Grammar all lying in the grate. That is against her will. She would prefer the children to be tidy. But on the other hand, it is her will which has left the children free to be untidy. The same thing arises in any regiment, or trade union, or school. You make a thing voluntary and then half the people do not do it. That is not what you willed, but your will has made it possible.

It is probably the same in the universe. God created things which had free will. That means creatures which can go either wrong or right. Some people think they can imagine a creature which was free but had no possibility of going wrong; I cannot. If a thing is free to be good it is also free to be bad. And free will is what has made evil possible. Why, then, did God give them free will? Because free will, though it makes evil possible, is also the only thing that makes possible any love or goodness or joy worth having. A world of automata—of creatures that worked like machines—would hardly be worth creating. The happiness which God designs for His higher creatures is the happiness of being freely, voluntarily united to Him and to each other in an ecstasy of love and delight compared with which the most rapturous love between a man and a woman on this earth is mere milk and water. And for that they must be free.

* * *

When we have understood about free will, we shall see how silly it is to ask, as somebody once asked me: "Why did God make a creature of such rotten stuff that it went wrong?" The better stuff a creature is made of—the cleverer and stronger and freer it is—then the better it will be if it goes right, but also the worse it will be if it goes wrong. A cow cannot be very good or very bad; a dog can be both better and worse; a child better and worse still; an ordinary man, still more so; a man of genius, still more so; a superhuman spirit best—or worst—of all.

How did the Dark Power go wrong? Here, no doubt, we ask a question to which human beings cannot give an answer with any certainty. A reasonable (and traditional) guess, based on our own experiences of going wrong, can, however, be offered. The moment you have a self at all, there is a possibility of putting yourself first—wanting to be the centre—wanting to be God, in fact. That was the sin of Satan; and that was the sin he taught the human race. Some people think the fall of man had something to do with sex, but that is a mistake. (The story in the Book of Genesis rather suggests that some corruption in our sexual nature followed the fall and was its result, not its cause.) What Satan put into the heads of our remote ancestors was the idea that they could "be like gods"—could set up on their own as if they had created themselves—be their own masters—invent some sort of happiness for themselves outside God, apart from God. And out of that hopeless attempt has come nearly all that we call human history—money, poverty, ambition, war, prostitution, classes, empires, slavery—the long terrible story of man trying to find something other than God which will make him happy.

* * *

. . . Terrific energy is expended—civilisations are built—excellent institutions devised; but each time something goes wrong. Some fatal flaw always brings the selfish and cruel people to the top and it all slides back into misery and ruin. In fact, the machine conks. It seems to start up all right and runs a few yards, and then it breaks down. They are trying to run it on the wrong juice. That is what Satan has done to us humans.

And what did God do? First of all He left us conscience, the sense of right and wrong: and all through history there have been people trying (some of them very hard) to obey it. None of them ever quite succeeded. Secondly, He sent the human race what I call good dreams: I mean those queer stories scattered all through the heathen religions about a god who dies and comes to life again and, by his death, has somehow given new life to men. Thirdly, He selected one particular people and spent several centuries hammering into their heads the sort of God He was—that there was only one of Him and that He cared about right conduct. Those people were the Jews, and the Old Testament gives an account of the hammering process.

Then comes the real shock. Among these Jews there suddenly turns up a man who goes about talking as if He was God. He claims to forgive sins. He says He has always existed. He says He is coming to judge the world at the end of time.

* * *

One part of the claim tends to slip past us unnoticed because we have heard it so often that we no longer see what it amounts to. I mean the claim to forgive sins: any sins. Now unless the speaker is God, this is really so preposterous as to be comic. We can all understand how a man forgives offences against himself. You tread on my toe and I forgive you, you steal my money and I forgive you. But what should we make of a man, himself unrobbed and untrodden on, who announced that he forgave you for treading on other men's toes and stealing other men's money? Asinine fatuity is the kindest description we should give of his conduct. Yet this is what Jesus did. He told people that their sins were forgiven, and never waited to consult all the other people whom their sins had undoubtedly injured. He unhesitatingly behaved as if He was the party chiefly concerned, the person chiefly offended in all offences. This makes sense only if He really was the God whose laws are broken and whose love is wounded in every sin. In the mouth of any speaker who is not God, these words would imply what I can only regard as a silliness and conceit unrivalled by any other character in history.

Yet (and this is the strange, significant thing) even His enemies, when they read the Gospels, do not usually get the impression of silliness and conceit. Still less do unprejudiced readers. Christ says that He is "humble and meek" and we believe Him; not noticing that, if He were merely a man, humility and meekness are the very last characteristics we could attribute to some of His sayings.

I am trying here to prevent anyone saying the really foolish thing that people often say about Him: "I'm ready to accept Jesus as a great moral teacher, but I don't accept His claim to be God." That is the one thing we must not say. A man who was merely a man and said the sort of things Jesus said would not be a great moral teacher. He would either be a lunatic—on a level with the man who says he is a poached egg—or else he would be the Devil of Hell. You must make your choice. Either this man was, and is, the

Son of God: or else a madman or something worse. You can shut Him up for a fool, you can spit at Him and kill Him as a demon; or you can fall at His feet and call Him Lord and God. But let us not come with any patronising nonsense about His being a great human teacher. He has not left that open to us. He did not intend to.

* * *

There are three things that spread the Christ life to us: baptism, belief, and that mysterious action which different Christians call by different names—Holy Communion, the Mass, the Lord's Supper. At least, those are the three ordinary methods. I am not saying there may not be special cases where it is spread without one or more of these. . . .

* * *

I cannot myself see why these things should be the conductors of the new kind of life. But then, if one did not happen to know, I should never have seen any connection between a particular physical pleasure and the appearance of a new human being in the world. We have to take reality as it comes to us: there is no good jabbering about what it ought to be like or what we should have expected it to be like. But though I cannot see why it should be so, I can tell you why I believe it is so. I have explained why I have to believe that Jesus was (and is) God. And it seems plain as a matter of history that He taught His followers that the new life was communicated in this way. In other words, I believe it on His authority. Do not be scared by the word authority. Believing things on authority only means believing them because you have been told them by someone you think trustworthy. Ninety-nine per cent of the things you believe are believed on authority. I believe there is such a place as New York. I have not seen it myself. I could not prove by abstract reasoning that there must be such a place. I believe it because reliable people have told me so. The ordinary man believes in the Solar System, atoms, evolution, and the circulation of the blood on authority—because the scientists say so. Every historical statement in the world is believed on authority. None of us has seen the Norman Conquest or the defeat of the Armada. None of us could prove them by pure logic as you prove a thing in mathematics. We believe them simply because people who did see them have left writings that tell us about them: in fact, on authority.

* * *

. . . Most people, if they had really learned to look into their own hearts, would know that they do want, and want acutely, something that cannot be had in this world. There are all sorts of things in this world that offer to give it to you, but they never quite keep their promise. The longings which arise in us when we first fall in love, or first think of some foreign country, or first take up some subject that excites us, are longings which no marriage, no travel, no learning, can really satisfy. I am not now speaking of what would be ordinarily called unsuccessful marriages, or holidays, or learned careers. I am speaking of the best possible ones. There was something we grasped at, in that first moment of longing, which just fades away in the reality. I think everyone knows what I mean. The wife may be a good wife, and the hotels and scenery may have been excellent, and chemistry may be a very interesting job: but something has evaded us. Now there are two wrong ways of dealing with this fact, and one right one.

(1) The Fool's Way.—He puts the blame on the things themselves. He goes on all his life thinking that if only he tried another woman, or went for a more expensive holiday, or whatever it is, then, this time, he really would catch the mysterious something we are all after. Most of the bored, discontented, rich people in the world are of this type. They spend their whole lives trotting from woman to woman (through the divorce courts), from continent to continent, from hobby to hobby, always thinking that the latest is "the Real Thing" at last, and always disappointed.

(2) The Way of the Disillusioned "Sensible Man."—He soon decides that the whole thing was moonshine. "Of course," he says, "one feels like that when one's young. But by the time you get to my age you've given up chasing the rainbow's end." And so he settles down and learns not to expect too much and represses the part of himself which used, as he would say, "to cry for the moon." This is, of course, a much better way than the first, and makes a man much happier, and less of a nuisance to society. It tends to make him a prig (he is apt to be rather superior towards what he calls "adolescents"), but, on the whole, he rubs along fairly comfortably. It would be the best line we could take if man did not live for ever. But supposing infinite happiness really is there, waiting for us? Supposing one really can reach the rainbow's end. In that case it would be a pity to find out too late (a moment after death) that by our supposed "common sense" we had stifled in ourselves the faculty of enjoying it.

(3) The Christian Way.—The Christian says, "Creatures are not born with desires unless satisfaction for those desires exists. A baby feels hunger: well, there is such a thing as food. A duckling wants to swim: well, there is such a thing as water. Men feel sexual desire: well, there is such a thing as sex. If I find in myself a desire which no experience in this world can satisfy, the most probable explanation is that I was made for another world. If none of my earthly pleasures satisfy it, that does not prove that the universe is a fraud. Probably earthly pleasures were never meant to satisfy it, but only to arouse it, to suggest the real thing. If that is so, I must take care, on the one hand, never to despise, or be unthankful for, these earthly blessings, and on the other, never to mistake them for the something else of which they are only a kind of copy, or echo, or mirage. I must keep alive in myself the desire for my true country, which I shall not find till after death; I must never let it get snowed under or turned aside; I must make it the

main object of life to press on to that other country and to help others to do the same."

Discussion Questions

1. How does Christianity differ from what Lewis calls Dualism?

2. How does Lewis conclude that everything can happen contrary to the will of a being with absolute power? Do you agree? Why or why not?

3. Do you think a creature can be free but have no possibility of going wrong? Why or why not?

4. Lewis defines *the problem* as follows: "A universe that contains much that is obviously bad and apparently meaningless, but containing creatures like ourselves who know that it is bad and meaningless." According to Lewis, what did God do to help us out?

5. Why can't Jesus, according to Lewis, be both not God and a great moral teacher? Do you agree? Why or why not?

6. What are the three things that spread the Christ life to us? On whose authority does Lewis believe this to be true?

7. What do most people want acutely, according to Lewis? What are the two wrong ways of dealing with this fact?

8. What is "the Christian Way"? What should be the appropriate response to it, according to Lewis?

E. AN EASTERN RELIGIOUS VIEW

Siddhartha Gautama Buddha: *Two Sermons*

Siddhartha Gautama Buddha (563?–483? B.C.) was born in the foothills of the Himalayas in what is now Nepal. Almost no authentic information exists about the details of Buddha's life. Among the facets of his life usually stressed are: 1) his youth living in luxury with his father; 2) his marriage to Princess Yasodhara; 3) his series of four visions at about age 29; 4) his life as a wandering monk; 5) his meditation under the bodhi tree; and 6) his preaching on how to overcome suffering.

Buddhism entails multifarious forms produced by the teachings of Gautama Buddha. All these forms center around the main doctrine of the four noble truths, the last of which enables one, in a series of eight stages, to reach Nirvana.

TWO SERMONS OF GOTAMA THE BUDDHA

The Sermon at Benares: The Four Noble Truths

Thus have I heard: at one time the Lord dwelt at Benares at Isipatana in the Deer Park. There the Lord addressed the five monks:

"These two extremes, monks, are not to be practised by one who has gone forth from the world. What are the two? That conjoined with the passions and luxury, low, vulgar, common, ignoble, and useless; and that conjoined with self-torture, painful, ignoble, and useless. Avoiding these two extremes the Perfect One has gained the enlightenment of the Middle Path, which produces insight and knowledge and tends to calm, to higher knowledge, enlightenment, Nirvana. . . .

"(1) Now this, monks, is the noble truth of pain: birth is painful, old age is painful, sickness is painful, death is painful, sorrow, lamentation, dejection, and despair are painful. Contact with unpleasant things is painful, not getting what one wishes is painful. In short the five groups of grasping (the five skandhas, which make up an individual) are painful.

"(2) Now this, monks, is the noble truth of the cause of pain: the craving which tends to rebirth, combined with pleasure and lust, finding pleasure here and there; namely, the craving for passion, the craving for existence, the craving for non-existence.

"(3) Now this, monks, is the noble truth of the cessation of pain, the cessation without a remainder of craving, the abandonment, forsaking release, non-attachment.

"(4) Now this, monks, is the noble truth of the way that leads to the cessation of pain: this is the noble Eightfold Way: namely, right views, right intention, right speech, right action, right livelihood, right effort, right mindfulness, right concentration. . . .

"And when, monks, in these four noble truths my due knowledge and insight. . . was well purified, then, monks. . . I had attained the highest complete enlightenment. This I recognized. Knowledge arose in me, insight arose that the release of my mind is unshakable; this is my last existence; now there is no rebirth."

Thus spoke the Lord, and the five monks expressed delight and approval at the Lord's utterance. And while this exposition was being uttered there arose in the elder Kondanna the pure and spotless eye of the doctrine that whatever was liable to origination was all liable to cessation. . .

Questions Not Tending To Edification: The Arrow Sermon

Thus have I heard.

On a certain occasion the Blessed One was dwelling at Savatthi in Jetavana monastery in Anathapindika's Park. Now it happened to the venerable Malunkyaputta, being in seclusion and plunged in meditation, that a consideration presented itself to his mind, as follows:

"These theories which the Blessed One has left unexplained, has set aside and rejected—that the world is eternal, that the world is not eternal, that the world is finite, that the world is infinite, that the soul and the body are identical, that the soul is one thing and the body another, that the saint exists after death, that the saint does not exist after death, that the saint both exists and does not exist after death, that the saint neither exists nor does not exist after death—these the Blessed One does not explain to me. And the fact that the Blessed One does not explain them to me does not please me nor suit me. Therefore I will draw near to the Blessed One and inquire of him concerning this matter. If the Blessed One will explain to me . . . in that case will I lead the religious life under the Blessed One. If the Blessed One will not explain to me . . . in that case I will abandon religious training and return to the lower life of a layman."

Then the venerable Malunkyaputta arose at eventide from his seclusion, and drew near to where the Blessed One was; and having drawn near and greeted the Blessed One, he sat down respectfully at one side. And seated respectfully at one side, the venerable Malunkyaputta spoke to the Blessed One as follows:

"Reverend Sir, it happened to me, as I was just now in seclusion, and plunged in meditation, that a consideration presented itself to my mind, as follows. . . .

"If the Blessed One knows that the world is eternal, let the Blessed One explain to me that the world is eternal; if the Blessed One knows that the world is not eternal, let the Blessed One explain to me that the world is not eternal. If the Blessed One does not know either that the world is eternal or that the world is not eternal, the only upright thing for one who does not know, or who has not that insight, is to say, 'I do not know; I have not that insight.'" . . .

"Pray, Malunkyaputta, did I ever say to you, 'Come, Malunkyaputta, lead the religious life under me, and I will explain to you either that the world is eternal, or that the world is not eternal . . . or that the saint neither exists nor does not exist after death'?"

"Nay, verily, Reverend Sir."

"Malunkyaputta, any one who should say, 'I will not lead the religious life under the Blessed One until the Blessed One shall explain to me either that the world is eternal, or that the world is not eternal . . . or that the saint neither exists for does not exist after death'—that person would die, Malunkyaputta, before the Perfect One had ever explained this to him.

"It is as if, Malunkyaputta, a man had been wounded by an arrow thickly smeared with poison, and his friends and companions, his relatives and kinsfolk, were to procure for him a physician or surgeon; and the sick man were to say, 'I will not have this arrow taken out until I have learnt whether the man who wounded me belonged to the warrior caste, or to the Brahmin caste, or to the agricultural caste, or to the menial caste.'

'Or again he were to say, 'I will not have this arrow taken out until I have learnt the name of the man who wounded me, and to what clan he belongs.'

"Or again he were to say, 'I will not have this arrow taken out until I have learnt whether the man who wounded me was tall, or short, or of the middle height.' . . .

"That man would die, Malunkyaputta, without ever having learnt this . . .

"The religious life, Malunkyaputta, does not depend on the dogma that the world is eternal; nor does the religious life, Malunkyaputta, depend on the dogma that the world is not eternal. Whether the dogma obtain, Malunkyaputta, that the world is eternal, or that the world is not eternal, there still remain birth, old age, death, sorrow, lamentation, misery, grief, and despair, for the extinction of which in the present life I am prescribing. . .

"Accordingly, Malunkyaputta, bear always in mind what it is that I have not explained, and what it is that I have explained. And what, Malunkyaputta, have I not explained? I have not explained, Malunkyaputta, that the world is eternal; I have not explained that the world is not eternal; I have not explained that the world is finite; I have not explained that the world is infinite; I have not explained that the soul and the body are identical; I have not explained that the soul is one thing and the body another; I have not explained that the saint exists after death; I have not explained that the saint does not exist after death; I have not explained that the saint both exists and does not exist after death; I have not explained that the saint neither exists nor does not exist after death. And why, Malunkyaputta, have I not explained this? Because, Malunkyaputta, this profits not, nor has to do with the fundamentals of religion, nor tends to aversion, absence of passion, cessation, quiescence, the supernatural faculties, supreme wisdom, and Nirvana; therefore have I not explained it.

"And what, Malunkyaputta, have I explained? Misery, Malunkyaputta, have I explained; the origin of misery have I explained; the cessation of misery have I explained; and the path leading to the cessation of misery have I explained. And why, Malunkyaputta, have I explained this? Because, Malunkyaputta, this does profit, has to do with the fundamentals of religion, and tends to aversion, absence of passion, cessation, quiescence, knowledge, supreme wisdom, and Nirvana; therefore have I explained it."

Discussion Questions

1. Explain the "Four Noble Truths" in your own words.

2. Show how the "Four Noble Truths" fit the fourfold pattern of a

doctor's analysis: observation (symptoms), diagnosis (disease), prognosis (cure), and prescription (treatment).

3. Show how the "Four Noble Truths" presuppose the principle of causality: if the cause (good or bad) is present, the corresponding effect is present, and if the cause is removed, the effect is removed.

4. Do you agree that Buddha's cure would completely solve all the pains and problems of life? Why or why not?

5. Do you think there is any exception to "the pure and spotless eye of the doctrine that whatever was liable to origination was all liable to cessation?"

6. What implicit answer to the question of the *summum bonum* (greatest good or final end) does Buddha give in his reason for not explaining any of the questions Malunkyaputta asks him?

7. In the light of what Buddha has and has not explained, should he be classified as a philosopher? Why or why not?

8. What similarity in attitude do you see in Buddha's Arrow Sermon and Pascal's critique of indifference and diversion (pp. 370)? Compare Jesus' teaching in Luke 13:23–24: "And some one said to him, 'Lord, will those who are saved be few?' And he said to them, 'Strive to enter by the narrow door.'"

COMMENT: Franz Kafka
The Problem of Our Laws

Our laws are not generally known; they are kept secret by the small group of nobles who rule us. We are convinced that these ancient laws are scrupulously administered; nevertheless, it is an extremely painful thing to be ruled by laws that one does not know. I am not thinking of possible discrepancies that may arise in the interpretation of the laws, or of the disadvantages involved when only a few and not the whole people are allowed to have a say in their interpretation. These disadvantages are perhaps of no great importance. For the laws are very ancient; their interpretation has been the work of centuries, and has itself doubtless acquired the status of law; and though there is still a possible freedom of interpretation left, it has now become very restricted. Moreover the nobles have obviously no cause to be influenced in their interpretation by personal interests inimical to us, for the laws were made to the advantage of the nobles from the very beginning, they themselves stand above the laws, and that seems to be why the laws were entrusted exclusively into their hands. Of course, there is wisdom in that—who doubts the wisdom of the ancient laws?—but also hardship for us; probably that is unavoidable.

The very existence of these laws, however, is at most a matter of presumption. There is a tradition that they exist and that they are a mystery confided to the nobility, but it is not and cannot be more than a mere tradition sanctioned by age, for the essence of a secret code is that it should remain a mystery. Some of us among the people have attentively scrutinized the doings of the nobility since the earliest times and possess records made by our forefathers—records which we have conscientiously continued—and claim to recognize amid the countless number of facts certain main tendencies which permit of this or that historical formulation; but when in accordance with these scrupulously tested and logically ordered conclusions we seek to orient ourselves somewhat towards the present or the future, everything becomes uncertain, and our work seems only an intellectual game, for perhaps these laws that we are trying to unravel do not exist at all. There is a small party who are actually of this opinion and who try to show that, if any law exists, it can only be this: The Law is whatever the nobles do. This party see everywhere only the arbitrary acts of the nobility, and reject the popular tradition, which according to them possesses only certain trifling and incidental advantages that do not offset its heavy drawbacks, for it gives the people a false, deceptive and overconfident security in confronting coming events. This cannot be gainsaid, but the overwhelming majority of our people account for it by the fact that the tradition is far from complete and must be more fully enquired into, that the material available, prodigious as it looks, is still too meager, and that several centuries will have to pass before it becomes really adequate. This view, so comfortless as far as the present is concerned, is lightened only by the belief that a time will eventually come when the tradition and our research into it will jointly reach their conclusion, and as it were gain a breathing space, when everything will have become clear, the law will belong to the people, and the nobility will vanish. This is not maintained in any spirit of hatred against the nobility; not at all, and by no one. We are more inclined to hate ourselves, because we have not yet shown ourselves worthy of being entrusted with the laws. And that is the real reason why the party which believes that there is no law has remained so small—although its doctrine is in certain ways so attractive, for it unequivocally recognizes the nobility and its right to go on existing.

Actually one can express the problem only in a sort of paradox: Any party which would repudiate, not only all belief in the laws, but the nobility as well, would have the whole people behind it; yet no such party can come into existence, for nobody would dare to repudiate the nobility. We live on this razor edge. A writer once summed the matter up in this way: The sole visible and indubitable law that is imposed upon us is the nobility, and must we ourselves deprive ourselves of that one law?

CHAPTER NINE
DO WE SURVIVE DEATH? THE PROBLEM OF IMMORTALITY

Death is surely our primary fear, as life is our primary gift. We label whatever is most important to us not "a matter of truth or falsehood" or even "a matter of good or evil" but "a matter of life or death." Death seems to remove forever not just some but all of the things we love. Thus the questions: Do we survive death? and Is there life after death? seem to be of crucial importance to us, for they seem to make the difference between long-range hope and long-range despair. To avoid this question by indifference or diversions, as Pascal describes in our first excerpt, is surely a mark of intellectual cowardice, and it is a sign of honesty that this formerly taboo topic of death and dying is once more surfacing for attention in our culture.

The history of thought shows six basic answers to the question: What, if anything, survives death? The first, typified by our excerpts from Lucretius in late Roman times and Bertrand Russell in our own, is the usual secular, or nonreligious answer: nothing survives except what we leave behind us on earth (our works, our descendants, our reputation). We, our selves, our consciousness or personality, die when the body dies. A second answer, more ancient than modern, is that a ghost or shadow-self survives, inhabiting a dark underworld (Hades, Sheol), less real and alive than this one. A third answer, reincarnation, contends that we live again in other bodies on this earth. Socrates and Plato teach a fourth answer: that the soul alone survives death, freed from its alien "prison-house" of the body. A fifth answer, found in Hinduism and Buddhism, contends that neither individual soul nor body survive death because both are illusory: the only reality is a single timeless Spirit, or cosmic consciousness. Finally, Christianity holds that by a divine miracle we live again after death in resurrected bodies in heaven.

Arguments pro and con concerning all six concepts would require more space than this introductory sample has available. Since the essential issue for most people in our culture is between position (1) and either (4) or (6), the excerpts are chosen to set up that essential dialog: Do I (as body and soul (6) or just soul (4)) survive death or not?

You may wonder just what *sort* of argument could help decide this issue. Apart from religious faith or mystical experience, what purely rational evidence is there? One very simple line of argument deduces our destiny from our nature. If our present nature can be explained simply in natural, temporal and material terms, then our destiny is not supernatural, eternal and spiritual. Thus Lucretius deduces the denial of immortality from a materialistic philosophy of the human person, which in turn is deduced from a materialistic metaphysics (that nothing except matter is *real*). A contrary destiny (immortality) presuppose a contrary philosophy of the person (soul or spirit as well as body), which in turn presupposes a contrary metaphysics (spirit as well as matter is real). This is an example of how a philosopher's metaphysical position determines the philosopher's position on other questions.

Of the many kinds of arguments for immortality, we have selected four here. The first and simplest is that if there is in us something other than body, it need not die when the body dies. Some call this 'soul,' others 'personality' or 'I.'

A second argument, from Plato, observes that souls are not destroyed by soul-evils or soul-sicknesses (ignorance and vice) as bodies are destroyed by body-evils (diseases). And since the diseases of one thing (body) do not destroy a different thing (soul), neither its own nor another thing's diseases can destroy the soul.

A third argument, from C.S. Lewis, deduces immortality from the two premises that (1) the *desire* for immortality is a natural desire and (2) that no natural desire is vain, i.e., every innate desire corresponds to some real object: hunger means food exists, curiosity means knowledge exists, etc. The first passage (from *The Problem of Pain*) describes the innate desire (premise (1)) and the second (from *The Pilgrim's Regress*) adds premise (2) and draws the conclusion. If you have ever experienced the desire Lewis describes, his argument will probably move you very powerfully; if not, it will probably puzzle you.

Our concluding "Comment" section offers a fourth and different sort of "argument": the personality, wisdom, and fearlessness of Socrates facing death in Plato's *Phaedo*. Many readers find such a personal, "lived proof" more persuasive than any other. C.S. Lewis' epitaph on his friend Charles Williams is applicable to Socrates here: "No event has corroborated my belief in the next world more than Williams did simply by dying. For when the idea of death and the idea of Williams thus met in my mind, it was the idea of death that was changed."

A. THE QUESTION OF DEATH

Blaise Pascal: "Against Indifference," *Pensees*

Blaise Pascal (1623-1662) was a brilliant French scientist and mathematician who invented, among many other things, the world's first working computer, vacuum cleaner, and city omnibus system. A nominal Catholic, his life was changed one night when he experienced what he called "FIRE—God of Abraham, Isaac and Jacob, not of the philosophers and scholars." He secretly sewed this account of his experience into his coat pocket and wore it wherever he went. His *Pensees* are the scattered notes for a projected apologetic, or defense, for Christianity. They manifest psychological canny and insight comparable only to Augustine's *Confessions*. The work was cut short by Pascal's early death after a lifetime of illness and suffering. His other publication, the *Provincial Letters,* is a brilliant and biting satire on Jesuit casuistry.

Imagine a number of men in chains, all under sentence of death, some of whom are each day butchered in the sight of the others; those remaining see their own condition in that of their fellows, and looking at each other with grief and despair await their turn. This is an image of the human condition.

* * *

I am no one's goal, nor have I the means of satisfying anyone; am I not ready to die?

* * *

The last act is bloody, however fine the rest of the play. They throw a little earth over your head and it is finished for ever.

* * *

Between us and heaven or hell there is only life half-way, the most fragile thing in the world.

* * *

The enchantment of vanity: to render passion harmless let us behave as though we had only a week to live.

* * *

Despite these afflictions man wants to be happy, only wants to be happy, and cannot help wanting to be happy.

But how shall he go about it? The best thing would be to make himself immortal, but as he cannot do that, he has decided to stop himself thinking about it.

* * *

We run heedlessly into the abyss after putting something in front of us to stop us seeing it.

* * *

The immortality of the soul is something of such vital importance to us, affecting us so deeply, that one must have lost all feeling not to care about knowing the facts of the matter. All our actions and thoughts must follow such different paths, according to whether there is hope of eternal blessings or not, that the only possible way of acting with sense and judgment is to decide our course in the light of this point, which ought to be our ultimate objective.

Thus our chief interest and chief duty is to seek enlightenment on this subject, on which all our conduct depends. And that is why, among those who are not convinced, I make an absolute distinction between those who strive with all their might to learn and those who live without troubling themselves or thinking about it.

I can feel nothing but compassion for those who sincerely lament their doubt, who regard it as the ultimate misfortune, and who, sparing no effort to escape from it, make their search their principal and most serious business.

But as for those who spend their lives without a thought for this final end of life and who, solely because they do not find within themselves the light of conviction, neglect to look elsewhere, and to examine thoroughly whether this opinion is one of those which people accept out of credulous simplicity or one of those which, though obscure in themselves, none the less have a most solid and unshakable foundation—as for them, I view them very differently.

This negligence in a matter where they themselves, their eternity, their all are at stake, fills me more with irritation than pity; it astounds and appals me; it seems quite monstrous to me. I do not say this prompted by the pious zeal of spiritual devotion. I mean on the contrary that we ought to have this feeling from principles of human interest and self-esteem. For that we need only see what the least enlightened see.

One needs no great sublimity of soul to realize that in this life there is no true and solid satisfaction, that all our pleasures are mere vanity, that our afflictions are infinite, and finally that death which threatens us at every moment must in a few years infallibly face us with the inescapable and appalling alternative of being annihilated or wretched throughout eternity.

Nothing could be more real, or more dreadful than that. Let us put on as bold a face as we like: that is the end awaiting the world's most illustrious life. Let us ponder these things and then say whether it is not beyond doubt that the only good thing in this life is the hope of another life, that we become happy only as we come nearer to it, and that, just as no more unhappiness awaits those who have been quite certain of eternity, so there is no happiness for those who have no inkling of it.

It is therefore quite certainly a great evil to have such doubts, but it is at least an indispensable obligation to seek when one does thus doubt; so the doubter who does not seek is at the same time very unhappy and very wrong. If in addition he feels a calm satisfaction, which he openly professes, and even regards as a reason for joy and vanity, I can find no terms to describe so extravagant a creature.

What can give rise to such feelings? What reason for joy can be found in the expectation of nothing but helpless wretchedness? What reason for vanity in being plunged into impenetrable darkness? And how can such an argument as this occur to a reasonable man?

'I do not know who put me into the world, nor what I am myself. I am terribly ignorant about everything. I do not know what my body is, or my senses, or my soul, or even that part of me which thinks what I am saying, which reflects about everything and about itself, and does not know itself any better than it knows anything else.

'I see the terrifying spaces of the universe hemming me in, and I find myself attached to one corner of this vast expanse without knowing why I have been put in this place rather than that, or why the brief span of life allotted to me should be assigned to one moment rather than another of all the eternity which went before me and all that which will come after me. I see only infinity on every side, hemming me in like an atom or like the shadow of a fleeting instant. All I know is that I must soon die, but what I know least about is this very death which I cannot evade.

'Just as I do not know whence I come, so I do not know whither I am going. All I know is that when I leave this world I shall fall for ever into nothingness or into the hands of a wrathful God, but I do not know which of these two states is to be my eternal lot. Such is my state, full of weakness and uncertainty. And my conclusion from all this is that I must pass my days without a thought of seeking what is to happen to me. Perhaps I might find some enlightenment in my doubts, but I do not want to take the trouble, nor take a step to look for it; and afterwards, as I sneer at those who are striving to this end, I will go without fear or foresight to face so momentous an event, and allow myself to be carried off limply to my death, uncertain of my future state for all eternity.'

Who would wish to have as his friend a man who argued like that? Who would choose him from among others as a confidant in his affairs? Who would resort to him in adversity? To what use in life could he possibly be turned?

It is truly glorious for religion to have such unreasonable men as enemies. . . .

Do they think that they have given us great pleasure by telling us that they hold our soul to be no more than wind or smoke, and saying it moreover in tones of pride and satisfaction? Is this then something to be said gaily? Is it not on the contrary something to be said sadly, as being the saddest thing in the world? . . .

There is no shame except in having none. There is no surer sign of extreme weakness of mind than the failure to recognize the unhappy state of a man without God; there is no surer sign of an evil heart than failure to desire that the eternal promises be true; nothing is more cowardly than to brazen it out with God.

Discussion Questions

1. How would Pascal reply to the charge that his concern with the question of death is morbid, especially in the first paragraph?

2. Spinoza wrote, "The free man never thinks of death, only of life." What do you suppose he may have meant? How do you think Pascal would reply to Spinoza?

3. Must one believe in life after death in order to agree with Pascal's main point? (What *is* his main point, or conclusion, by the way? Formulate it.)

4. Formulate Pascal's essential argument for this conclusion. Then evaluate it in the three ways suggested.

5. Do you think the "argument" Pascal puts into the mouth of his opponent on page 370 truly represents the implicit philosophy of many people? If so, how could they be so unreasonable? If not, how would they reply to Pascal?

B. A DENIAL OF IMMORTALITY

Lucretius: *De Rerum Natura*

Lucretius (94?-55 B.C.) was a Roman philosophical poet whose chief work, *De Rerum Natura (On the Nature of Things)*, is both a great poem and a statement of a major metaphysical thesis. This book is based on the philosophy of Epicurus, which taught that the world is without divine design or rule. *De Rerum Natura* is concerned with how all the objects and events that make up the world we live in can be explained through an appeal to matter (atoms) in motion. Moreover, Lucretius seeks to show the consequences which this materialist view of reality has for human life. He stresses that much of the suffering of human beings results from religious superstitution. Lucretius explained his arguments with vivid word pictures which, he said, were like honey on the rim of a cup of bitter medicine.

Lucretius' full name was Titus Lucretius Carus. He was born in Rome. Very little is known of his life.

. . . if men saw that a term was set to their troubles, they would find strength in some way to withstand the hocus-pocus and intimidations of the prophets. As it is, they have no power of resistance, because they are haunted by the fear of eternal punishment after death. They know nothing of the nature of the spirit. Is it born, or is it implanted in us at birth? Does it perish with us, dissolved by death, or does it visit the murky depths and dreary sloughs of Hades? Or is it transplanted by divine power into other creatures? . . .

I have already shown what the component bodies of everything are like; how they vary in shape; how they fly spontaneously through space, impelled by a perpetual motion; and how from these all objects can be created. The next step now is evidently to elucidate in my verses the nature of mind and of life. In so doing I shall drive out neck and crop that fear of Hell which blasts the life of man from its very foundations, sullying everything with the blackness of death and leaving no pleasure pure and unalloyed. . . .

First, I maintain that *the mind,* which we often call the intellect, the seat of the guidance and control of life, *is part of a man,* no less than hand or foot or eyes are parts of a whole living creature. . . .

. . . mind and spirit are both composed of matter. . . . You see the mind sharing in the body's experiences. . . . When the nerve-racking impact of a spear gashes bones and sinews . . . there ensues faintness and . . . a turmoil in the mind. . . . The substance of the mind must therefore be material, since it is affected by the impact of material weapons. . . .

My next point is this: you must understand that *the minds of living things and the light fabric of their spirits are neither birthless nor deathless. . . .*

Please note that both objects are to be embraced under one name. When, for instance, I proceed to demonstrate that 'spirit' is mortal, you must understand that this applies equally to 'mind', since the two are so conjoined as to constitute a single substance.

First of all, then, I have shown that spirit is flimsy stuff composed of tiny particles. Its atoms are obviously far smaller than those of swift-flowing water or mist or smoke, since it far outstrips them in mobility and is moved by a far slighter impetus. . . .

Now, we see that water flows out in all directions from a broken vessel and the moisture is dissipated, and mist and smoke vanish into thin air. Be assured, therefore, that spirit is similarly dispelled and vanishes far more speedily and is sooner dissolved into its component atoms once it has been let loose from the human frame. . . .

Again, we are conscious that mind and body are born together, grow up together and together decay. With the weak and delicate frame of wavering childhood goes a like infirmity of judgment. The robust vigor of ripening years is accompanied by a steadier resolve and a maturer strength of mind. Later, when the body is palsied by the potent forces of age and the limbs begin to droop with blunted vigor, the understanding limps, the tongue falters and the mind totters; everything weakens and gives way at the same time. . . .

Furthermore, as the body suffers the horrors of disease and the pangs of pain, so we see the mind stabbed with anguish, grief and fear. What more natural than that it should likewise have a share in death? . . . Since the mind is thus invaded by the contagion of disease, you must acknowledge that it is destructible. For pain and sickness are the artificers of death. . . .

Again, when the pervasive power of wine has entered into a man and its glow is dispersed through his veins, his limbs are overcome by heaviness; his legs stagger and stumble; his speech is blurred, his mind besotted; his eyes swim; there is a crescendo of shouts, hiccups, oaths; and all the other symptoms follow in due order. Why should this be, if not because the wanton wildness of the wine has power to dislodge the vital spirit within the body? And when things can be dislodged and arrested, this is an indication that the inroad of a slightly more potent force would make an end of them and rob them of a future. . . .

Conversely, we see that the mind, like a sick body, can be healed and directed by medicine. This too is a presage that its life is mortal. . . . By this susceptibility both to sickness (as I have shown) and to medicine, the mind displays the marks of mortality. . . .

Again, we often see a man pass away little by little, and lose his vital sensibility limb by limb. . . . Since the vital spirit is thus dispersed and does not come out all at once in its entirety, it must be regarded as mortal. . . .

No one on the point of death seems to feel his spirit retiring intact right out of his body. . . . On the contrary, he feels that it is failing. . . . If our mind were indeed immortal, it would not complain of extinction in the hour of death, but would feel rather that it was escaping from confinement and sloughing off its garment like a snake. . . .

Moreover, if the spirit is by nature immortal and can remain sentient when divorced from our body, we must credit it, I presume, with the possession of five senses. In no other way can we picture to ourselves departed spirits wandering through the Infernal Regions. So it is that painters and bygone generations of writers have portrayed spirits in possession of their senses. But eyes or nostrils or hand or tongue or ears cannot be attached to a disembodied spirit. Such a spirit cannot therefore be sentient or so much as exist. . . .

Next, if the spirit is by nature immortal and is slipped into the body at birth, why do we retain no memory of an earlier existence, no impress of antecedent events? If the mind's operation is so greatly changed that all record of former actions has been expunged, it is no long journey, in my judgment, from this experience to annihilation. So you must admit that the pre-existent spirit has died and the one that is now is a new creation.

Let us suppose, for argument's sake, that the vital force of mind is introduced into us when the body is already fully formed, at the moment when we are born and step across the threshold of life. This theory does not square with the observed fact that the mind grows with the bodily frame and in the very blood. It would imply that the mind lived in solitary confinement, alone in its cell, and yet at the same time the whole body was shot through with sentience. Here then is proof upon proof that spirits are not to be regarded as birthless, nor yet as exempt from the law of death. If they were slipped into our bodies from outside, it cannot be supposed that the two would be so closely interlocked as they are shown to be by the clearest evidence. . . .

From all this it follows that *death is nothing to us* and no concern of ours . . . when we shall be no more—when the union of body and spirit that engenders us has been disrupted—to us, who shall then be nothing, nothing by any hazard will happen any more at all. . . . If the future holds travail and anguish in store, the self must be in existence, when that time comes, in order to experience it. But from this fate we are redeemed by death, which denies existence to the self that might have suffered these tribulations. Rest assured, therefore, that we have nothing to fear in death. One who no longer is cannot suffer . . .

As for all those torments that are said to take place in the depths of Hell, they are actually present here and now, in our own lives. There is no wretched Tantalus, as the myth relates, transfixed with groundless terror at the huge boulder poised above him in the air. But in this life there really are mortals oppressed by unfounded fear of the gods and trembling at the impending doom that may fall upon any of them at the whim of chance. . . .

What is this deplorable lust of life that holds us trembling in bondage to such uncertainties and dangers? A fixed term is set to the life of mortals, and there is no way of dodging death. . . . So long as the object of our craving is unattained, it seems more precious than anything besides. Once it is ours, we crave for something else. So an unquenchable thirst for life keeps us always on the gasp . . .

Discussion Questions

1. Is Lucretius sad or happy that there is no life after death? Why?

2. Does he argue *from* "no fear of Hell" *to* "no life after death," or vice versa?

3. Lucretius gives evidence from experience that the soul is material. Does his argument take the form "materialism is an *adequate* hypothesis to explain all the facts of experience" or the form "materialism is necessary, the only hypothesis to explain these facts"? If the former, wherein lies the superiority of the materialistic hypothesis to the equally possible dualistic hypothesis (mind and body as two different realities)? If the latter, what makes materialism necessary and dualism impossible?

4. How would a believer in the spirituality and immortality of the soul (or mind or spirit) explain the evidence Lucretius uses in each of his arguments against immortality (pages 373-74). Each paragraph is a separate argument; can you imagine an answer to each one?

5. Are there any features of our experience that Lucretius' materialism seems unable to explain?

6. Does the conclusion necessarily follow that "death is nothing to us"? Why or why not?

7. Do you agree that "lust for life" is "deplorable"? Why or why not? Why do you suppose Dylan Thomas wrote "Do not go gentle into that good-night/Rage, rage against the dying of the light"? And Moses' "I have set before you life and death, blessing and curse; therefore choose life" (Deuteronomy 30:19)—from what opposite premises do Lucretius and Moses draw such opposite conclusions, do you think? Which side is Buddha on? (See pages 361-63.)

C. ANOTHER DENIAL OF IMMORTALITY

Bertrand Russell: *Mysticism and Logic*

Bertrand Russel (1872-1970) was perhaps twentieth-century England's closest approximation to the Renaissance ideal of the universal genius, or to the Enlightenment figure of Voltaire. Russell was an atheist and political renegade who wrote witty satires on religion and the political establishment. But he also made major contributions to epistemology and, with A.N. Whitehead, co-authored *Principia Mathematica,* "the Bible of mathematical logic."

A FREE MAN'S WORSHIP

To Dr. Faustus in his study Mephistopheles told the history of the Creation, saying:

"The endless praises of the choirs of angels had begun to grow wearisome; for, after all, did he not deserve their praise? Had he not given them endless joy? Would it not be more amusing to obtain undeserved praise, to be worshipped by beings whom he tortured? He smiled inwardly, and resolved that the great drama should be performed.

"For countless ages the hot nebula whirled aimlessly through space. At length it began to take shape, the central mass threw off planets, the planets cooled, boiling seas and burning mountains heaved and tossed, from black masses of cloud hot sheets of rain deluged the barely solid crust. And now the first germ of life grew in the depths of the ocean, and developed rapidly in the fructifying warmth into vast forest trees, huge ferns springing from the damp mould, sea monsters breeding, fighting, devouring, and passing away. And from the monsters, as the play unfolded itself, Man was born, with the power of thought, the knowledge of good and evil, and the cruel thirst for worship. And Man saw that all is passing in this mad, monstrous world, that all is struggling to snatch, at any cost, a few brief moments of life before Death's inexorable decree. And Man said: 'There is a hidden purpose, could we but fathom it, and the purpose is good; for we must reverence something, and in the visible world there is nothing worthy of reverence.' And Man stood aside from the struggle, resolving that God intended harmony to come out of chaos by human efforts. And when he followed the instincts which God had transmitted to him from his ancestry of beasts of prey, he called it Sin, and asked God to forgive him. But he doubted whether he could be justly forgiven, until he invented a divine Plan by which God's wrath was to have been appeased. And seeing the present was bad, he made it yet worse, that thereby the future might be better. And he gave God thanks for the strength that enabled him to forgo even the joys that were possible. And God smiled; and when he saw that Man had become perfect in renunciation and worship, he sent another sun through the sky, which crashed into Man's sun; and all returned again to nebula.

"'Yes,' he murmured, 'it was a good play; I will have it performed again.' "

Such, in outline, but even more purposeless, more void of meaning, is the world which Science presents for our belief. Amid such a world, if anywhere, our ideals henceforward must find a home. That Man is the product of causes which had no prevision of the end they were achieving; that his origin, his growth, his hopes and fears, his loves and his beliefs, are but the outcome of accidental collocations of atoms; that no fire, no heroism, no intensity of thought and feeling, can preserve an individual life beyond the grave; that all the labours of the ages, all the devotion, all the inspiration, all the noonday brightness of human genius, are destined to extinction in the vast death of the solar system, and that the whole temple of Man's achievement must inevitably be buried beneath the debris of a universe in ruins—all these things, if not quite beyond dispute, are yet so nearly certain, that no philosophy which rejects them can hope to stand.

Only within the scaffolding of these truths, only on the firm foundation of unyielding despair, can the soul's habitation henceforth be safely built.

Discussion Questions

1. What consequences does Russell deduce from the denial of immortality?

2. Would Pascal agree that these are indeed the consequences that follow if immortality is denied? Give evidence from Pascal's excerpted writings to support your answer.

3. Why do you think Lucretius is more optimistic about the consequences of the denial of immortality than Russell is? How might these two philosophers carry on an argument between themselves on this issue?

4. Russell's excerpt has two parts: the myth or story of the divine "play" and the philosophy in the last paragraph. Compare them; do they say the same thing (if so, what?) in different ways (if so, how?)?

5. Would a believer in God disagree with anything in Russell's characterization of God? How might the argument between the two proceed?

6. Point out the irony or sarcasm in Russell's account of the divine "play."

D. AN ARGUMENT FOR IMMORTALITY

Peter Kreeft: *Love is Stronger than Death*

Peter Kreeft (b. 1937), an American philosopher, is one of the editors of this book. He is the author of several articles on the philosophy of religion and of six books, including *Heaven: The Heart's Deepest Longing* (1978) and *Love Is Stronger than Death* (1977), from which this selection is taken.

Death removes everything in us that is unfree, passive, and accidental, everything tht we receive from this world through the umbilical cord of our body: our heredity, our environment, our possessions, our social status, our wealth. What remains is what is free, what we have freely made ourselves into, out of this worldly raw material, the person we have freely chosen to become. The clothes the world gave us now rot away; we stand as naked *I*'s in death: "Naked I came into this world; naked I return."

In the Latin rite for the burial of an Austrian emperor, the people carry the corpse to the door of the great monastic church. The door is locked. They strike the door and say "Open!" The abbot inside says, "Who is there?" "Emperor Karl, King of X and Y and Z." "We know no such person here." Strike again. "Who is there?" "Emperor Karl." "We know no such person here." Strike a third time. "Who is there?" "Karl." The door is opened.

You can't take it with you—any "it." You can only take *you.*

The distinction between the free, naked *I* and everything else puts us in a position to see why we must be immortal. A person not only *is* a body but *has* a body; that is, the "haver" is more than the "had." This "more" that every person is, is usually called the soul, or the spirit. What's that? Perhaps the best answer is that it is not a *what* at all; unlike everything else in the world, a person is not a *what* but a *who,* not an object but a subject. *What* I am is all my worldly clothes; *who* I am is their wearer, the naked self underneath. My heredity and environment have determined my *what* (for example, my race, sex, temperament, and taste for olives), but my free choices have determined my *who.* I am my own co-creator. Of course, my *what* has conditioned my *who;* that is, it has influenced it, both to limit it and to help it. But influencing is not forcing; conditioning is not determining. The world, which has given me my *what* by this determining, can and does take it all away in death. But since it has not given me my *who,* it cannot take it away, not even by death. If I am a person, I am immortal; if I am not immortal, I am not a person. *What* I am is not stronger than death, but *I* am. If I am not stronger than death, then I am not an I.

Another way of seeing this is that my anything and everything can die because it is possessed; it is what I *have.* There is a gap between me and what I have. The gap can become final, can become death. But I do not *have* my *I;* I *am* my *I.* There is no gap between I and I, as there is between me and mine; there is no place for death to fit, no "deathspot." Death can separate me from everything, but not from myself.

Still another way is that a *what* is made of parts; therefore it is dissolvable into its parts; therefore, it can die. Not so with a *who.* Death is separation. Separation presupposes separable parts. The body dies because it is made of separable parts. Man dies because he is made of separable parts; that is, body and soul. But my soul, my *who,* my *I,* does not fall apart and die because it is one: it is me.

Discussion Questions

1. *What* does this passage try to prove is immortal? (paragraphs 1 and 2)

2. Formulate in your own words the three arguments used (paragraphs 4, 5, and 6).

3. Which seems strongest to you? Why? Which seems weakest? Why?

4. How would Lucretius or Russell reply to the first argument?

E. ANOTHER ARGUMENT FOR IMMORTALITY

Plato: *The Republic*

Plato (428-348 B.C.) was the first systematic philosopher. No one knows how much in his thirty dialogs came from his master, Socrates, who wrote nothing, and how much from Plato, who used Socrates as his literary mouthpiece; but in these dialogs nearly every major question in the next 2400 years of Western philosophy is raised. Thus Ralph Waldo Emerson says that "Plato is philosophy and philosophy is Plato," and Alfred North Whitehead calls the whole history of Western philosophy "a series of footnotes to Plato."

BOOK 10

Are you not aware, I said, that the soul of man is immortal and imperishable?

He looked at me in astonishment, and said: No, by heaven: And are you really prepared to maintain this?

Yes, I said, I ought to be, and you too—there is no difficulty in proving it.

I see a great difficulty; but I should like to hear you state this argument of which you make so light.

Listen then.

I am attending.

There is a thing which you call good and another which you call evil?

Yes, he replied.

Would you agree with me in thinking that the corrupting and destroying element is the evil, and the saving and improving element the good?

Yes.

And you admit that every thing has a good and also an evil; as ophthalmia is the evil of the eyes and disease of the whole body; as mildew is of corn, and rot of timber, or rust of copper and iron: in everything, or in almost everything, there is an inherent evil and disease?

Yes, he said.

And anything which is infected by any of these evils is made evil, and at last wholly dissolves and dies?

True.

The vice and evil which is inherent in each is the destruction of each; and if this does not destroy them there is nothing else that will; for good certainly will not destroy them, nor again, that which is neither good nor evil.

Certainly not.

If, then, we find any nature which having this inherent corruption cannot be dissolved or destroyed, we may be certain that of such a nature there is no destruction?

That may be assumed.

Well, I said, and is there no evil which corrupts the soul?

Yes, he said, there are all the evils which we were just now passing in review: unrighteousness, intemperance, cowardice, ignorance.

But does any of these dissolve or destroy her?—and here do not let us fall into the error of supposing that the unjust and foolish man, when he is detected, perishes through his own injustice, which is an evil of the soul. Take the analogy of the body: The evil of the body is a disease which wastes and reduces and annihilates the body; and all the things of which we were just now speaking come to annihilation through their own corruption attaching to them and inhering in them and so destroying them. Is not this true?

Yes.

Consider the soul in like manner. Does the injustice or other evil which exists in the soul waste and consume her? do they by attaching to the soul and inhering in her at last bring her to death, and so separate her from the body?

Certainly not.

And yet, I said, it is unreasonable to suppose that anything can perish from without through affection of external evil which could not be destroyed from within by a corruption of its own?

It is, he repleid.

Consider, I said, Glaucon, that even the badness of food, whether staleness, decomposition, or any other bad quality, when confined to the actual food, is not supposed to destroy the body; although, if the badness of food communicates corruption to the body, then we should say that the body has been destroyed by a corruption of itself, which is disease, brought on by this; but that the body, being one thing, can be destroyed by the badness of food, which is another, and which does not engender any natural infection—this we shall absolutely deny?

Very true.

And, on the same principle, unless some bodily evil can produce an evil of the soul, we must not suppose that the soul, which is one thing, can be dissolved by any merely external evil which belongs to another?

Yes, he said, there is reason in that.

Either, then, let us refute this conclusion, or, while it remains unrefuted, let us never say that fever, or any other disease, or the knife put to the throat, or even the cutting up of the whole body into the minutest pieces, can destroy the soul, until she herself is proved to become more unholy or unrighteous in consequence of these things being done to the body; but that the soul, or anything else if not destroyed by an internal evil, can be destroyed by an external one, is not to be affirmed by any man. . . .

If the inherent natural vice or evil of the soul is unable to kill or destroy her, hardly will that which is appointed to be the destruction of some other body, destroy a soul or anything else except that of which it was appointed to be the destruction.

Yes, that can hardly be.

But the soul which cannot be destroyed by an evil, whether inherent or external, must exist for ever, and if existing for ever, must be immortal?

Certainly.

Discussion Questions

1. Why must Plato define "good" and "evil" first in the way that he does?

2. How do you think Plato might have replied to the following criticism? "You use 'evil' or 'illness' or 'corruption' ambiguously. Physical or bodily evils come to the body from without; spiritual or moral evils come from within the soul. Bodily evils are suffered; moral evils are committed."

3. Are there any unstated premises or implicit assumptions in Plato's argument?

4. Which part of the argument appeals to experience? Which part appeals to a logical analysis of the meaning of terms? How would (a) a ratonalist (b) an empiricist evaluate these two parts?

5. What practical consequences for ethics does Plato see in the immortality of the soul? Point out the passage.

F. A THIRD ARGUMENT FOR IMMORTALITY

C.S. Lewis:
The Problem of Pain and *The Pilgrim's Regress*

C.S. Lewis (1898-1963) was not a professional philosopher but taught medieval and Renaissance English literature at Oxford and Cambridge. He produced over 40 volumes of philosophy, theology, apologetics, poetry, letters, formal and informal essays, literary history and criticism, fantasy, science fiction, a historical novel, an autobiography, allegory, Biblical studies, sermons, a spiritual diary, short stories, and children's novels (the already-classic *Chronicles of Narnia*). He was probably the most influential and effective Christian apologist of the century.

THE PROBLEM OF PAIN

We are very shy nowadays of even mentioning heaven. We are afraid of the jeer about "pie in the sky," and of being told that we are trying to "escape" from the duty of making a happy world here and now into dreams of a happy world elsewhere. But either there is "pie in the sky" or there is not. If there is not, then Christianity is false, for this doctrine is woven into its whole fabric. If there is, then this truth, like any other, must be faced, whether it is useful at political meetings or not.

. . . There have been times when I think we do not desire heaven but more often I find myself wondering whether, in our heart of hearts, we have ever desired anything else. You may have noticed that the books you really love are bound together by a secret thread. You know very well what is the common quality that makes you love them, though you cannot put it into words; but most of your friends do not see it at all, and often wonder why, liking this, you should also like that. Again, you have stood before some landscape, which seems to embody what you have been looking for all your life; and then turned to the friend at your side who appears to be seeing what you saw—but at the first words a gulf yawns between you and you realise that this landscape means something totally different to him, that he is pursuing an alien vision and cares nothing for the ineffable suggestion by which you are transported. Even in your hobbies, has there not always been some secret attraction which the others are curiously ignorant of—something, not to be identified with, but always on the verge of breaking through, the smell of cut wood in the workshop or the clap-clap of water against the boat's side? Are not all lifelong friendships born at the moment when at last you meet another human being who has some inkling (but faint and uncertain even in the best) of that something which you were born desiring, and which, beneath the flux of other desires and in all the momentary silences between the louder passions, night and day, year by year, from childhood to old age, you are looking for, watching for, listening for? You have never *had* it. All the things that have ever deeply possessed your soul have been but hints of it—tantalising glimpses, promises never quite fulfilled, echoes that died away just as they caught your ear. But if it should really become manifest—if there ever came an echo that did not die away but swelled into the sound itself—you would know it. Beyond all possibility of doubt you would say "Here at last is the thing I was made for." We cannot tell each other about it. It is the secret signature of each soul, the incommunicable and unappeasable want, the thing we desired before we met our wives or made our friends or chose our work, and which we shall still desire on our deathbeds, when the mind no longer knows wife or friend or work. While we are, this is. If we lose this, we lose all.

THE PILGRIM'S REGRESS

The experience is one of intense longing. It is distinguished from other longings by two things. In the first place, though the sense of want is acute and even painful, yet the mere wanting is felt to be somehow a delight. Other desires are felt as pleasures only if satisfaction is expected in the near future: hunger is pleasant only while we know (or believe) that we are soon going to eat. But this desire, even when there is no hope of possible satisfaction, continues to be prized, and even to be preferred to anything else in the world, by those who have once felt it. This hunger is better than any other fullness; this poverty better than all other wealth. And thus it comes about, that if the desire is long absent, it may itself be desired, and that new desiring becomes a new instance of the original desire, though the subject may not at once recognise the fact and thus cries out for his lost youth of soul at the very moment in which he is being rejuvenated. This sounds complicated, but it is simple when we live it. 'Oh to feel as I did then!' we cry; not noticing that even while we say the words the very feeling whose loss we lament is rising again in all its old bitter-sweetness. For this sweet Desire cuts across our ordinary distinctions between wanting and having. To have it is, by definition, a want; to want it, we find, is to have it.

In the second place there is a peculiar mystery about the object of this Desire. Inexperienced people (and inattention leaves some inexperienced all their lives) suppose, when they feel it, that they know what they are desiring. Thus if it comes to a child while he is looking at a far-off hillside, he at once thinks 'if only I were there'; if it comes when he is remembering some event in the past, he thinks 'if only I could go back to those days.' If it comes (a little later) while he is reading a 'romantic' tale or poem of 'perilous seas and faerie lands forlorn', he thinks he is wishing that such places really existed and that he could reach them. If it comes (later still) in a context with erotic suggestions he believes he is desiring the perfect beloved. If he falls upon literature (like Maeterlinck or the early Yeats) which treats of spirits and the like with some show of serious belief, he may think that he is hankering for real magic and occultism. When it darts out upon him from his studies in history or science, he may confuse it with the intellectual craving for knowledge.

But every one of these impressions is wrong. The sole merit I claim for this book is that it is written by one who has proved them all to be wrong. There is no room for vanity in the claim; I know them to be wrong not by intelligence but by experience, such experience as would not have come my way if my youth had been wiser, more virtuous, and less self-centered than it was. For I myself have been deluded by every one of these false answers in turn, and have contemplated each of them earnestly enough to discover the cheat. . . .

Every one of these supposed *objects* for the Desire is inadequate to it. An easy experiment will show that by going to the far hillside you will get either nothing, or else a recurrence of the same desire which sent you thither. A rather more difficult, but still possible, study of your own memories, will prove that by returning to the past you could not find, as a possession, that ecstasy which some sudden reminder of the past now moves you to desire. Those remembered moments were either quite commonplace at the time (and owe all their enchantment to memory) or else were themselves moments of desiring. . . . As for the sexual answer, that I suppose to be the most obviously false . . . of all. On whatever plane you take it, it is not what we were looking for. Lust can be gratified. Another personality can become to us 'our America, our New-found-land.' A happy marriage can be achieved. But what has any of the three, or any mixture of the three, to do with that unnameable something, desire for which pierces us like a rapier at the smell of a bonfire, the sound of wild ducks flying overhead, the title of *The Well at the World's End,* the opening lines of *Kubla Khan,* the morning cobwebs in late summer, or the noise of falling waves?

It appeared to me, therefore, that if a man diligently followed this desire, pursuing the false objects until their falsity appeared and then resolutely abandoning them, he must come out at last into the clear knowledge that the human soul was made to enjoy some object that is never fully given—nay, cannot even be imagined as given—in our present mode of subjective and spatio-temporal experience. This Desire was, in the soul, as the Siege Perilous in Arthur's castle—the chair in which only one could sit. And if nature makes nothing in vain, the One who can sit in this chair must exist. I knew only too well how easily the longing accepts false objects and through what dark ways the pursuit of them leads us; but I also saw that the Desire itself contains the corrective of all these errors. The only fatal error was to pretend that you had passed from desire to fruition, when, in reality, you had found either nothing, or desire itself, or the satisfaction of some different desire. The dialectic of Desire, faithfully followed, would retrieve all mistakes, head you off from all false paths, and force you not to propound, but to live through, a sort of ontological proof.

Discussion Questions

1. Have you ever had the experience of unsatisfiable desire that Lewis describes? If so, what occasioned it? Did you draw the same conclusion Lewis did?

2. What do you suppose Lewis would reply to the following argument? "Nature is a cheat. She satisfies all our other desires except this one, the greatest one of all. How could you possibly disprove that, or prove your premise that no natural desire is vain?"

3. Why is the desire felt to be more valuable than any other satisfaction?

4. Do you know of any characters or stories in literature or life which exemplify Lewis's "dialectic of desire," or lived "ontological proof" in the last paragraph?

5. Compare Lewis's argument here (especially the last paragraph) with the passage from Aquinas on pages 249–60. Are they making the same essential point? If so, explain how.

6. Does the argument indicate anything about the *nature* of heaven, immortality, life after death, or God? Could these things be just anything at all? If not, what can be deduced from the argument about their nature?

COMMENT: Plato
"The Death of Socrates" from *Phaedo*

A man of sense ought not to say, nor will I be very confident, that the description which I have given of the soul and her mansions is exactly true. But I do say that, inasmuch as the soul is shown to be immortal, he may venture to think, not improperly or unworthily, that something of the kind is true. The venture is a glorious one, and he ought to comfort himself with words like these, which is the reason why I lengthen out the tale. Wherefore, I say, let a man be of good cheer about his soul, who having cast away the pleasures and ornaments of the body as alien to him and working harm rather than good, has sought after the pleasures of knowledge; and has arrayed the soul, not in some foreign attire, but in her own proper jewels, temperance, and justice, and courage, and nobility, and truth—in these adorned she is ready to go on her journey to the world below, when her hour comes. You, Simmias and Cebes, and all other men, will depart at some time or other. Me already, as a tragic poet would say, the voice of fate calls. Soon I must drink the poison; and I think that I had better repair to the bath first, in order that the women may not have the trouble of washing my body after I am dead.

When he had done speaking, Crito said: And have you any commands for us, Socrates—anything to say about your children, or any other matter in which we can serve you?

Nothing particular, Crito, he replied: only, as I have always told you, take care of yourselves; that is a service which you may be ever rendering to me and mine and to all of us, whether you promise to do so or not. But if you have no thought for yourselves, and care not to walk according to the rule which I have prescribed for you, not now for the first time, however much you may profess or promise at the moment, it will be of no avail.

We will do our best, said Crito: And in what way shall we bury you?

In any way that you like; but you must get hold of me, and take care that I do not run away from you. Then he turned to us, and added with a smile:—I cannot make Crito believe that I am the same Socrates who have been talking and conducting the argument; he fancies that I am the other Socrates whom he will soon see, a dead body—and he asks, How shall he bury me? And though I have spoken many words in the endeavour to show that when I have drunk the posion I shall leave you and go to the joys of the blessed,—these words of mine, with which I was comforting you and myself, have had, as I perceive, no effect upon Crito. And therefore I want you to be surety for me to him now, as at the trial he was surety to the judges for me: but let the promise be of another sort; for he was surety for me to the judges that I would remain, and you must be my surety to him that I shall not remain, but go away and depart; and then he will suffer less at my death, and not be grieved when he sees my body being burned or buried. I would not have him sorrow at my hard lot, or say at the burial, Thus we lay out Socrates, or, Thus we follow him to the grave or bury him;

for false words are not only evil in themselves, but they inflict the soul with evil. Be of good cheer then, my dear Crito, and say that you are burying my body only, and do with that whatever is usual, and what you think best.

When he had spoken these words, he arose and went into a chamber to bathe; Crito followed him and told us to wait. So we remained behind, talking and thinking of the subject of discourse, and also of the greatness of our sorrow; he was like a father of whom we were being bereaved, and we were about to pass the rest of our lives as orphans. When he had taken the bath his children were brought to him (he had two young sons and an elder one); and the women of his family also came, and he talked to them and gave them a few directions in the presence of Crito; then he dismissed them and returned to us.

Now the hour of sunset was near, for a good deal of time had passed while he was within. When he came out, he sat down with us again after his bath, but not much was said. Soon the jailer, who was the servant of the Eleven, entered and stood by him, saying:—To you, Socrates, whom I know to be the noblest and gentlest and best of all who ever came to this place, I will not impute the angry feeling of other men, who rage and swear at me, when, in obedience to the authorities, I bid them drink the poison—indeed, I am sure that you will not be angry with me; for others, as you are aware, and not I, are to blame. And so fare you well, and try to bear lightly what must needs be—you know my errand. Then bursting into tears he turned away and went out.

Socrates looked at him and said: I return your good wishes, and will do as you bid. Then turning to us, he said, How charming the man is: since I have been in prison he has always been coming to see me, and at times he would talk to me, and was as good to me as could be, and now see how generously he sorrows on my account. We must do as he says, Crito; and therefore let the cup be brought, if the poison is prepared: if not, let the attendant prepare some.

Yet, said Crito, the sun is still upon the hill-tops, and I know that many a one has taken the draught late, and after the announcement has been made to him, he has eaten and drunk, and enjoyed the society of his beloved: do not hurry—there is time enough.

Socrates said: Yes, Crito, and they of whom you speak are right in so acting, for they think that they will be gainers by the delay; but I am right in not following their example, for I do not think that I should gain anything by drinking the poison a little later; I should only be ridiculous in my own eyes for sparing and saving a life which is already forfeit. Please then to do as I say, and not to refuse me.

Crito made a sign to the servant, who was standing by, and he went out, and having been absent for some time, returned with the jailer carrying the cup of poison. Socrates said: You, my good friend, who are experienced in these matters, shall give me directions how I am to proceed. The man answered: You have only to walk about until your legs are heavy, and then to lie down, and the poison will act. At the same time he handed the cup to Socrates, who in the easiest and gentlest manner, without the least fear or change of colour or feature, looking at the man with all his eyes. Echecrates, as his manner was, took the cup and said: What do you say about making a libation out of this cup to any god? May I, or not? The man answered: We only prepare, Socrates, just so much as we deem enough. I understand, he said: but I may and must ask the gods to prosper my journey from this to the other world—even so—and so be it according to my prayer. Then raising the cup to his lips, quite readily and cheerfully he drank off the poison. And hitherto most of us had been able to control our sorrow; but now when we saw him drinking, and saw too that he had finished the draught, we could no longer forbear, and in spite of myself my own tears were flowing fast; so that I covered my face and wept, not for him, but at the thought of my own calamity in having to part from such a friend. Nor was I the first; for Crito, when he found himself unable to restrain his tears, and got up, and I followed; and at that moment, Apollodorus, who had been weeping all the time, broke out in a loud and passionate cry which made cowards of us all. Socrates alone retained his calmness: What is this strange outcry? he said. I sent away the women mainly in order that they might not misbehave in this way, for I have been told that a man should die in peace. Be quiet then, and have patience. When we heard his words we were ashamed, and refrained our tears; and he walked about until, as he said, his legs began to fail, and then he lay on his back, according to directions, and the man who gave him the poison now and then looked at his feet and legs; and after a while he pressed his foot hard, and asked him if he could feel; and he said, No; and then his leg, and so upwards and upwards, and showed us that he was cold and stiff. And he felt them himself, and said: When the poison reaches the heart, that will be the end. He was beginning to grow cold about the groin, when he uncovered his face, for he had covered himself up, and said—they were his last words—he said: Crito, I owe a cock to Asclepius; will you remember to pay the debt? The debt shall be paid, said Crito; is there anything else? There was no answer to this question; but in a minute or two a movement was heard, and the attendants uncovered him; his eyes were set, and Crito closed his eyes and mouth.

Such was the end, Echecrates, of our friend; concerning whom I may truly say, that of all men of his time whom I have known, he was the wisest and justest and best.